Language and Literature

LANGUAGE

Wentworth K. Brown

Sterling P. Olmsted

Rensselaer Polytechnic Institute

AND LITERATURE

Harcourt, Brace & World, Inc.
New York · Burlingame

P
105
B78
c. 2

Preface

The present book, developed over an eight-year period in an experimental basic course in language and literature, has grown out of a conviction that language and its nature and functions should be a major concern, if not the core, of an undergraduate course in English. Whether the course stress reading or writing, skill or content, language must be viewed as the central subject under examination.

The questions we raise here are fundamental. What *is* language? What purposes does it serve? How are these purposes related to the rest of human endeavor? How is language related to the complex business of "knowing" and of storing and transmitting knowledge? Are the traditional distinctions between kinds of literature perhaps related to even more fundamental distinctions between kinds of knowledge or ways of knowing? How are the many varieties of informal word-using related to the various kinds of formal word-using that we call literature? How is literature related to the equally familiar nonverbal symbolisms that we also use in learning, communicating, and expressing? What are the relative advantages and disadvantages of verbal and nonverbal symbolisms? By what criteria do we judge literary works and other symbolic forms? How do these criteria differ from one another? And *why* do they differ? In what ways does literature that is concerned with "facts" and "ideas" differ from literary art? And how do both differ from literature intended to change people's attitudes and hence their actions? How does one's method of dealing with one kind of language and literature differ from his approach to other kinds?

These are some of the questions around which this book is organized and which it invites students to consider. On a level that can only be called philosophical, they ask the student to think about the whole business of language and its cousins, the nonverbal symbolisms. Many of the answers are unknown at this stage in man's investigations. Even where answers of a sort are available, they are offered here as hypotheses only. The emphasis is on language as a phenomenon still in the process of being understood, not upon a set of rigid principles.

Our experience with earlier versions of this work indicates that it is a highly practical as well as "theoretical" book, in some ways almost a "how-to-do-it" book. The theory presented and the abstract questions raised have important utilitarian implications and applications for both readers and writers. These practical conclusions and principles are explicitly adduced and applied in the numerous exercises scattered throughout the book and can be used with almost any supplementary reading material.

We wish to acknowledge a few of our many indebtednesses. We appreciate the patience of Rensselaer students during the several years in which this book has been evolving. We are grateful for the patience, and especially for the positive contributions, of so many of our colleagues in the Department of Language and Literature. We have also received many helpful criticisms and suggestions from Professors Maynard Mack of Yale University, Howard Dean of Montana State College, Laurence Perrine of Southern Methodist University, Alvin Kernan of Yale University, and Donald Sears of Upsala College. We owe a special debt, deeper than we can express here, to Professor Douglas H. Washburn, also of our department, who collaborated with us on the first two versions of the book. Finally, we are grateful to Mrs. Sylvia Gerhard for her untiring help in preparing the manuscript.

WENTWORTH K. BROWN

STERLING P. OLMSTED

Troy, New York
January 3, 1962

Contents

Language and Literature

1. Two Kinds of Knowledge

> As scientists we realise that colour is merely a question of the wave-lengths of aethereal vibrations; but that does not seem to have dispelled the feeling that eyes which reflect light near the wave-length of 4800 are subject for rhapsody whilst those which reflect wave-length 5300 are left unsung. We have not yet reached the practice of the Laputans, who, "if they would for example, praise the beauty of a woman, or any other animal, they describe it by rhombs, circles, parallelograms, ellipses, and other geometrical terms." The [man] who is convinced that all phenomena arise from electrons and quanta and the like controlled by mathematical formulae, must presumably hold the belief that his wife is a rather elaborate differential equation; but he is probably tactful enough not to obtrude this opinion in domestic life.[1]
>
> A. S. EDDINGTON, *The Nature of the Physical World*

A Fable

What follows is a fable of two men and of two kinds of knowledge. It is an inconclusive, undramatic fable, and it is offered simply as a starting point for a discussion of language, in a very broad sense of that term, and of literature, in an equally broad sense of *that* term.

The two men are Henry Haines and Dr. Norman Keene. Henry Haines is a lifelong resident of the town of Deep River; Dr. Keene

[1] FROM *The Nature of the Physical World* by A. S. Eddington, by permission of the Cambridge University Press.

is an outsider, brought in by the chamber of commerce to do a preliminary study of the community as part of a redevelopment project. Henry Haines has lived in Deep River for over seventy years. For twenty years he was postmaster, and he represented Deep River for three terms in the state legislature. His father, grandfather, and great grandfather were born in the town and are buried there; and most of the descendants of the old families of Deep River are his kin. He may be said to know Deep River as an insider in the community. Dr. Keene, on the other hand, never saw the community until he was invited by a committee to come for an interview. A professor of economics at the state university, well grounded also in political science and sociology, he has made similar studies of small industrial communities. What he brings to Deep River is a detailed factual knowledge of several towns like Deep River, a theoretical understanding of communities and how they operate, and a wide knowledge of the mechanisms of society.

After six weeks of reading in the local records and talking with local people—city officials, businessmen, and long-time residents (including Henry Haines)—Dr. Keene has built up a very clear picture of Deep River. He now has a kind of knowledge which no one inside the community possesses. He understands the make-up of the population by age group, ethnic and national origin, level of educational attainment, and economic status, and he knows a good deal about population trends over the past fifty years. Dr. Keene has written, chiefly for himself, an economic history of Deep River, covering its industrial development as a mill town in the latter part of the nineteenth century and its gradual economic decay over the past twenty years. He has also pieced together a picture of the internal conflicts in the town, some of which help explain the decline. All these developments and conflicts he has placed in both regional and national contexts.

Yet Dr. Keene does not know Deep River in the way Henry Haines does—a fact which Henry is quick to point out. Henry himself has very little formal knowledge of social, economic, or political theory, but he has been a part of Deep River, and Deep River has been a part of him, for three quarters of a century. He has lived many of the events which Dr. Keene has recounted in his little economic history; and the slow decay of the town, which for Dr. Keene is a documented fact, is to Henry Haines a bitter personal experience. Henry sees Deep River in terms of individuals, their ambitions, and their disappointments. And he sees the conflicts in the community not from outside but from inside, as a participant: many of the people of Deep River are his close friends; some are bitter enemies. In other words, much of Henry's knowledge is first-hand (as is some of Dr. Keene's knowledge by now), but he also has a good deal of secondhand knowledge. He too has investigated the history of Deep River, though *investigate* is perhaps the wrong word for the kind of storing up of legend and tradition which has made Henry an interesting reteller of the tales told him by his father and grandfather. His own life and the life of the community, past and present, are closely bound together. Perhaps the best symbol of this relation is the monument Henry has had set up in the Haines family plot in the cemetery: it is a granite millstone which had been used in one of the very early mills established in Deep River.

Yet for all his participation in the life of Deep River, for all his feeling for the people who make the community, Henry Haines does not know Deep River as Dr. Keene does. The two men have two different kinds of knowledge. Dr. Keene will put his knowledge of Deep River into a report, complete with tables, maps, and graphs. If Henry Haines were a writer—which he is not—he would be more likely to put his knowledge into a novel or play.

Needed: A Pair of Terms

This story might be unnecessary if the English language had convenient labels for the two kinds of knowledge possessed by Dr. Keene and Henry Haines. The verb *to know* is used in English to cover all kinds of knowing. We might have less difficulty in French or German, both of which have pairs of words, *connaître* and *savoir* in French, *kennen* and *wissen* in German. *Wissen* and *savoir* fit fairly well Dr. Keene's kind of knowing, *kennen* and *connaître* Henry Haines'. In English, the closest common expressions are perhaps *to know* and *to know about*. Henry Haines, we say, *knows* Deep River; Dr. Keene *knows about* it. But because this terminology is awkward when applied not to the act of knowing but to knowledge itself, we will use another pair of terms, calling Dr. Keene's kind of knowledge *conceptual*, Henry Haines' kind of knowledge *experiential*.

However, since fables, like the one we have just used, have a way

of generating unintended and often confusing ideas, it may be well
to add that in using the terms *conceptual* and *experiential* we are
talking only about the dominant characteristic of each man's knowledge. Though Henry Haines knows very little about the concepts
used by social scientists, a great deal of his knowledge of Deep
River is conceptual. And Dr. Keene, in six weeks, has acquired
sympathies and resentments, images and feelings, sense impressions
and intuitions, which give his knowledge an experiential coloring.
Personal clashes with several strong personalities, daily contact with
the sights and sounds and smells of the town, and especially a long
walk beside the river, have given him a sense of the fierce attach-
ments which drive men and women to try to revive a declining
community.

Some Extra Pairs

The distinction we have just made is not a new one, and the two
kinds of knowledge we have been talking about have been labeled
in a number of different ways. For example, Will Herberg, a contemporary theologian and philosopher, uses the terms *playing-field*
knowledge (for the experiential) and *spectatorial* knowledge (for
the conceptual), a terminology that fits very well the situations
of Henry Haines and Dr. Keene. Herberg's illustration, however,
is a football game. A player taking part in the game naturally knows
it in a different way than does a spectator in the grandstand, especially if the spectator has no connection with either team, no money
bet on the outcome, and no interest except to observe as accurately
as he can in order to write a newspaper account of the game. Dr.
Herberg also suggests another pair of terms: *engaged* knowledge,
for the player's understanding of the game, in contrast to *disen-
gaged* knowledge, for the spectator's.

Dr. Herberg is sympathetic to the contemporary philosophical
movement known as existentialism, a movement which has been
much concerned with the difference between these two kinds of
knowledge. Existentialists strongly favor the experiential (they
call it existential) as opposed to the conceptual (they call it objective, analytic, rationalist, or scientific).

On a somewhat different intellectual plane, another contemporary
movement has also declaimed against conceptual knowledge and

in favor of the experiential. The Beatnik's word for knowing experientially is *to dig*. To dig jazz or poetry or people is to understand them with your whole heart and body, not merely with your mind. The Beatnik's aim is to dig all of life; whereas (he feels) the "organization" world is all too content with facts, figures, and other such intellectual falsifications and sterilizations of reality.

Experiential knowledge is not, of course, the invention either of Beatniks or of existentialists. Both groups simply happen, at the moment, to be highly articulate about it. But there have always been men and women who have found their primary values in the richness of sensation and feeling, in the quality of personal relations, and in the immediate texture of life—in other words, in experiential knowledge.

But Why Talk About It?

Since this is a book about language and literature, it might be reasonable to ask at this point why we should devote so much space, and at the very outset, to a discussion not of writing but of two kinds of knowledge. Part of the answer will have to wait until later in the book. For the moment, however, it is worth noting that the key to the importance of this distinction has already been implied in the statement that Dr. Keene's knowledge of Deep River will be embodied in a report, while Henry Haines' knowledge would be better embodied in a novel or play. In other words the distinction between conceptual and experiential knowledge is at the root of certain basic distinctions between the purposes which language and literature serve.

This point will be discussed more fully in Chapter 2, but it may be well to take a preliminary look at it at this point, both as an indication of what we are doing in this chapter and as a way of reinforcing our sense of the distinction itself. Here, for example, is a passage from the article on chemical warfare in the *Encyclopaedia Britannica*:

> In July 1917 the Germans began using mustard gas, which caused severe, slow-healing burns on the skin and damage to the respiratory tract. It was difficult to provide effective protection against this agent, which accounted for the majority of gas casualties. Next to mustard gas, chlorine and chlorine-phosgene mixtures were the greatest **gas**

casualty producers. The number of gas casualties as compared to casualties from other means (bullets, high explosives, disease, etc.) increased in the last months of the war, although deaths among gas casualties were few.[2]

What this statement conveys is primarily conceptual knowledge. There is, of course, something inherently horrible in the idea of gas warfare, and some of this horror may come through from the subject itself, but, for the most part, we are aware, as we read, not of suffering people but of "casualties" with damaged respiratory tracts; and we are led to think of bullets, high explosives, disease, and gas as means, or as casualty-producing agents.

By way of contrast, here is a poem which started with the same historical "fact"—the use of poison gas in World War I. It is Wilfred Owen's "Dulce et Decorum Est," the title of which is taken from a line by Horace which, in its entirety, may be translated as, "It is sweet and fitting to die for one's country."

Dulce et Decorum Est

Bent double, like old beggars under sacks,
Knock-kneed, coughing like hags, we cursed through sludge,
Till on the haunting flares we turned our backs,
And towards our distant rest began to trudge.
Men marched asleep. Many had lost their boots,
But limped on, blood-shod. All went lame, all blind;
Drunk with fatigue; deaf even to the hoots
Of gas-shells dropping softly behind.

Gas! Gas! Quick, boys!—An ecstasy of fumbling,
Fitting the clumsy helmets just in time,
But someone still was yelling out and stumbling
And floundering like a man in fire or lime.—
Dim through the misty panes and thick green light,
As under a green sea, I saw him drowning.

In all my dreams before my helpless sight
He plunges at me, guttering, choking, drowning.

If in some smothering dreams, you too could pace
Behind the wagon that we flung him in,
And watch the white eyes writhing in his face,
His hanging face, like a devil's sick of sin;
If you could hear, at every jolt, the blood

[2] FROM "Gas Warfare," reprinted from *Encyclopaedia Britannica*, 11th edition. By permission of *Encyclopaedia Britannica*.

Come gargling from the froth-corrupted lungs,
Bitten* as the cud
Of vile, incurable sores on innocent tongues,—
My friend, you would not tell with such high zest
To children ardent for some desperate glory,
The old Lie: *Dulce et decorum est
Pro patria mori.*[3]

(WILFRED OWEN, 1893–1918)

* Some editors suggest *bitter* instead of *bitten*.

Owen's poem, in contrast to the encyclopedia story, gives us very little conceptual knowledge. We do not know what the chemical agent was, nor when the attack occurred, nor where. We do not even know whether Owen actually witnessed such an attack. And the question is, of course, irrelevant. What the poem gives us is a stark and terrible image of war, compounded of pictures, sensations, and emotions, dominated by a growing anger directed, not against an enemy, nor against chemical warfare, nor even against war itself, but rather against the lofty heroic vision of death in war as sweet and fitting. In other words, what we get from Owen's poem is experiential knowledge; what we get from the *Britannica* account is conceptual knowledge. An understanding of these facts, and of the two kinds of knowledge themselves, is basic to an understanding of these two pieces of writing—and of many others.

Some Possible Misconceptions

Before we try to do any more with the notion of two kinds of knowledge, we should deal with some of the ways in which this distinction is often misunderstood. For once we move beyond a simple recognition of difference, it is very easy to come to wrong conclusions.

In the first place, some authorities on this subject contend that conceptual knowledge is valid and useful because it is "objective," while experiential knowledge, being "subjective," is uncertain and useless except perhaps for entertainment. Their argument is that conceptual knowledge is in some way external to the mind, that it

[3] "Dulce et Decorum Est" by Wilfred Owen, from *The Poems of Wilfred Owen.* All rights reserved. Reprinted by permission of New Directions, Publishers.

is concerned with a substantial "real world" as opposed to the world of idea or imagination. This position is, of course, a thoroughly respectable one, although in this book we shall argue against it. From the point of view taken here, both kinds of knowledge exist, in the first place, only in the mind. And although we may honestly believe that many of our perceptions have a source outside of ourselves, our primary data are experiences. From these experiences we infer the existence of an external world. From these experiences we also derive ideas or concepts, the conceptual knowledge we have been talking about in this chapter, which we use in the further interpretation of experience. From this point of view, then, both experiential knowledge and conceptual knowledge are valuable and useful, both exist in the first place in our own minds, and each is in a sense dependent on the other. The knowledge in the *Britannica* article and the knowledge in the poem may both increase the meaning of experience. The question of truthfulness is relevant, of course, but it must be asked about both kinds of knowledge, and both are concerned with "reality" although in somewhat different ways.

A second misconception concerns the sources of the two kinds of knowledge. It would be easy to conclude that conceptual knowledge is always secondhand and bookish, experiential knowledge firsthand and immediate. We have already seen, however, that Dr. Keene and Henry Haines each have both firsthand and secondhand knowledge of Deep River. Concepts may be the immediate result of firsthand experience; and much experiential knowledge comes to us secondhand, through literature and other works of art.

A third misconception about these two kinds of knowledge arises chiefly when we try to embody them in writing or in some other form. Experiential knowledge must be, one would expect, more detailed than conceptual knowledge. If we want to generate experiential knowledge, the logical thing to do is to put in more details. But this is not necessarily so. A map, which is usually a vehicle for conceptual knowledge, is not made more experiential by the addition of greater detail. Nor is a painting less experiential when it is less "realistic" and more "nonobjective."

A fourth misconception has to do with the personal element in experiential knowledge—especially in the expression of it. Amateur writers, trying to create experiential knowledge, sometimes feel that all they need to do is to write in the first person; and it is true that some very effective experiential narratives *are* written in the first person. But the statement "I was very hungry" does not create experiential knowledge any more effectively than does the statement "He was very hungry." Both really convey conceptual knowledge. They tell us *about* someone's experience, but they do not create experience. Wilfred Owen does not say in his poem, "I was angry when I saw a man dying of gas, and I thought bitterly of the idea that death in war is a sweet and fitting sacrifice to patriotism." This would be a conceptual report *about* an experience, whereas what Owen manages to do is to *create* an experience.

What, Then, Is the Difference?

But if these are misconceptions, what *is* the difference between the two kinds of knowledge? Most basically the difference lies in the mental faculties which are operating. We "know" not only with our intellects but also with our senses, our feelings, our imaginations, and our intuitions—to use traditional though rather vague terms. We sense things which we cannot formulate in conceptual terms. We do conceptual thinking most successfully when we isolate our intellectual faculties from the others. We then find ourselves thinking *about* things instead of being aware of them directly and immediately. It is perfectly possible, for example, to think about the color red in terms of wave lengths without experiencing any sensation. We have reduced the experience of red to an intellectual concept. This process of reduction may be very useful, but it yields a kind of knowledge which stands to the rest of knowledge as the skeleton does to the body as a whole.

A second way of seeing this distinction is in terms of the personal and the impersonal. Experiential knowledge is always to some extent personal and private, although an artist may be able to convey it or to produce it in others, as Wilfred Owen does with his poem. Conceptual knowledge on the other hand is much more impersonal and public. Though it is always based to a degree on the personal experience of someone, and though it can exist only in the minds of individuals, it is social as well as individual. The English philosopher Bertrand Russell has described this aspect of knowledge in these words:

> The community knows both more and less than the individual: it knows, in its collective capacity, all the contents of the encyclopedia

and all the contributions to the proceedings of learned bodies, but it does not know the warm and intimate things that make up the color and texture of an individual life. When a man says, "I can never convey the horror I felt on seeing Buchenwald" or "No words can express my joy at seeing the sea again after years in a prison camp," he is saying something which is strictly and precisely true: he possesses through his experience, knowledge not possessed by those whose experience has been different, and not completely capable of verbal expression. If he is a superb literary artist, he may create in sensitive readers a state of mind not wholly unlike his own, but if he tries scientific methods the stream of his experience will be lost in a dusty desert.[4]

A third way of seeing the distinction is suggested by Russell's remark that a "superb literary artist" may *create* experiential knowledge for someone else. The point is that superb artistry is required only for the creation of experiential knowledge. Almost any literate person can learn to convey conceptual knowledge reasonably well, but the transmitting of experiential knowledge, even rather badly, is difficult.

Which Kind Is Better?

There is no really good way of classifying the contents of our minds, yet we can give a rough, metaphorical account that will perhaps show us something of the relation of the two kinds of knowledge to each other. Everyone, it would appear, carries around with him a bundle of assorted concepts and beliefs, impressions, memories, images, and attitudes. And to this bundle we add other concepts, beliefs, impressions, images and attitudes as we go along. But we do not add indiscriminately, for what is already there influences the selection and rejection of new items. At the same time, what is added may change radically the content and structure of the whole.

Dr. Keene, in our fable, is equipped with a systematic collection of concepts, derived from many people's (including his own) experience of communities in action. And because he has these concepts he is able to see the social processes of Deep River differently than will an untrained person. But the concepts which he uses in this way are not necessarily permanently fixed. If Dr. Keene is a

[4] FROM *Human Knowledge* by Bertrand Russell. Copyright 1948 by Bertrand Russell. By permission of Simon and Schuster, Inc.

scholar as well as a practical investigator, he will not only write a report for the chamber of commerce but will use what he learns about Deep River as the basis for an article or even a book that may modify his set of concepts and those of other social scientists.

But Dr. Keene's knowledge of Deep River includes some of the experiential variety. He does not deal exclusively in concepts, for no one can. Experiential knowledge and conceptual knowledge never remain wholly separate. They interact in various ways. Concepts affect experiences; and experiences affect concepts.

Experiential knowledge, at the same time, acts on other experiential knowledge—whether of the firsthand kind or the kind embodied in various art forms. A work of art may intensify or sharpen experience. It may make us more sensitive, more aware. At the same time, the state of our experiential knowledge affects profoundly our reaction to a work of art or to any other experience. We may see nothing in a poem or painting at one time in our lives but at another time be profoundly moved by it.

What we have just said reinforces the point made earlier, that conceptual knowledge is not necessarily better than experiential knowledge and vice versa. There is a strong tendency in our own time to overemphasize conceptual knowledge. And conceptual knowledge is certainly indispensable to the "practical" side of living: it helps provide us with food, shelter, hydrogen bombs, and some of the deterrents to keep us from destroying ourselves with hydrogen bombs. Furthermore, quite aside from these practical values, conceptual knowledge satisfies our fundamental desire for reasonable, logical, intellectual explanations of phenomena, even when these explanations have no conceivable practical application. This emphasis on the conceptual is strengthened by the fact that experiential knowledge is much harder to talk about, and merely talking about it—in conceptual terms—is never wholly satisfactory. So literature courses in school and college often become courses *about* literature. One does not always get from them the experiential knowledge which literature is capable of creating, but only knowledge about works, authors, movements, periods, and sources.

Some instances of reaction against this overemphasis have already been mentioned. A few people—artists, Bohemians, existentialists— come to feel on their side that only experiential knowledge is of real value, that conceptual knowledge is mere dry bones.

Both these positions suggest that we must choose between the two kinds of knowledge. Actually, there is no need to choose. In fact we cannot live completely with either kind of knowledge alone. They are really complementary, a point which is made abundantly clear in the following passage from Joseph Conrad's Preface to *The Nigger of the Narcissus.*

Impressed by the aspect of the world the thinker plunges into ideas, the scientist into facts—whence, presently, emerging they make their appeal to those qualities of our being that fit us best for the hazardous enterprise of living. They speak authoritatively to our commonsense, to our intelligence, to our desire of peace or to our desire of unrest; not seldom to our prejudices, sometimes to our fears, often to our egoism—but always to our credulity. And their words are heard with reverence, for their concern is with weighty matters: with the cultivation of our minds and the proper care of our bodies, with the attainment of our ambitions, with the perfection of the means and the glorification of our precious aims.

It is otherwise with the artist.

Confronted by the same enigmatical spectacle, the artist descends within himself, and in that lonely region of stress and strife, if he be deserving and fortunate, he finds the terms of his appeal. His appeal is made to our less obvious capacities: to that part of our nature which, because of the warlike conditions of existence, is necessarily kept out of sight within the more resisting and hard qualities—like the vulnerable body within a steel armour. His appeal is less loud, more profound, less distinct, more stirring—and sooner forgotten. Yet its effect endures forever. The changing wisdom of successive generations discards ideas, questions facts, demolishes theories. But the artist appeals to that part of our being which is not dependent upon wisdom: to that in us which is a gift not an acquisition—and, therefore, more permanently enduring. He speaks to our capacity for delight and wonder, to the sense of mystery surrounding our lives; to our sense of pity, and beauty, and pain; to the latent feeling of fellowship with all creatures—and to the subtle but invincible conviction of solidarity that knits together the loneliness of innumerable hearts, to the solidarity in dreams, in joy, in sorrow, in aspirations, in illusions, in hope, in fear, which binds men to each other, which binds together all humanity—the dead to the living and the living to the unborn.[5]

Despite the somewhat old-fashioned eloquence of Conrad's style, this Preface is still one of the most magnificent statements of professional faith which any artist has given us. It also reinforces a point already suggested about the relationship of these two kinds

[5] FROM "Preface," reprinted from *The Nigger of the Narcissus* by Joseph Conrad. By permission of J. M. Dent & Sons Ltd.

of knowledge: they are not always as separate and distinct as we have perhaps made them appear. On the contrary, they naturally tend to merge with one another. All first-rate writers deal in both kinds of knowledge. Most good literature exhibits evidence of both kinds. Furthermore, as we shall see in Chapter 3, the nature of language itself makes their complete separation all but impossible, at least as far as writing is concerned.

The passage from Conrad is itself an excellent example of this merging of the conceptual and the experiential. Conrad is giving us both his intellectual knowledge and his felt knowledge of the different but complementary roles played by the thinker-scientist and the artist.

From Knowledge to Language

Our attention throughout this chapter has been focused on knowledge rather than on language. At various times, however, we have found it necessary to look at examples of language and literature—the *Britannica* article and the Owen poem, for instance. And we have seen that language is one means of conveying or creating conceptual and experiential knowledge. But we should also notice that the relations between knowledge and language are much more complex than this discussion has been able so far to show. For language is not merely the neutral vehicle by which knowledge is conveyed from one person to another. It is itself something to be experienced, and it is also a tool by which we experience and conceptualize. We have said that Dr. Keene brings certain concepts to his study of Deep River and that these concepts enable him to see things which are not apparent to others. But these concepts are, in all probability, embodied in some kind of language. In a very real sense it is Dr. Keene's command of the language of the social sciences which makes it possible for him to acquire conceptual knowledge of Deep River. As Dr. Keene puts things down on paper, he sees other things more clearly. Thus language enables him to conceptualize and to theorize.

In a similar way language is used not only, or even primarily, to convey experiential knowledge to an audience, but to fix it, to clarify it, to make it real for the writer himself. Poets and novelists may write for themselves as much as for some hypothetical reader;

and the best of them probably do not begin with an already crystallized body of experiential knowledge which they then seek to convey intact to someone else. They realize their own experience as
they write, just as Dr. Keene works out some of his concepts as
he writes. From the poem itself we can't tell what Wilfred Owen
began with, whether with an incident on the front, or with a reading of Horace's poem, or whatever. Any attempt to probe his mind,
to discover some "real intention," is useless, probably worse than
useless, because it focuses attention on the wrong thing. What we,
as readers, should be interested in is the experience itself. We need
not ask whether Owen felt it completely before he wrote the poem,
or whether the poem clarified and fixed an experience for him as
he worked on it. It is there for us to get if we know how.

But the more detailed consideration of the relation of language
and literature to knowledge must be left to the next chapter.

EXERCISES

A. Think about the following questions for class discussion:
   1. Can you suggest any additional pairs of terms for the two kinds
      of knowledge? (See p. 4.)
   2. Cite some additional examples of *conceptual* knowledge of
      Deep River which Dr. Keene may well have and Henry Haines
      may not; also cite some additional examples of *experiential*
      knowledge of the community which Henry Haines probably
      has and Dr. Keene does not have.
   3. Can you think of examples of *conceptual* knowledge which
      Henry Haines has, and of experiential knowledge which Dr.
      Keene has?
   4. A few basic differences between the two kinds of knowledge
      are mentioned on pages 9–10. Can you suggest any others?

B. Write two different accounts of the same event, place, thing, or person which you have experienced firsthand. In one account try to
present only conceptual knowledge; in the other try to convey something of the experience itself. (Remember that in the second account
you are not bound to "stick to the facts"; you may find it necessary
to ignore or to modify many of them.)

C. Having completed Exercise B, write a short analysis of how your two
versions differ.

D. Write another fable, like the one about Henry Haines and Dr. Keene, which also illustrates the distinction between the two kinds of knowledge.

E. Try to write a purely conceptual version of Owen's poem "Dulce et Decorum Est." Then explain what problems you ran into.

F. Do the same thing (as in E) with the passage from Conrad.

G. Write an imaginary conversation between Dr. Keene and Henry Haines.

ADDITIONAL READINGS

A. J. Ayer, *Language, Truth, and Logic.*
Kenneth E. Boulding, *The Image.*
A. S. Eddington, *The Nature of the Physical World.*
Archibald MacLeish, "The Poet and the Press," *Atlantic Monthly,* March, 1959.
Benjamin Lee Whorf, "An American Indian Model of the Universe," *Language, Thought, and Reality.*

2. The Uses of Language

> Like the colors of the spectrum merging into one
> another from the extremes of ultraviolet to infrared, the
> different uses of language overlap and merge into one
> another, running all the way from everyday conver-
> sational discourse, through law and religion, liturgy
> and homily, poetry, science and philosophy, to logic
> and mathematics.
>
> JOSHUA WHATMOUGH, *Language: A Modern Synthesis*

Language in Use

It is difficult and, for our purposes, probably pointless to classify
and label the many uses to which language is put, but it may be
worthwhile to look briefly at a few examples.

The lady balances her teacup, smiles pleasantly, and says, "I'm
so glad to meet you." The presiding officer at the commencement
ceremony tells the new graduates that he is not only conferring
certain degrees upon them but admitting them "to all the rights and
privileges thereunto appertaining." The lawyer, drawing up a deed,
inserts a string of almost synonymous words, "do give, grant, bar-
gain, sell and confirm . . ." Abraham Lincoln tells his audience at
Gettysburg, "It is rather for us to be here dedicated to the great
task remaining before us . . ." Robert Frost concludes a famous
poem with the lines,

> But I have promises to keep,
> And miles to go before I sleep,
> And miles to go before I sleep.[1]
>
> (ROBERT FROST, 1874–   )

[1] FROM "Stopping by Woods on a Snowy Evening" by Robert Frost, from
Complete Poems of Robert Frost. Copyright 1923, 1930, 1939 by Holt, Rine-

Albert Einstein writes, "Physical space and the ether are only different names for the same thing; fields are physical conditions of space." The taxi driver slams on his brakes and relieves his feelings with a barrage of words, some of them identical with those used by the clergyman as he spreads his hands in blessing. The sergeant moves his platoon off with a series of commands: "Right FACE! . . . Forward MARCH! . . . Column right MARCH!" And the headline writer compresses a column of newsprint into the words, "PRESIDENT WARNS RED THREAT WILL BE MET."

These are only samples, of course, but they indicate the variety of ways in which words are used. Some of the uses are informal; others are formal. Some transmit or create knowledge; others provide an outlet for feelings, lend dignity to ceremonial occasions, or simply oil the wheels of sociability. In this book we shall concern ourselves very little with those uses which are themselves little concerned with knowledge—except to recognize here and now that they exist and that they are legitimate and often indispensable functions of language.

Our attention will be focused on only three uses of language: the *informative,* the *creative,* and the *persuasive,* represented in our rapid introductory survey by a sentence each from Einstein, Frost, and Lincoln. These three uses, however, account for the greater part of our formal writing and speaking, and most of the things we read belong to one or another of these uses or to some combination of them. Our ability to handle language, either as readers or writers, depends largely upon our ability to recognize and understand these three uses, in relatively pure forms and in various combinations. C. S. Lewis begins *A Preface to Paradise Lost* with the following apt sentences:

> The first qualification for judging any piece of workmanship from a corkscrew to a cathedral is to know *what* it is—what it was intended to do and how it was meant to be used. After that has been discovered, the temperance reformer may decide that the corkscrew was made for a bad purpose, and the communist may think the same about the cathedral. But such questions come later. The first thing is to understand the object before you: as long as you think the corkscrew was meant for opening tin cans or the cathedral for entertaining tourists, you can say nothing to the purpose about them.[2]

hart and Winston, Inc. Copyright 1936 by Robert Frost. Copyright renewed 1951 by Robert Frost. Reprinted by permission of Holt, Rinehart and Winston, Inc.

[2] FROM *A Preface to Paradise Lost* by C. S. Lewis. Reprinted by permission of Oxford University Press, Inc.

Mr. Lewis is actually talking here not so much about corkscrews and cathedrals as about pieces of writing, and though his emphasis is on the problems of judging language, his remarks apply equally well to the problems of understanding and using it.

Informing and Creating

We have already looked at examples of two of these uses of language, but under the rubric of knowledge rather than of language. The *Britannica* article on chemical warfare is *informative;* what we get from it is *conceptual* knowledge. Wilfred Owen's "Dulce et Decorum Est" is *creative;* what we get from it is *experiential* knowledge. (This poem happens also to be persuasive, as we shall see later.)

Our basic generalization here is that *informative writing conveys conceptual knowledge while creative writing generates experiential knowledge.* But, like most sweeping generalizations, this one needs to be qualified. Most creative writing is to some extent *built on* conceptual knowledge; and it often *conveys* conceptual knowledge as well, though this is never its primary aim. On the other hand, the kind of informative writing which endures usually generates experiential knowledge as well. By means of its language and form it establishes a tone, evokes images and feelings that reinforce the conceptual knowledge which is still its principal ingredient, and it even establishes "character," in the person of a sensitive, thoughtful author. Finally, the two kinds of knowledge are themselves complementary, as we have already seen. We should not be surprised, therefore, if we sometimes find them so thoroughly blended in a single piece of writing as to make classification sheer nonsense.

The careful study of relatively pure examples, however, is *not* nonsense. There are vast literatures which are largely informative, and others which are largely creative. And even if pure examples were very rare, it would be worthwhile to search them out and look at them for what they could reveal about blends and combinations. We shall get to these blends and combinations later, and later, also, to the third use of language with which we are concerned in this book, the *persuasive.* From the point of view of knowledge, it is less basic than the other two. There is, for example, no such thing as a third, or persuasive, kind of knowledge. Persuasion must, therefore, build on and use either conceptual or experiential knowledge or both. It follows that persuasive writing can be best understood against the background of informative and creative writing.

Two New Examples

Most of the general characteristics of informative and creative writing could probably be deduced from the *Britannica* article and from "Dulce et Decorum Est," but it may be more interesting to work with fresh examples. Besides, "Dulce et Decorum Est" can be considered in still another way. We shall have occasion to return to it at the end of the chapter.

Our first example is from a *New Yorker* article, one of a series called "The Annals of Medicine," written by Berton Roueché:

> Most authorities place the incidence of delirium tremens among American alcoholics at about five per cent. It thus hits, on the average, one steadfast drinker in twenty. Its mortality rate is less easily reckoned, since it depends entirely on the circumstances of the case. In patients receiving the best of hospital care, the rate is seldom more than four or five per cent. Among those who suffer unattended—the solitary or the homeless—it is many times that. Current estimates range from twenty to twenty-five per cent. One reason for the high death rate among untreated victims is that an attack of delirium tremens is often precipitated by some other disease (pneumonia is a common catalyst) or by a serious physical injury. Another is that delirium tremens can be warmly hospitable to many dangerous diseases. The terrifying hallucinations that it induces in its victims are a third. . . . In the frenzied victim's efforts to flee the horrors that seem to threaten him, he may, unless closely watched and restrained, kill himself by plunging through a window or tumbling down a flight of stairs.[3]

This is, basically, informative writing. The spirit in which Roueché writes is, "Here, to the best of my knowledge and of my ability to transmit it, are some possibly interesting current facts and figures on this subject." His writing tells us about his subject as a map tells us about a territory, a schematic diagram tells us about a radio circuit, a table of organization tells us about a company, or a flow chart tells us about an industrial process. The writing is clear, pre-

[3] FROM "Alcohol" by Berton Roueché, reprinted from *The New Yorker*, January 23, 1960. By permission of the author and the publisher.

cise, restrained. It is even elegant in spots. Some words and phrases, especially toward the end, such as "frenzied victim" and "horrors that seem to threaten," are more vivid, however, than the subject matter absolutely demands. And the phrases "steadfast drinker" and "warmly hospitable" are elegantly ironic, clothing distinctly unpleasant ideas in pleasant language. Nevertheless, in the sense in which the word *creative* is being used in this book, Roueché is not writing creatively; and the experiential knowledge which comes through from his vivid and ironic phrases is normal in any informative writing which the author has tried to make interesting.

For a second example we turn to a passage from Samuel Clemens' *Huckleberry Finn.* This is, in a very general way, on the same subject as Roueché's paragraph, though it is perhaps misleading to think of creative writing as being "on a subject." It would be better to say that Clemens is working with the same rather special area of human experience—an attack of delirium tremens. The victim is Huck's father, the village drunkard, who has locked both Huck and himself into an isolated woods cabin, while he attends to a jug of liquor. The story is told in the first person, from Huck's point of view:

> I don't know how long I was asleep, but all of a sudden there was an awful scream and I was up. There was pap looking wild, and skipping around every which way and yelling about snakes. He said they was crawling up his legs; and then he would give a jump and scream, and say one had bit him on the cheek—but I couldn't see no snakes. He started and run round and round the cabin, hollerin' "Take him off! Take him off! He's biting me on the neck!" I never seen a man look so wild in the eyes. Pretty soon he was all fagged out, and fell down panting; then he rolled over and over wonderful fast, kicking things every which way, and striking and grabbing at the air with his hands, and screaming and saying there was devils a-hold of him. He wore out by and by, and laid still awhile, moaning. Then he laid stiller, and didn't make a sound. I could hear the owls and the wolves away off in the woods, and it seemed terrible still. He was laying over by the corner. By and by he raised up part way and listened, with his head on one side. He says, very low:

> "Tramp—tramp—tramp; that's the dead; tramp—tramp—tramp; They're coming after me; but I won't go. Oh, they're here! Don't touch me—don't! hands off—they're cold; let go. Oh, let a poor devil alone!

Then he went on all fours and crawled off, begging them to let him alone, and he rolled himself up in his blanket and wallowed in under the old pine table, still a-begging; and then he went to crying. I could hear him through the blanket.

Doctors have praised this passage as a classic description of delirium tremens, but the conceptual knowledge it contains is certainly incidental and subordinate to the experiential. This is not a dressing up of clinical symptoms in order to make them more interesting. The passage was not written for the sake of the symptoms; the symptoms are there for the sake of the passage—or, more precisely, as one element in the total experience the passage evokes. What we get from the passage is a whole scene, an imaginary event in which Pap and his problems play an important part. We see Pap and hear him and perhaps even pity him a little; but mostly we feel, in imagination, what Huck is going through—the mixed emotions of shock, horror, fear, and helplessness. We never quite become Huck, however, because we also see Huck within the situation, and we sense, as he does not, the grotesque, comic side of the picture.

Some Generalizations

Using these two passages as examples, we can try to generalize some of the differences between informative and creative writing. Both passages, we have said, convey or create knowledge—mostly conceptual knowledge in Roueché's case, mostly experiential knowledge in Clemens'. And, as with the examples in the first chapter, the *appeal* of each is clear. Roueché's passage appeals primarily to our intellectual faculties—our sense of fact, our logical powers, our reason. Except in so far as all words are sense stimuli, there is relatively little appeal to our senses, our imagination, or our emotions. Clemens' passage, on the other hand, appeals directly to these non-intellectual faculties. We hear the words as we read them. We see and feel the imaginary world they evoke, including Huck as imaginary narrator.

Thus our *response* to these two passages is basically different. Reading Roueché, we concentrate on grasping his facts and figures: we take away a package of information, small or large, depending mainly on our interest in the subject. We may also feel a certain fascinated horror as the recital goes on, but this is a secondary response. With Clemens' passage, however, the emotional and imaginative response is primary. We experience the words, the scene which they bring into being, and the sensations and emotions which are the products of words and scene.

If Roueché were a less meticulous and subtle informative writer than he is, these differences in appeal and in response would be sharper. Sharper, too, would be another difference—a difference in the relative *roles* of knowledge and language.

Conceptual knowledge is reducible finally to the reasonably neat and manageable units we call *facts* and *ideas*. These units are separable from the language in which they are conveyed, though there is no doubt that an informative writer—especially in the earlier stages of his writing—may learn something about his subject matter from the actual attempt to put it into words. In a very real sense, however, his facts and ideas have an existence quite apart from the piece of writing in which they are ultimately presented. Experiential knowledge cannot be so easily separated from the language through which it is created. As readers we invariably go wrong when we try to separate it out, when we try to paraphrase or summarize a piece of creative writing. Experiential knowledge exists *in* images and metaphors, *in* characters and scenes, *in* dialogue and action. Thus, an abstract of a scientific article may be a useful document, but a summary of *Hamlet*—or a comic-book version of *Hamlet*—is bound to be a travesty on the original. It stands to the original as a "simplified" and truncated version of a symphony would to the original composition.

What this means is that an informative writer like Roueché is able to concentrate most of his attention on the knowledge he has to convey, whereas a writer like Clemens must give his primary attention to the thing he is making, to each of its parts and to the work as a whole. This does not imply, of course, that Roueché can be careless of his words, or that Clemens can take an irresponsible attitude toward the truth of human experience. But the informative writer's first concern is for his subject matter, the creative writer's for the poem or story, play or novel, he is composing.

We have already noted the possibility of paraphrasing or summarizing informative writing, the practical impossibility of doing the same with creative writing. The differing roles of knowledge and language may be shown even more clearly if we try the device of rephrasing. Even as subtle an informative writer as Roueché can often be rephrased almost completely without altering significantly either the conceptual knowledge or our response to it. Here, for example, is one of Roueché's sentences:

> Its mortality rate is less easily reckoned, since it depends entirely on the circumstances of the case.

This sentence may be rewritten in these words:

> The death rate is not so easy to compute, because it is wholly dependent on the conditions in each instance.

Only the words *rate, it, on, the,* and *is* have been retained, yet the sense of the passage has not been significantly altered. Roueché's meaning here lies in the conceptual knowledge he is conveying; conceptual knowledge is separable from the words used to convey it, therefore the words may be changed without affecting it. This does not mean that one word or phrase in informative writing may not be more apt or natural than another. It does, however, demonstrate the relative importance of subject matter, the relatively lesser importance of the language used to convey it. And the ease of changing from one set of English words to another set of English words suggests that the passage could probably also be translated out of English into, say, French or Russian or Japanese without seriously impairing its meaning.

Huckleberry Finn cannot be treated in so high-handed a fashion. Here are the first three sentences of the passage; let's see what happens when we try to revise them.

> I don't know how long I was asleep, but all of a sudden there was an awful scream and I was up. There was pap looking wild, and skipping around every which way and yelling about snakes. He said they was crawling up his legs; and then he would give a jump and scream, and say one had bit him on the cheek—but I couldn't see no snakes.

And here is an "improved" version:

> I don't know how long I had been asleep; but suddenly, hearing a frightful scream, I sprang out of bed. There was father, looking frantic, whirling about the room, and declaiming about snakes. He insisted that they were crawling up his legs; he leaped about and cried out and protested that one had sunk its fangs in his cheek; but I must say, I failed to perceive any snakes.

The changes in wording in this revised version are not nearly so drastic as those which were made on the sentence from Roueché.

Huck's bad grammar has been corrected, and the whole passage made more proper and schoolmarmish. But these changes alter completely the effect of the passage. They affect our image and estimate of Huck and, through him, our response to the entire scene. The emphasis is on the writing, not on a separable subject matter.

The rephrasing test is an almost sure way of determining emphasis: if in doubt, rewrite. In the process the spots in a piece of informative writing where experiential knowledge plays a part will become clear. Thus, if we had selected a different sentence from Roueché, we might have found rewording more difficult—this sentence, for example:

It thus hits, on the average, one steadfast drinker in twenty.

"Steadfast drinker," is, as we noted earlier, an ironic phrase. Change it to "habitual drinker" or "alcoholic," and the effect of the sentence is changed.

Another generalization which we can make from these two passages concerns *value* and *standards of judgment*. The primary value of Roueché's piece, as of all informative writing, lies in the conceptual knowledge which it contains. It is capable, at least theoretically, of extending our own conceptual knowledge. Our final standard of judgment, therefore, is "truthfulness." Are the statements in the passage, taken individually, true (or probably true), or are they false (or probably false)? Taken together, do they appear to represent the subject fairly and impartially, or do they add up to a slanted, biased picture? If we are reading at all critically, we check what the author asserts against what we happen to know about the subject, and we look for internal evidence of bias or prejudice. But we also judge the passage on its qualities as writing. We admire an informative piece for its clarity, precision, variety of prose style, polish, and readability. These are important qualities, but they are important chiefly as the means by which conceptual knowledge is conveyed. In fact, we are more likely to notice their absence than their presence—a further indication of where our own attention focuses as we read.

The question of the value of *Huckleberry Finn*, as of all creative work, is much more complex; but the value must lie primarily in the quality of the experience which the work offers and in the capacity of that experience to extend our imaginative sense of life. This, of course, is the value of experience itself: experience gives meaning to experience. "Truthfulness" is still a criterion, but it is not truthfulness in the conceptual sense, for this or any other piece of creative writing. Huck and Pap and all the other elements in the novel, whatever their source in Clemens' own experience, are make-believe. The truth we look for is experiential truth, not literal truth but life*like*ness. We also feel and note the qualities of vividness, drama, and humor, and the "organic" way in which everything seems to play a part in the total effect which the scene produces. At this point the best we can probably do is to suggest that *richness* and *unity* are important criteria for creative writing. We shall return to this complex problem, however, in later chapters.

From Knowledge to Action

In spite of all their differences, and we have so far noted only a few, both informative and creative writing deal ultimately with knowledge. In Roueché's article it is primarily conceptual knowledge, in Samuel Clemens' novel primarily experiential knowledge. There is no sign that either author cares particularly what we *do* with the knowledge he has to offer. From the passages we have looked at, it would be impossible to guess where either Clemens or Roueché stands on the issue of whether alcohol is in general a blessing or a curse. Yet this *is* an issue which has inspired an enormous amount of "persuasive" literature, both worthy and cheap. And either Roueché's passage or Clemens' *could* be built into a temperance tract and used explicitly for persuasive purposes, and either, under the right circumstances, might be effective. The cartoons about Popeye the Sailorman have been known to persuade children to eat their spinach. But this is certainly not why the cartoonist created Popeye, nor is there, in the passages from Roueché and Clemens, any sign of persuasive purpose.

But knowledge does not always remain simply knowledge. Knowledge involves belief, and belief can take the form of conviction—even fiercely held conviction. And if a conviction is strong enough, it tends toward action. The ultimate goal of our third use of language is action—not necessarily immediate, overt, physical action, but a change in response, in attitude, in orientation. The persuasive writer—and who is *not* one on occasion?—moves others to act on the knowledge he has to offer. Serious persuasion—and this is the sort we are concerned with here, just as we are concerned here with serious informative writing and serious creative writing—deals in knowledge, but it goes one step further: it moves from knowledge toward action, and if it is effective it moves us along with it.

Persuasive writing, then, should be viewed not as an entirely separate use of language but as a natural extension of the informative and the creative uses. This point is perfectly illustrated in a work which we looked at in Chapter 1—Wilfred Owen's "Dulce et Decorum Est." We examined this poem earlier for the experiential knowledge which it generates, and we then described it as an example of creative writing, which it certainly is. But the nightmarish experience with which it begins, becomes, halfway through, the base for persuasive appeal. Even the point of view shifts, from the third person to the second:

> If in some smothering dreams, you too could pace
> Behind the wagon that we flung him in,
> And watch the white eyes writhing in his face,
> His hanging face, like a devil's sick of sin;
> If you could hear, at every jolt, the blood
> Come gargling from the froth-corrupted lungs,
> Bitten as the cud
> Of vile, incurable sores on innocent tongues,—
> My friend, you would not tell with such high zest
> To children ardent for some desperate glory,
> The old Lie: *Dulce et decorum est*
> *Pro patria mori.*[4]

It would be hard to find a more powerful indictment of the romantic glorification of war. But note: when Owen's attention turns from creation for its own sake to persuasion, he does not, thereby, stop being a poet. He adds to the making of the poem a second purpose. His experience demands action, and he points his poem toward action—not a specific, particular action, but one which will vary depending upon what we have been doing and saying. For the "you" of the poem, it is a demand to stop glamorizing war in ignorant oratory; for the rest of us it may be simply a demand that we stop listening to such talk.

This piece of serious persuasion is obviously on the creative-experiential side. Intellectually, Owen's argument is simple enough:

---

[4] FROM "Dulce et Decorum Est" by Wilfred Owen, from *The Poems of Wilfred Owen*. All rights reserved. Reprinted by permission of New Directions, Publishers.

"You [the war propagandist] say death in war is a noble sacrifice; I say it is a hellish death. And I know, because I was there." It would be possible to quote other persuasive writers on the same subject whose arguments are more conceptual than experiential. For the two kinds of knowledge and the two basic kinds of writing (informative and creative) naturally tend to produce two modes of persuasion, quite different—in their purer forms—in the kind of forcefulness they achieve, although they are more often found in various combinations.

It may be more interesting, however, at this point, to quote another writer who is also more on the experiential than on the conceptual side, and who is also dealing with war. The writer is Lincoln, and the piece of writing is the Gettysburg Address.

Fourscore and seven years ago our fathers brought forth on this continent a new nation, conceived in liberty, and dedicated to the proposition that all men are created equal. Now we are engaged in a great civil war, testing whether that nation, or any nation so conceived and so dedicated, can long endure. We are met on a great battlefield of that war. We have come to dedicate a portion of that field, as a final resting place for those who here gave their lives that that nation might live. It is altogether fitting and proper that we should do this. But, in a larger sense, we cannot dedicate—we cannot consecrate—we cannot hallow—this ground. The brave men, living and dead, who struggled here, have consecrated it, far above our poor power to add or detract. The world will little note, nor long remember, what we say here, but it can never forget what they did here. It is for us the living, rather, to be dedicated here to the unfinished work which they who fought here have thus far so nobly advanced. It is rather for us to be here dedicated to the great task remaining before us,—that from these honored dead we take increased devotion to that cause for which they gave the last full measure of devotion—that we here highly resolve that these dead shall not have died in vain—that this nation, under God, shall have a new birth of freedom—and that government of the people, by the people, for the people, shall not perish from the earth.

This, again, is persuasion, one of history's supremely great calls to action, matched only by such masterpieces as Winston Churchill's inspired oratory during World War II. As a persuasive writer and speaker, Lincoln is seeking to inspire his listeners and readers to intensify their efforts, whatever these may be, toward victory for the Union. This is the "action" he is asking for; and it will vary from one person to another. For some it undoubtedly means death.

But Lincoln never for a moment pretends that it is "sweet and fitting to die for one's country," though his belief in America is so deep that he identifies its destiny with the destiny of mankind. His faith in the cause is equaled by the depth of his awareness of the suffering and tragedy that his plea entails. We doubt that even Wilfred Owen would have objected to this plea for greater sacrifice in time of crisis.

We have in the Address then, as in Owen's poem, persuasion of a high order, precisely because it grows out of, and bases its appeal on, knowledge. What Lincoln does is to share with his audience at Gettysburg his vision of America, of the war, of the meaning of the battle, and of the implications of these things for the future of the human race. There is more of an intellectual argument in Lincoln than in Owen, but the knowledge is still essentially experiential.

In a later section of this book we shall look more closely at persuasive writing, including various kinds of informative or conceptual persuasion as well as of creative persuasion, and various combinations of the two modes. We shall also look at the kind of persuasion which focuses its attention not upon knowledge at all but upon the response of the audience. Persuasion of this kind is primarily manipulative. At the moment we will say only that it does not deserve to be taken seriously by critical readers—for exactly the same reason that the great mass of inferior informative and creative writing does not deserve to be taken seriously: none of this mass literature, whatever use of language it represents, has much to do with knowledge. Some, of course, is the product of sincere but mediocre people who have very little to say; but a large part of it—whether informative, creative, or persuasive—is put together out of an essentially cynical sense of what the mass reader wants, and of how he can best be manipulated. This does not mean that manipulative writing can be safely ignored by the critical reader. It bulks large in the reading matter of the world, and the persuasive variety, at least, has great potential dangers.

As for serious persuasive writing, we can say at this stage simply that the points made about informative and creative writing of the serious sort also apply to the modes of persuasion which grow out of them. If the persuasion is basically informative, we approach it much as we do informative writing; if it is of the more creative kind—as are Owen's poem and Lincoln's speech—we approach it much as we would any creative writing, judging it on the validity of the experiential knowledge which it creates, and thinking in terms of its richness and unity. And to the extent that a persuasive article mixes conceptual and experiential knowledge, we will look at it from both points of view. In addition we cannot, and should not, refrain from noticing that knowledge, of either kind, has in persuasion become instrumental. If the action toward which the work points is relevant to us today, we are bound to consider it in the light of our own general system of values, though we should be able to see its worth even when we are not able or willing to follow where it leads us.

Summary

In this chapter, after a brief look at the range of purposes which language serves, we have focused our attention on what are probably its three most important formal public uses: the *informative,* the *creative,* and the *persuasive.* The first two are directly related to the two kinds of knowledge discussed in Chapter 1; informative writing deals chiefly with conceptual knowledge, creative writing with experiential knowledge. The two kinds of writing overlap, however, just as the two kinds of knowledge do. Persuasive writing, in its serious forms, grows directly out of the informative and the creative. It therefore may occur in two modes (though the modes are probably more often combined in various ways) because persuasion goes beyond knowledge for its own sake, tending to transform knowledge into attitudes and—ultimately—into action.

Perhaps these relationships can be most easily summed up in a simple chart. The horizontal axis represents the range of knowledge, from experiential on the left to conceptual on the right; the vertical axis represents the range of purpose, from knowledge for its own sake, at the top, to knowledge in the service of action, at the bottom. The circles, which stand for the three chief uses of language, overlap:

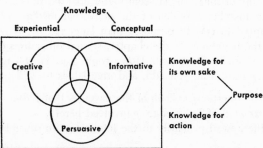

The analyses of specific passages have, so far, been very general, partly because the analysis of language for any purpose is a quite technical matter. Before we can do much with the details of any piece of writing, we must first become conversant with a few technical concepts. These will be the business of the next two chapters.

EXERCISES

A. Think about the following questions for class discussion:
   1. Reread the passage by Berton Roueché (p. 19). At what specific points and in exactly what ways does this writing seem to you more (or less) than purely informative?
   2. Is there any sense in which the passage from *Huckleberry Finn* might be called informative? Just what sort of information does it contain?
   3. Can you venture any guesses, at this stage, as to just *how* Samuel Clemens makes the scene in the cabin "come to life"?
   4. At the end of "Dulce et Decorum Est," Wilfred Owen uses as his example of "the old Lie" a very famous line from a revered Latin poet, Horace, rather than a quotation from a contemporary orator. What is the effect here of bringing in this allusion to a classical author?
   5. What is the conceptual content—that is, the *intellectual* argument—in the Gettysburg Address? Try translating it into informative (conceptual) language.
   6. What are some of the ways in which Lincoln's Address resembles poetry?
   7. Nothing has been said in this chapter about *nonverbal* media of communication and expression, such as painting, photography, sculpture, architecture, the motion picture, music, and the graphic arts. Can you cite examples of the same three purposes —informative, creative, and persuasive—in any of these media? Do any of these media seem better adapted to certain purposes than to others? Which of the nonverbal media seem less well adapted to certain purposes than language is? Why?
   8. At the beginning of the chapter, several other uses of language were briefly illustrated. How would you label each of these other uses? Can you add, and give labels to, still further uses?

B. Apply these questions to each of the passages that follow:
   1. What kind of knowledge is involved here?
   2. Is the appeal primarily to the intellect or to other faculties?

3. What sort of response would the passage normally elicit?
4. What are the relative roles of language and "subject matter"? Why does one absorb our attention more than the other? Or are they of equal importance?
5. What is your judgment of the passage, and what criterion or criteria did you use?

Passages:

a. There is a dress designed for every woman. Her problem is to find it and to know it when she has found it. To be well dressed, any woman needs knowledge of the optical illusion of line, of becoming color, of fitness of purpose. First, consider becoming line. There are five general types of figures: 1. The very tall and slim; 2. the short; 3. the stout; 4. the narrow hipped and wide shouldered; 5. the wide hipped and narrow shouldered. Types 1 and 4 are considered ideal now, and many clothes are designed with them in mind. They do not have as hard a problem. Type 1 should choose dresses with horizontal lines, with shoulder breadth, full sleeves, blouses and jackets contrasting with the color of the skirt to cut the height, never tight or slim skirts but wide, flared, or pleated in wide pleats. . . .[5]

(*Encyclopedia Americana*)

b. *Upon Julia's Clothes*

Whenas in silks my Julia goes,
Then, then, methinks, how sweetly flows
The liquefaction of her clothes!

Next, when I cast mine eyes and see
That brave vibration each way free,
—O how that glittering taketh me!
(ROBERT HERRICK, 1591–1674)

c. I can make myself sick at any time with comparing the dazzling splendor wherewith our gentlewomen were embellished in some former habits, with the gut-foundered goosedom wherewith they are now surcingled and debauched. We have about five or six of them [fashionably dressed women] in our colony; if I see any of them accidentally, I cannot cleanse my fancy of them for a month after. I . . . purposed lately to make a step over to my native country for a yokefellow: but when I consider how women there have tripe-

[5] FROM "Principles of Good Dress" by Kay Hardy, reprinted from *The Encyclopedia Americana*. By permission of *The Encyclopedia Americana*.

wifed themselves with their cladments, I have no heart to the voyage, lest their nauseous shapes and the sea should work too sorely upon my stomach. . . . As for such a woman, I look at her as the very gizzard of a trifle, the product of a quarter of a cipher, the epitome of nothing, fitter to be kicked, if she were of a kickable substance, than either honored or humored.

(NATHANIEL WARD, 1578–1652)

d. The fluid ripple of pleats below a smoothly shaped bodice . . . the yoke a simple curve of flattery in this textured silk dress by Georgia Bullock that moves gracefully forward into summer . . . red or black . . . 10 to 16 sizes 98.95.

(From an advertisement in the *New Yorker* magazine)

C. Find three or four more good examples of informative, creative, and persuasive writing on some one subject, and try out the questions in Exercise B on them.

D. Try the rewording test on the following pair of passages:

1. The fire beyond the belt of woods on the farther side of the creek, reflected to earth from the canopy of its own smoke, was now suffusing the whole landscape. It transformed the sinuous line of mist to the vapor of gold. The water gleamed with dashes of red, and red, too, were many of the stones protruding above the surface. But that was blood; the less desperately wounded had stained them in crossing. On them, too, the child now crossed with eager steps; he was going to the fire. As he stood upon the farther bank he turned about to look at the companions of his march. The advance was arriving at the creek. The stronger had already drawn themselves to the brink and plunged their faces into the flood.

(AMBROSE BIERCE, 1842–1914?, "Chickamauga")

2. The fury of Bragg's assault spent itself uselessly on the heroic divisions under Thomas, who remained on the field until night and then withdrew in good order to Rossville. Here he remained on the 21st, imposing respect upon the victors. On the 22nd Rosecrans had re-established order, and Thomas fell back quietly to Chattanooga, whither Bragg slowly pursued. . . . The losses in the battle bear witness to a severity in the fighting unusual even in the American Civil War. Of 70,000 Confederates engaged at least 18,000 were killed and wounded, and the Federals lost 16,000 out of about 57,000.[6]

("Chickamauga Creek," *Encyclopaedia Britannica*)

[6] FROM "Chickamauga Creek," reprinted from *Encyclopaedia Britannica,* 11th edition. By permission of *Encyclopaedia Britannica.*

E. Before turning to Chapter 3, explain as well as you can the difference in wording between a passage which conveys conceptual knowledge and one which creates experiential knowledge.

F. After reading Chapter 1, you wrote a double account of some object, place, event, or person. If the subject is at all suitable, try turning one of your accounts into a piece of persuasion. If it is not suitable, write a new informative or creative account and turn it into persuasion. Then explain how the persuasive version differs from the one on which it was based.

3. Words and Meaning

> Symbolization is . . . the starting point of all intel-
> lection in the human sense, and is more general than
> thinking, fancying, or taking action. For the brain is
> not merely a great transmitter, a super-switchboard; it
> is better likened to a great transformer. The current of
> experience that passes through it undergoes a change
> of character . . . by virtue of a primary use which is
> made of it immediately: it is sucked into the stream
> of symbols which constitutes a human mind.[1]
>
> SUSANNE K. LANGER, *Philosophy in a New Key*

Language as Symbol

Before we can share our knowledge, whatever kind it may be
or whatever our purpose in sharing it, we must first embody it in
symbols. Some thinkers even contend that nothing can truly be
called knowledge until it has somehow been crystallized in symbolic
form. Man has devised various methods of symbolizing his experience. Gestures and other bodily movements are used as simple
modes of expression and are formalized in pantomime, dance, ritual,
and the whole complex art of acting. Objects, also, are used as
symbols—crowns and crosses, tombstones and medallions, cathedrals
and courtrooms, cars and clothes, even houses and their furnishings.
More obviously symbolic, perhaps, are music and painting, sculpture and drawing, photography, and mathematics. Even entire occasions, such as ceremonial events or stage performances, are symbolic
constructions, usually employing many different modes of symbolism working together.

[1] FROM *Philosophy in a New Key* by Susanne K. Langer. Reprinted by permission of Harvard University Press.

Above all there is language. That language occupies a special place among modes of symbolism is fairly obvious. It is universal: all societies, no matter how "primitive," have fully developed languages; and all normal people (and even some mentally handicapped people) can learn to use language. It is versatile: it can be made either audible or visual—in Braille even tactile; it is portable, always at hand and ready for use without special equipment of any kind; it is relatively unobtrusive in itself. It also has one other great advantage: it is capable of embodying both experiential and conceptual knowledge. This is not true of all modes of symbolism. Music and architecture, for instance, are not good vehicles for conceptual knowledge, despite their power to generate experience; nor are mathematics and graphics, though most satisfactory for dealing with conceptual knowledge, of much use in creating experiential knowledge. Language, however, can do both jobs. Just how this is possible is the theme of this chapter and the next.

Three Aspects of Meaning

Unlike most kinds of symbolism, language has a "vocabulary." It is made up of a great many very small units (words), each of which is independently meaningful. Separate musical notes, or colors, or stones in a building do not have "meaning" in this sense. An account of meaning in language might well begin, therefore, with a moment in which a single word takes on meaning.

A child, out walking in the country with his father, suddenly has a startling experience. He sees something long and black slithering through the grass at his feet.

"What's that?" he asks.

"That's a blacksnake," his father tells him.

"What's a blacksnake?" the child asks.

"That—the thing you just saw," his father says, not without some annoyance.

"But what *is* a blacksnake?" the child persists.

"Oh," his father says, catching on at last to the sort of question the child is asking, "it's one kind of snake. You know what a snake is. A blacksnake is harmless to people . . . eats toads and mice. Some of them get to be five or six feet long."

The child stares at the place where the snake was. "I don't like blacksnakes!" he decides.

This imaginary conversation reflects only one of several processes by which we learn the "meaning" of words. It does, however, illustrate three aspects of meaning: two of them, which we will call *conceptual* meaning and *evocative* meaning, are *kinds* of meaning; the third, *denotation,* is best thought of not as a kind of meaning but as a *source* of meaning. We will consider first the aspect which our fable of the child and the snake began with—denotation.

Denotation

In the simplest terms, the denotation of a word is what it names, that for which it is an accepted label. But the moment we try to expand this simple definition, we run into philosophical problems. What *is* it that a word names or labels? An easy—but much oversimplified—answer is that what a word names is an object or event, an external "thing" that has its own independent existence in time and space, wholly apart from any observer's experience of it. From this point of view, the denotation of *blacksnake* includes the object which the child saw and all other objects roughly like it. This is perhaps the most common way of viewing denotation, but it presents certain problems, both practical and theoretical.

On the practical side, this simplified, "objective" view of denotation implies that only nouns have denotations. Thus, the noun *snake* clearly labels a class of "things," but how about the adjective *snakelike?* The noun *plain* obviously names the kind of thing we have in mind when we speak, for example, of the Great Plains, but how about the adjective *plain?* And yet both of these adjectives, *snakelike* and *plain,* do name qualities or characteristics which we have all experienced, which we can talk about without totally misunderstanding each other, and which we would readily agree are therefore "real."

More seriously, the simplified way of looking at denotation tends to imply that the only "real" things are those which have an existence outside ourselves. It suggests, for example, that *blacksnake* and *pulpit* denote "realities," whereas *pain* and *boredom,* since they do not refer to external, observable entities, lack any real denotation. And yet pain and boredom are both terribly real experiences.

As a final example, the simplified view tends to suggest that the only "real" entities are things which we can apprehend with our senses, even though modern science has made it very clear that our sensory apparatus has serious limitations. Thus, from the "objective" point of view, *snake* and *metal* are somehow more "real" than *gene* and *electron.*

Now, it seems too bad to define a useful term like *denotation* in such a way as to introduce such practical and philosophical limitations. The authors of this book cannot accept any of the three implications mentioned above: in our view, it is most useful to be able to apply the term *denotation* to other words besides nouns; there may or may not be "things" which "really" exist independent of our experience of them; and our sense of reality includes "things" which cannot be perceived by the senses.

In short, men know very little about what philosophers have sometimes called "things-in-themselves." Men are, however, acquainted, through experience of all sorts, with a vast variety of phenomena. In this book, therefore, we shall see *denotation,* not in terms of objects and events, or of "things," but in terms of phenomena (in the broadest sense of that term), and we shall define the denotation of a word as *all the phenomena, taken individually or collectively, for which the word is an acceptable name.* From this point of view, it is possible to say that the words *snake, snakelike, plain* (as noun), *plain* (as adjective), *pulpit, pain, boredom, metal, gene,* and *electron* all have denotations.

As we have said at the beginning, denotation is not a kind of meaning, but a source of meaning. Denotation is what brings a word to mind; meaning is what a word brings to mind. Except in fairy tales, the use of a word cannot produce its denotation. The word *toothache* cannot, fortunately, produce a toothache, the phenomenon which the word denotes. The word *toothache* can, however, produce meaning.

Two Kinds of Meaning

We can distinguish two basically different kinds of meaning. For one thing, a word can bring to mind an idea or concept. It is this kind of meaning that the child is after when he asks, "What *is* a blacksnake?" He wants an idea, or set of ideas, which he can associate with both the new word *blacksnake* and the phenomenon to which his father has applied the word. Like most of us, his father is an amateur at answering this sort of question. It is far easier to attach labels than it is to state their meanings. But he does at least try to suggest part of the idea which *blacksnake* stands for, as he understands it. A good dictionary would, of course, do a much better job. This first kind of meaning, the kind collected in dictionaries, we will call *conceptual meaning*.

But even the best dictionary definition could never include all of the meaning which the term *blacksnake* is beginning to acquire for the child. Seeing the snake did more than merely arouse the child's intellectual curiosity. It was a startling experience, and apparently somewhat unpleasant: "I don't like blacksnakes!" It will almost certainly leave a residue of memories, including certain mental pictures, or images—of the phenomenon snake, of the snake wriggling through the grass, perhaps of the whole episode, including this walk with his father. Some of these images may remain for some time in the child's mind, always associated with the word *blacksnake*. And these memories will also have, in this case, an emotional coloration, including attitudes of fear, disgust, revulsion. All of these associated images, feelings, and attitudes constitute a second kind of meaning which the word *blacksnake* is beginning to take on for the child. We will lump together all these associations, including memories of the denotation, under the general term *evocative meaning*.

No word, probably, acquires definite and permanent meanings on first encounter. The conceptual meaning of *blacksnake* outlined roughly by the child's father will be refined and developed later. Even if the child never sees another blacksnake, he will hear and read about them. Similar changes will also take place in the evocative meaning of the word, as the child adds to his experience of the phenomenon called *snake* or develops from other sources associations with the word or with its denotation.

A Pair of Definitions

A discussion of the denotation of the term *blacksnake* does not belong in this book, but in a book on reptiles. However, the two kinds of meaning we have seen the word take on are very much our concern. And we should make sure that we understand the conceptual meanings of *conceptual meaning* and *evocative meaning*:

1. The *conceptual meaning* of a word is the idea for which the word stands and which it is therefore capable of bringing to mind. A good dictionary definition is a statement of a word's conceptual meaning.
2. The *evocative meaning* of a word is everything else which the word is capable of bringing to mind. This "everything else" may include images and other memories of the word's denotation. It may also include various other images, feelings, and attitudes which are associated with the word or with its denotation. Dictionary definitions usually tell us very little about the evocative meaning of words.

All genuine words have at least one conceptual meaning, and most words have more than one. Even so simple a word as *a* brings to mind the idea of oneness; even an interjection like *ah* brings to mind the idea of sudden, strong feeling (*Webster's* suggests "regret, contempt, delight," etc.).

Similarly, all words are capable of carrying evocative meaning for at least some people, and some words are highly evocative for most people. Evocative meaning will naturally vary a great deal more from person to person than will conceptual meaning. And, as we shall see later, exactly what a word evokes depends far more on how a word is used than on any inherent evocativeness it may possess. This is one reason why dictionaries make little attempt to deal with evocative meanings.

In the rest of this chapter we will explore a few questions raised by these three aspects of meaning.

Conceptual Meaning and Denotation

We know very little about how most words originally came to be associated with the particular phenomena they denote. One exception is the relatively few words which are obviously onomatopoeic (which sound like what they denote) such as *buzz, whiz, bang, jolt*. Another exception is words which were coined so recently that their full history can be known. And, of course, we do know where a great many words came from in the sense that we can trace their derivation from other words, belonging sometimes to other languages. But in general the connection between particular words and their denotation seems arbitrary.

We can, however, explain some parts of the process by which words initially came to denote and to have meaning. A word begins to acquire conceptual meaning at the same time that it is first used to denote certain phenomena. Someone notices at least one instance (usually several instances) of a particular phenomenon. He senses that this phenomenon is unique or that it represents a new class of phenomena. If other people share his sense of discovery, some label will be found for this new phenomenon or class. It comes to be called *blacksnake* or *democracy* or *pain* or *grief*. At the same time, people are, of course, beginning to recognize the characteristics of this new class of phenomena—the features which its members have in common and which distinguish it from all other classes. These characteristics become the core of the new label's conceptual meaning. Thereafter, a phenomenon will be accepted as part of the word's denotation only if it fits the general idea of the class (the word's conceptual meaning). But if a new member differs even slightly from other members of the class, its inclusion will at the same time slightly modify the idea of the class (the word's conceptual meaning). Theoretically, then, a sense of what a word denotes and a sense of the word's conceptual meaning develop simultaneously.

This process is illustrated by our incident of the child and the snake. The child encountered a (to him) new phenomenon. The father, however, was already acquainted with this phenomenon and was able to furnish a ready-made label for it, even able to add a crude definition of the word's conceptual meaning. In fact all of us, especially in our younger years, learn many new words in precisely this way. More often, probably, we meet an unfamiliar word at a time when no instance of its denotation is present, or when no one is around to point to it. Or the denotation may be such that it cannot be pointed to anyway. We read the word, or hear it, and then try to decide what it denotes, what its conceptual meaning must be. Usually we succeed, after a fashion, especially if the word happens to be used several times. Or we may look it up in a dictionary or ask someone about it. We may then discover that we are already acquainted with the class of phenomena it denotes. Or we may not encounter an instance of the denotation until later, perhaps never. A great many of the words that any educated person uses all his life he understands, both conceptually and evocatively, without ever experiencing the phenomena that they denote. And, of course, it is pleasant to avoid personal knowledge of the denotations of some words: *war, shipwreck, anguish.*

Any extension of the denotation of a word modifies its total conceptual meaning. Many of the technical terms used in baseball, for example, are ordinary, nontechnical words whose usual denotation has been extended metaphorically. Words like *fly, bat, home, steal, out, field,* and *foul* have thus taken on additional conceptual meanings (as the dictionary shows).

A final point about conceptual meaning and denotation: the more intimate and extensive our acquaintance with the denotation of a word, the more definite, detailed, and inclusive will be our awareness of its conceptual meanings. And, conversely, the better we understand a word's conceptual meanings, the more likely we are to apply it correctly as a name or label.

Evocative Meaning and Denotation

Up to a point, the statements just made about conceptual meaning also apply here—that is, close and repeated familiarity with the denotation of a word should enrich our sense of the word's evocative meanings. This is no doubt one reason why good writers prefer to deal with what they know well firsthand.

It is also possible, however, to become so habituated to some experiences that they become stale for us: we are no longer capable of responding to them emotionally or imaginatively. For example, Dr. Keene, the social scientist of our fable, may be able to respond more freshly to life in Deep River than Henry Haines does, simply because Deep River is new to him. And many professional writers, even though they like to write about the familiar, also like to get away from the familiar, at least temporarily. The same principle applies to language: words which may seem commonplace technical terms to the baseball fan may appear as colorful, imaginative, even poetic, to a person attending his first game. And one important function of literature is to refresh our feelings and imaginations. Creative writing in particular serves to restore our sensitivity to both experience and language.

If there seems to be an inconsistency here, we should remember that evocative meaning encompasses many kinds of mental events. One component of evocative meaning is image, and it is pretty hard to store up vivid images without having some knowledge of a term's denotation. But evocative meaning also involves feelings and attitudes, both of which can be dulled by prolonged acquaintance either with words or with what the words stand for.

A Note on Abstraction

One aspect of the relation between evocative meaning and denotation deserves special treatment. Some words have denotations which give rise to rather specific and memorable images or other sense impressions. Other words have such varied and far-reaching denotations that the images attached to them are indistinct or even nonexistent. The word *cow*, for example, produces a far more distinct image than does the term *farm animal*. This is because the denotation of the word *cow* consists of a great number of phenomena, all pretty much alike. Any one instance is fairly representative of the class as a whole. On the other hand, the denotation of *farm animal* consists of an even larger number of phenomena many of which are quite unlike each other. The word, therefore, does not call to mind any single, distinct image.

This example illustrates the distinction people usually have in mind when they talk about *concrete* terms and *abstract* ones, though these two words are rather tricky and imply differences which are only relative. Thus though *cow* may be more concrete than *farm animal, farm animal* is probably more concrete than *agricultural asset*. Some words, furthermore, are so very abstract that any single instance of the denotation bears no recognizable relation to the concept as a whole. Thus the phenomena which give rise to a concept such as electron—that is, which belong to its denotation—are certain "pointer readings" (marks on a dial and shapes on an oscilloscope). It is not memories of these pointer readings, however, which are called to mind by the word, but the concept. If any images arise, they have been put there by analogy: we have seen models of the atom, and hence of electrons. But we have no images of electrons "as such."

The words we have discussed so far are, basically, nouns. But the principle of abstraction applies also to words used as verbs, adjectives, and adverbs. Thus an action verb like *amble* is more concrete than a verb like *proceed;* an adjective like *scarlet* is more concrete than one like *colored.*

What we have just said suggests a very rough rule: in general, since the more concrete word carries more precise and vivid images, it is more evocative than a less concrete word. But it would be wrong to assume that the more concrete term is *in all respects* more evocative. A word can be evocative in more than one way: it can call to mind images; it can evoke attitudes; it can arouse strong feelings. For example, many very abstract terms are highly evocative because we feel strongly about the very concepts they call to mind—*justice, progress, democracy, totalitarianism* are all examples. And in any case, as we shall see in the next chapter, far more important than any intrinsic evocative power of words is their power to evoke because of the context in which they appear.

Language as Mold

Our discussion so far in this chapter may suggest that words are simply names for bits of experience. Many modern scholars oppose this view. Language, they point out, also tends to determine *what* we will experience and what meaning we will find in it: language is in part a mold which shapes experience itself. Some Eskimo tribes have many different words for different kinds of snow—but no word for a general phenomenon snow. A person brought up in this language presumably does not experience the general phenomenon of snow at all; instead he sees particular forms of snow, as determined by the stock of names in his vocabulary. If this seems strange and primitive to us, we might reflect that the same condition exists in our own culture. In discussing communication, for example, we have a great number of terms—such as painting, music, mathematics, sculpture, gesture, and pantomime—but no generic term which embraces them all: the best we can do at the moment is to label them negatively as *nonverbal media.* And this lack of a general term hinders both discussion and perception.

Not only the terms but the very structure of a language may determine the way the user understands the world he lives in. The Hopi Indian language makes no distinction between past, present, and future, either in vocabulary or in verb forms. Men using such a language probably would have great difficulty in seeing history as most of us see it. They might have less difficulty than we do in understanding the theory of relativity. Our own language, on the other hand, is rich in transitive verbs: we tend to see a subject as doing something to an object. And it is certainly conceivable that our action-conscious culture is conditioned by this characteristic of our language. In fact, the reason we have been so long in recognizing the effects of language structure on thought is probably our limited acquaintance, until very recently, with languages which are structurally unlike our own. Latin, Greek, French, German, and Spanish are all first cousins of English, and hence embody the same structures and concepts.

How Meaning Changes

An additional point is suggested by the cultural approach to language to which we have just referred. The group of languages just mentioned—along with a number of others—are known to be descended from a common but remote ancestor. Their very diversity, however, clearly demonstrates that languages are not fixed but changing. And the changes which are reflected in the differences between, let us say, English and Latin are still operating today. Even the best dictionary gives only a fragmentary view of a language at a particular moment in its history. There is really no such thing as an "unabridged" dictionary: every new edition is out of date before it even reaches the presses.

New words are coined every day; pronunciations change; even spellings change. And so, of course, do the meanings of words. Among the many causes both for additions to the general vocabulary and for changes in meaning, we shall look here at three: the need for new labels, shifts in attitudes and values, and the influence of literature.

Need for New Labels. Man is forever discovering or creating new categories for which he needs labels. Sometimes he makes up a label, but it is usually more convenient to borrow one which already exists. We can see both the invention and borrowing of labels most clearly in slang, which is one of the growing edges of language. For example, when a new group of young rebels-against-society began to make themselves heard after World War II, someone labeled them the "Beat" generation, though the evocative meanings of the slang word *beat* (defeated, exhausted, apathetic) were quite inappropriate to the new group. (The term was actually taken over from jazz: the new group were trying to feel the beat, to "get with it.") Then in 1957, the first Russian satellite went into orbit, and the Russian word *sputnik* came into the English vocabulary. Shortly thereafter, newspapers began to refer to members of the beat generation as *Beatniks*—a coinage expressing disapproval and suggesting sardonically an unfavorable comparison with the Russians: they had their *sputniks;* we had our *Beatniks.*

Shifts in Attitude. In the example just given, new concepts and shifts in attitude are perhaps both at work. It may be well, however, to look at a few other examples—also from slang—which chiefly reflect changing attitudes. A few years ago the slang word *hot* was a complimentary term (as applied to people); today *cool* is much more complimentary. *Square* used to be an adjective of approval; today it has become a noun of derision. *Sharp,* in slang, used to imply dishonesty; now it implies intelligence or neatness of appearance. Thus the meanings of words, especially their evocative meanings, constantly change in accordance with shifts in attitude and value.

Influence of Literature. Most of the day-by-day changes in the meanings of words take place in a world quite outside of literature, the world of informal spoken language. But occasionally a writer happens along who uses a word or phrase so effectively and so originally that he permanently changes its meaning. The name Babbitt was not invented by Sinclair Lewis. Besides being a family name, it was the name for an antifriction alloy; but Lewis made it, by writing a novel, a powerful symbol for a particular kind of modern middle-class person and a whole set of bourgeois values. The term *wasteland* was nothing new to English in the 1920's; but it did not have the power to suggest spiritual sterility until T. S. Eliot used it as the title of a long poem. The phrase *brave new world* goes back at least as far as Shakespeare—in fact, it was from Shakespeare's play *The Tempest* that Aldous Huxley borrowed it as a name for his novel about a socialistic-scientific utopia of the future. And it has now become, with all its ironic overtones, an everyday part of the language.

Public and Private Meanings

By their very nature, as intellectual abstractions from experience, conceptual meanings tend to be far more stable than evocative meanings. They are also, for the same reason, more public or impersonal. All of us do, of course, occasionally find that we "misunderstand" the conceptual meaning of some term. We have a *private* notion of its meaning which is different from the *public* notion. When this happens, we are likely to misuse the word. This kind of mistake naturally tends to correct itself rather quickly. But even when we don't actually make mistakes of this sort, our individual sense of the conceptual meaning of a term may not correspond exactly to someone else's. Because people's experience and education always differ at least slightly, they never classify all phenomena in exactly the same way. Two men, asked to pick out the boats from a number of conveyances along a waterfront, might not make exactly the same selection. One man might include a canoe but exclude a raft; another might exclude both. This indicates that the two men have at least slightly different notions of the idea which *boat* stands for.

In general, however, our sense of conceptual meanings tends toward conformity with the public, conventional sense. Our sense of evocative meanings, on the other hand, will vary much more from one person to another, as a result of variations in personal experience with both the word's denotation and the word itself. To one man the word *Negro* may have one set of evocative meanings, while to another it will have an almost opposite set. To a man of little education the word *Babbitt* might have none of the evocative force which it had for Lewis and has for people who have read his novel.

Evocative meanings do vary greatly from one person to another, yet in a particular culture at a particular time there is also rather more public agreement about what particular words mean evocatively than we sometimes recognize. In fact, if this were not so— if many words did not tend to carry similar evocative meanings for most people—neither poetry nor propaganda would be possible. All writers who depend heavily on the evocative power of language have to assume a large degree of agreement about evocative meanings. They have to assume that most of their readers will sense, for example, a difference in evocative meaning between words with similar conceptual meaning: *thrifty* and *stingy*, *firm* and *stubborn*, *chopped sirloin* and *hamburger*, *tuxedo* and *monkey suit*, *leader* and *boss*, *diplomat* and *apple-polisher*.

Words as "Things"

Semanticists (people who study the science of meaning) are fond of pointing out that "the word is not the thing." And, of course, they are right; a word is not the thing itself—whatever the thing is—but a symbol for it. However, words are "things" in their own right: they are sounds and visible notations for sounds. All good writers take into account the sound of their words and sentences; and in some uses of language the "thingness" of words becomes an important part of the writer's resources. Rhythm and rhyme call attention to the sounds of words, as does the repetition of initial sounds (alliteration) exemplified in the phrase "full fathom five." Many words also are onomatopoeic, sounding like the phenomena they name—*hiss, howl, clang*. Even the visual appearance of words on a page may contribute to the meaning of a piece of writing. Most words, however, possess little value as "things" until they are made to interact somehow with the other words around them.

How We Determine Meaning

Considering some of the aspects of language which we have noted in this chapter, it may seem almost miraculous that we manage to communicate at all. Words have meanings in such different ways, their meanings are all so changeable, and they vary so much from person to person—how are we ever able to figure out what the other fellow is talking or writing about?

There can be no doubt that denotation often helps pin down meaning. In many situations, the most practical test of whether two people are in fact using a word in the same way is not to compare conceptual meanings (definitions), which sometimes only complicates matters, but to compare denotations. For example, we might best decide whether we are all using the word *red* in the same way by picking out the "reds" from an array of color samples. In practice, we seldom go to this much trouble in dealing with words which denote the simple and tangible, but we often do precisely this in dealing with words whose denotations are more complex. The most sensible approach to the problem of what the word *tragedy* means might well be to look at specific literary works which we could agree are all part of the denotation of *tragedy*. We could then go on to develop a mutually acceptable statement of the term's conceptual meaning.

If it is not possible to "point," in this fashion, to instances of denotation, we can always resort to a good dictionary. This will not help us much to get at whatever evocative meanings may be intended, but it will at least define the *range* of probable conceptual meanings. And this can definitely help, assuming, of course, that the word is being used literally and in some conventional sense. If it is being used in a special way, or if—as so often in poetry—it is being used not literally but figuratively, even the best dictionary may not give us the main clues, nor would citing examples of denotation.

In such cases, we have to depend entirely upon what is, after all, our one habitual aid in the determination of meaning—context. For in practice, the basic way in which we get at the full and precise meaning of words is by noting their interaction with the words around them. This principle is so fundamental to an understanding of how words actually operate in their various uses that we shall devote a separate chapter to it.

EXERCISES

A. Think about the following questions for class discussion:
1. Name several kinds of symbolism which are likely to be involved in a typical stage performance.
2. In theory, which comes first: the use of a word to denote certain phenomena *or* the formulation of its conceptual meaning?
3. Which comes first in practice?
4. For a given person, might a word acquire evocative meaning before it acquires conceptual meaning?

5. Cite some examples of words whose meanings you understand quite well but whose denotations you have never experienced firsthand. Are there other words whose denotations you have never even experienced vicariously through imaginative literature or art?

6. Which of the two sets of words you were able to list in 5 have stronger evocative meanings?

B. Make a collection of objects which constitute a part of the denotation of a term. (Your instructor may ask you to present these on a display board.) What characteristics would a new object need to have in order to become a legitimate member of this collection?

C. Write a description of the characteristics which the objects collected for Exercise B have in common. How is your description related to the conceptual meaning of the word which names the objects?

D. The scene is anywhere. The characters are the teacher and the pupil. The pupil understands no English except the words *yes, no, I, me, you, see, this.* The teacher is trying to add the following words to the pupil's vocabulary; *paper, strong, weak, flat, curved, bend, very, cloth, wood,* and *sadly.* (Your instructor may suggest a different list.) Assume that the necessary "props" are available. Write up, in play form, the scene in which the teacher teaches the pupil the new words. Place stage directions in parentheses. You may use each new word, as it is learned, to help explain the other words.

E. The problem here is to define a new word, *tripset*. Of the figures pictured below, C, D, E, and F are tripsets, whereas A, B, G, and H are not tripsets. Write a formal definition of *tripset* which would enable someone else to divide the group correctly into tripsets and non-tripsets. Then draw a new tripset.

A   B   C   D   E   F   G   H

F. Show that the over-all impression given by the following news story depends in part on the evocative meanings of certain words and phrases. Suggest synonyms for these words which would have made the story a more objective piece of writing than it now is.

Harvard's Dr. Helen Deane Markham, who has been in and out of her job as assistant professor of anatomy because of her refusal to say whether she is or has ever been a Communist, was in again. When Dr. Markham clammed up before the Jenner Subcommittee last March, the Corporation of the University cleared her of Red affiliations, announced she would keep her job. Then an FBI undercover agent identified Dr. Markham and her husband as Communists; Harvard reopened the case, suspended her with pay.

Last week, in a masterful bit of fence-straddling, the Corporation reinstated her, but announced she would not be reappointed when her present term expires next June. Cried the Boston *Herald:* "A ponderous pussyfooting . . . You can no more be partially loyal than you can be partially pregnant." [2]

(*Time* magazine)

G. Below are four English versions of the Twenty-third Psalm. Which verses seem to you to have noticeably different meanings in the different translations? To what extent is this difference caused by variations in conceptual meaning? Evocative meaning? Other factors?

King James	*Douai*
The Lord is my shepherd; I shall not want.	The Lord ruleth me: and I shall want nothing.
He maketh me to lie down in green pastures;	He hath set me in a place of pasture.
He leadeth me beside the still waters.	He hath brought me up on the water of refreshment:
He restoreth my soul;	He hath converted my soul,
He leadeth me in the paths of righteousness for his name's sake.	He hath led me on the paths of justice, for his own name's sake.
Yea, though I walk through the valley of the shadow of death	For though I would walk in the midst of the shadow of death
I will fear no evil: for thou art with me; Thy rod and Thy staff they comfort me.	I will fear no evils, for thou art with me; Thy rod and Thy staff, they have comforted me.
Thou preparest a table before me in the presence of mine enemies:	Thou has prepared a table before me, against them that afflict me.
Thou anointest my head with oil; my cup runneth over.	Thou has anointed my head with oil; and my chalice which inebriateth me, how goodly it is!
Surely goodness and mercy shall follow me all the days of my life:	And thy mercy will follow me all the days of my life.
And I will dwell in the house of the Lord forever.	And that I may dwell in the house of the Lord unto length of days.

[2] "In Again, Temporarily." Reprinted by permission from *Time* The Weekly Newsmagazine; copyright Time, Inc., 1953.

Monsignor Knox	Moffat
The Lord is my shepherd: how can I lack anything?	The Eternal shepherds me, I lack for nothing;
He gives me a resting place where there is green pasture,	He makes me lie in meadows green.
Leads me out to the cool water's brink, refreshed and content.	He leads me to refreshing streams, He revives life in me.
As in honour pledged, by sure path he leads me;	He guides me by true paths as he himself is true.
Dark be the valley about my path,	My road may run through a glen of gloom,
Hurt I fear none while he is with me;	But I fear no harm, for thou art beside me;
Thy rod, thy crook are my comfort	Thy club, thy staff—they give me courage.
Envious my foes watch, while thou dost spread a banquet before me;	Thou art my host, spreading a feast for me, while my foes have to look on.
Richly thou dost anoint my head with oil, well filled my cup.	Thou hast poured oil upon my head, my cup is brimming over.
All my life thy loving favor pursues me;	Yes, and all through my life goodness and kindness wait on me,
Through the long years the Lord's house shall be my dwelling-place.[3]	The Eternal's guest within his house evermore.[4]

H. Analyze the part played by the meaning of individual words, both conceptual and evocative, in the general effect of each of the following passages. Consider especially the italicized words and phrases.

1. TOUJOURS MOI . . . *Conceived, born, and bred in Paris* for you whose *instinct* leads to the most *alluring* in everything you wear. No other perfume *lingers so long and lovingly* . . . so *seductively* adds a new dimension to your charm.

2. GIANTS *MURDER* INDIANS

3. We, the People of the United States, in order to form *a more perfect* Union, *establish* Justice, insure domestic *Tranquility*, *provide* for the *common* Defense, promote the *general Welfare*, and *secure* the *Blessings of Liberty* to ourselves and our posterity,

[3] "The Twenty-third Psalm," from the *Old Testament,* Volume II, in the translation of Monsignor Ronald Knox, Copyright 1950, Sheed & Ward, Inc., New York. Permission to use the Knox translation was given by His Eminence the Cardinal Archbishop of Westminster and by Burns & Oates Ltd.

[4] "The Twenty-third Psalm," from: *The Bible: A New Translation* by James Moffatt. Copyright 1922, 1935 and 1950 by Harper & Brothers. Used by permission.

do *ordain* and *establish* this CONSTITUTION for the United States of America.

I. Below are two versions of a sonnet, Shakespeare's original version and a "modernization." How does the language of the two versions differ, in general? What part do conceptual meanings play in these differences? Evocative meanings?

1. When, in disgrace with Fortune and men's eyes,
    I all alone beweep my outcast state,
    And trouble deaf heaven with my bootless cries,
    And look upon myself and curse my fate,
    Wishing me like to one more rich in hope,
    Featur'd like him, like him with friends possess'd,
    Desiring this man's art, and that man's scope,
    With what I most enjoy contented least;
    Yet in these thoughts myself almost despising,
    Haply I think on thee, and then my state,
    Like to the lark at break of day arising
    From sullen earth, sings hymns at heaven's gate;
    For thy sweet love rememb'red such wealth brings
    That then I scorn to change my state with kings.

                    (WILLIAM SHAKESPEARE, 1564–1616)

2. When times are hard and old friends fall away
    And all alone I lose my hope and pluck,
    Doubting if God can hear me when I pray,
    And brood upon myself and curse my luck,
    Envying some stranger for his handsome face,
    His wit, his health, his chances, or his friends,
    Desiring this man's brains and that man's place,
    And vexed with all I have that makes amends,
    Yet in these thoughts myself almost despising—
    By chance I think of you; and then my mind,
    Like music from deep sullen murmurs rising
    To peals and raptures, leaves the earth behind:
    For if you care for me, what need I care
    To own the world or be a millionaire?

4. Context

"But 'glory' doesn't mean 'a nice knockdown argument,'" Alice objected.

"When I use a word," Humpty Dumpty said in
rather a scornful tone, "it means just what I choose it
to mean—neither more nor less."

"The question is," said Alice, "whether you can make
words mean so many different things."

"The question is," said Humpty Dumpty, "which is
to be Master—that's all."

LEWIS CARROLL, *Through the Looking Glass*

No Word Is an Island

It is always a little misleading to talk about meaning in terms of
individual words, as we did in the last chapter; for words seldom
act alone but function rather as members of teams. In the passage
from *Through the Looking Glass*, Humpty Dumpty is much too
arbitrary; but Alice is much too academic: she assumes that dictionaries tell the whole story and that dictionaries are always correct.
Humpty Dumpty assumes that he can change the meaning of a
word simply by deciding to change it. And so long as he is talking
to himself, he can, of course, assign any meanings he pleases. But
for communicating with others, neither Humpty Dumpty's arbitrary point of view nor Alice's academic one is adequate. In actual
use it is neither arbitrary decisions nor dictionary definitions which
control the meaning of a word, but the context in which it appears—
the other words which appear with it.

Now, in a broad sense, the context of a word includes not only
all the words which are used with it, but the social and physical

53

setting in which it is used as well. The single word *Fire!* means one thing when shouted on the rifle range and quite another thing when shouted in a crowded auditorium. But we shall focus our attention here only on verbal contexts.

Suppose we were to choose at random a few dozen words from a dictionary and write them down, in random order, like this:

> acrolith xanthous alderman vocative antidote towboat banker tarrier blackamoor sprouting bore shoulder by sandwort celibacy risible clearing rebuff conniption pump cornerstone prate crotch pinkeye deathbed perfect dilution orthodox easterner naiad erewhile miff fatherhood life front lax harmonize knot histoid instrumentation housemaid imprimatur.

This "passage" is not utterly meaningless. Each word is *per se* capable of conveying some kind of meaning. Even the words which we have never seen before may suggest other words which we do know, and thus bring something to mind. Quite by accident, a few of the words may even work together, in a rudimentary way: for example, *celibacy* and *risible* may suggest a crude joke; *rebuff* and *conniption* may suggest cause and effect; *perfect* and *dilution* go together as adjective and noun, as do *orthodox* and *easterner;* and *naiad* and *erewhile* are not wholly unrelated, because both sound archaic and vaguely "poetic."

Thus the random passage should bring to mind, for each reader, *some* assortment of ideas, images, feelings, and miscellaneous associations. But the assortment will be quite different for each reader, and none of the assortments will in any sense represent a "communication" from any writer to any reader. The passage thus tells us nothing about the content of a *writer's* mind, though study of a reader's response to the passage might tell a skilled psychologist some very interesting things about the content of that particular *reader's* mind. As a matter of fact, psychologists often use tests which are based on exactly this kind of "free association."

But language which is genuinely meaningful—which does represent a deliberate act of communication or expression—is not free but controlled. The control may be conscious or unconscious or—most likely—a mixture of the two. The basic meaningful units (words) are selected and arranged to form larger meaningful units (phrases, clauses, sentences), which in turn are selected and arranged to form still larger meaningful units (paragraphs, stanzas, scenes, etc.). No writer or speaker chooses a word simply for itself, but rather with an eye to the words that precede and will follow it. And a reader who wants the full meaning of what he reads attends not only to the separate words but to their interaction.

Context: An Elastic Concept

The context of a word is its verbal environment at any given time and place, the unique fabric of other words of which it is a part each time it is used. The context of a word is never exactly the same twice. Even when a word appears in two identical sentences, which happens for example when certain lines of a poem are repeated exactly, the sentences which surround these sentences are bound to differ at least slightly. In a poem the very fact that the line is repeated gives it a different context and changes the meaning of its parts.

How much of a word's context affects its meaning varies greatly, though. Sometimes only a few words, those immediately adjacent to the word in question, really matter; at other times, the entire piece of writing must be considered significant context. Here is an example of the first case:

BEETLES—The Japanese and rose beetle are the most destructive members of this large group of chewing insects. The former attacks the buds, flowers and foliage of many plants; the latter definitely prefers the buds and partially opened flowers of the rose.

We know as soon as we encounter them, without even thinking about it, what *rose* and *beetle* mean here. Context in the narrowest sense of the term is enough to put us straight. But what about *rose* and *worm* in this poem, by William Blake?

The Sick Rose

O Rose, thou art sick!
The invisible worm
That flies in the night,
In the howling storm,

Has found out thy bed
Of crimson joy,
And his dark secret love
Does thy life destroy.

(WILLIAM BLAKE,
1757–1827)

This is the whole poem, and we need every bit of it to decide what Blake means here by his key words. In fact, because this is an extreme case (Blake is the kind of poet who employs highly personal symbols), we may even need to go beyond this one poem and read more of his work, or at least some competent criticism, in order to feel sure what meanings the key words are supposed to carry. Is *Rose,* for example, a flower, a girl, anything beautiful and innocent? Is the *worm* a literal worm, or is it anything evil and sinister? Why is it invisible?

Thus, in some kinds of writing—especially the purely informative sort—the relevant context is nothing more than a few nearby words. In other kinds of writing, notably creative literature, the entire poem or essay, story or play, must be thought of as the relevant context. In the former case, context performs its role of determining meaning almost automatically; in the latter case, context may operate in very complex and subtle ways and require close attention. But whether context functions in a simple or complicated fashion, and whether we are conscious of its role or not, it is always at work, helping not only to control but also to create meaning.

In the next few pages we will note a few of the specific ways in which context functions.

Context Sets the LEVEL of Meaning

One important *general* service which context performs is to tell us *how literally* to interpret the words which comprise it. The passages cited above, from a book on gardening and from Blake, span the range of language from the barest, most literal prose to the most highly figurative poetry. Most writing falls somewhere within this range, and the reader has to decide what to take literally and what figuratively. Context provides the only reliable clues, because even when we know a writer's previous work very well we cannot be sure that he may not be deviating from his usual level of literalness. Most good authors experiment with various different styles and levels, and we must rely on the specific context in approaching each work.

Sometimes, of course, there is really no problem. This is especially true when, as with the roses and the beetles or worm, the level obviously lies close to either extreme. For instance, here is a sentence from an auto instruction manual:

When a fuse has blown out, it is not sufficient merely to replace it with a new one.

The very fact that this sentence does appear in a manual indicates that it is to be taken literally. But even if we see the sentence (as we do here) apart from its whole context, we are unlikely to look for any figurative meanings. *Fuse* here clearly refers to a device for interrupting the flow of electrical current; *blown out* refers to the melting of the fuse; and so on. The specific context neither requires nor invites us to "read anything into" these words.

But here for contrast is another sentence:

> The force that through the green fuse drives the flower
> Drives my green age.[1]
>
> (DYLAN THOMAS, 1914–53)

If we recognize this as the opening lines of a poem (which it is) we will naturally expect the words to have figurative meanings. But even without this clue, the immediate context clearly calls for figurative interpretation. Strange though it seems, *fuse* must now be taken to mean stem; and yet *fuse* also seems to carry the more ordinary associations of something connected with power and with possible explosiveness, short-circuiting, and the prevention of these. The first time *green* appears we can accept it literally, as having the usual dictionary meaning of a color, because the live stems of flowers are green; but in the context of "Drives my green age," *green* becomes figurative, suggesting youth, inexperience, and all the rampant and potentially self-destructive vitality of young and growing things, including people. As to what kind of meaning we should attach to *force,* we can't be sure until, as in reading Blake's "The Sick Rose," we have seen the whole context, the entire poem. But in view of the general figurativeness of Dylan Thomas's language here, we will expect *force* to have a far less literal meaning than it does, for example, in this bit of versified physics:

> There is no force however great
> Can stretch a cord however fine
> Into a horizontal line
> That shall be absolutely straight.
>
> (WILLIAM WHEWELL, 1794–1866)

Curiously, readers have been known to see in this scientific quatrain all sorts of symbolic, even mystical meanings, simply because the form is verse. Most people expect verse to be figurative. The same readers would be likely to deal too literally with anything written in prose, such as the opening sentence of Jane Austen's *Pride and Prejudice:*

> It is a truth universally acknowledged, that a single man in possession of good fortune must be in want of a wife.

If the reader accepts this literally, as a statement of a fact which Miss Austen believes, merely because on the surface it looks like one, he is already on the wrong track. Instead, he must recognize that Jane Austen is speaking ironically here. What she means is:

> In the kind of society I am about to introduce you to, any wealthy man who is still a bachelor must expect to be pursued ruthlessly by every unmarried girl in the neighborhood, and by her parents, whether he is at all interested in acquiring a wife or not.

In other words, Jane Austen's very first sentence sounds the opening note of the wonderful irony that permeates this novel. Properly read, the sentence sets the tone for the entire novel.

Thus one must beware of jumping to wrong conclusions about the level of meaning simply on the basis of the general type of literature to which a work belongs. Context in the broad sense can be a useful clue, but it can also mislead us unless we also attend to the specific context. And even then we may run into problems, especially in the kind of writing which is neither extremely literal nor extremely figurative, but somewhere in between. The most common problem cases occur in the sort of fiction and drama which are partly realistic, partly symbolic. For instance, here is the first sentence of Franz Kafka's strange novelette *Metamorphosis:*

> As Gregor Samsa awoke one morning from a troubled dream, he found himself changed in his bed to some monstrous kind of vermin.

Unless we interpret this as the start of a rather gruesome fairy tale, which the rest of the story will not allow us to do, we have to decide how much of the detail to take literally (that is, as realism) and how much to take figuratively (as symbol). The basic situation— that a man has overnight been changed into a bug—we conclude has to be symbolic, though just what it symbolizes we will not know until we have read much further. But how about *awoke, one morning, troubled dream,* and *bed?* Are these also figurative? Or are they merely realistic bedrock for a more general symbolism to rest on? Even if we already know some of Kafka's other work, our solution to such problems rests finally on our sense of context—the context being in this case, as in Blake's poem, the whole work.

One final point about level of meaning: despite some current critical fashions, it is usually unwise to look for more elaborate interpretations than the context demands. We can normally assume that a good writer is never any more abstruse than he has to be. Only inexperienced writers try for obscurity and symbolism for their own sake; and only inexperienced readers insist on more far-fetched interpretations than are necessary.

The principle here is the same one that scientists follow: the simplest interpretation that will still explain all of the data is always the preferred one. In literature the data is the full context, in all of its complexity and richness. And the test of any "interpretation" is how adequately it accounts for all the words and all of their undeniable interrelationships. Any explanation which is "farther out" (more esoteric) than the context demands is automatically suspect. By way of an example, here is a modern elegy by the American poet and critic John Crowe Ransom:

> ### Bells for John Whiteside's Daughter
>
> There was such speed in her little body,
> And such lightness in her footfall,
> It is no wonder that her brown study
> Astonishes us all.
>
> Her wars were bruited in our high window,
> We looked among orchard trees and beyond,
> Where she took arms against her shadow,
> Or harried unto the pond
>
> The lazy geese, like a snow cloud
> Dripping their snow on the green grass,
> Tricking and stopping, sleepy and proud,
> Who cried in goose, Alas,
>
> For the tireless heart within the little
> Lady with rod that made them rise
> From their noon apple-dreams, and scuttle
> Goose-fashion under the skies!
>
> But now go the bells, and we are ready;
> In one house we are sternly stopped
> To say we are vexed at her brown study,
> Lying so primly propped.[2]
>
> (JOHN CROWE RANSOM, 1888–   )

Readers have been known to believe that this poem could not possibly be about so "trivial" a subject as the death of a little girl, and they have proposed unnecessary theories to explain the poem's "real meaning": the little girl symbolizes an impassioned reformer trying without avail to prod the lazy geese (a reluctant public) into progressive action; the poem is an allegory of the Civil War, the little girl standing for our Southern citizenry taking arms, tragically, against their shadow (their Northern compatriots). These are ingenious theories, but two things are wrong with them: the interpretations are far more figurative than the context demands; and neither interpretation makes nearly as much sense of the poem *as a whole* as would a more literal reading of it.

Context Controls Conceptual Meaning

Context tells us whether the words should be taken literally or figuratively or sometimes one way and sometimes the other. It also tells us which literal meaning to assign to each word.

As the dictionary makes abundantly clear, most words have more than one conceptual meaning. How do we know which one is intended in a given use of the word? We know from the context, usually without even thinking about it. The following sentence is perfectly clear even though the same common word is used in six different senses:

On a *fair* day, feeling pretty *fair* myself, I went to the *fair*, where I met a *fair*-haired girl, and we rode together on the roller coaster, which, if you are *fair*, you will have to admit is a *fair* enough pastime.

We know without conscious effort that the first *fair* means sunny; the second, healthy; the third, an agricultural exposition; the fourth, blond; the fifth, just; and the sixth, pleasant or reasonable.

So strongly does context indicate what a word's conceptual meaning should be that it often enables us to supply words which are actually missing, as in a telegram ("Mother ill come home father"), or mentally to correct words which are patently wrong, as in the epigram "A smill is a curve that can straighten out a lct of things."

When the context fails to help us decide which of two or more conceptual meanings is intended, we have what is called ambiguity. A newspaper statement, "The judge ran down the Mayor's program point by point," may leave us in some doubt as to the meaning of *ran down*. Did the judge merely comment on the program item by item in order to give information to his audience? Or did he sneer at it and oppose it? Similarly the headline "GOVERNOR ATTACKS BUDGET" may mean either that the Governor has set to work preparing a budget or that he is objecting publicly to one that has been prepared by someone else. Ambiguities of this kind may be the result of inept writing. They could be corrected either by changing the ambiguous word or by changing the context in which it appears. Sometimes, of course, ambiguity is intentional: the writer wants to mislead the reader.

And very often a writer wants a word to carry more than one conceptual meaning, but not for the purpose of confusing or misleading the reader. He wants the reader to be fully aware of two or more conceptual meanings at the same time. One of the most obvious examples is a particular variety of pun, in which the humor—if there is any—lies entirely in the double meaning of a word or phrase; for example, the epitaph of a man convicted of murder by his sweetheart's testimony, "He hung on her words," or the remark of the young woman who returned from Europe to report that she had found nothing there but "old ruins with fallen arches." We all recognize such puns as a form of humor which can stand very little repeating. But creative writing, and especially poetry, is full of a similar kind of word play, some of it extremely rich and complex.

When we first meet Shakespeare's Hamlet, he is a figure apart in the glitter of King Claudius' first formal court gathering after his coronation and marriage to Gertrude, Hamlet's mother. Hamlet is a brooding, introspective figure, still openly grieving for his late father and deeply resentful of his mother's "o'er hasty" remarriage. Gertrude joins her new husband in admonishing her son to leave off this excessive mourning, in these words:

> Good Hamlet, cast thy nighted color off,
> And let thine eye look like a friend on Denmark.
> Do not forever with thy vailed lids
> Seek for thy noble father in the dust:
> Thou knowest 'tis common: all that lives must die,
> Passing through nature to eternity.

Hamlet's answer is

> Ay, madam, it is common.

We know, from the context, that he means *common* not only in Gertrude's sense of natural, inevitable, customary, but also in another dictionary sense: indecent, vulgar, unbecoming the noble estate of man. Furthermore, Hamlet's *common* refers not only to the fact of death, but also to the practice of limiting one's show of grief to a socially prescribed period of mourning. Finally, his *common* also refers to his mother. In short, Shakespeare purposely brings several conceptual meanings of the word *common* into play here, but at the same time he warns us, by means of context, not to try to choose among them but to see all of them operating at once.

Context Determines the DEGREE of Evocativeness

Context not only controls conceptual meaning, however. It also determines the relative weights of conceptual and evocative meaning. It is true, as we noted in Chapter 3, that some words are inherently more evocative than others. But far more important than their natural evocativeness is how they are made to function in context. Context can either enhance or suppress the natural evocativeness of a word. Most of us would agree, for instance, that the word *liberty* is a "loaded" word, highly evocative in the sense that it has the power to arouse feelings and attitudes. In the opening sentence of the Gettysburg Address, this evocative power is apparent to anyone:

> Fourscore and seven years ago our fathers brought forth on this continent a new nation, conceived in liberty, and dedicated to the proposition that all men are created equal.

But in another context the word *liberty* might have very little evocative effect:

> Liberty is the state of exemption from slavery, bondage, imprisonment, or control of another.

> The Statue of Liberty can be seen from the Staten Island Ferry.

> Gentlemen: may I take the liberty to remind you that . . .

Even more important, by control of context a writer can make a quite tame, neutral word carry rich evocative meaning. For ex-

ample, consider how the words *root, leaves,* and *flower* differ in the
following pair of passages:

> The soil immediately adjacent to the roots of roses should be packed
> in firmly. Hardy roses should be set out in the fall if practicable. It
> is desirable to get them out as soon as they have shed their leaves. If
> not then, they may be planted in early spring. Setting them out early
> is preferable to waiting till they are in leaf and flower.

Because the emphasis here is on "facts," and very practical ones at
that, few readers would be likely to see any of these words as
especially evocative. Even any strong private memories and feelings
about roses and gardening tend to be excluded by context. The
passage is not likely to bring to one reader's mind his vivid recollec-
tion of being badly pricked by a rose thorn yesterday, or to another
his strong distaste for gardening, or to another his passionate interest
in all plants and especially roses, or to still another her dread of
the day when spring planting will begin. Any or all of these associations *could* be brought into play by the passage, because no writer
can ever completely exclude private evocative meanings. However,
if they are evoked here it is purely accidental; the context invites
only a conceptual response to each word.

But here are the same three words in a four-line poem by William
Butler Yeats:

The Coming of Wisdom with Time

> Though leaves are many, the root is one;
> Through all the lying days of my youth
> I swayed my leaves and flowers in the sun;
> Now I may wither into the truth.[3]
> (WILLIAM BUTLER YEATS, 1865–1939)

In this context the key words take on meanings which no dictionary
will mention. *Leaves* and *flowers* here suggest not only man's youth
but also sensual pleasures, a mood of carefreeness, a life lived from
day to day, the ephemeral existence of the body, and a total lack of
concern for such problems as what life is all about. *Root,* on the
other hand, suggests here old age, the exhaustion of the senses, a
serious interest in things of the mind, a more philosophic concern

[3] "The Coming of Wisdom with Time" by William Butler Yeats. Copyright,
1912 by The Macmillan Company. Copyright, 1940 by William Butler Yeats. Reprinted with permission of The Macmillan Company, New York, The Macmillan Company of Canada, Ltd., A. P. Watt & Son, London, and Mrs. William
Butler Yeats from *The Collected Poems of William Butler Yeats.*

for the meaning of life. *Leaves* and *flowers* are thus both good and bad, fruitful and deathbound; but *root* is also good and bad, the fountain of truth and wisdom though also a kind of withering. Yeats is not coming out in favor of one and against the other: he is reconciling himself to old age on the ground that it brings wisdom, but he retains a tempered regret for his youth. He is accepting the wisdom of experience, but this wisdom includes the knowledge that truth compensates only in part for the passing of youth and its pleasures.

Of course, the gardening manual and Yeats' poem represent extremes of the literal and the figurative. It is possible, however, for words to be used in a quite literal sense and still take on fairly strong evocative meanings from context. For instance, notice *trees* and *leaves* in this passage from *Huckleberry Finn:*

> The sun was up so high when I waked that I judged it was after eight o'clock. I laid there in the grass and cool shade thinking about things, and feeling rested and ruther comfortable and satisfied. I could see the sun out at one or two holes, but mostly it was big trees all about, and gloomy in there amongst them. There was freckled places on the ground where the light sifted down through the leaves, and the freckled places swapped about a little, showing there was a little breeze up there. A couple of squirrels set on a limb and jabbered at me very friendly.

In the gardening manual, then, we have context functioning so as to damp all evocative meanings; in Clemens, context produces vivid but conventional evocative meanings; and in Yeats it creates rich and highly original evocative meanings. But all three writers are also careful of their words' conceptual meanings. Words are by nature vehicles for concepts, whatever other meanings they may also carry in particular contexts. And no writer can ever dispense with conceptual meaning entirely, even if he wants to. This fact can be seen most clearly in what is called nonsense verse, which is never utterly nonsensical. As good an example as any is Lewis Carroll's famous poem, "Jabberwocky":

> 'Twas brillig, and the slithy toves
>   Did gyre and gimble in the wabe:
> All mimsy were the borogoves,
>   And the mome raths outgrabe.
>
> "Beware the Jabberwock, my son!
> The jaws that bite, the claws that catch!

Beware the Jubjub bird, and shun
    The frumious Bandersnatch!"

He took his vorpal sword in hand;
    Long time the manxome foe he sought—
So rested he by the Tumtum tree,
    And stood awhile in thought.

And, as in uffish thought he stood,
    The Jabberwock, with eyes of flame,
Came whiffling through the tulgey wood,
    And burbled as it came!

One, two! One, two! And through and through
    The vorpal blade went snicker-snack!
He left it dead, and with its head
    He went galumphing back.

"And hast thou slain the Jabberwock?
    Come to my arms, my beamish boy!
O frabjous day! Callooh, Callay!"
    He chortled in his joy.

'Twas brillig, and the slithy toves
    Did gyre and gimble in the wabe:
All mimsy were the borogoves
    And the mome raths outgrabe.

(LEWIS CARROLL, 1832–98)

It is obvious from the opening line of "Jabberwocky" that evocative meaning is of prime importance here. And yet the poem has a perfectly intelligible conceptual pattern: the "plot" can be synopsized and the "characters" described. Artists have even made illustrations for the poem, showing what the various strange creatures and objects "look like."

Context Controls the KIND of Evocativeness

Context does more than determine the relative importance of conceptual and evocative meanings; it also determines the *kind* of evocative meaning which a word has in a given instance. Here, for example, is a poem by Samuel Hoffenstein in which the word *little* changes in evocative meaning as the context changes:

Love Song

Your little hands,
Your little feet,
Your little mouth—
Oh, God, how sweet!

Your little nose,
Your little ears,
Your eyes, that shed
Such little tears!

Your little voice,
So soft and kind;
Your little soul,
Your little mind! [4]

(SAMUEL HOFFENSTEIN,
1890–1947)

To illustrate this point more fully, it will perhaps be easiest to use not one passage but a series of passages in which the same common word appears in several different contexts. The word is *apple*, and the first passage is from Hemingway's short story "The Three-Day Blow":

The rain stopped as Nick turned into the road that went through the orchard. The fruit had been picked and the fall wind blew through the bare trees. Nick stopped and picked up a Wagner apple from beside the road, shiny in the brown grass from the rain. He put the apple in the pocket of his Mackinaw coat. [5]

Here, what the word *apple* evokes is primarily an image—a vivid mental picture of a very concrete object in all its round redness, wetness, and coolness. The image is mainly visual, and is sharpened by the contrasting picture of the brown grass; but it is also a tactile image, because of the rain and the fall wind. If one were to read the whole story, he might conclude that this apple may also be a vague symbol for the male pleasures of comradeship and hunting which Nick has salvaged from the debacle of his summer romance with a girl, but this reading may well be farfetched.

Now see what happens to *apple* in this poem by Wilfred Owen:

[4] "Love Song" by Samuel Hoffenstein. From: *A Treasury of Humorous Verse* by Samuel Hoffenstein. By Permission of Liveright, Publishers, New York. Copyright © 1947 by Liveright Publishing Corporation.

[5] FROM "The Three-Day Blow" by Ernest Hemingway, from *In Our Time* by Ernest Hemingway. Reprinted by permission of Charles Scribner's Sons.

Arms and the Boy

Let the boy try along this bayonet-blade
How cold steel is, and keen with hunger of blood;
Blue with all malice, like a madman's flash,
And thinly drawn with famishing for flesh.

Lend him to stroke these blind, blunt bullet-heads
Which long to nuzzle in the hearts of lads,
Or give him cartridges of fine zinc teeth,
Sharp with the sharpness of grief and death.

For his teeth seem for laughing round an apple.
There lurk no claws behind his fingers supple;
And God will grow no talons at his heels,
Nor antlers through the thickness of his curls.[6]

Here, too, there is a visual image, of the boy stretching his jaws around the fruit. But this time the apple is much more than an imagined object. It suggests the normal, healthy, harmless life of boyhood itself, in contrast to the madness of war. It implies the boy's innocence and his lack of the predatory instincts of some animals, instincts which are themselves seen in the poem as natural and even God-approved by comparison with the unnaturalness and ungodliness of man-made wars. Thus an apple is what a boy should hold in his hands, and not bayonet blades, rifles, and bullets. Hemingway's apple is neither a good thing nor a bad one; Owen's is clearly a good thing, almost a symbol for moral goodness itself.

But how about these apples, in a poem by Emerson?

Days

Daughters of Time, the hypocritic Days,
Muffled and dumb like barefoot dervishes,
And marching single in an endless file,
Bring diadems and faggots in their hands.
To each they offer gifts after his will,
Bread, kingdoms, stars, and sky that holds them all.
I, in my pleached garden, watched the pomp.
Forgot my morning wishes, hastily
Took a few herbs and apples, and the Day
Turned and departed silent. I, too late,
Under her solemn fillet saw the scorn.

(RALPH WALDO EMERSON, 1803–82)

Here apples scarcely exist as sense objects at all; they are merely members, along with *faggots* and *bread,* of the class of lesser values which a careless and unambitious man settles for, as opposed to the higher values which life offers, represented here by *diadems, kingdoms, stars,* and "sky that holds them all."

Emerson's apples stand for all that is ordinary, commonplace, even ignoble. And yet in this stanza from Dylan Thomas's "Fern Hill" *apple* helps to suggest the special, precious quality of childhood:

> Now as I was young and easy under the apple boughs
> About the lilting house and happy as the grass was green,
>   The night above the dingle starry,
>   Time let me hail and climb
>   Golden in the heydays of his eyes,
> And honored among wagons I was prince of the apple towns
> And once below a time I lordly had the trees and leaves
>   Trail with daisies and barley
>   Down the rivers of the windfall light.[7]

William Blake, on the other hand, uses an apple to suggest evil and sin:

A Poison Tree

> I was angry with my friend:
> I told my wrath, my wrath did end.
> I was angry with my foe:
> I told it not, my wrath did grow.
>
> And I watered it in fears
> Night and morning with my tears,
> And I sunned it with smiles
> And with soft deceitful wiles.
>
> And it grew both day and night,
> Till it bore an apple bright,
> And my foe beheld it shine,
> And he knew that it was mine—
>
> And into my garden stole
> When the night had veiled the pole;
> In the morning, glad, I see
> My foe outstretched beneath the tree.

[7] FROM "Fern Hill" by Dylan Thomas. From *The Collected Poems of Dylan Thomas.* Copyright © 1957 by New Directions. Reprinted by permission of New Directions, Publishers, and J. M. Dent & Sons, Ltd.

Blake's apple is the fruit of secret anger and of hypocrisy, and it is poisonous. Had the foe not got to it first, it would presumably have killed the speaker in the poem.

One more example is probably enough. Gregor Samsa, the young man in Kafka's *Metamorphosis* who was turned into a giant cockroach, continued to exist in this form, locked in his room in his parents' apartment, until one day he ventured to crawl out into the family living room and was attacked by his father, who began to hurl fruit at him:

> Paralyzed with terror, Gregor stayed still. It was useless to continue his course, now that his father had decided to bombard him. . . . These little red apples rolled about on the floor as if electrified, knocking against each other. One lightly-thrown apple struck Gregor's back without doing any harm, but the next one literally pierced his flesh. . . . The apple which none dared draw from Gregor's back remained imbedded in his flesh as a palpable memory, and the grave wound which he now had borne for a month seemed to have reminded his father that Gregor, despite his sad and terrible change, remained nonetheless a member of the family and must not be treated as an enemy; on the contrary, duty demanded that disgust should be overcome and Gregor be given all possible help.

Involved here is a Freudian conflict between father and son, perhaps also a larger conflict between God and man. The apple is a curse of some sort, which wounds and festers; it is both an insult hurled from outside and the pain of a conscience injured from within. However one interprets it, this *apple* carries evocative meanings of a sort never dreamed of by the man who wrote

> An apple a day
> Keeps the doctor away.

Context and "Thingness"

One of the great virtues of language as a mode of symbolism is the relative unobtrusiveness of words as things. The sound and shape of most words bear little relation to their basic meanings, either conceptual or evocative. An exception, of course, is the onomatopoeic word, which in its sound suggests what it means (*whiz, buzz, bang, wham, murmur,* etc.). And sometimes writers—especially creative writers—find it useful to exploit onomatopoeia, because the ear is another way of bringing the imagination into play.

But not many words are onomatopoeic. If a writer wants to exploit the sound of language he usually has to do it by context. He arranges words in rhythmic patterns, makes some of the words rhyme or half rhyme or not rhyme when we would expect them to, picks words which are alliterative, and so on. Usually the words involved would not be especially "thingful" in themselves; but placed in the right context, their sound, rhythm, and even appearance can be very expressive. We shall have occasion later (in the chapter on lyric poetry) to look at some examples of how context operates to emphasize and even to produce "thingness."

If, on the other hand, a writer wants to push the words themselves into the background—as the informative writer often does—he will avoid contextual arrangements which might call attention to thingness. He will avoid rhymes, obtrusive alliteration, and even the regular rhythms of poetry.

A Pair of New Terms

We have been discussing a number of different ways in which context affects and even creates meaning. Before we can bring what we have noted to bear on our three uses of language, we probably should try to condense what has been said so far. One convenient way to do this is by introducing a couple of new terms. These are *monosign* and *plurisign*, and we will define them as follows:

MONOSIGN—A word (or any unit of language) so used that only one fairly standard conceptual meaning is brought into play and no evocative meaning is important.

PLURISIGN—A word (or any unit of language) so used that it has more than one meaning at the same time. A plurisign may involve both conceptual and evocative meaning; or two or more conceptual meanings may be operating simultaneously, with or without evocative meanings as well; and any or all of these meanings may be quite unorthodox and not even implied by any dictionary definition.

It is important to note that *monosign* and *plurisign* refer to words *in context*, not to words by themselves. That is to say, it is not true that certain words are by nature monosigns, others by nature pluri-signs, though people sometimes talk as if this were so. Hence arises the notion, for instance, that certain words are inherently more "poetic" than others. This is true only to a very limited extent. Any word can function as either a monosign or a plurisign, depending on its context. This should be apparent from some of the examples cited in this chapter, such as *rose, worm, root, leaves, flowers,* and *apple.*

Quite often, in fact, a word changes from monosign to plurisign in the course of a single piece. This is precisely what happens, for instance, to *wall* (and its synonym *fence*) in Robert Frost's "Mending Wall."

> Something there is that doesn't love a wall,
> That sends the frozen ground-swell under it,
> And spills the upper boulders in the sun;
> And makes gaps even two can pass abreast.
> The work of hunters is another thing:
> I have come after them and made repair
> When they have left not one stone on a stone,
> But they would have the rabbit out of hiding,
> To please the yelping dogs. The gaps I mean,
> No one has seen them made or heard them made,
> But at spring mending-time we find them there.
> I let my neighbor know beyond the hill;
> And on a day we meet to walk the line
> And set the wall between us once again.
> We keep the wall between us as we go.
> To each the boulders that have fallen to each.
> And some are loaves and some so nearly balls
> We have to use a spell to make them balance:
> "Stay where you are until our backs are turned!"
> We wear our fingers rough with handling them.
> Oh, just another kind of outdoor game,
> One on a side. It comes to little more:
> There where it is we do not need the wall:
> He is all pine and I am apple-orchard.
> My apple trees will never get across
> And eat the cones under his pines, I tell him.
> He only says, "Good fences make good neighbors."
> Spring is the mischief in me, and I wonder
> If I could put a notion in his head:
> "*Why* do they make good neighbors? Isn't it
> Where there are cows? But here there are no cows.

Before I built a wall I'd ask to know
What I was walling in or walling out,
And to whom I was like to give offense.
Something there is that doesn't love a wall,
That wants it down!" I could say "elves" to him,
But it's not elves exactly, and I'd rather
He said it for himself. I see him there,
Bringing a stone grasped firmly by the top
In each hand, like an old-stone savage armed.
He moves in darkness, as it seems to me,
Not of woods only and the shade of trees.
He will not go behind his father's saying,
And he likes having thought of it so well
He says again, "Good fences make good neighbors." [8]

Plurisigns are not, of course, found only in poetry, nor monosigns only in prose. But it is true that informative writers tend to use words in such a way that they function mostly as monosigns, and creative writers tend to use them as plurisigns, whether they are writing poems or plays, essays or short stories, novels, or anything else. And the reason is clear enough: informative writers, being concerned primarily with conceptual knowledge, are most interested in the conceptual meanings of words and usually in their standard dictionary senses; creative writers, on the other hand, in their effort to embody or create experiential knowledge, inevitably work words a great deal harder. They not only employ standard conceptual meanings but even extend these dictionary meanings in all directions; they make words carry more than one conceptual meaning at once; they use or create all kinds of evocative meanings; and they take advantage of the thingness of words.

As for persuasive writers, their language may consist mostly of monosigns or it may be as full of plurisigns as poetry, depending on whether the persuasion grows out of and appeals to knowledge which is largely conceptual or knowledge which is largely experiential.

But whatever the purpose of language, it will be lean or rich in plurisigns as a result of the writer's manipulation of context. It is context that makes a word, or any other piece of language, a monosign or a plurisign.

[8] FROM *Complete Poems of Robert Frost*. Copyright 1923, 1930, 1939 by Holt, Rinehart and Winston, Inc. Copyright 1936 by Robert Frost. Copyright renewed 1951 by Robert Frost. Reprinted by permission of Holt, Rinehart and Winston, Inc.

EXERCISES

A. Think about the following questions for class discussion:
1. What do you think of the claim of some writers that they write meaningful literature "spontaneously" or without imposing any deliberate control over their language?
2. Explain what evocative meaning the word *apple* carries in "Bells for John Whiteside's Daughter" (p. 59).
3. Explain the characters and the action in "Jabberwocky" (pp. 64–65).
4. What is the difference between an ambiguous expression and a plurisign?

B. In the following groups of sentences explain how the meanings of the italicized words are controlled by the context:
1. Turn *right* at the next corner.
   My country *right* or wrong.
   In economic matters he is on the extreme *right*.
   The *right* to work and the *right* to vote are not quite the same thing.
   Might makes *right*.
   For each share of stock you get one *right*.
   Go *right* down the street until you get to the first traffic light.
   The keys are on the shelf *right* over the sink.
   You are *right*.
   Right you are.
2. The weather has been very *dry* lately.
   You'd better have that suit *dry*-cleaned.
   Blitzen beer is a light, *dry* beer.
   He had a *dry* sense of humor.
   Under local option most of the small towns are still *dry*.
   The style of the article is *dry*.
   I feel *dry*.

C. Make up or find a number of sentences which show how context may control the meaning of the following words:

1. light	4. suit	7. red
2. pink	5. set	8. treat
3. strong	6. shot	9. race

D. In the following passage from *Novum Organum* by Sir Francis Bacon (1561–1626), try to determine from the context what Bacon means by *idols of the tribe, idols of the den,* and *idols of the market*.

The idols of the tribe are inherent in human nature and the very tribe or race of man; for man's sense is falsely asserted to be the standard of things; on the contrary, all the perceptions both of the senses and the mind bear reference to man and not to the universe, and the human mind resembles those uneven mirrors which impart their own properties to different objects, from which rays are emitted and disfigure them.

The idols of the den are those of each individual; for everybody (in addition to the errors common to the race of man) has his own individual den or cavern, which intercepts and corrupts the light of nature, either from his own peculiar and singular disposition, or from his education and intercourse with others, or from his reading, and the authority acquired by those whom he reverences and admires, or from the different impressions produced on the mind, as it happens to be preoccupied and predisposed, or equable and tranquil, and the like so that the spirit of man (according to its several dispositions), is variable, confused, and as it were, actuated by chance; and Heraclitus said well that men search for knowledge in lesser worlds, and not in the greater or common world.

There are also idols formed by the reciprocal intercourse and society of man with man, which we call idols of the market, from the commerce and association of men with each other; for men converse by means of language, but words are formed by the will of the generality, and there arises from a bad and unapt formation of words a wonderful obstruction to the mind. Nor can the definitions and explanations with which learned men are wont to guard and protect themselves in some instances afford a complete remedy—words still manifestly force the understanding, throw everything into confusion, and lead mankind into vain and innumerable controversies and fallacies.

E. Handle each of the following two sets of short passages separately. In each set, one word reappears in every passage: *water* in the first set and *tree* in the second. Show how the evocative meanings of these two words vary from passage to passage as a result of the interaction of the word with the other words of the context. In your analyses, explain, insofar as you can, how other words in the context act to control the evocative meanings of the word you are considering.

   Set 1: Analyze the evocative meanings of *water* in each of these contexts.

   a.   Day after day, day after day
   We stuck, nor breath nor motion;
   As idle as a painted ship
   Upon a painted ocean.

Water, water, everywhere,
And all the boards did shrink;
Water, water, everywhere,
Nor any drop to drink.

The very deep did rot: O Christ!
That ever this should be!
Yea, slimy things did crawl with legs
Upon the slimy sea.

b. More water glideth under the mill
Than wots the miller of.

c. A flock of sheep that leisurely pass by,
One after one; the sound of rain and bees
Murmuring; the fall of rivers, winds, and seas,
Smooth fields, white sheets of water, and pure sky;
I have thought of all by turns, and yet do sleepless lie.

d. Ho, everyone that thirsteth, come ye to the waters, and he
that hath no money; yes, come ye, buy and eat; yea, come
buy wine and milk without money and without price.

e. The ship laboured without intermission amongst the black
hills of water, paying with this hard tumbling the price of
her life.

Set 2: Analyze the evocative meanings of *tree* in each of these
contexts.

a. A tall tree tossed by the autumn winds.
b. Under the greenwood tree.
c. A pine tree stands so lonely
In the North where the high winds blow.
d. Down where the taproots of New England trees
Suck bare existence from the broken stones.
e. The trees in the streets are old trees used to living with
people
Family-trees that remember your grandfather's name.
f. Loveliest of trees, the cherry now
Is hung with bloom along the bough.

5. Conceptual Knowledge and Informative Language

> The only subject presented to me for study is the content of my consciousness. You are able to communicate to me part of the content of your consciousness which thereby becomes accessible in my own. For reasons which are generally admitted, though I should not like to have to prove that they are conclusive, I grant your consciousness equal status with my own; and I use this second-hand part of my consciousness to "put myself in your place." Accordingly my subject of study becomes differentiated into the contents of many consciousnesses, each content constituting a *view-point*. Then there arises the problem of combining the view-points. . . .[1]
>
> A. S. EDDINGTON, *The Nature of the Physical World*

The Long Conversation

Eddington's statement points up the importance of informative communication of every kind. We are all engaged in a lifelong conversation—with our friends, our families, our associates in school and at work, with a host of writers and speakers whom we know mostly through their words, with audiences who know us mostly through our words, and even with ourselves. Through this continual conversation we extend, refresh, share, and test our knowledge. We make part of our private consciousness available to others, and we test what we think we know by their reactions to what we

[1] FROM *The Nature of the Physical World* by A. S. Eddington, by permission of the Cambridge University Press.

say. At the same time, we take into our consciousness what they say, and test it against what we think we know.

The communications we use in this conversation are immensely varied. They include things as long and elaborate as the *Encyclopaedia Britannica,* or Toynbee's *A Study of History,* things as sketchy as a map drawn on the back of an envelope, and things as brief and transitory as the remark that "it looks like rain." They include formulations which are so simple and so definite that no one would think to question them ("I broke another dish tonight") and theories which are so speculative and so tentative that the formulators are ready to change them even as they state them. They include simple records—casual diaries, lab notes, ships' logs, the minutes of meetings. They also include fully developed discussions—essays, critical studies, interpretive histories, news analyses, scientific articles and reports, textbooks, feature stories in newpapers and magazines, and those extended pieces of modern journalism which are currently called "reportage."

In these three chapters we shall look at some of these kinds of informative communication, beginning with a discussion of the conceptual knowledge which they contain, and going on to consider a few of the more important principles which informative writers use—consciously or unconsciously—in organizing and presenting conceptual knowledge. In the third chapter in this section, we shall look at the whole process from the reader's point of view.

Word-Groups, Statements, and Propositions

One good place to begin this discussion is with the notion of context. We have seen already that meaning is largely a matter of the interaction of words in groups, and in the last chapter we distinguished two kinds of word-groups, the *creative* kind ("His teeth seemed for laughing round an apple," "O, Rose, thou art sick," "The force that through the green fuse drives the flower/Drives my green age,"), and the *informative* kind ("The Japanese and rose beetles are the most important members of this large group of chewing insects," "When a fuse has blown out, it is not sufficient merely to replace it with a new one"). We noted a difference between these two groups, but we saw it mostly as a difference in how the symbols operate—whether figuratively or literally, as plurisigns or as monosigns.

These two kinds of word-groups differ, however, in still another way. In the creative examples, the words interact as both symbols and sounds, and in a great variety of ways. The informative word-groups, on the other hand, *assert relationship.* One contemporary philosopher, Philip Wheelwright, characterizes the creative word-group as "a tension among plurisigns," the informative word-group as an "assertion about monosigns."

At this point, a few additional word-groups of the informative kind may be useful: "New York is about 250 miles from Washington," "All men are created equal," "There is a bell ringing somewhere," "The square on the hypotenuse of a right triangle is equal to the sum of the squares on the other two sides," "Rembrandt is probably the world's greatest painter," "A rhombus is an oblique-angled equilateral parallelogram," "The mayor's sole object is to get re-elected." Word-groups of this kind constitute what we shall call *statements.* Statements are the essential components of informative language.

It may be well, however, to point out—not quite in passing—that statements need not be composed of words at all. Any kind of symbol group can function as a statement. Indeed, at least two of the verbal statements just listed can be put into nonverbal form: The distance from New York to Washington could be shown on a map; the Pythagorean theorem could be expressed algebraically as "$a^2 = b^2 + c^2$." Conceptual knowledge is, as a matter of fact, often cast in nonverbal forms. Maps, diagrams, blueprints, charts, tables, graphs, mathematical and chemical equations, and even pictures may serve as informative statements. Many of these nonverbal statements can be converted into verbal statements or from one nonverbal form to another. (We have already noted that most informative statements of the verbal kind can be rephrased in other words.)

Now the possibility of rephrasing a statement, or even of recasting it in an entirely new form, introduces a distinction which is basic to an understanding of informative language: this is the distinction between *statements* and *propositions.* Cohen and Nagel, in *An Introduction to Logic and Scientific Method,* make this point quite clearly in the following passage (using *sentence,* however, where we are using *statement*).

A proposition is not the same thing as the sentence which states it. The three sentences, "I think, therefore I am," "*Je pense, donc je suis,*" "*Cogito, ergo sum,*" all state the same proposition. A sentence is a group of words, and words, like other symbols, are in themselves physical objects, distinct from that to which they refer or which they symbolize. . . . But the proposition of which a sentence is a verbal expression is distinct from the visual marks or sound waves of the expression. Sentences may or may not conform to standards of usage or taste. But they are not true or false. Truth or falsity can be predicated only of the propositions they signify.[2]

To return to our own examples, the two statements "The square on the hypotenuse is equal to the sum of the squares on the other two sides of a right triangle" and "$a^2 = b^2 + c^2$" both express the same set of relationships (providing, of course, that a, b, and c in the equation designate respectively the hypotenuse and two legs of a right triangle); that is, the two *statements* embody a single *proposition*. To put the matter another way: a proposition is a piece of thought; a statement is a piece of language. Or, to state the distinction more formally:

A *proposition* is a basic unit of conceptual knowledge. It consists of a single thought, fact, idea, principle, assertible relationship. (It may be general or particular, precise or approximate; credible, questionable, or dead wrong; of permanent value or of only passing interest.)

A *statement* is a basic unit of informative language. It consists of a sentence (or clause or phrase) which conveys a proposition.

It should now be clear—if it was not before—why it is often possible to rephrase the statements in informative writing. Statements are to propositions as words are to concepts. Just as a word's conceptual meaning can be expressed in other words (in a synonym, for example), so a proposition can usually be stated in some other form. Here is one more sample revision. This passage:

In order to establish the effects of radiation on posterity, comparative studies have been made between the descendants of doctors who have used X-ray apparatus over a period of years and the descendants of doctors who have not,

could be recast in this form:

Scientific comparisons between the children and grandchildren of medical practitioners long accustomed to working with X-ray equipment and those of practitioners who have seldom employed it have been carried out. The object of this research was to determine how much effect exposure to radiation might have on one's descendants.

[2] FROM *An Introduction to Logic and Scientific Method* by Morris R. Cohen and Ernest Nagel. Reprinted by permission of Harcourt, Brace & World, Inc.

Most of us would probably agree that the first version is "better" than the second, meaning that it is less wordy and perhaps somewhat clearer; but we would probably also agree that the two passages contain about the same conceptual knowledge. The *propositions* remain essentially unchanged. But the *statements* differ greatly —in the number of sentences, in the order in which information is presented, in the number of words, and in the specific words used.

Where Propositions Come From

Any piece of informative writing, of whatever kind, length, or importance, consists of statements, which embody propositions. Before we go on to consider how statements and groups of statements are put together, we might ask: "Where do the propositions come from?"

It is possible to work out a rather elaborate answer to this question. Many propositions are apparently based on observation: "There's a bell ringing somewhere," "New York is about 250 miles from Washington." Other propositions seem to be derived from other sources as well. Some propositions are inferences from observations: "The roof seems to be leaking again" may contain a proposition of this kind. Some are inferences concerning the contents of another person's mind: "The mayor's sole object is to get re-elected." Some are definitions: people have agreed to call an "oblique-angled equilateral parallelogram" a rhombus. Some are value judgments: "Rembrandt is probably the world's greatest painter." Some may be taken simply as working assumptions; possibly the statement that "all men are created equal" contains a proposition of this sort, though Jefferson calls the statement a "self-evident truth," meaning a proposition derived from the natural operation of reason.

In actual practice however, this kind of systematic classification does not work very well. For example, the value judgment about Rembrandt may be based partly upon observation, partly upon certain criteria of greatness, which may themselves be definitions, assumptions, or perhaps "self-evident truths." Furthermore, all but the very simplest observational propositions—and even these exceptions are doubtful—involve inferences as well as observations. The assertion that "New York is about 250 miles from Washington" is based ultimately upon a number of measurements that have been put together to give this result. And even a very precise-sounding statement, such as "the metal rod is 3.62 cm. long," involves assumptions—that the measuring instrument was accurate, that the measurers were competent and meticulous, and that the rod does not vary in length because of changes in temperature—and inferences from these assumptions.

Back in Chapter 3 the authors of this book confessed to a rather basic skepticism: they admitted that they do not know what the world is "really" like, what the bits and pieces "really" are, and how they are "really" related to each other. This skeptical position is very like that expressed by Sir Arthur Eddington in the quotation at the beginning of this chapter. Such skepticism does not imply a paralyzing uncertainty. It does imply that a proposition should be taken as something "put forth" (as the derivation of the word suggests)—a tentative and, at first, private formulation. Converted into a statement, a proposition is thus made public. It now has value for others as a record of one man's thinking; but it also enables the proposer to check his conceptual knowledge against other people's. Even so simple a statement as "The roof is leaking again" may lead other members of the household to check on our observation and inference, and to correct or confirm the proposition. (They may even help fix the roof; but this further practical consequence comes later.) And the man who remarks, "There's a bell ringing somewhere," may actually be looking for reassurance: something unusual is going on in his head; he will feel better about it if he can be assured that other people hear it too.

All this adds up to the fact that propositions are, basically, hypotheses. They are tentative formulations. This does not mean, of course, that they are all equally tentative; nor does it mean that they are all offered in a tentative way. Many propositions are presented simply as reports. The writer or speaker is astonished and thoroughly annoyed if his propositions are questioned: "I ought to know—I was there." But in the long conversation all propositions function in a more or less tentative fashion, and some propositions are plainly labeled "hypothesis."

One further point should be noted. The distinction between propositions and statements may suggest that all the informative writer has to do is find verbal clothes for ready-made propositions: the ideas are all there in his head; he needs merely to put them into words. This is, however, a much oversimplified view. Putting a proposition into words is not only a way of communicating it, of making it public; it is also a way of formulating it. In fact, we often check our private knowledge first by putting it into statements intended for ourselves alone. Once we have found phrases for our thoughts, we may need no audience to tell us that we are wrong. Therefore, we should recognize that part of the answer to "Where do propositions come from?" is that to some extent they come from the statements which are used to express them.

Level of Generality

Let us look now at another distinction among propositions—one which is essential for the understanding both of conceptual knowledge and informative writing. Here are three statements, all having to do with the game of chess:

(1) Chess is a game of skill.
(2) The bishop in chess moves only along the diagonal.
(3) On the sixth move the bishop captured the king's rook.

Now the propositions which these three statements express differ in what we shall call generality: The first proposition is at a high level of generality: it is concerned with the over-all principles and characteristics of the game. The second proposition is somewhat less general: it has to do not with over-all principles and characteristics but with a rule which governs the movements of a particular piece, the bishop. The third proposition is even less general: it is a report of what happened at a specific point in a specific game. We often describe this kind of range by using the word *general* for the first proposition and the word *particular* for the third. The second is thought of as being more general than the third, less general than the first (or more particular than the first, less particular than the third).

Let us look at another example, also illustrating three levels:

(1) Men are mortal.
(2) Human longevity has increased twenty-eight years in the past century.
(3) Mr. Johnson died yesterday afternoon.

The first proposition is at a very high level of generality: it is presumably applicable to all men, in all times and places; it asserts, therefore, a condition of human existence. The second proposition is a kind of vital statistic. It covers a tremendous number of people, is based presumably on a vast quantity of data, and covers a time-span of a century. It is a generalization, but the level of generality is not so high as in the first. The third proposition, on the other hand, deals with a specific instance of human mortality, the death yesterday afternoon of a man named Johnson.

There is, of course, nothing sacred here about the number three. We can sometimes distinguish four, five, or even more levels of generality in the propositions which together constitute a conceptual subject matter. "All life is transitory," for example, expresses a proposition which is more general than "Men are mortal"; "the play-principle is deeply rooted in human nature" is more general than "chess is a game of skill."

But this sorting out of propositions by level of generality is not merely itself an interesting game: the principle has been introduced here for two reasons. First, the development of conceptual knowl-edge involves movement from one level of generality to another. The classic summary of this point occurs in Francis Bacon's *Novum Organum:*

> There are and can be only two ways of searching into and discover-ing truth. The one flies from the senses and particulars to the most general axioms, and from these principles, the truth of which it takes for settled and immovable, proceeds to judgment and to the discovery of middle axioms. . . . The other derives axioms from the senses and particulars, rising by a gradual and unbroken ascent, so that it arrives at the most general axioms last of all.

Logicians often call these two thought processes deductive reason-ing and inductive reasoning, respectively—deduction proceeding from the general to the particular, induction from the particular to the general. However, as a close look at Bacon's statement will show, this neat separation tends to oversimplify the way our minds actually work. The notion of multiple levels of generality, among which the mind moves at will in either direction, is both more ac-curate and more useful.

Second, not only the development of conceptual knowledge but its presentation requires the writer to pay attention to levels of generality. Any complex subject exhibits several levels of generality, which must somehow be gotten across to a reader. To understand the game of chess, for example, a man must know some rather general things (principles, rules, and over-all strategy); some slightly less general things (tactics—what to do in particular situations); and some very specific or particular things (the possibilities and probabilities at each stage of an actual game). A writer who wants to convey these things must decide where to begin and how to move from one subject to another. And even if the subject itself is not so varied as chess, if for instance the essential knowledge can all be compressed into a few very high-level generalizations (as in some philosophical discussions), the writer must still decide how to develop these generalizations: usually, he will find it expedient to introduce some other propositions—at a lower level—which will help the reader climb to the principles he is really interested in. On the other hand, even if the essential information consists of a lot of rather particular propositions, most writers will find it useful to invent a more general framework into which they will fit and which will help to relate them to the reader's previous knowledge.

Levels of Generality and Conceptual Knowledge

Let us look now at two examples which show something of the relation of levels of generality to the actual working out of conceptual knowledge. These two examples are, at the same time, examples of informative writing—the special kind of informative writing which seeks to involve the reader directly in the writer's own thought processes.

The first is from Plato's *Republic*. Socrates is in the process of working out the characteristics which the ruling class, the guardians, must possess in the ideal commonwealth he is describing. He is moving toward the idea that these guardians must be, among other things, philosophers, and that they must be gentle toward their friends and dangerous toward their enemies. The discussion has moved onto a high level of generality. Socrates, as Plato presents the account, now brings it down by stages and then back up again (the "I" in the dialogue is always Socrates):

> My friend, I said, no wonder that we are in a perplexity; for we have lost sight of the image we had before us.
> What do you mean? he said.
> I mean to say that there do exist natures gifted with those opposite qualities.

And where so you find them?

Many animals, I replied, furnish examples of them; our friend the dog is a very good one; you know that well-bred dogs are perfectly gentle to their familiars and acquaintances, and the reverse to strangers.

Yes, I know.

Then there is nothing impossible or out of the order of nature in our finding a guardian who has a similar combination of qualities?

Certainly not.

Would not he who is fitted to be a guardian, besides the spirited nature, need to have the qualities of a philosopher?

I do not apprehend your meaning.

The trait of which I am speaking, I replied, may be also seen in the dog, and is remarkable in the animal.

What trait?

Why, a dog, whenever he sees a stranger, is angry; when an acquaintance, he welcomes him, although the one has never done him any harm, nor the other any good. Did this never strike you as curious?

The matter never struck me before; but I quite recognize the truth of your remark.

And surely this instinct of the dog is very charming:—your dog is a true philosopher.

Why?

Why, because he distinguishes the face of a friend and of an enemy by the criterion of knowing or not knowing. And must not an animal be a lover of learning who determines what he likes and dislikes by the test of knowledge and ignorance?

Most assuredly.

And is not the love of learning the love of wisdom, which is philosophy?

It is perhaps unnecessary to point out all the shifts in level. The reader may find it worthwhile to try to work them out himself. The principal point, however, is that the analogy of the dog is here a device for leading the other participants in the dialogue—and through them the audience—to think out the characteristics of the guardians.

Our second example is very different in form and method, but it is also concerned with the development of conceptual knowledge, and it also makes striking use of several levels of generality. The writer is Sir John Lubbock, a nineteenth-century British naturalist. In two paragraphs he reports on experiments he has conducted to find out whether ants (like Plato's philosopher-dogs) can distinguish between friends and strangers:

A number of small yellow ants (*L. flavus*) were out feeding on some honey. I took five of them, and also five others of the same species, but from a different nest, chloroformed them, and put them close to the honey, and on the path which the ants took in going to and from the nest, so that these could not but see them. The glass on which the honey was placed was surrounded by a moat of water. This, I thought, would give me an opportunity of testing both how far they would be disposed to assist a fellow-creature, and what difference they would make between their nest companions and strangers from a different community of the same species. The chloroformed ants were put down at 10 in the morning. For more than an hour, though many ants came up and touched them with their antennae, none did more. At length one of the strangers was picked up, carried to the edge of the glass, and quietly thrown, or rather dropped into the water. Shortly afterwards a friend was taken up and treated in the same way. By degrees they were all picked up and thrown into the water. One of the strangers was, indeed, taken into the nest, but in about half an hour she was brought out again and thrown into the water like the rest. I repeated this experiment with fifty ants, half friends and half strangers. In each case twenty out of the twenty-five ants were thrown into the water as described. A few were left lying where they were placed, and these also, if we had watched longer, would no doubt have been treated in the same way. One out of the twenty-five friends, and three out of the twenty-five strangers were carried into the nest, but they were all brought out again and thrown away like the rest. Under such circumstances, then, it seems that ants make no difference between friends and strangers.

It may, however, be said, as to this experiment, that since ants do not recover from chloroform, and these ants were, therefore, to all intents and purposes dead, we should not expect that much difference would be made between friends and strangers. I therefore tried the same experiment again, only, instead of chloroforming the ants, I made them intoxicated. This was rather more difficult. No ant would voluntarily degrade herself by getting drunk, and it was not easy in all cases to hit off the requisite degree of this compulsory intoxication. In all cases they were made quite drunk, so that they lay helplessly on their backs. The sober ants seemed much puzzled at finding their friends in this helpless and discreditable condition. They took them and carried them about for a while in a sort of aimless way, as if they did not know what to do with their drunkards, any more than we do. Ultimately, however, the results were as follows. The ants removed twenty-five friends and thirty strangers. Of the friends twenty were carried into the nest, where no doubt they slept off the effect of the spirit—at least we saw no more of them—and five were thrown into the water. Of the strangers, on the contrary, twenty-four were thrown into the water; only six were taken into the nest, and four at least of these were afterwards brought out again and thrown away. The difference in the treatment of friends and strangers was therefore most marked.

Lubbock's little experiments may leave us with some questions still unanswered, mostly about matters of procedure and methods of identifying ants. Also, are Lubbock's ants also philosophers, like Socrates' dogs? But we are here less concerned with the quality of Lubbock's science than we are with the form of his presentation. He begins at a very low level of generality: the first three sentences are quite particular reports of his experimental procedure. There follows, in one sentence, a more general statement of the purpose of the experiment—to test how far ants would be disposed to help their fellow creatures and what distinctions they would make between friends and strangers. Lubbock then goes on to report results in a series of statements which are again at a low level of generality, and at length concludes his first paragraph, and his first two experiments, with a general but tentative conclusion: "Under such circumstances, then, it seems that ants make no difference between friends and strangers." He begins the next paragraph, still at a high level of generality, speculating about the validity of his experiments, since the ants were to all intents and purposes dead. Recounting his experiments now with intoxicated ants, he sticks to particulars—jumping to a higher level merely to comment on the ways of ants and men. And he concludes with another general statement, summarizing the results of his second experiment: "The difference in the treatment of friends and strangers was therefore marked." (Incidentally, his whole procedure is a fair example of Francis Bacon's second method: "The other derives axioms from the senses and particulars, rising by a gradual and unbroken ascent, so that it arrives at the most general axioms last of all." Lubbock, of course, never gets to general axioms in these experiments. But he does take his reader with him as far as he goes. He is developing conceptual knowledge, and inviting the reader to follow the development and even to repeat the experiment if he cares to.)

Levels of Generality and Informative Writing

It is clear that both Lubbock and Plato are not only developing conceptual knowledge, they are also writing informatively. Plato's dialogues imitate the long conversation, but they are certainly not a transcript of an actual discussion. For Plato, the dialogue is a method of presentation, one that is designed to involve the reader in a thinking process. Similarly Lubbock is not merely working out a conclusion: he is presenting his conclusion and the evidence which backs it up. Nevertheless these two passages, although they are examples of informative writing, give us too limited a view of the field.

We should begin by noting that much informative writing is far simpler in its structure, and in its use of levels of generality, than are the two passages we have looked at. A great deal of informative writing makes no effort to work out conceptual knowledge, or even to lead the reader through the different levels of a subject. Journals, log books, lab notes, chronicle histories, and the simpler forms of narrative and descriptive writing consist of statements—most of them at a very low level of generality—organized to follow a pattern set by the subject itself: the chronology of events in time, the arrangement of parts in space. One example will be sufficient. The following passage is from the *Journal of the Pilgrims,* an anonymous work. The time is December, 1620.

> Friday the 22, the storm still continued, that we could not get a-land, nor they come to us aboard; this morning Good wife *Alderton* was delivered of a sonne, but dead borne.
>
> Saturday the 23. so many of us as could went on shore, felled and carried timber, to provide themselves stuff for building.
>
> Sunday the 24. Our people on shore heard a cry of some Savages (as they thought) which caused an Alarm, and to stand on their guard, expecting an assault, but all was quiet.
>
> Munday the 25. day, we went on shore, some to fell timber, some to saw, some to rive, and some to carry, so no man rested all that day, but towards night some as they were at work, heard a noise of some *Indians,* which caused us all to go to our Muskets, but we heard no further, so we came aboard again, and left some twenty to keep the court of guard; that night we had a sore storm of wind and rain.
>
> Munday the 25. being Christmas day, we began to drink water aboard, but at night the Master caused us to have some Beer, and so on board we had diverse times now and then some Beer, but on shore none at all.
>
> Tuesday the 26. it was foul weather, that we could not go ashore.
>
> Wednesday the 27. we went to work again.

Some of the statements in this passage are, of course, slightly more general than others: "So on board we had diverse times now and then some Beer," is a more general statement than the one which precedes it, "But at night the Master caused us to have some Beer." Nevertheless the over-all effect is of a sequence of statements at a very low level of generality. The *Journal* is a record of what happened, as it appeared to one man. He states no general principles; he draws no conclusions; and he organizes his statements in the simplest manner possible, following the events in a chronological order.

Let us look now at another example, one which *does* involve varying levels of generality. This is a two-paragraph definition of "law," from Dorothy Sayers' *Mind of the Maker*:

The word "law" is currently used in two quite distinct meanings. It may describe an arbitrary regulation made by human consent in particular circumstances for a particular purpose, and capable of being promulgated, enforced, suspended, altered, or rescinded without interference with the general scheme of the universe. In this sense we may talk of Roman "Law," the "laws" of civilized warfare, or the "laws" of cricket. Such laws frequently prescribe that certain events shall follow upon certain others; but the second event is not a necessary consequence of the first: the connection between the two is purely formal. Thus if the ball (correctly bowled) hits the wicket, the batsman is "out." There is, however, no inevitable connection between the impact of the ball upon three wooden stumps and the progress of a human body from a patch of mown grass to a pavilion. The two events are really separable in theory. If the Marylebone Cricket Club chose to alter the "law," they could do so immediately, by merely saying so, and no cataclysm of nature would be involved. The l.b.w. rule has, in fact, been altered within living memory, and not merely the universe, but even the game, has survived the alteration. Similarly, if a twentieth-century Englishman marries two wives at once, he goes to prison—but only if he is found out; there is no necessary causal connection between over-indulgence in matrimony and curtailment of human liberty (in the formal sense, that is; in another sense, one may say that to marry even one wife is to renounce one's freedom); in Mohammedan countries any number of wives up to four is, or was, held to be both lawful and morally right. And in warfare, the restrictions forbidding the use of poison-gas and the indiscriminate sowing of mines must, unfortunately, be regarded rather as pious aspirations than as "laws" entailing consequences even of a conventional kind.

In its other use, the word "law" is employed to designate a generalized statement of observed fact of one sort or another. Most of the so-called "laws of nature" are of this kind: "If you hold your finger in the fire it will be burnt"; "if you vary the distance between an object and a source of light, the intensity of the light at the surface of the object will vary inversely as the square of the distance." Such "laws" as these cannot be promulgated, altered, suspended, or broken at will; they are not "laws" at all in the sense that the laws of cricket or the laws of the realm are "laws"; they are statements of observed facts inherent in the nature of the universe. Anybody can enact that murder shall not be punishable by death; nobody can enact that the swallowing of a tumblerful of prussic acid shall not be punishable by death. In the former case, the connection between the two events is legal—that is, arbitrary; in the latter, it is a true causal connection, and the second event is a necessary consequence of the first.[3]

Miss Sayers, like Sir John Lubbock, is primarily interested in the generalization she is trying to explain, a generalization which may be separated from the more particular propositions and stated all at once in the following sentences:

The word "law" is currently used in two quite distinct meanings. It may describe an arbitrary regulation made by human consent in particular circumstances for a particular purpose, and capable of being promulgated, enforced, suspended, altered, or rescinded without interference with the general scheme of the universe. In its other use, the word "law" is employed to designate a generalized statement of observed fact of one sort or another.

Most of the remaining statements in Miss Sayers' paragraphs are at several lower levels of generality. They illustrate and clarify. It is doubtful whether the high-level statements which have been taken out and assembled above would make the distinction as clear to the reader as it is when they are combined with lower-level generalizations. But the lower-level generalizations in Miss Sayers' paragraphs are *not* designed, like those in Sir John Lubbock's paragraphs, to "prove" the high-level generalizations. The reader can see this for himself if he will try to do with Lubbock's high-level generalizations what we have just done with those of Miss Sayers.

Now, most informative writers use levels of generality in the way

[3] FROM *Mind of the Maker,* copyright 1942 by Dorothy L. Sayers. Reprinted by permission.

Miss Sayers does rather than in the way Sir John Lubbock does. But they do not all go about it in the same way. Miss Sayers begins with the most general statements and then, in each paragraph, goes on with the particulars. This is a very common method—one of the conventional ways, in fact, of constructing a paragraph: the most general statement is the topic sentence, which is then "spelled out" or illustrated in the rest of the paragraph. This method has the advantage of giving the reader a general framework into which ideas can be easily fitted. The effect on the reader is as if he were watching a man draw a map, beginning with the over-all layout. The reverse procedure may be used, however: it is then as if we were watching the map-maker place a few interesting and startling details on the paper first; we look at them and wonder what the final pattern is going to be. Many writers use this method, at least for variation, beginning with particulars which focus attention and arouse interest. Here is the opening paragraph of a book on prison reform by John Bartlow Martin, called *Break Down the Walls:*

> One quiet Sunday evening in the spring of 1952 Harold W. Tucker, the captain in charge of guards on the 2-to-10 shift at the state prison in Jackson, Michigan, answered the telephone at the Main Office in the rotunda just inside the prison gates and heard a man say, "This is Ward talking in 15-block." Tucker knew Earl Ward and he knew Earl Ward shouldn't be talking on the telephone; he should be locked in his cell that he never left except once a week to take a bath. Ward was a homicidal psychopath, considered one of the most dangerous convicts in the institution.

Martin's book continues to stick fairly close to particulars for several paragraphs, arriving at his generalizations only quite late in the discussion. The effect obviously is to arouse interest and focus attention well in advance of the writer's most important propositions.

One additional use of levels of generality is worth noticing. Many skillful writers who are not scientists use a method of presentation which looks a good deal like Sir John Lubbock's. They convert the exposition of an idea into a narrative in which they recount how they personally discovered something. Their presentations are made up largely of particulars; in fact, the reader may be left to draw his own conclusions. Besides its dramatic interest, the method adds credibility to the main idea because the reader feels that he is formulating it by himself. One example will illustrate this kind of presentation, the opening of an article called "Settling the Colonel's Hash," by Mary McCarthy:

> Seven years ago, when I taught in a progressive college, I had a pretty girl student in one of my classes who wanted to be a short-story writer. She was not studying writing with me, but she knew that I sometimes wrote short stories, and one day, breathless and glowing, she came up to me in the hall, to tell me that she had just written a story that her writing teacher, a Mr. Converse, was terribly excited about.
>
> "He thinks it's wonderful," she said, "and he's going to help me fix it up for publication."
>
> I asked what the story was about; the girl was a rather simple being who loved clothes and dates. Her answer had a deprecating tone. It was just about a girl (herself) and some sailors she had met on the train. But then her face, which had looked perturbed for a moment, gladdened.
>
> "Mr. Converse is going over it with me and we're going to put in the symbols."
>
> Another girl in the same college, when asked by us in her sophomore orals why she read novels (one of the pseudo-profound questions that ought never to be put) answered in a defensive flurry: "Well, *of course,* I don't read them to find out what happens to the hero!"
>
> At the time, I thought these notions were peculiar to progressive education: it was old-fashioned or regressive to read a novel to find out what happens to the hero or to have a mere experience empty of symbolic pointers. But I now discover that this attitude is quite general, and that readers and students all over the country are in a state of apprehension, lest they read a book or story literally and miss the presence of a symbol.[4]

Summary

In this chapter we have seen informative communication as a means by which we manage to build up for ourselves and others a body of conceptual knowledge. We have drawn a distinction between propositions, the basic units of conceptual knowledge, and statements, the basic units of informative communication. We have

[4] FROM "Settling the Colonel's Hash" by Mary McCarthy, reprinted from *Harper's Magazine.* By permission of the publisher.

also looked at levels of generality and the way in which they are employed both in thought processes and in informative writing.

But the working out of informative structures and the selection of words in which to clothe ideas is more complicated than the analysis so far would indicate. In the next chapter we shall consider some other problems that the informative writer inevitably has to face and solve.

EXERCISES

A. Collect five examples of word-groups, which, from their context, appear to be statements, and five others which do not. In order to determine whether your judgment is correct, try to reword the statements without affecting the propositions they contain. Try to do the same thing with the word-groups which you think are not statements. Be ready to discuss your results.

B. Convert the following semiverbal communications into purely verbal language:

1.   TUDOR AND STUART DYNASTIES

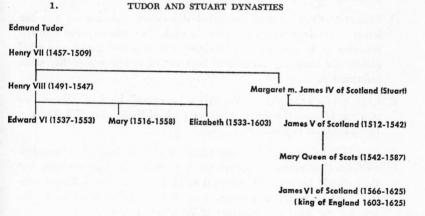

2.   ORGANIZATION CHART

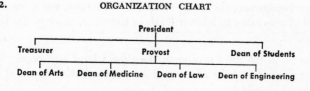

3.

HOUSE PLAN

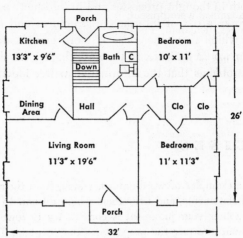

C. Find two examples of symbolic forms, both nonverbal, but one informative and the other creative. (A map and a painting would be good choices.) Discuss the differences between them: Do the symbols function as monosigns or plurisigns? Do both examples contain propositions? Try to state verbally the propositions in each.

D. Collect five examples of nonverbal statements and discuss: (1) the kinds of symbols which are used in each, (2) whether the symbols function as monosigns or plurisigns, (3) whether these nonverbal statements have any advantage over verbal statements of the same information.

E. Collect five examples of the "record-keeping" kind of informative writing. Discuss the organization of each of these examples. Do you find variations in generality?

F. Collect three examples of the more developed kind of informative writing. (Individual paragraphs will probably be long enough, but they should be carefully selected so that they are on different subjects and have different structures.) Analyze these examples to determine the level of generality of each proposition.

G. Write two paragraphs on the same subject. In one, move from a high level of generality to a lower level; in the other, move in the opposite direction.

H. Rewrite, in the form of a news story for a local newspaper, the following minutes of the meeting of an organization. (You need not include all details.)

The Glenridge Taxpayers' Association held its monthly meeting on June 21, in the Glenridge High School Auditorium. One hundred and five members were present.

Mr. James Benjamin, President, called the meeting to order at 8:10 P.M.

The minutes of the last meeting were read by the Secretary. Mrs. Herman Giddings pointed out that the minutes were in error: she had not opposed the appointment of a new by-laws committee. The minutes were corrected, and, there being no further objection, were accepted as revised.

The President called for a report of the Nominating Committee.

Mr. Harold Francis, Chairman of the Nominating Committee, reported the following nominations:

> President: Mr. James Benjamin
> Vice-President: Mr. George Lewis
> Secretary: Mr. Myron Young
> Treasurer: Dr. Lewis Kendall

Mr. Francis moved that the secretary be instructed to cast one ballot for the slate. The President asked if there were any further nominations and, hearing none, called for a vote on the motion. Carried unanimously.

The President stated that he was gratified at this vote of confidence and pledged to continue to work for the interests of the Taxpayers' Association.

The President appointed a committee, consisting of Dr. Kendall, Miss Helen Ames, and George Newsom, to meet with the Mayor to discuss the Association's stand on the new city budget.

The meeting adjourned at 9:45 P.M.

6. Structure and Style in Informative Writing

> "Logic! Good gracious! What rubbish!" exclaimed
> E. M. Forster's Old Lady. "How can I tell what I
> think till I see what I say?"
>
> CURTIS AND GREENSLET (EDITORS),
The Practical Cogitator

Selection and Arrangement

Inexperienced writers are likely to assume that nearly the whole problem, in informative writing, is to work out statements which will express ready-made propositions, to spell out some pre-established outline. This is not true, for several reasons. Except in the simplest, most factual kind of informative communications, very few of even the main propositions will have been fully thought out ahead of time: they achieve final clarity and precision only in the process of being stated in words. Furthermore, their arrangement—the outline—changes as the writing proceeds. As for the minor propositions, many—sometimes most—of these will scarcely exist in the writer's mind until they are forced into consciousness by the writing process itself. And finally, any but the most routine informative writing involves important strategy decisions which go well beyond merely putting facts and ideas into words.

One of these basic strategy decisions we have already talked about. Most informative writers decide, rather early in the writing process and usually quite consciously, whether to begin with an over-all view, a statement of major principles, the basic theory of the subject, their conclusions; or to begin instead with examples, applications, incidents, the story of how they reached their conclusions. They decide, in other words, whether to start at a high level of generality or at a low level of generality. They also decide what levels of generality to maintain throughout the rest of the writing, a decision which depends primarily on the nature of the audience and the space available. And even when they have finished a rough draft, perhaps the first thing they will check is their levels. Are more examples and applications needed? Have the proper conclusions been drawn so that all the "back-and-fill" is given significance? Such questions are primarily a matter of the selection and arrangement of material, questions about conceptual knowledge, about what propositions to include and to exclude and what order to present them in. In some ways, such strategy decisions are the most important ones a writer has to make. And they are not merely preliminary decisions, nor decisions which can be made once and for all and then stuck to, because what happens as the writing goes along is bound to modify even the basic strategy.

All this, of course, explains why in the last chapter we devoted so much time to levels of generality. But there are a number of other very fundamental principles which are useful as guide lines to writing. In this chapter we will consider a few of the more important ones, all of them closely related to the theory of language developed in this book.

Abstraction

A couple of chapters back we defined *abstraction,* almost in passing. We said that an abstract term is one which brings to mind no clear and distinct image or other sense impression. Now, this is a very rough definition, and also a somewhat oversimplified one.

We have seen that most words have both conceptual meanings and evocative meanings. We have also seen that usually one of the principal sources of a word's meaning is its denotation. (Remember the boy and the blacksnake.) A term's conceptual meaning is derived from instances of its denotation; but the term may also call to mind instances of its denotation, in the form of images. However, words vary a great deal in the relation between the images they evoke and the conceptual meanings which they also bring to mind. If the boy in our story never sees another blacksnake, and never talks or reads about blacksnakes again, the chances are that his memory of this one blacksnake—preserved as an image—will be very close to his concept of blacksnake; in fact, even if he subsequently sees many more blacksnakes, the instances will be so much alike that there will still be a close correspondence between image and concept. But suppose the word is not *blacksnake* but *animal.* Here the instances of the denotation will differ so greatly among themselves that the word will call no clear and distinct image to mind.

In general, we use the term *abstract* for a word like *animal* and the opposite term, *concrete,* for a word like *blacksnake.* But this is clearly not an either-or distinction. There are gradations of abstractness: we can go from the concrete to the abstract along a line from *blacksnake,* to *snake,* to *reptile,* to *animal,* to *life.* At some point along this line, instances of the denotation become so unlike each other that the word no longer is capable of a distinct image. For convenience we speak of the image-bearing words as concrete, those which are not image-bearing as abstract; but there are clearly levels of abstraction within each group. *Reptile* perhaps produces only a vague image, but it is less abstract than *animal; snake* may evoke an image, but it is less concrete than *blacksnake.* Yet the notion of image-bearing words as concrete, and of non-image-bearing words as abstract, provides a very useful distinction for the writer to keep in mind.

One other point needs to be added, however. In Chapter 3 we had to think of level of abstractness as an attribute of individual words, because we had not yet introduced the notion of context. But context can change abstraction level significantly. The word *animal* may call to mind no distinct image, but put it in the phrase "a small, furry animal with a pointed nose and a scaly tail," and the image is quite clear.

For practical purposes, then, the notion of abstraction applies only to words in context. The question is whether the words taken together are capable of producing a picture or other sense impression, a scene which we can visualize, or an event in which we in effect take part. In Mary McCarthy's account of her conversation with the story-writing student, few of the words themselves are especially concrete, but they evoke a scene, conflicts among characters, setting, dialogue. This part of the passage is therefore relatively concrete as compared with her last paragraph, in which she draws the moral.

A couple of additional examples may be useful at this point.

Though both come from philosophers, the first is almost wholly abstract, the second much more concrete. The first is from Immanuel Kant's *Metaphysics of Ethics:*

> Because the universality of the law according to which effects are produced constitutes what we really mean by *nature* in the most general sense (according to form), that is, the existence of things in so far as it is determined by universal laws, the universal imperative of duty may read thus: *Act as if the maxim of your action by your will were to become a universal law of nature.*

This brings no images, pictures, scenes to mind. But philosophers are not always so abstract, as witness this statement from the Greek Stoic philosopher Epictetus:

> On no occasion call yourself a philosopher, nor talk at large of your principles among the multitude, but act on your principles. For instance, at a banquet do not say how one ought to eat, but eat as you ought. Remember that Socrates had so completely got rid of the thought of display that when men came and wanted an introduction to philosophers, he took them to be introduced; so patient of neglect was he. And if a discussion arise among the multitude on some principle, keep silent for the most part; for you are in great danger of blurting out some undigested thought. And when someone says to you, "You know nothing," and you do not let it provoke you, then know that you are really on the right road. For sheep do not bring grass to their shepherds and show them how much they have eaten, but they digest their fodder and then produce it in the form of wool and milk. Do the same yourself; instead of displaying your principles to the multitude, show them the results of the principles you have digested.

Not only do a number of words in this passage carry fairly distinct images—*grass, shepherds, fodder, show, wool, milk;* but the situation is easy to visualize: we see Epictetus at a banquet "eating as he ought," sitting among a multitude and keeping silent, and being rebuked for his silence. We also see Socrates meekly taking his visitors off to meet some philosophers.

Abstraction and Generality

At first glance it may seem that this new principle, the principle of abstraction, is just generality under a new name; and where the terms are used very loosely, they are often equated. It is quite true also that there is a natural relationship between the general and the abstract, on the one hand, and the particular and the concrete, on the other; so that many statements which convey general propositions are quite abstract, while many statements which convey less general propositions are fairly concrete.

But in spite of this approximate relationship, the ideas are essentially different: *generality is a matter of propositions; abstraction is a matter of the language which is used to convey propositions.* It is therefore possible for a statement to convey a general proposition in rather concrete terms, or a less general proposition in abstract terms. "The ax is a sharp-headed tool with a wooden handle and is used for cutting down trees," conveys a general proposition in fairly concrete language. "The temperature at 6 A.M. was 62° F" conveys a particular proposition in abstract language. We could change the level of abstraction without changing the generality of the second proposition by saying, "The mercury in the thermometer stood at 62 degrees Fahrenheit when the village clock struck six in the morning." This sentence gives us a picture which is not given by the first one.

Use of Abstraction Levels in Writing

The important fact about abstraction levels is that their existence gives a writer another way of organizing his writing and of developing ideas. He can use levels of generality *and* levels of abstraction.

But before we look at some examples, a common misunderstanding must be cleared up. Many people have the idea that creative writing—especially poetry—is quite abstract; and that informative writing is correspondingly concrete. As a matter of fact, these notions should be almost reversed. Poetry—and creative writing in general—are usually quite concrete: they produce images, pictures, scenes. Informative writing on the other hand always *tends toward* the abstract. Since we have already seen that all informative writing is not equally abstract, and since we are about to look at ways of varying the abstraction level in informative writing, it may be well to explain this statement.

The point is that informative writers are more concerned with the concepts which they are trying to convey than with the sense characteristics of phenomena. If the informative writer uses image-bearing words—as he sometimes does—it is usually either because his subject matter requires that he use such words (he is talking about things that we can touch and see) or because he wants us to see and feel as a prelude to understanding intellectually. We can grasp this point most clearly perhaps if we think of a piece of *non-*verbal communication, such as a map. Most of the symbols on a map—lines, colors, conventional "culture symbols"—have picturable denotations. But unless the map is intended chiefly as a wall-decoration or as a piece of advertising (as maps sometimes are), the symbols serve principally to identify features of the territory, not to evoke images of them. The production of images, if it takes place, is almost incidental, and it may even be confusing: it would be unfortunate if a person looking at a map concluded that the Indiana landscape must be red because the state is colored red on the map.

Turning now to the verbal equivalent of a map, we can see the same point again. A man explaining where he lives writes:

> My house is the third on the left after you pass the stone bridge. You can see it from the bridge. It's almost at the top of the hill.

Not only do the words *house, hill, stone bridge,* and perhaps even *left,* carry picturable images, but the statements as a whole give us a picture of the landscape. Still their purpose is simply to identify landmarks so that the reader can find the place; and as long as he does find it, it matters very little whether the scene actually corresponds to his imaginings. He may have pictured a neat Cape Cod cottage, only to find a run-down Victorian mansion. He may have thought of three houses in a row on a paved highway, only to find them widely scattered and set far back from a dusty country road. None of these "mistakes," however, matters very much: they were not "misconceptions" only "mis-imaginings"; and in this case, conceptual meanings were what counted, not evocative ones.

Nevertheless, images remain as characteristics of many words. And good informative writers, though they keep their eyes focused on concepts, make use of images as a means of explaining or of reinforcing their concepts, or simply to make them more palatable.

Some writers do this by introducing statements which present pictures or which at least contain image-bearing words. In the last chapter we looked at a couple of paragraphs on law written by Dorothy Sayers. A great deal of the interest in these paragraphs is in the more concrete statements:

Thus if the ball (correctly bowled) hits the wicket, the batsman is "out." There is, however, no inevitable connection between the impact of the ball upon three wooden stumps and the progress of a human body from a patch of mown grass to a pavilion. . . . "If you hold your finger in the fire, it will be burnt."

In the passage as a whole, what Miss Sayers does is to move up and down between levels of abstraction. And this is a very common and useful way of working out a concept. If we want to see the converse effect, of a passage in which level of abstraction is not changed, we have only to look again at the selection from Kant (p. 99). (Kant does not, of course, always stay on such a high level of abstraction.)

A second way of using the principle of abstraction is illustrated in the following passage from *Creative Evolution* by another philosopher, Henri Bergson:

> Duration is the continuous progress of the past which gnaws into the future and which swells as it advances. And as the past grows without ceasing, so also there is no limit to its preservation. Memory . . . is not a faculty of putting away recollections in a drawer or of inscribing them in a register. There is no register, no drawer; there is not even, properly speaking, a faculty, for a faculty works intermittently, when it will or when it can, whilst the piling up of the past on the past goes on without relaxation. In reality the past is preserved by itself, automatically. In its entirety, probably, it follows us at every instant; all that we have felt, thought, and willed from our earliest infancy is there, leaning over the present which is about to join it, pressing against the portals of consciousness that would fain leave it outside.

This is a particularly interesting passage, because its propositions are all high-level generalizations. Bergson is talking about time, duration, the past, the present; and he is making very general statements about them. Yet one's impression is that his language is remarkably concrete. However, Bergson does not *move* between levels of abstraction, as Dorothy Sayers does, but puts his very general propositions in language which is partly metaphorical. He wants us to see duration as an organic process; he uses words therefore which create in our minds a picture of some kind of organism— something which *gnaws* and *swells* and *grows,* which *follows us at every instant,* which *leans over the present,* and *which presses against the portals of consciousness.* This picture is less a result of individual words than of cumulative metaphor. Bergson never says the past is like an organism; he creates that impression largely through a series of verbs.

Comparison and Contrast

Bergson's use of metaphor suggests another principle which is much used in informative discussion—the principle of comparison and contrast. In later chapters we shall see comparison and contrast as a universal characteristic of creative form, in fact of all artistic form. But it appears also in informative writing, not as an inevitable ingredient but as a valuable device for developing and explaining ideas.

As an example of how comparison and contrast work in informative writing, let us start this time not with a finished example but with a problem. A writer has been asked to explain in a short paper the meaning of democracy. Now democracy is a difficult concept, and it is almost certain that the writer will want to use various levels of both generality and abstraction in explaining it. He will want to give examples, to cite instances of democracy in action. (He may even decide to *begin* with such examples—a town meeting, perhaps; an election; an instance of equality of treatment in the courts.) And he will probably want to go back into history, both to collect statements about democracy by such men as Jefferson and Lincoln, and also to find more examples of democracy in action. But he will not be able to present an adequate picture unless he also compares and contrasts democracy with some other systems—totalitarianism perhaps, or anarchy. Or he may want to work out the differences between a democracy and a representative republic. Or he may compare several democratic institutions and try to derive from this comparison a more adequate definition. At any rate, comparison and contrast, including comparisons at various levels of generality and in language which varies in abstractness, is likely to be one of the devices the writer will use.

The plain fact is that we understand anything best when we see it in relation to something else. We have to see how it is like certain other things and how it differs from them. In formal definitions, the standard system is to place the term to be defined in a larger framework—that is, to set down the general class to which it belongs. It is then differentiated from other members of the class. The class provides the framework in which comparison can be made; setting the term apart from other members of the class involves contrast. Here is a dictionary definition of history: "the branch of knowledge dealing with past events." History is first put in a larger category: it is a branch of knowledge. It is then differentiated from other branches of knowledge by its subject matter, which is past events.

But comparison and contrast are often used in much more complex ways. We have already seen one such use in Dorothy Sayers' paragraphs on law. These constitute an informal definition. Miss Sayers is clearly interested in the distinction between two kinds of law; but even if she were interested in only one kind, the method she employs would be useful. Had she confined her discourse to only one meaning of law, and employed no comparison, it would hardly have been very memorable.

In fact, comparison and contrast are so useful that informative writers sometimes develop contrasts which are not really necessary. An author either invents or describes one point of view—often what he imagines to be the reader's—and then dismantles it bit by bit, thus replacing it with his own point of view. If the point of view to be destroyed is an invented one, this device is sometimes called the "straw man" technique. It is of course a common device in persuasion; but it can also be used merely as a background against which to present ideas which might otherwise seem rather tame. Here is an example, primarily informative, from an essay on Ibsen by H. L. Mencken:

> Twenty years ago [Ibsen] was hymned and damned as . . . symbolist, seer, prophet, necromancer, maker of riddles, rabble-rouser, cheap shocker, pornographer, spinner of gossamer nothings. Fools belabored him and fools defended him; he was near to being suffocated and done for in the fog of balderdash. I know of no sure cure for all the sorrows of the world, social, political or aesthetic, that was not credited to him, read into him, forced into his baggage. And I know of no crime against virtue, good order and the revelation of God that he was not accused of. The product of all this pawing and bawling was the Ibsen legend, that fabulous picture of a fabulous monster . . . drenching the world with scandalous platitudes from a watch-tower in the chilblained North. The righteous heard of him with creepy shudders; there was bold talk of denying him the use of the mails. . . .
>
> No such Ibsen, of course, ever really existed. The genuine Ibsen was anything but the Anti-Christ thus conjured up by imprudent partisans and terrified opponents. On the contrary, he was a man whose salient quality was precisely his distrust of, and disdain for,

any and all such facile heresies; a highly respectable gentleman of the middle class, well-barbered, ease loving and careful in mind; a very skilful practitioner of a very exacting and lucrative trade; a safe and sane exponent of order, efficiency, honesty and common sense. From end to end of his life there is no record that Ibsen ever wrote a single word or formulated a single idea that might not have been exposed in a newspaper editorial. He believed in all the things that the normal, law-abiding citizen of Christendom believes in, from democracy to romantic love, and from the obligations of duty to the value of virtue, and he always gave them the best of it in his plays. And whenever, mistaking his position, someone charged him with flouting these things or with advocating some notion that stood in opposition to them, he invariably called the plaintiff to book, and denied vehemently that he was guilty, and protested bitterly that it was outrageous to fasten any such wild and naughty stuff upon a reputable man.[1]

Surely, without the use of contrast here Mencken would have had trouble, not only in trying to make so respectable a figure interesting, but even in defining Ibsen's actual relation to the world of radical ideas. Incidentally, Mencken's language here represents a level of concreteness which is about as far from—say—Kant's language as informative writing is likely to get.

Comparison is often used in another way also: the writer sets up an *analogy* between something which is hard to understand (his subject), and something which is easy to understand. He then works out the difficult concept in terms of the easy one. Einstein once presented the principle of the conversion of mass into energy by means of the following analogy:

> The atom M is a rich miser who, during his life, gives away no money (*energy*). But in his will he bequeaths his fortune to his sons M' and M'' on condition that they give to the community a small amount, less than one thousandth of the whole estate (*energy or mass*). The sons together have somewhat less than their father had (*the mass sum $M' + M''$ is somewhat smaller than the mass M of the radioactive atom*). But the part given to the community, though relatively small, is still so enormously large (*considered as kinetic energy*) that it brings with it a great threat of evil. Averting that threat has become the most urgent problem of our time.

And Plato, in *The Republic* (from which we quoted a short passage in the last chapter) uses a similar method much more ex-

[1] Reprinted from the Introduction to the *Eleven Plays of Henrik Ibsen*. By permission of Random House, Inc.

tensively, constructing his imaginary state on the analogy of the individual soul. He is investigating the meaning of Justice, and when he cannot find it in the operations of an individual soul, he builds an ideal state and looks for it there. And he constructs his state on the analogy of the individual with his separate faculties: the ruling class, called the guardians, are analogous to the rational element in the soul; the auxiliaries (who act as an army and police force) are the spirited element; the artisans and merchants are the appetites. And Justice turns out, by this reasoning, to consist of a proper relation among the three classes in the state, and a proper relation among these elements in the soul. (In the passage about the philosopher-dog, Plato is, of course, using still another analogy.)

As all these examples indicate, analogies are usually drawn between relatively general propositions and relatively particular ones, and they usually lead us to see a relationship in terms of a picture. In this way comparison and contrast is combined with the use of levels of generality and of levels of abstraction.

One more point should be made about the use of analogy: it is usually safer as a means of presenting propositions than as a means of working them out. Reasoning by analogy can be dangerous business, especially if we do not know how far the analogy holds. And even presentation by analogy can lead to misconceptions. Sometimes the farfetched analogy—as in Einstein's example—is safer than the close one: it does not invite an unwarranted extension. False analogy is nicely represented by the following editorial comment, quoted earlier, on a university's indecisiveness in handling the case of a teacher suspected of communism:

> "A ponderous pussy-footing . . . You can no more be partially loyal than you can be partially pregnant."

Some Further Notes on Style

Several additional points can now be made about the language of informative writing. Back in Chapter 4 we noted that symbols tend to function as monosigns in informative discussion: they focus attention not only on conceptual meaning but on a single conceptual meaning. Nevertheless, as we have also seen, many of the words used in informative writing do generate images as well as concepts: that is, they have some evocative meaning as well. We need always to remember that words in general retain all their *potential* meanings, both conceptual and evocative, no matter where they appear. Images and feelings as well as concepts may be brought to mind. And although the informative writer often does need to avoid words which have strong evaluative associations, he can never focus attention entirely on concepts: the words are still there.

What he can do is watch his contexts, avoiding combinations of words whose evocative effects reinforce each other except for special purposes, some of which we have already seen—for example, the passages from Bergson and Mencken. And he tries, also through control of context, to avoid concentrating attention on the "thingness" of his words. Informative prose, for example, is seldom noticeably alliterative, because the repetition of opening sounds—or of any other sounds—has the effect of attracting attention to the words instead of permitting the reader to go through to the concepts. Even too rhythmical or too balanced a style may distract the reader. On the other hand, this avoidance of undue emphasis on language does not imply a disregard for language. A crabbed or awkward style diverts attention from the propositions to the words just as surely as does writing which emphasizes thingness and evocative effects, and usually with far more serious results.

To use an analogy of our own, the language of informative writing functions as a transparent glass *through* which concepts and propositions may be seen. If it is either opaque in spots, or imperfect and scratched, it tends to get in the way: one sees *it* instead of seeing what is underneath it. On the other hand it can function to channel attention, to point out relationships, to highlight essential points. It then becomes not merely a transparent substance through which we look but a kind of overlay which guides our seeing.

As this analogy should suggest, informative writing actually varies a great deal in style and tone. Some of it approaches so close to the creative that the words are used with attention to their thingness and their evocative meanings simply because conceptual and experiential knowledge are joined. (We shall have more to say about this combination in Chapter 13.) But even in the kind of writing which aims principally at conceptual knowledge, great variations are possible—in formality, objectivity, seriousness, and elegance.

Let's look at a few contrasting sentences, all of them from pieces of informative writing. Here is Darwin writing with great formality:

Authors of the highest eminence seem to be fully satisfied with the view that each species has been independently created.

And here is Captain Joshua Slocum writing in much less formal language about a visit to Buenos Aires:

In all the years away from his native home Howard had not forgotten the art of making fish chowders; and to prove this he brought along some fine rockfish and prepared a mess fit for kings.

Here is Sir James Jeans writing in a thoroughly objective vein:

The mathematical laws of the quantum theory show that radiant energy is transferred by complete quanta.

And here is Edmund Gosse giving his highly personal impressions of a religious meeting he attended as a child:

An elderly man, fat and greasy, with a voice like a bassoon, and an imperturbable assurance, was denouncing the spread of infidelity, and the lukewarmness of professing Christians who refrained from battling with the wickedness at their doors.

And here is George Meredith writing with the greatest seriousness:

One excellent test of the civilization of a country, as I have said, I take to be the flourishing of the Comic idea and Comedy; and the test of true Comedy is that it shall awaken thoughtful laughter.

And here is Eddington summarizing his argument for various ways of knowing:

I suppose that humor can be analyzed to some extent and the essential ingredients of the different kinds of wit classified. Suppose that we are offered an alleged joke. We subject it to scientific analysis as we would a chemical salt of doubtful nature, and perhaps after careful consideration of all its aspects we are able to confirm that it really and truly is a joke. Logically I suppose our next procedure would be to laugh. But it may certainly be predicted that as a result of this scrutiny we shall have lost all inclination we may ever have had to laugh at it.[2]

In some informative writing, there is a conscious striving for the memorable phrase. We remember words as well as ideas; and it may be the words which make the ideas memorable. Memorable expressions are usually apt, balanced, witty, and neatly arranged.

[2] FROM *The Nature of the Physical World* by A. S. Eddington, by permission of the Cambridge University Press.

The chances are that some of us will recall the following sentence from Dorothy Sayers long after we have forgotten the details of her argument:

> Anybody can enact that murder shall not be punishable by death; nobody can enact that the swallowing of a tumblerful of prussic acid shall not be punishable by death.

At the same time, this very particular, very concrete, nicely balanced, vivid, and witty sentence brings together the two meanings of law which Miss Sayers is trying to convey. We can even reconstruct her distinction from this one sentence—a good example of the usefulness of memorable phrasing.

The Writing Process Again

The analysis which we have worked out in these two chapters may leave the reader with the impression that writing is both more mechanical and more difficult than is actually the case. We have been concerned with principles, and they are the sort of principles which, properly used, can help the writer to understand what he is doing, to work out ideas, and to fill in gaps in his presentation. They can even help the tongue-tied beginner, who starts out by putting everything he has to say into three rather unclear sentences and then wonders what to do next. To him it says: Are you sure this is the way to begin? Have you thought of working through to these conclusions instead of beginning with them? How about some examples? (Or, conversely, What does it all add up to anyway?) Can you be more concrete in your language without falsifying the propositions you are trying to get across? Have you thought of comparing and contrasting? Would an analogy help? Does your language focus attention on the important ideas without getting in the way? Are all of your words and all of your other devices truly functional in terms of your informative purpose?

But these questions are over-all guides: things to think about before you start to write—occasionally while you are writing—and most especially after you have something down on paper. The actual putting things down on paper, however, may be much simpler than these questions would suggest. An informative writer has at his disposal an instrument which is more valuable than any system—

his own thinking mind. And it is valuable because it probably works very much like his reader's mind.

Writing is not a matter of planting ideas on the blank surface of someone else's consciousness. In the first place, the surface is never really blank: there is already something there, though it may be part of the writer's job to connect what is there with what *he* has to say. In the second place, as ideas are presented they generate other ideas. The reader questions, anticipates, objects, agrees. He says in effect: "Give me an example," "What do you conclude from all this?" "How is what you are talking about like this other thing? How is it different?" And these are precisely the kinds of questions we have been suggesting that the writer ask of himself as he writes—and afterwards.

But in practice, much of the development is worked out almost automatically. The writer's own statements, as he makes them, suggest the need for examples, for explicit conclusions, for comparisons and contrasts. And the language which he uses—the very form of his sentences—suggests the language which should follow. Writers do not sit down ordinarily and plan their phrasing: a pattern which has already been established calls for what comes next. A figure of speech—for example Bergson's organic metaphor—dictates a continuation of the same figure. A word which is particularly important clearly needs to be repeated, perhaps thereby tying together a whole paragraph.

By way of conclusion, let us look at a few more examples. We shall present them with very little comment. The reader will do well to examine them closely with all the principles suggested in these two chapters in mind.

Here is a passage from L. Susan Stebbing's *Thinking to Some Purpose:*

> Some forms of ineffective thinking are due to our not unnatural desire to have confident beliefs about complicated matters with regard to which we must take some action or other. We are sometimes too lazy, usually too busy, and often too ignorant to think out what is involved in the statements we so readily accept. Few true statements about a complicated state of affairs can be expressed in a single sentence. Our need to have definite beliefs to hold on to is great; the difficulty in mastering the evidence upon which such beliefs ought to be based is burdensome; consequently, we easily fall into the habit of accepting compressed statements which save us from the trouble of thinking. Thus arises what I shall call "Potted Thinking." This metaphor seems to me to be appropriate, because potted thinking is easily

accepted, is concentrated in form, and has lost the vitamins essential to mental nourishment. You will notice that I have continued the metaphor by using the word "vitamins." Do not accept the metaphor too hastily: it must be expanded. Potted meat is sometimes a convenient form of food; it may be tasty, it contains some nourishment. But its nutritive value is not equivalent to that of the fresh meat from which it was potted. Also, it must originally have been made from fresh meat, and must not be allowed to grow stale. Similarly, a potted belief is convenient; it can be stated briefly, sometimes also in a snappy manner likely to attract attention. A potted belief should be the outcome of a belief that is not potted. It should not be held on to when circumstances have changed and new factors have come to light. We should not allow our habits of thought to close our minds, nor rely upon catch words to save ourselves from the labour of thinking. Vitamins are essential for the natural growth of our bodies; the critical questioning at times of our potted beliefs is necessary for the development of our capacity to think to some purpose.[8]

Besides looking at this passage in terms of the main principles suggested in this chapter and the last, the reader should also notice repetitions, either of sentence and phrase forms or of words.

The second passage is from an article by George Whicher called "Frost at Seventy."

Frost's distinction is precisely that he has maintained during a time of general disillusionment his instinctive belief in the tradition which lies at the core of our national being, the tradition of liberal democracy.

> *As long as the Declaration guards*
> *My right to be equal in number of cards,*
> *It is nothing to me who runs the Dive.*

No reader of his poems can suppose that Frost's serenity is the product of an easy optimism. He has known what it is to feel himself swept and shaken, he has been acquainted with dark hours, he has experienced poverty and injustice. His power of neighborly sympathy with others is attested beyond the possibility of contravention in "The Death of the Hired Man," "A Servant to Servants," "The Self-Seeker," "The Hill Wife," and "Out, Out—" among many other poems. But Frost is more than a mass of sensibilities,

> *I have a mind myself and recognize*
> *Mind where I meet it in any guise.*[4]

[8] FROM *Thinking to Some Purpose* by L. Susan Stebbing. Reprinted by permission of Penguin Books, Ltd.
[4] FROM "Frost at Seventy" by George F. Whicher, reprinted from *The American Scholar*, Autumn, 1945. By permission of the author and the publisher.

Our final example is very short, and most interestingly constructed; it is from an article, "The Place of Religion and Ethics in a Civilization Based on Science," by Raymond Cattell. He is arguing for the existence and the significance of what he calls the "group mind":

> There is one other way in which the group mind differs signally from the individual mind: it is potentially immortal. The individual dies; society lives on. There is a wood near London that the Romans spoke of. All the trees are different but the wood is still there.

EXERCISES

A. Collect three examples of informative writing in which you can see levels of abstraction, levels of generality, comparison and contrast, and other principles of organization at work. (Paragraph-length examples will do if they are sufficiently varied.) Analyze the examples in detail.

B. The following statements assert highly general propositions. Make each the basis of a paragraph which also contains particulars.
   1. Communication media operate through the senses—sight, hearing, and sometimes touch.
   2. Democracy has political, social, and economic aspects.
   3. There is a basic conflict between freedom and security.

C. Rewrite each of the paragraphs you wrote for B, trying to make your original language more concrete wherever you can.

D. Write three paragraphs on subjects of your own choice, using comparison and contrast in one, levels of generality in the second, and levels of abstraction in the third.

E. Write an informal definition of one of the following terms: *academic freedom, the welfare state, liberalism.* Develop your definition using comparison and contrast, levels of generality, and levels of abstraction, but do not confine yourself to these devices if you find others that are useful.

F. Write an informal definition of a term of your own choice, employing the same principles mentioned in E.

G. Prepare a topical outline of a scientific report, a scholarly article, a piece of "reportage," or some other formal kind of informative writing already in print. Try to decide what principles of organization are operating. (Your instructor may assign different articles to each student and ask for a comparison and discussion in class.)

H. Using the discussion of the philosopher-dog as your model (or better yet, using a whole Socratic dialogue—your instructor may specify), write a Socratic dialogue on one of the following topics:
    1. The limitations of freedom
    2. Pleasure as the end of life
    3. The aims of the good society
    4. Science and censorship
    5. Conscience and the state
These topics are all too large for complete development in a short dialogue: treat only one aspect of the topic you choose and develop it carefully. Create your own characters as participants in the dialogue, and try to make your discussion as interesting as possible.

I. Write a Socratic dialogue on a subject of your own choosing.

J. Rewrite either of the dialogues in H or I above as an essay.

7. Reading Informative Literature

> We must be content, then, in speaking of such subjects and with such premises to indicate the truth roughly and in outline, and in speaking about things which are only for the most part true and with premises of the same kind to reach conclusions which are no better. In this spirit, therefore, should each type of statement be received; for it is the mark of an educated man to look for precision in each class of things just so far as the nature of the subject admits; it is evidently equally foolish to accept probable reasoning from a mathematician and to demand from a rhetorician scientific proofs.
>
> ARISTOTLE, *The Nichomachean Ethics*

The Amateur's Role in the Long Conversation

In the formal, published part of the long conversation, most of us are, of course, amateurs. We make only sporadic and rather modest contributions as writers and speakers. But as readers and as members of the audience we take part in the long conversation all our lives. And our role as readers and listeners is by no means a passive one. The intelligent reader and listener is constantly engaged in the very demanding activities of understanding and of passing judgment—activities which are (or should be) interrelated, since we cannot judge intelligently until we understand.

In this chapter we shall consider a few of the less obvious aspects of this double task of understanding and evaluating informative literature.

114

An Example to Work With

Informative literature is so diverse in all its characteristics that no single piece nor even a number of samples would illustrate all the problems involved in reading it. We would have to include news stories, news analyses, historical studies, scientific reports, technical and scholarly articles of all sorts, critical essays, and philosophical treatises. Excerpts from many of these informative species have been quoted in the last two chapters, and we shall refer back to them as we need to. But it may be well to have, in addition, one complete and fairly complex informative work—of the kind which definitely poses some problems in understanding, interpreting, and evaluating. The following example, presented as a radio address by Joseph Wood Krutch, professor emeritus of dramatic literature at Columbia University, is entitled "The Modern View of Man":

Our own age began as the age when man seemed to be coming finally into his own.

Never before in the history of civilization had it been so generally taken for granted that man's freedom, his dignity, his happiness, even what we call his "prosperity," were the only things that count. Never before had statesmen and philosophers laid so much stress on the importance of any and all men. Never before had they professed to take so little account of, for example, the glory of God, or the glory of the church, or the glory of the political and military state, considered as things to which the welfare of the individual man might properly be sacrificed.

An ancient Greek philosopher said that "Man is the measure of all things," but we took that statement more literally and more absolutely than his contemporaries did. We applied it not so much to man in the abstract as to men—to our fellow citizens and our fellow citizens of the world.

That means, among other things, that our age began as also the great age of the humanitarian. To the ancient question, "Am I my brother's keeper?" we answered with an unequivocal "Yes." And by being his keeper we usually meant, not so much responsible for the welfare of his soul, or for guiding his steps in the direction we thought he should take, as simply responsible for his health, his comfort, his general welfare.

If in certain preceding ages it was generally thought that the privileged had done enough when they persuaded the less fortunate to be content with the circumstances into which it had pleased God to put them, we found that little more than hypocrisy. We professed, at least, to want to see to it that every man was fed when he was hungry, housed when he was cold, treated when he was ill, and given an opportunity to learn when he was ignorant. We wanted to provide him with the maximum of comfort and convenience it was possible to give him. We were almost fanatically concerned with what we call his "standard of living."

As recently as two generations—perhaps even one generation—ago, it seemed to most of us that our enterprise had achieved a good deal of success and was destined to achieve a good deal more. But by no means everyone is nearly so confident today. Over a large part of the area once occupied by "the most advanced civilizations" there is, to put it bluntly, less welfare than there was a few years ago. Most of the men in those areas are worse fed, worse clothed, and worse housed than they were. What is perhaps even more important is that "man's inhumanity to man" has reached what seems almost unparalleled proportions. There has been more violence, more brutality, more cold, calculated ferocity than at any time since the end of those ages which we complacently call "dark." Men have shown themselves capable of organized outrages of a kind we thought no group of men would any longer be capable of.

Now so far as the decline in the "standard of living" is concerned, that is obviously the result of two world wars. But both of those wars were no less obviously connected with an idea of man; and so are the unofficial wars, cold and hot, which continue to rage. Fascism and Communism both wage war in the name of what we call an "ideology," and in both the ideology involves an idea of what man *is* and what he *ought to be*.

Sometimes we recognize this fact and try to simplify the problem by saying that all we need to do is to defeat the powers which represent the fascist and Communist ideologies and then resume the march of progress which they interrupted so catastrophically. Perhaps it would be as simple as that if these "ideologies" were everywhere and entirely as antithetical to ours as their consequences seem antithetical to the consequences we would like to produce—if, for example, a Communist or a Fascist was a man who proposed to revive the divine right of kings or the temporal power of the church, and who professed to believe that the welfare of the individual man was of no great importance.

But the uncomfortable fact is that many of his professed premises are very similar to ours. He too professes to believe that the material welfare of mankind is of supreme importance. And if many persons all over the world are seduced by his promises, it is partly because these promises involve many of the same goods we promise. He says merely that his way, not ours, will bring that higher standard of living for all which we have failed to provide.

If this is true, then it seems as though an important part of our struggle against fascism and Communism might have in the end to turn around the subject of this present talk: namely, the modern idea of man. It may become necessary to ask what really is the difference between our idea of man and that professed by our enemies. Or, more subtly, what aspects of our idea made it possible for our enemies to transform it into the fascist and Communist ideas?

Perhaps it would be well for us to re-examine our concept of man and to redefine it in some way which would distinguish it more clearly from that of the totalitarians and render impossible any suspicion that it must, or even could, justify a totalitarian philosophy or a totalitarian state.

When we ask these questions, I think that the answers become simpler and clearer than we might have supposed they would. The questions remind us immediately that there is a paradox hidden in our definition of man and that as long as that paradox remains unresolved the definition can lead us either in the direction of free democracy or in the direction of totalitarianism. Let us see if we can examine the paradox.

When I began a few moments ago to describe the modern attitude, I really described only half of it. I said that we had made man's welfare the measure of all things. What I did not say was that along with that increasing stress upon the importance of men's rights and privileges, along with that tendency to glorify him, went another tendency to belittle him. Less than perhaps any other age do we really think of him as a free agent, as the captain of his own soul, and capable of making his own choices. We call him "the product of his environment." We say that the society in which he lives makes him what he is. We talk about his psychological and his sociological "conditioning."

Now, of course, Marxism, as the Communists interpret it, is the philosophy which justifies this tendency in its most absolute and dogmatic form. It is the theory that a man never is and never can be *anything except* the product of social, and especially of economic, conditions; that his philosophy, his code of ethics, his religion, even his tastes and preferences, are not, as he thinks, his free choice, but simply what he must believe because of the environment in which he has grown up. Thus it makes man nothing in himself.

Few Americans believe quite this. But it can hardly be denied that a great deal of sociological and political thinking, whether it is Marxian or not, has tended to lay more and more stress upon what can be done *to* men, less and less upon what they are capable of in themselves.

We have, for instance, very little faith in moral discourse, a great deal in what can be done to condition the youth. We have very little faith in the individual's power to solve his own spiritual problems, a great deal in the effect of counselors and psychologists. We talk a great deal about the importance of education, the molding of public opinion, sometimes of "propaganda," and we make very little distinction between the three.

We have much less faith than our forefathers had in the native ability of the individual man to arrive at good and sensible decisions. We think a good deal more than our forefathers did about what instruments can be used to sway public opinion in this direction or that.

Now this is the aspect of the modern attitude which has made it possible for that attitude to develop the democracies on the one hand and the totalitarian states on the other.

Accept without qualification the belief that man is always "nothing but" the product of the sociological and psychological factors which operate upon him, and nothing could be more logical than the totalitarian methods.

If we can make man what we think he ought to be by making an environment which will produce the kind of man we want, then we, the rulers, must be able to manipulate that environment; and we cannot do so unless everything, from literature to wages, which might affect a man is under control.

Democrats may protest against such a totalitarian system in the name of freedom and in the name of the unique, sacred individual. But how can an individual be either unique or sacred if he is merely the product of his environment? What can freedom mean if the individual is not himself capable of it? The very ideal of political liberty is absurd unless the individuals who exercise it are themselves free. If they are not—if they are merely what circumstances make them—then *from* what or *for* what can they possibly be free?

This, then, is the paradox of the modern idea of man. On the one hand it has exalted, on the other it has debased, him. It has exalted him by saying that his welfare is the only thing which counts; it has debased him by tending, at least, to deny that he possesses any of the powers or capacities upon which any real dignity or importance can be founded. It regards him as both more and less than he was ever before taken to be.

You may say, if you like, that at the present moment the struggle between democracy and totalitarianism is a struggle between those who are most aware of the "more" which the modern idea makes man, and those who are most aware of the "less." But just because the modern idea itself does present these two aspects, just because one may so easily pass from stress on the one to stress on the other, the struggle is confused. Were it not for that confusion, it would not be possible for the totalitarian states to claim that they actually accomplish what we only pretend to want, and it would not be possible for a few Americans to agree with them.

Perhaps the struggle will never be decided until the confusion is cleared, and it cannot be cleared until the paradox in the modern idea of man is somehow resolved. Perhaps we can never state our own case clearly until we have ourselves decided how much more than what the Communists call him we believe that a man actually is; until we can say clearly and firmly that our idea of man includes a real belief in his dignity, in the uniqueness of the individual, in something residing in him, which makes him capable of thinking rather than of merely "rationalizing," of believing rather than of being merely conditioned to believe, of exercising choice and determination rather than simply obeying his conditioned reflexes.

The nineteenth century was much concerned with the conflict between science and religion. That conflict turned around such questions as the inspiration of the Bible, the genuineness of miracles, evolution versus special creation, etc. Today it is often said that this conflict is over. In a sense it is. For a great many, perhaps for the majority of men, the issues are no longer very much alive, and for at least a large section of the public they are no longer alive because religion ended by accepting science's judgment concerning the majority of the specific points at issue.

But there is a sense in which the struggle between science and religion does continue. On the whole it is religion which has tended to reaffirm its belief in man as an infinitely complex and mysterious creature who is somehow and to some extent the captain of his soul. On the whole it is science which has tended to see him in mechanical terms, to describe him as some kind of machine operating in accordance with laws which make it possible to predict and control his behavior.

In so far as biology, psychology, and sociology actually have tended in the direction of mechanism, materialism, and determinism, just to that extent these sciences have encouraged an interpretation of the modern idea of man compatible with the theories and methods of totalitarianism. If man is a machine, then there is very little justification for treating him as though he were not. It is no accident that Pavlov, the great exponent of the conditioned reflex as the key to the understanding of human behavior, should be the great Soviet hero of science.

In the surviving democracies there is an articulate minority which has based upon these facts the simple dogmatic contention that there is no choice before us except that between Communism and a return to some form of Christian orthodoxy. That opinion is a defensible one, but perhaps it narrows the choices too much. Perhaps it would be truer to say, no choice except some form of rigidly planned, scientifically engineered society in which the concept of freedom will have lost its meaning and one based upon some "idea of man" which includes in our definition of him the characteristics and powers not recognized by any science which sees him only in terms of the dialectic materialism of Marx or the conditioned reflex of the behaviorist.

It may be that, in the end, science will itself find some way of recognizing the reality behind the concepts to which religion has persistently clung. Perhaps in this case, therefore, the conflict between the two will be resolved by science's taking over something from religion instead of, as before, by religion's taking over much from science. Indeed, there are already signs, especially in the sciences of physics and biology, that this is happening.

In atomic physics it is now almost universally recognized that even material particles do not behave in a way which the classical conception of the mechanical can account for. Observed fact has made it necessary for the physicist to acknowledge mysteries at least as repugnant to the old hard-headed materialist as the concepts of "free-will," "independent judgment," and the absolute validity of moral standards are repugnant to the hard-headed sociologist and psychologist. Mechanisms are not as mechanical and matter is not as material as each was once supposed to be. Mechanisms are not as mechanical because individual atoms are unpredictable and do not always behave in accordance with any definable law. Matter is not so material because it can be transformed into energy—despite the fact that matter and energy were once supposed to be as eternally different as the physical, which the scientist studied, and the so-called "spiritual" which the moralist insisted upon assuming to be somehow inherent in the operations of the physical man.

Similarly, many of the most eminent contemporary students of biology have come to believe that neither the so-called "body machine" nor the evolutionary process which created it is completely understandable in terms of the mechanically determined phenomena which were once thought adequate. Even more important is the fact that medicine is at the moment much concerned with what it calls "psychosomatic" phenomena. If the mind can affect the body no less surely than the body can affect the mind, then the mind must be in some sense an independent reality and the psyche quite as substantial as the brain or the nervous system.

As a matter of fact, the medical concept of the psychosomatic is entirely incompatible with that interpretation of the modern idea of man which would make him what the totalitarian as opposed to the democrat assumes him to be. It reconfers upon him something corresponding to the theological concept of the soul—at least to the extent that it makes possible an "idea of man" compatible with the democratic, as opposed to the totalitarian, conception of how he should be treated and dealt with.

Perhaps the clarification which we have been searching for will find in the psychosomatic concept its beginning. A democracy which hopes to promote human welfare and yet retain faith in the dignity of the individual and the freedom of which he is capable cannot do without a sort of psychosomatic theory of his nature. Perhaps the most modern idea of man is the psychosomatic idea.

If and when such a psychosomatic idea of man is clearly defined, then it will be more sharply differentiated than it is now from the idea of man held by the Marxian Communists. And we shall then be better able than we now are to defend democracy.[1]

Although intended for a radio audience, this address requires fairly close attention. The reader cannot sit passively and take it in; he must do some work.

Getting at the Knowledge

The first thing to do with any piece of informative writing is to try to understand the conceptual knowledge which it contains. With much writing this is no problem. Most informative writers present knowledge which is fairly easy to take in: in fact, some of it is so diluted that we can gulp it down without noticing it. This is probably true of the bulk of what we find in newspapers and magazines, and even in general reference books and textbooks. But necessity—or, sometimes, intellectual curiosity—also forces us on occasion to tackle informative material of a more demanding sort. At any time we may find ourselves listening to an address or reading something which is as disturbing in its sweeping paradoxes as Mr. Krutch is here.

Literature of this sort is not just an organized collection of "facts"

[1] "The Modern View of Man" by Joseph Wood Krutch, reprinted from *Man's Right to Knowledge.* By permission of the author and Columbia University Press.

but an educated experiment in analysis, interpretation, speculation. It is a record of intellectual exploration—often tentative, usually questioning, and always probing. Getting at the knowledge in this kind of informative writing—and we should remember that it *is* informative because it involves conceptualizing—often poses a real problem. For convenience we shall split this problem into three parts: *identifying the subject, recognizing the key propositions,* and *spotting the unstated propositions.*

Identifying the Subject

Conceptual knowledge can be thought of as "skeletal" knowledge. Often our first question is, "What creature is this a skeleton of?" What, in other words, is the subject? At first glance it appears fairly easy to decide what Krutch is talking about: his address is entitled "The Modern View of Man." But he actually gives only a very sketchy view of man; he attacks at least part of the view he presents, and he spends much of his time also attacking behaviorism, mechanistic philosophy, totalitarianism. And he is clearly much interested in a paradox—"the modern idea of man . . . on the one hand it has exalted, on the other it has debased, him"—which seems to be central to his whole approach. (As we go on with our analysis, we may find ourselves wondering how the two parts of the paradox are really related to each other. What, if anything, do they have in common?)

Not all readers will, of course, see the subject of this, or any other complex piece of informative writing, in quite the same way. This difference of interpretation is most likely when, as in Krutch's address, the propositions are general and the language is relatively abstract. In the beginning each reader should certainly try to identify and formulate the subject in a way which makes sense to him; but he should keep his mind open, and be ready to change his formulation. No interpretation is adequate unless it accounts for all of an author's main points and respects his emphases. The reader must be particularly careful not to allow his own bias to distort the text completely.

Krutch is treading on a lot of cherished opinions, and giving aid and comfort to a lot of others: the democratic materialist may object to being put in the camp with the Communist; on the other hand the humanist or the religious man may be inordinately pleased, each assuming that Krutch really agrees with him; either the opponent or the exponent of the "welfare state" may jump to the rather hasty conclusion that Krutch is against humanitarian measures. Having formed his quick prejudice either for or against, any of these readers may fail to grasp Krutch's true position.

This quite natural tendency of the reader to go off on a tangent—thus in effect rewriting his author to suit himself—is perhaps the prime cause of serious misinterpretation of philosophic literature. We should distinguish between what the author has said and what *we* would have said on the subject. Furthermore, tangential reading is always insulting to the writer: it implies that he was incompetent to say what he meant. A more reasonable assumption is that any good writer both has said what he meant and means what he has said, which suggests that the reader's first job is to attend to what the author has actually written—*all* of it.

Recognizing the Key Propositions

Having, at some point, decided tentatively what the subject is, we next need to find out what the author has to *say about* this subject: we need to isolate his main ideas. As we do so, we may have to revise our notion of the subject itself and our new definition of the subject may, in turn, modify our sense of which propositions are the main ones, and so on. The situation is analogous to that of an archeologist who, having uncovered a few buried bones, makes a preliminary guess as to the creature they belong to, only to uncover new bones that require him to revise his hypothesis. And this process may be repeated several times until he has unearthed all the major bones, at which point he may discover that what he has assembled is the skeleton of a creature previously unknown to science—or possibly just the remains of Mrs. Wilson's long lost cow.

The big bones in a piece of informative writing are the key propositions, and digging them out is often fairly easy. Much expository prose is clearly organized into introduction-body-conclusion: we can't help knowing where we are and what the author is trying to get across. At the level of the paragraph also, the key proposition is likely to be either at the beginning or the end. And the fact that some species of informative writing are constructed on a standard pattern may make reading easy. The typical news story places the main facts first, the details later. Similarly much narrative and descriptive exposition begins with a summary view followed by a more detailed treatment. And all these aids may be supplemented by various typographical devices designed to make the key propositions stand out.

Yet even a very well-organized piece may have to be studied a bit before its essential shape becomes clear to us. This is especially true of highly condensed and general writing like Krutch's. If we really care to learn what Krutch is saying, our best recourse is to try to mark what seem to be key propositions, or even to set them down in their proper relation to one another. Such a précis of Krutch's address might read something like this, sticking as close as possible to his own wording:

> Never before [our own age] had statesmen and philosophers laid so much stress on the importance of [the general welfare] of any and all men. [And yet] there is . . . less welfare than there was a few years ago [largely because of war between the democracies and the totalitarian powers]. Fascism and Communism both wage war [as we do] in the name of . . . an "ideology" . . . [which] involves an idea of what man *is* and what he *ought to be.*
>
> Many of [the totalitarian's] professed premises are very similar to ours. He too professes to believe that the material welfare of [all] mankind is of supreme importance. Perhaps it would be well for us to re-examine our concept of man and to redefine it in some way which would distinguish it more clearly from that of the totalitarian.
>
> There is a paradox hidden in [the modern] definition of man. . . . On the one hand it has exalted, on the other it has debased him. It has exalted him by saying that his welfare is the only thing that counts; it has debased him by denying that he possesses any of the powers or capacities upon which any real dignity or importance can be founded. Were it not for [this] confusion, it would not be possible for the totalitarian states to claim that they actually accomplish what we only pretend to want.
>
> Perhaps we can never state our own case clearly until we have ourselves decided how much more than what the Communists call him we believe that a man actually is. . . . If man is a machine, then there is very little justification for treating him as though he were not.
>
> It may be that . . . science will itself find some way of recognizing the reality behind the concepts to which religion has persistently

clung. Indeed, there are already signs, especially in the sciences of physics and biology, that this is happening.

A democracy which hopes to promote human welfare and yet retain faith in the dignity of the individual and the freedom of which he is capable cannot do without a sort of psychosomatic theory of his nature.

If and when such a psychosomatic idea of man is clearly defined . . . we shall then be better able than we now are to defend democracy [as the true means to the true welfare of all men].

Debatable though this précis may be (other readers would no doubt select as key ideas somewhat different ones), and vague though many of Krutch's generalizations may seem in this naked form, such an abridgement can be very helpful: it separates the central ideas from the peripheral ones; it shows how the main ideas hitch together; and it indicates what the key terms are (which is why we tried to use Krutch's own language).

But it is not enough merely to pick out the key propositions: we need also to understand them. And the surest way of grasping the difficult ones is to try to restate them in our own words. This would be the next thing to do with our précis. In particular, we should try to find our own synonyms or definitions for the key terms. As the précis clearly shows, one such term in Krutch's address is *welfare*. The reader might test *his* definition of this word against Krutch's frequent use of it.

Only when we can, at least crudely, rephrase an author's central ideas in our own language are we fairly sure we understand, in the sense that we have partially accommodated his knowledge to ours. Try, for instance, rewording this passage from Krutch:

Perhaps we can never state our own case . . . until we can say clearly and firmly that our idea of man includes a belief in his dignity, in the uniqueness of the individual, in something residing in him which makes him capable of thinking rather than merely "rationalizing," of believing rather than of being merely conditioned to believe, of exercising choice and determination rather than simply obeying his conditioned reflexes.

If our rewording is correct, the intended meaning should be the idea which our version and the author's express in common. The rewording test may also reveal that an author is merely writing words, or is not clear in his own mind, or is actually writing not informatively but persuasively.

Spotting the Unstated Propositions

No writer attempts to state *all* he knows about any subject. Even the most exhaustive treatment leaves many things unsaid; and what is left out may be important.

The kind of omission which produces "slanting" we will discuss later. At the moment our concern is with basic assumptions and other background propositions which remain unstated—the submerged part of the iceberg on which the visible part floats. The author is not necessarily trying to hide these assumptions: he has not stated them perhaps because he simply takes them for granted, or, possibly, because his subject is so large that he cannot develop it completely. It is important to recognize these assumptions, however, for an impressively worked-out pattern of stated propositions may rest on unstated propositions which we cannot accept. Furthermore, it is sometimes the unstated propositions which give logical coherence to a piece of writing which might otherwise seem fragmentary and disorganized.

Mr. Krutch's stated propositions clearly rest on a basic belief in what is sometimes called "free will." He is certain that man is not a machine whose actions can be wholly explained by the laws of physics and chemistry: man is somehow able to initiate actions himself. This seems to imply the existence of a directing entity, a "soul" or spirit—though Krutch uses the word *soul* rather hesitantly: "something corresponding to the theological concept of the soul." This is one of his basic, underlying assumptions. An even more fundamental assumption concerns Krutch's implicit faith in *ideas*. He assumes that if man can somehow formulate a fresh idea of man, this intellectual feat could affect the course of history. But Krutch is by training and turn of mind a philosopher. A purely practical Communist might well deny that any new idea could have so crucial an effect on man's destiny, which is—according to Marxist doctrine—historically predetermined.

Krutch also seems to be making other assumptions, though these are less certain. We may not be quite sure, for example, what Mr. Krutch thinks about the other half of the modern view, the humanitarian half. He talks about man's coming into his own and about resuming progress; but he seems to see the humanitarian half as equally materialistic: note the quotation marks around *prosperity*, and note the remark that we are almost fanatically concerned with what we call the "standard of living." We shall have to return to this half of the paradox later.

In general, we spot unstated assumptions and background ideas by pulling away from the text far enough to see it in some perspective. We may then try to trace a particular line of reasoning until we can see clearly what premises are taken for granted.

Evaluating the Knowledge

In most informative writing it is no problem at all to get at the knowledge: the subject is obvious; the main statements stand out clearly, the propositions they contain can be easily pulled out and rephrased if necessary; the unstated propositions are not hard to spot. Yet even the simplest kind of informative writing poses another problem—that of evaluating the knowledge.

In theory, evaluating conceptual knowledge can become very complex. Whole textbooks, even whole courses in logic are devoted to this problem. In practice, however, even if we are very conscientious we seldom apply much of our knowledge of logical analysis to our daily reading. A great deal of the conceptual knowledge we encounter does not require or deserve this close attention: it is too trivial, too ephemeral, too stale, too well-established, or too remote from our immediate concerns to matter that much. Furthermore, a great deal of information has already been competently checked out for us—by publishers' readers, research assistants, editors, and others. We quite rightly take for granted the "truth" (or probable truth) of much that is printed *as* information in responsible newspapers, magazines, and books.

On the other hand, the critical reader nearly always has some doubts and reservations. More important, he likes to understand *why* he doubts this fact or feels uneasy about that idea. Furthermore, there are times when the truth of what an informative writer says is vitally important to us, for personal or professional reasons—especially when it may affect our decisions, either practical or intellectual, or when the knowledge itself is notably fresh, original, unfamiliar, or controversial.

For many reasons we may wish to evaluate what Mr. Krutch has to say. He is suggesting things about our own philosophy which can be disturbing, implying that the seeds of totalitarianism are present in our view of man. And he seems to be asking us to change a point of view which has had scientific sanction for a long time. He seems to be implying that we must either reject some basic implications of science or wait hopefully for science to change its mind. Meanwhile there is still the problem of combatting totalitarianism. And there is also the question about the materialistic basis for our twentieth-century humanitarianism. We wonder whether we can deny one half of the modern view without denying the other also. Can we see progress in such simple, materialistic terms if we abandon the simple materialistic view of man? These are important issues, and they suggest that we would be wise to ask some questions before accepting or rejecting Mr. Krutch's view.

The kinds of questions we may want to ask will probably fall under two main headings: *credibility* and *usefulness*. The two are related but not identical; we shall treat them separately.

Credibility

Perhaps the best way of approaching the problem of credibility is through a set of questions an experienced reader is likely to ask himself—consciously or unconsciously—as he reads.

1. *Who is this writer?* We almost always prejudge a piece of informative writing on the basis of its authorship. We are predisposed to accept what we read in a respected encyclopedia, newspaper or magazine, or in a book by a reputable author; and we instinctively view with suspicion the "knowledge" we find in tabloid papers and pulp magazines. This seems a reasonable approach, but it is dangerous for at least two reasons. First, even respected authors don't always stick to what they know. Second, undue respect for established authors and publishers may shut us off from newcomers with something important to say.

Nevertheless, it is always legitimate to ask: "Who is this author? By what right does he presume to inform us on this subject?" If we ask these questions about Joseph Wood Krutch, we shall discover that he is a very eminent teacher, literary scholar, and drama critic; that his main professional field of interest is drama, but that he has ranged widely over the whole area of human affairs. We may want to ask whether he is professionally qualified to speak on so large a subject, involving so many diverse specialties—from physics to political philosophy. (On the other hand, we may wonder whether anyone is *better* qualified, since no one can profess to be a specialist in all the areas involved.) At least we will discover that Krutch has given a great deal of attention to the implications of social philosophy.

Sometimes it is necessary to ask questions not only about the man but about the publication in which his work appears, or the organization which is sponsoring him. How much initial credence can be granted because of the nature of the publication? What is its general reputation? Is it known to have editorial biases on this particular subject? On other subjects? Mr. Krutch's lecture was part of an international symposium on "Man's Right to Knowledge," conducted in commemoration of the two-hundredth anniversary of the founding of Columbia University. Fellow speakers included the Chinese philosopher and statesman Hu Shih, the British historian Arnold Toynbee, and the president of Columbia, Grayson Kirk, among others. All the talks were later published in book form by Columbia. These facts are relevant, and they certainly do not detract from the authoritativeness of Mr. Krutch's statements. (We might ask whether we would feel differently about his talk if it had been given at a political meeting of some kind.)

2. *For whom is he writing?* Our sense of the intended audience will also affect our judgment of the information offered. A scientific article written for a layman will naturally be less detailed and precise than one intended for fellow scientists. If we don't know who the intended audience is we can often guess—from the appearance of a book, the nature of the advertisements in a magazine, or the general style.

Once we have sized up the audience, we may ask: "Does the writer seem to be making unjustified concessions to this audience? Are there signs that he may be distorting what he believes to be true for the sake of giving his readers a version of the truth which will suit them better?" This kind of misrepresentation should be distinguished from such legitimate concessions as avoiding technical jargon, using simple analogies, and omitting masses of detail which a lay audience would have trouble understanding.

Mr. Krutch presents his propositions lucidly and simply. If we sense additional complications which he has not touched on, we need not feel that his simplifications are an attempt to conceal anything from his audience. Nor need we feel that the omission of supporting data of the kind which would be included if this were a book instead of a radio talk is a serious oversight: a speaker could scarcely be expected to do more within the prescribed limits of a half-hour radio program.

3. *Where do the propositions come from?* Nevertheless, we have every right to ask where Mr. Krutch's propositions came from. How does he know these things?

Back in Chapter 5 we listed a number of propositions of various kinds, and though we avoided systematic classification, we did suggest that propositions come from various sources. Some of them are based on observation; when they are, it is pertinent to ask whether the author did the observing himself or whether he depended on someone else. And if he depended on someone else, what are his *source's* credentials? Other propositions are based on inferences from observations. Some may be based simply on hunches.

If we look closely at Mr. Krutch's statements we will see that the propositions which they contain are of several different kinds. Most important perhaps are a number of high-level generalizations, many of them presumably going back to someone's observation at some time. Take for example the series of statements beginning with: "We have little faith in moral discourse, a great deal in what can be done to condition youth." Some, on the other hand, are inferences derived essentially from an analysis of ideas: "Accept without qualification the belief that man is always 'nothing but' the product of sociological and psychological factors which operate upon him, and nothing could be more logical than the totalitarian methods."

Now some philosophers give the highest marks for credibility only to propositions which are "verifiable," and much scientific writing is designed to indicate the possibility of verification and to make verification itself easy. Sir John Lubbock, in his experiments with the ants, does not merely give us his conclusions (as, in a sense, Mr. Krutch does); he tells us what methods he used, and what specific results he obtained. (If we wish we can go and watch ants too.)

But we should not expect all propositions to be of the same easily verifiable kind. Even a fairly simple assertion such as, "The Declaration of Independence was signed on July 4, 1776," is beyond *experimental* verification: all we can do is to compare the reports of various witnesses—all of them now dead. We should remember that different standards of precision are called for by different kinds of propositions. In Aristotle's words, "it is evidently equally foolish to accept probable reasoning from a mathematician and to demand from a rhetorician scientific proofs." We expect a news story to be primarily observational—and accurate in its particulars; on the other hand, we expect a columnist interpreting the same events to make general statements involving inferences. And we do not expect Mr. Krutch to proceed as if he were reporting a scientific experiment.

There are two classes of propositions, however, which deserve special attention here. When we first discussed propositions back in Chapter 5 we included in our list "The mayor's sole object is to get re-elected." An inference of this kind—we might call it a *psychological inference*—is rather different from other kinds of inference. It may be based on careful observation and reasoning, but it is always at least a little suspect: "Just how did the writer know what another man was thinking, or what his real motives were?" The other kind of proposition which requires special attention is the *value judgment:* "Rembrandt is probably the world's greatest painter." When such judgments are presented explicitly, they hardly present a problem. When they are implicit, either as assumptions behind stated propositions or in the wording of a statement, they may cause trouble, however. In fact, the most troublesome part of Mr. Krutch's address is in the implied value judgments in the quotation marks around the word *prosperity* and in the characterization of our concern for the standard of living as *fanatical*. We suspect that Mr. Krutch is not altogether happy with the materialistic bias in our humanitarianism. The problem is not, however, that he is using some kind of veiled persuasion: we are just not quite sure what he is saying and to what extent he feels that the ambiguity of the modern view of man applies to both parts of his paradox.

4. *Does he include all sides?* This question is most pertinent to material on controversial subjects. The omission of relevant information is what is commonly called *slanting*. A piece is slanted when it presents only one part of the picture. The term, however, is applied usually only to the kind of writing which is at a low level of generality. An author who is giving his analysis of events and the philosophy behind them—as Mr. Krutch does—is certainly not obliged to present the arguments *against* his analysis. He is an interpreter and expects to be taken as such. A newspaper reporter, on the other hand, who gives only those facts in a case which support one side is presenting a slanted story. We are counting on him to give us a report of what happened—to tell the whole truth. What

he has given us may be the truth as far as it goes—that is, all his propositions may be credible—and yet, because of the omissions, they may add up to a one-sided view. We may often suspect slanting in a news story or other supposedly straightforward piece of reporting, but we can be sure of it only if we can check other accounts of the same events.

Slanting does not, of course, prove intent to deceive. The author's knowledge may simply be incomplete. But usually slanting is grounds for suspicion that the writer or the publication has an ax to grind.

5. *Do the propositions hang together?* When we ask this kind of question we are concerned not with the relation of the propositions to observable phenomena, but with their relation to each other. Do they make sense when we consider them together, or is there some inconsistency? When they form a reasoned argument, is the reasoning valid?

Questions of this kind often lead us back to the unstated propositions—the submerged portion of the iceberg. We have already noted two problems of this kind in Mr. Krutch's remarks, but it may be well to look at them again: First, do the two halves of the central paradox, one of which glorifies man while the other debases him, rest on the same materialistic premise? If they do, is Mr. Krutch willing to reject both, or does he want to keep the liberal welfare programs while he rejects control, manipulation, propaganda, conditioning? And if the latter, can he do this logically? Second, supposing determinism is the logical conclusion of all our science, do we reject it simply because of its human consequences? Or must we accept it as "truth," and take the consequences? These are hard questions, and on their answer depends our judgment about the coherence of the propositions.

6. *Do any of the propositions seem dubious?* Looking at all of the propositions together is an excellent way of seeing relationships, but it may have the effect of blinding us to the inadequacy of individual propositions. It is usually worthwhile to trust our own feelings far enough at least so that we will ask why we feel uneasy about some propositions—if we do.

The present authors do not happen to feel uneasy about any of Mr. Krutch's propositions with the exceptions already noted. That is, some of the generalizations about current American thinking seem to rest only on the most casual kind of observation. We would like to know whether they are really so.

7. Is the LEVEL of credibility appropriate? This is perhaps the most important of all the questions we can ask about the "truthfulness" of informative writing. Information is a fabric of hypotheses, not a collection of absolute truths. The New York *Times* does *not* publish "All the news that's fit to print," but a selection of the more plausible hypotheses, on a few subjects, which happen to be of interest at the moment. There is not even such a thing as a "complete weather report." In very few areas of inquiry is there any large body of conceptual knowledge which is not subject to revision and replacement at any time, because of new formulations, new hypotheses.

We would be wrong to demand full documentation in the Krutch address. It is offered as one man's view of the situation. Mr. Krutch is presenting some opinions and, in a way, a solution, to a problem. His address is certainly persuasive in part—and consciously so, though its principal purpose is clearly to inform—to tell us how the world looks to Mr. Krutch. Beyond that he simply asks us to think about man and to try to see the relation of our view of man to the worldwide conflict between totalitarianism and democracy. What he offers is questions and hypotheses. We must do most of the thinking about what we believe ourselves.

Usefulness

Equally important—in fact, sometimes more important than credibility—is the usefulness of conceptual knowledge. In one sense, there is no such thing as useless knowledge. Even misinformation can be of value, if it is recognized as such: a "wrong" hypothesis, if it leads to a genuine investigation, may be just as useful as a "right" hypothesis. But it is still possible to distinguish degrees and kinds of usefulness.

At one extreme there is "practical" knowledge: The information in a publication like *Consumer Reports* may help us to buy more intelligently; a pamphlet from the League of Women Voters or some other nonpartisan group may lead us to vote more rationally; Dr. Spock's book on baby care may at least reassure us that nothing much is wrong with the child.

At the other extreme, human beings also collect—and often publish—great masses of conceptual knowledge which is of no imaginable utilitarian value to anyone. Some of this was gathered simply to satisfy a few people's intellectual curiosity. People who pride themselves on their practicality sometimes boast of never reading anything which is not useful information. Most of them, however, will admit that they do skim the newspapers—hardly conscious of the fact, perhaps, that newspapers are full of impractical information. The point is that knowledge, even of the most impractical kind, satisfies the urge to know "what's going on." The same urge that compels us to read the newspaper compels the scientist to try to find out "what's going on" in outer space.

Now much information—even of the practical variety—does not consist of verifiable propositions at all. Many propositions which could not possibly be verified are useful as organizers of our thinking processes. They give meaning to the contents of our minds. They help us to "understand," and they also stimulate us to think.

This is the kind of value which is most evident in Mr. Krutch's talk. It really does not matter whether a detailed survey would show that the tendencies to belittle man are as strong in our own society as Mr. Krutch says they are. (Most of us will probably admit that they are to some extent there.) The important thing is, first, that Mr. Krutch's remarks make us aware of the relation between ideas and institutions—between the conclusions of science, for example, and the social structure. Most of us have a strong tendency to keep such different matters in logic-tight compartments; Mr. Krutch says in effect that the divisions between compartments do not really divide: what the physicist thinks about matter and energy, what the biologist thinks about body and mind, have a great deal to do with the political conflict that has divided the world. Second, Mr. Krutch's hypotheses—this is what they clearly are—give us a framework within which we can study our own society, totalitarian societies, our own thought processes. And finally, the very incomplete, tentative and paradoxical nature of Mr. Krutch's remarks forces us to think about a great many diverse matters.

But do we have to agree with Mr. Krutch in order to find his formulations useful? Not at all. We may feel that his nonmechanist solution to the ideological problem is not justified by the evidence. We may feel that psychosomatic theory is a tenuous hope on which to pin the possibility of developing a coherent, "democratic" view of man. We may feel that Mr. Krutch, to be consistent, should be less concerned about material progress than he seems to be. But we can still find many of his formulations useful without agreeing with all of them.

And this is an important point about the usefulness of conceptual knowledge. Unsophisticated readers are sometimes horrified to discover that the author they are reading is apparently a socialist, an agnostic, a member of a sect or a party with which they violently disagree—and they promptly assume that they can learn nothing from him. This simply is not true.

In many fields, we are even coming to be tolerant of multiple explanations. Even within the physical sciences, where the most rigorous methods of verification are used, we find physicists working with two different and apparently incompatible theories of light, wave theory, and particle theory. Each works better in some situations than does the other, and is accordingly used without serious question as to which is "true." Similarly in psychology, a student may become acquainted with a stimulus-response kind of analysis and a Freudian kind of analysis—and he may use both to clarify his thinking on a specific case. And in economics he may find a Marxist labor theory of value useful even though in general he himself sees economic processes predominantly in classical or in Keynesian terms.

This does not mean that we give all views equal status: we are perpetually trying for more comprehensive, more adequate formulations.

EXERCISES

A. Read a fairly general piece of informative writing, preferably of the theoretical or speculative sort. Then try to state the subject of this article (or essay or chapter) in not more than four or five sentences. If possible, compare your statement of the subject with other people's statements.

B. Find news stories about the same event in two or more different newspapers. Write a brief analysis in which you compare the stories as to their credibility. This exercise will be most useful if you select stories from newspapers of differing quality and if you stick to staff-written stories (avoiding wire-service material).

C. Write a thorough analysis (1500 to 2000 words) of a single, relatively difficult informative piece, applying all of the principles discussed in this chapter.

D. Write a research report (1200 to 1500 words) on some one source of information on contemporary affairs. Examples: a newspaper or magazine; an editor, commentator, columnist, publisher, or organizer; a news-gathering agency, syndicate, publishing house, radio network, newspaper chain.

Remember that you are yourself acting as an informative writer. The rest of the class is your audience. Here are some specific suggestions:

1. If you are studying a publication, you will want to know its nature, purpose, and background: Who runs it? What is its intended audience? What kinds of material does it contain? What connection does it have with other publications, and with organizations? You will probably find the following sources of information useful:

   a. One or more issues of the publication for sample content, format, indications of audience, statements of ownership, editorial staff, statements of policy.

   b. Ayer's *Directory of Newspapers and Periodicals* for information about circulation.

   c. Moody's *Industrial Manual* for information about the business organization behind the publication if it is a fairly large one.

   d. *Who's Who in America* for information about editors, publishers, and regular contributors.

   e. *Reader's Guide to Periodical Literature* and the New York *Times Index* for references to the publication.

2. If you are studying a man, what you want to know is his role as a source of information: who he is, what jobs he has held, what he has written, what organizations he has been active in, what other people have to say about him. (Always consider, however, who the other people are; and try to avoid "guilt by association"; keep your eye on relationships which actually exist.) The following sources—in addition, of course, to some of the author's own writings—may be useful:

   a. *Who's Who* or some of the more specialized directories.

   b. *Biographical Index* and *Reader's Guide to Periodical Literature*.

   c. New York *Times Index*.

   d. *Current Biography*.

   e. *Book Review Digest*, for critical comments on books he has written.

3. If you are studying a business organization (publishing house, news-gathering agency, syndicate, or radio network) you want to know first what this organization is, what it does, and who runs it. Later you may want to know what kind of control it exercises. The following sources of information, all of them

mentioned before, may be useful: Moody's *Industrial Manual,* Ayer's *Directory* (for information about publications if it is a publishing house), *Reader's Guide to Periodical Literature,* and *Who's Who* (for information on officers, owners, etc.).

4. If you are studying a pressure organization, you want to know what the purpose of the organization is and how it goes about it, what it publishes, and who is active in it. *Reader's Guide, Who's Who,* and Ayer's *Directory* may be helpful, but you will probably have to start with publications of the organization, including letters with a letterhead list of officers, and paid advertisements; or with the New York *Times Index.*

Whatever your subject, try to find references which are both favorable and unfavorable. Also be especially careful to date your information. Remember that publications, organizations, and men change their points of view.

In writing your report, try to be as accurate a reporter as possible. It is important to make clear the sources of your information. Since most of the information will come from various printed material, complete documentation is necessary. You will undoubtedly have a great many footnotes. (Consult a standard handbook for the form of footnote and bibliographical references.) Follow the rule of labeling your *own* propositions as to source.

E. Following some of the principles suggested in Chapters 5 and 6, edit or rewrite, for a high school audience, two paragraphs of the address used as an example in this chapter. Writing for this new audience, do you make more use of comparison and contrast? Do you add different levels of generality? Do you change the level of abstraction?

8. The Creative Use of Language

> My task which I am trying to achieve is, by the
> power of the written word to make you hear, to make
> you feel—it is, before all, to make you *see*. That—and
> no more, and it is everything. If I succeed, you shall
> find there according to your deserts: encouragement,
> consolation, fear, charm—all you demand—and, perhaps,
> also that glimpse of truth for which you have forgot-
> ten to ask.[1]
>
> JOSEPH CONRAD, Preface to
> *The Nigger of the Narcissus.*

Relation of the Creative and Informative Uses

For simplicity's sake, little has been said in the last two chapters
about the creative use of language. Informative writing has been
treated as if it were a wholly separate species, having nothing to
do with the art of literature or with experiential knowledge.

This, of course, is not true: all of the uses of language overlap;
only certain rather specialized types of informative writing deal exclusively with conceptual knowledge; the best informative authors,
in every field, exhibit talent both as observers and thinkers *and* as
literary artists. Many first-rate reporters, historians, philosophers,
and scientists who publish their work not only know how to adapt
the methods and devices of creative literature to informative purposes, but, more important, they instinctively add experiential richness to their writing even when the material is primarily conceptual. So it is not strange that we have a large body of literature

[1] FROM "Preface," reprinted from *The Nigger of the Narcissus* by Joseph
Conrad. By permission of J. M. Dent & Sons Ltd.

138

which one can no more classify as purely informative or purely creative than one can draw a dividing line between north and south. In Chapter 13 we shall take a look at some typical blends and fusions of informative and creative writing, of conceptual and experiential knowledge.

On the other hand, a poem *is* different from a news story, a novel from a history, a play from the transcript of a court trial, a short story from a case study, a literary essay from a technical report. And even though these differences are not absolute, they are real— so real we have to "shift gears," as readers, in moving from one genre to another. A reader who knows what he is doing simply does not approach *Hamlet* in the same spirit nor with the same assumptions and expectations that he does—say—Sir Ernest Jones' book *Hamlet and Oedipus*, which is a brilliant Freudian analysis of Shakespeare's play.

Three Misconceptions of Creative Writing

The trouble is that readers do not always know what they are doing. Creative writing poses a peculiar problem. It causes difficulties precisely because it is made out of words. Susanne Langer makes the point well in her book *Feeling and Form:*

> Literature is one of the great arts, and is more widely taught and studied than any other, yet its artistic character is more often avowed than really discerned and respected. The reason why literature is a standard academic pursuit lies in the very fact that one can treat it as something other than art. Since its normal material is language, and language is, after all, the medium of discourse, it is always possible to look at a literary work as an assertion of facts and opinions.[2]

All printed texts tend to look somewhat alike simply because all of them, regardless of purpose, employ the same medium, language. It is far too easy, therefore, as Mrs. Langer notes, to misread creative writing as if it were supposed to be informative. This common basic mistake about creative literature is most likely to be made by quite serious readers, partly because they are overanxious to prove the value of poetry, fiction, and drama, and partly because it is always much easier to talk about informative writing than about creative

[2] FROM *Feeling and Form* by Susanne K. Langer. Reprinted by permission of the publishers, Charles Scribner's Sons.

writing, about conceptual knowledge than about experiential knowledge.

Even teachers trained in literature sometimes approach poems and novels and plays as if these were really collections of propositions—inconvenient collections, granted, because the propositions lie buried under a lot of irrelevant material, and because creative writers invariably fail to furnish handy indexes. Taught from this angle, Hardy's novel *The Return of the Native,* for example, becomes a somewhat eccentric way of presenting certain philosophical ideas—a kind of obstacle course to test the student's skill as a proposition detector. Hardy certainly did have a "philosophy" and it is reflected in his novels and poems, as a literary artist's ideas usually are. But in *The Return* Hardy's philosophy is implicit rather than explicit and is not formulated and developed in conceptual fashion; it is merely one strand in a complex fictional fabric. And, in our day, when people read *The Return,* it may even be in spite of Hardy's ideas about the universe rather than because of them. In other words, the presentation of a metaphysic was only one of Hardy's objectives in this novel, the other and more important aims being not informative at all but something else.

Another basic mistake which even conscientious readers make is to confuse creative writing with persuasion. They feel that if the poet's or playwright's purpose is not to teach, it must at least be to preach. From this standpoint the thing to do with a creative work is to find the "moral." If one can't unearth a moral, or if the apparent moral turns out to be unsound, the work either is not much good or it is downright bad. But if an acceptable moral can be found, and especially if the moral is explicitly stated, then the work is worth reading. Thus teachers sometimes give the impression that a high point of *Hamlet* is Polonius' rather sententious speech of fatherly advice to Laertes on the eve of the latter's return to Paris:

> Neither a borrower nor a lender be;
> For loan oft loses both itself and friend,
> And borrowing dulls the edge of husbandry.
> This above all, to thine own self be true
> And it must follow, as the night the day,
> Thou canst not then be false to any man.

Similarly teachers have been known to imply that the whole of Coleridge's "The Rime of the Ancient Mariner" culminates and is summed up in the famous little sermon, which pupils sometimes have to memorize:

He prayeth best, who loveth best
All things both great and small;
For the dear God who loveth us,
He made and loveth all.
(SAMUEL TAYLOR COLERIDGE,
1772–1834)

Now this stanza is certainly a part of the poem, put there by Coleridge in deliberate imitation of the old-fashioned folk ballad, which by tradition often ends with a moral. But as poetry it is certainly one of the least admirable stanzas in a great poem and it does not deserve to be singled out for special attention. To do so is to lose sight of the poem in searching for a "point"—treating creative writing as if it were persuasive.

Still another basic mistake which readers often make is to assume that creative writing has no serious purpose at all, that it is merely "entertainment." Sometimes this mistake springs from simple ignorance: many people don't know enough about creative artists and their activities to realize how seriously most of them take their profession. More often, the "So what?" attitude probably arises from overexposure to the informative and persuasive fallacies: an intelligent reader soon discovers that in fact good creative literature often contains little or no information or persuasion, that what it does contain is frequently as banal as Hardy's deterministic "philosophy" or the ancient Mariner's sermon, and that, if such ideas and appeals really are the *main* point of novels and poems, then writings of this sort tend to be pretty inefficient forms of communication. Such a reader naturally concludes that only a fool or someone who owns stock in the company would take creative literature seriously. This conclusion is further reinforced by the obvious fact that the great bulk of popular, mass-media fiction, poetry, and drama *is* frivolous, is intended to do nothing more than help its readers pass the time painlessly.

Literature as an Art Form

Good creative writing is not dolled-up information or persuasion, nor is it merely prefabricated pipedreams. It is, as Susanne Langer says, a mode of art. In other words, *creative writing stands much closer, in many important ways, to the nonverbal arts than it does to other kinds of writing.* Good novels and poems, plays and short stories, have far more in common with paintings and symphonies and sculpture and creative architecture than they do with either reports and treatises or sermons and editorials.

But, it can be argued, not all creative writers think of themselves as artists. True enough. Yet every creative writer does practice the art of literature, whether he sees his work in those terms or not. Walter Allen, the English novelist and critic, puts the point this way:

> Novelists have given many reasons for writing novels: Richardson believed he did so to inculcate right conduct, Fielding to reform the manners of the age, Dickens to expose social evils, Trollope to make money by providing acceptable entertainment. The reasons were genuine enough but rationalizations after the event.[3]

As Allen sees it, novelists write novels because they are novelists, just as composers write music because they are composers. In short, artists create works of art primarily because they are artists, whatever public excuses, strange or plausible, they may offer for their profession.

But what do we mean by "art"? And in what sense can poets and playwrights and fiction writers be called artists? These are questions which invite fierce differences of opinion, and we can only suggest partial answers here. However, before we make any more generalizations it might be well to have in front of us a concrete example of creative writing and a brief account of how it came into being.

Case History of a Poem

The writer is Robert Frost, and the work is his poem "Stopping by Woods on a Snowy Evening." Frost himself has described how he composed this poem.

He had been working all night on a very long poem of a quite different sort. Just as he finished, there suddenly came to him four lines of a brand new poem. They sounded promising, so he turned to a fresh page of his notebook and wrote them down:

> Whose woods these are I think I know.
> His house is in the village though;
> He will not see me stopping here
> To watch his woods fill up with snow.[4]

[3] FROM *The English Novel* by Walter Allen. Reprinted by permission of E. P. Dutton & Company, Inc., and Phoenix House, Ltd.

[4] FROM "Stopping by Woods on a Snowy Evening" by Robert Frost, from

Though this stanza was based on a real-life experience of Frost's, he had not consciously recalled the incident until now. Nor, at this beginning stage, did he have any idea where his poem was going, what "meaning" it would finally take on. On the contrary, the lines he had been "given" (presumably by his subconscious mind) interested him primarily as a technical problem in versification. As Frost tells the story,

> That [the first stanza] went off so easily that I was tempted into the added difficulty of picking up my 3 [that is, the end sound of the third line,—*ere*] for my 1-2-4 to go on with in the next stanza.

In other words, the first stanza suggested to Frost that he experiment with the difficult rhyme scheme aaba-bbcb-ccdc-etc. He accepted the challenge, and managed to complete the poem at a single sitting, but not without running into some problems along the way. Here is a facsimile of his manuscript of the remaining stanzas, showing the changes he made as the poem gradually evolved its own form *and meaning:*

Complete Poems of Robert Frost. Copyright 1923, 1930, 1939 by Holt, Rinehart and Winston, Inc. Copyright 1936 by Robert Frost. Copyright renewed 1951 by Robert Frost. Reprinted by permission of Holt, Rinehart and Winston, Inc.

[5] Facsimile of draft of last three stanzas of "Stopping by Woods on a Snowy Evening" by Robert Frost. Reproduced by permission of Holt, Rinehart and Winston, Inc.

And here is the finished poem:

Stopping by Woods on a Snowy Evening

Whose woods these are I think I know.
His house is in the village though;
He will not see me stopping here
To watch his woods fill up with snow.

My little horse must think it queer
To stop without a farmhouse near
Between the woods and frozen lake
The darkest evening of the year.

He gives his harness bells a shake
To ask if there is some mistake.
The only other sound's the sweep
Of easy wind and downy flake.

The woods are lovely, dark and deep.
But I have promises to keep,
And miles to go before I sleep,
And miles to go before I sleep.

The manuscript shows clearly that, after the first stanza, only a few lines came out right the first time. It may be instructive to look at some of Frost's revisions and to try to guess why he made them.

Line five originally read,

The steaming horses think it queer,

because, on the real-life occasion which was the "source" of the poem, Frost was actually driving a *team* of horses. Had Frost been writing informatively here, he probably would have felt obliged to "stick to the facts." However, a poem is not a report but a work of art, and art demands a different kind of truth. Perhaps Frost sensed that one horse would better fit the atmosphere of quiet and solitude which he was after. Also, the adjective *steaming*, for all its descriptive accuracy, called too much attention to the animals, especially their physical aspect, and detracted from the mood. For some such reasons as these, he changed the line to

The horse begins to think it queer.

But *begins* really added nothing to the poem, and besides Frost wanted to individualize the horse. So the line became

My little horse must think it queer.

The smallness of the horse also added to a contrast which the scene was beginning to evoke, between a miniature world of animate things and a larger world of inanimate forest and snow.

Line seven also underwent revision, from

> Between a forest and a lake

to

> Between the woods and frozen lake.

The word *woods* served to link this line to both the first stanza and the last. Also, the overtones of *woods* may have seemed more appropriate to the mood than those of *forest*—perhaps *woods* sounded warmer, more intimate, more inviting. And the new adjective *frozen* helped to particularize the lake and to prepare for and strengthen the next line, with its evocation of wintriness:

> The darkest evening of the year.

Line nine is interesting. The manuscript shows that Frost once considered turning the horse into a mare, but then for some reason decided against it. Did he perhaps want to avoid any suggestion that his aesthetic pleasure in the winter scene was somehow feminine, a feeling too delicate to be decently male?

Line twelve first read

> Of easy wind and falling flake,

but then became

> Of easy wind and downy flake.

Maybe Frost felt that *falling* was trite and added nothing. Perhaps he also disliked the too obvious alliteration of *falling flake*. In any case, the new word *downy* is wonderfully right in this context—visually and tactually evocative, soft, inviting, and parallel in sound and overtone to *easy*.

Through the first twelve lines Frost apparently encountered no serious problems. Then, with stanza four, came trouble. He first wrote:

> The woods are lovely dark and deep
> But I have promises to keep
> That bid me give the reins a shake . . .

But that third line would not do: he should not reuse the rhyme *-ake* so soon after *lake-shake-mistake-flake;* and he certainly could not repeat the identical word *shake* so soon. So he changed the line to

> That bid me on, and there are miles . . .

But this was still wrong. In the rhyme scheme of the poem, the new word would tend to imply that a fifth stanza was to follow, and Frost sensed by now that his poem had just about run itself out, that this fourth stanza had to be the last. Then all at once the solution struck him. As we study his manuscript, we can picture him excitedly crossing out both earlier versions of line fifteen and quickly winding up the poem with a repeat ending:

> And miles to go before I sleep
> And miles to go before I sleep.

As we shall see shortly, this simple repetition of the penultimate line not only solved his technical problem but added to the poem new levels of meaning which he had not anticipated.

Here, then, is an example of the creative writer in action. "Stopping by Woods" is not perfectly typical of the creative process in general, nor even of Robert Frost's poetic method. But this poem, and the process that produced it, do illustrate certain basic principles of all creative literature. If we can grasp a few of these principles we will begin to understand what Susanne Langer means by the "artistic character" of this kind of writing and we will be in a much better position to read it intelligently.

"Virtual Life"

One promising place to begin is with the question, "What exactly was Frost trying to 'create' in writing this poem?" It seems quite obvious that he did *not* set out, as an informative writer would have, to transmit a package of facts and ideas. Frost started, not with a series of propositions, but with a piece of a poem—in this case it happened to be the whole first stanza. And his immediate concern was simply to work out the rest of the poem.

Part of the answer to our question, then, is that Frost was trying to create the kind of verbal structure, the sort of thing-made-of-words, which we call a poem. Like any other artist, a creative writer is first of all a "maker," in his case a composer of poems or novels or plays or stories.

So far so good. But words, as we have seen, are symbols, and therefore stand for something beyond themselves. What does a poem like "Stopping by Woods" stand for? If it does not embody propositions, what does it embody? The easiest answer is "experience": a writer like Frost wants the verbal structure he is making to constitute an experience. This is undoubtedly true, not only of Frost but of any other creative writer. But this notion of "creating experience" is a fuzzy one at best, and it can be highly misleading.

It may, for example, be taken to mean the sort of thing which the hack writer does, when he says to himself, "Now let's see—how can I most effectively make my readers feel happy or pleasantly sad? What formula will induce them to laugh or to shudder or to want to make love? What gimmick will thrill them? Shock them? Let them feel larger than life-size? In short, what are the gaps in my customers' actual lives which I can fill in with make-believe experience, to their pleasure and my profit?"

All of this is the sort of direct experience-creating by which cheap literature makes its living. In every case, the purpose of such writing is to take us out of reality and into a never-never land in which "life" is more intense, more glamorous, more suspenseful, more comfortable, more just, and more gratifying in every way than real life can ever be. Above all, this make-believe world must be as different as possible from our pedestrian everyday existences. This is why cheap fiction and drama—we might call it pseudocreative writing—is often called "escape" literature.

Genuine or serious creative writing, however, offers no such deliberate gratification of our need for vicarious experience. It does, of course, create make-believe worlds, but it does so in order to show us the real world. Its aim is not to help us forget reality nor to compensate for the deficiencies of actual living, but to take us closer to reality and to life than we would normally get on our own. Its purpose, in short—as we noted earlier in this book—is to extend, clarify, organize, and deepen our experiential knowledge of human nature and of the human situation.

This being so, the notion that the artist creates experience is perhaps a dangerous one. It might be better to say that what he creates—besides verbal objects—is *virtual life*. The phrase is Susanne Langer's, and this is how she explains it:

The appearances of events in our actual lives are fragmentary, transient and often indefinite like most of our experiences—like the space we move in, the time we feel passing, the human and inhuman forces that challenge us. The poet's business is to create the appearance of "experiences," the semblance of events lived and felt, and to organize them so that they constitute a purely and completely experienced reality, a piece of *virtual life*.

The piece may be great or small—as great as the Odyssey, or so small that it comprises only one little event, like the thinking of a thought or the perception of a landscape. But its distinguishing mark, which makes it quite different from any actual segment of life, is that the events in it are simplified, and at the same time much more fully perceived and evaluated than the jumble of happenings in any person's actual history.[6]

(We should beware of a possible misunderstanding here: Mrs. Langer is *not* arguing that art is always "realistic"—that virtual life always resembles real life down to the smallest detail. Fantasy, satire, allegory, and other nonrealistic modes of literature also create virtual life; they differ from "realism" in the *level* on which they resemble life.)

Here, then, is the sense in which a literary artist creates experience: what he actually makes is a verbal structure which will evoke a segment of virtual life. As readers, what we experience is a combination of the verbal thing itself *and* the virtual life it generates. This unit of virtual life, in all of its organized richness, is the "meaning" of the poem or novel, story or play.

This seems to describe exactly what Frost was doing as he wrote "Stopping by Woods." Every move he made was in the direction of unifying and enriching *both* the poem itself and the virtual world it calls into being. The most important point about this whole process is that in creative writing we cannot separate the verbal structure from the virtual life. The two are inextricably fused. This explains several peculiarities of creative writing. For instance, it explains why literary art, especially poetry, is so difficult to translate from one language to another. It also explains why no paraphrase of a poem, abridgement of a novel, cut version of a play, or synopsis of a story can ever replace the original. And, finally, it explains why creative writers sometimes take almost incredible pains with the details of their work.

[6] FROM *Feeling and Form* by Susanne K. Langer. Reprinted by permission of the publishers, Charles Scribner's Sons.

Likeness-and-Difference

We have watched Robert Frost make a poem; and we have tried to state what a piece of creative literature really is. But so far we have not considered the general principles involved in this kind of writing.

As we saw in Chapter 6, there is nothing very mysterious about how an informative writer goes at his job. All of us have tried to do this kind of writing. We started with a collection of propositions, a "subject matter" which was more or less settled beforehand, or at least we thought it was. We tentatively organized these propositions according to some sort of logical plan. And we then set about converting these facts and ideas into the verbal formulations called statements. As we proceeded, we discovered that our original plan, our working outline, kept changing: certain headings disappeared entirely, new headings appeared, some topics divided into two or three, others merged into one; headings which we had expected to be major turned out to be minor, and vice versa; we had to revise the order of topics here and there; some subjects needed more elaboration than anticipated, others less; all sorts of alterations became necessary as we developed a clearer picture of our intended readers; the very process of trying to express our thoughts in words tended to modify the thoughts themselves; some ideas turned out to be silly or fruitless and had to be discarded, others proved surprisingly "true" or useful and had to be expanded; if we were lucky, we even enjoyed occasional moments of sudden insight—brief inspirations like that which gave Frost his repeat ending—when ideas, or ways of putting them, suddenly emerged out of nowhere; and so on.

We are all acquainted with this general procedure. To turn information into language may be laborious and sometimes even quite complex, but the process is seldom very mysterious. Suppose, though, that one's task as a writer is not the formulation and discussion of propositions but the creation of literary art—that is, of verbal structures which will evoke virtual life. Most of us have had little experience with this sort of writing. How does one proceed?

The question cannot be answered easily, nor by setting down simple rules which will apply across the board. Creative writers do not

follow any one standard procedure, any more than composers, paint-
ers, or sculptors do. We cannot even say with certainty what a
novelist or poet begins with. In writing "Stopping by Woods" Robert
Frost was lucky enough to start with an entire finished stanza, but
not all his poems have begun this way. A creative writer may start
with only a single phrase or line or image; or merely with an impression or mood; or with one character or a set of characters; or
with a scene, a place, a conversation, a situation; with an isolated
incident or with the outline of an entire plot. Occasionally he may
even, like an informative writer, begin with an intellectual problem, with a single fact or idea, or even with a whole system of
propositions—a set of moral convictions, a theology, or a pattern
of social, political, historical or economic data or belief. He may
start with a metaphor or a myth, with something out of his own
experience (as Frost did) or with something borrowed from other
people's lives or from older literature, with something taken from
reality or with something which is pure invention.

Thus there are no recipes which the creative writer invariably
follows. There are, however, some general principles which appear
to operate in creative writing whether the writer thinks in terms
of these principles or not. One of them we have already discussed
in connection with words and meaning: *a creative writer "works"*
words far harder than an informative writer does. He forces words
to function as plurisigns and he takes fuller advantage of the "thingness" of language. Frost's poem clearly illustrates this extra attention to individual words and to language in general.

But "Stopping by Woods" also illustrates a second basic principle, which has not yet been mentioned and which is not quite
so obvious. This one has to do with *form.* A creative writer is much
more concerned with form—which means structure or pattern or
organization—than an informative writer usually is. Partly this is
simply because he is far more conscious of himself as a maker of
things, of verbal structures; partly it is because he must attend
to what his reader will experience moment by moment rather than
simply to what package of information the reader will take away
at the end; but more important than either of these reasons is his
sense that only through form can he create virtual life.

In most of the other arts—in music, architecture, and abstract
painting and sculpture—form is, in fact, almost the only thing
the artist has to work with. And if we are to appreciate any art, as
art, we must recognize the crucial importance of form. Perhaps the

first step is to understand the kind of form that one finds in art. This is not easy, but a useful approach to the problem is suggested in the following passage by Eric Bentley:

> In analyzing *form*, a good starting point is the logical proposition that things must be either like or unlike each other. The technique of a playwright may be seen in the way he uses parallelism (likeness) and contrast (unlikeness). Through words and through the other arts of the theatre, he devises situations and incidents which will bring out the similarity or the difference. He creates all possible ironies, inter-actions, relationships. Repetition, juxtaposition, inversion, alternation, "counterpoint" are his stock in trade.

Bentley is talking here about dramatic form, but his description applies just as well to form in poetry and fiction. As a matter of fact, what he is explaining in rather broad and loose terms is the essence of *all* artistic form, whether the medium be language or musical sound or color and line and shape. *The artist—including the creative writer—selects and organizes his material according to the formal principle of likeness-and-difference, parallelism-and-contrast, repetition-and-variation, symmetry-and-asymmetry, harmony-and-conflict, congruity-and-incongruity.* The principle can be expressed in innumerable ways because it shows up in innumerable ways, which differ somewhat from one art to another. We shall usually refer to it as the principle of likeness-and-difference.

Now, all writers use this principle on occasion. We have already noted, for instance, that comparison and contrast are useful tools of the informative writer. However, in creative literature likeness-and-difference is not just a tool, but the fundamental principle of selection and arrangement. As such, it ranks in importance with the verbal principles of the plurisign and of thingness. These principles together constitute the chief means by which writers create both verbal structures and virtual life.

There has probably never existed a creative writer who thought of his work in precisely these terms. Like most artists, poets and fiction makers and playwrights depend far more on aesthetic sense than on critical theory. However, we readers have a perfect right to try to formulate the artist's working principles, even when these may be unconscious, and to analyze his works in the light of them.

Thus it probably never occurred to Robert Frost that in shaping "Stopping by Woods" he was following the principle of likeness-and-difference. But the poem clearly shows this principle in all sorts of ways. The most obvious example is the tension which crystallizes in the last stanza. The speaker in the poem (we may as well think of him as Frost in this case) is momentarily caught between two forces, between the attraction of the winter scene around him and his need to get going, between the woods (so "lovely, dark and deep") and the "promises" he has to keep. This is difference, disharmony, conflict. But it is merely the culmination of a contrast which has been building up since the opening stanza, between two opposing sets of values. One set is represented by the village man who owns the woods, by the impatient horse, and perhaps by the people who have been "promised"; the other set is represented by the poet, who can enjoy the woods without owning them, who is willing to interrupt his travel to watch them fill up with snow, and who can see other possibilities in life besides the keeping of promises.

But this obvious conflict is not all. The poem begins when a journey is briefly halted; it ends with the (implied) resumption of the journey. The man and his horse are contrasted in a way, but they also unite to make a living tableau in an otherwise deserted snow-scape. Their tinyness is contrasted with the breadth of the background. The tinkle of the harness bells serves to emphasize, by contrast, the silence of the scene. The first three stanzas are alike in their rhyme scheme and hence contrast with the fourth stanza, where all the lines rhyme and one line is repeated exactly.

And these are only the more conspicuous instances of likeness-and-difference in this poem. The minor revisions we noted earlier almost all resulted from Frost's trying, however unconsciously, for more parallels or more contrasts or, more precisely, for both at once. In fact, from this point of view the entire work is a surprisingly complex fabric of similarities-and-differences, repetitions-and-variations. Almost every feature of the poem, from its smallest detail to its over-all structure, displays this kind of form in one way or another. But "Stopping by Woods" is by no means unique in this respect; during the next four chapters we shall find the same formal principle at work in other poems and in fiction as well.

The Idea of Plurisign Extended

We have already seen that in creative writing words tend to function as plurisigns: they usually carry more than one meaning, and often different kinds of meaning, at the same time. It is hardly surprising, therefore, that this principle of multiple meaning also applies to the larger units of creative language—to phrases, sentences, lines, paragraphs, stanzas, scenes, chapters, and so on. In fact, at their best, entire poems, stories, and plays really operate as plurisigns.

"Stopping by Woods" illustrates this fact very well, even though most readers would agree that this is a relatively simple poem. On one level it does nothing more than bring to life a momentary interlude in the journey of a country man who suddenly notices the beauty of a winter scene and stops briefly to admire it. This is the poem at its most literal level, though as we have seen it is not a "factual" kind of literalness. But here is how John Holmes, who is also a poet in his own right, interprets "Stopping by Woods":

> It can be thought of as a picture: the whites, greys, and blacks of the masses and areas of lake, field, and woods, with the tiny figure of the man in the sleigh, and the horse. And it can be thought of as a statement of man's everlasting responsibility to man; though the dark and nothingness tempt him to surrender, he will not give in. Like several of Frost's poems, this one is built on the image of the pull of wildness and lawlessness against man's conscious will and the promises he has made to be kept.

Now, it is entirely possible to disagree with Holmes here. He implies that the man's decision to resume his journey represents a triumph. Might it not also be seen as a surrender? Is the final mood of the poem one of self-righteousness or is it perhaps one of resignation? Is the world which is symbolized by the snow-filling woods necessarily a "wild" and "lawless" one, or may it equally well be a world of higher values than those represented by the practical obligations, the routine promises?

We probably could debate the issue at length; the point is that there *is* an issue. People do disagree about works of art. They are bound to, and they should. A good creative work affects one's consciousness much as a tossed pebble does a pool of water. The words and other elements set up concentric circles of meaning, like the waves that spread out from the spot where the pebble hits the pool. If the pool is tiny, only a few and only small circles can form; if the pool is sizable, many circles will form, and some will reach great breadth. If the pool (the reader's awareness) should somehow grow larger, the same pebble would produce more and larger circles;

but if the pool happens to be frozen over (if, for instance, the reader has a deep prejudice against all poetry), then no circles at all will form. None of the circles is necessarily the one and only right one; more likely, the writer hoped his readers would be aware of many circles at once, including some which he had not consciously intended. This is what Robert Frost meant by his famous statement, "The poet has a right to anything the reader can find in him"; that is, there may be circles of meaning of which the poet himself was not aware. Frost did *not* mean to imply that all interpretations of a poem—or of any creative work—are equally valid. It is not true that the interpretation of literature is merely a matter of individual opinion. Interpretations must always be checked back against the work of art itself. They are acceptable only in so far as they take into account what was actually written. Frost in this statement was referring to meanings which are present for the reader to find, not to meanings dragged in from outside the poem.

Fusion of Form and Meaning

Thus, a good creative work is itself a plurisign. But its multiplicity of meaning depends only in part on a fuller use of words. It also depends on form. "Stopping by Woods" is an unusually clear example of this point. Most of the wider circles of meaning which readers have found in the poem—Holmes' interpretation is only one of a great many—are the direct result of Frost's happy solution of a formal problem—namely, how to finish his fourth stanza. Before he happened on his repeat ending, the virtual life this poem was creating possessed nothing like the universal significance which most readers now sense in it. Everything hinges on the repetition of line fifteen:

> And miles to go before I sleep.

The first time we encounter them, these "miles" are just ordinary lengths of country road which the man must travel to get home, where he has (perhaps) promised to be by 7 P.M. in order to take his wife to the church social. But once the line repeats, both it and the whole poem instantly take on meanings wider than their literal ones. The "miles" are still 5280-foot units, but somehow they have now also become all the years the man has left to live; the "promises" now include not only his pledge to his wife (or whatever) but all of his obligations and commitments; "sleep" means not only rest after a long day but death; and the "woods" are not only a lovely moment in the day's journey but all the temptations that may divert a man from his "promised" course.

Thus the virtual man and his virtual moment of minor decision have come to symbolize all men and a perennial human dilemma: should we continue to play out the roles—sometimes onerous—we find ourselves in, or should we rebel against them? Does manhood itself depend on the keeping of promises, or is it perhaps more manly to assert our independence, to strike out on our own? To what extent should we submit to the centripetal force of our commitments? To what extent have we a right to yield to the also powerful centrifugal force of diversions, new callings, chance avenues of escape?

Frost does not really try to resolve the dilemma: that is the moralist's job, not the artist's. As a poet, Frost is content merely to present the dilemma, to allow it to become one dimension of the virtual life his poem evokes. But the poem achieves this dimension because Frost solved the formal problem as he did. "Stopping by Woods" thus becomes a perfect example of the interdependence of form and meaning in creative writing.

Some Practical Implications

This chapter has attempted to introduce only a few basic principles of creative literature. We have focused on a handful of very general ideas which serve three purposes: they apply to all types of creative writing and help to define its difference from other kinds of writing; they suggest various analogies between literary art and the nonverbal arts; and they have important practical implications.

We might conclude by pointing out some of these implications:

1. Poetry, fiction, and drama should be approached in the same spirit that we approach any other mode of art. Like music, painting, and other arts, creative writing is a product and source of experiential knowledge.

2. Our business with a creative piece, as with any work of art, is simply to experience it, as fully and sensitively and intel-

ligently as we can. This means taking in both the verbal structure itself and the virtual life it generates, in all of their unified
richness.

3. We must be prepared for a richer kind of word-using than we
normally find in informative literature, and we must be willing
to respond to this language in all of its multiplicity of meanings.

4. We must also be prepared for a far greater emphasis on form,
and for a different kind of form, than we usually encounter
in informative writing. Specifically, we must keep our senses,
our minds, and our imaginations alert to every conceivable
kind of likeness-and-difference.

In the next four chapters we will further test and refine some of
these general principles by applying them to various aspects and
types of creative literature, starting with poetry and then moving
on to prose.

EXERCISES

A. Think about the following questions for class discussion:
1. Can you cite other uses of the word *virtual* which resemble its
use in the phrase *virtual life?*
2. According to popular mythology, poetry is supposed to be based
on "inspiration." To what extent did "inspiration" figure in
Frost's writing of "Stopping by Woods"?
3. How might modern psychology explain the phenomenon of
"inspiration"?
4. Can you cite examples of inspiration from your own experience
(not necessarily literary experiences)?
5. Using the ideas presented in this chapter, how would you distinguish between fiction which is pornographic and fiction which
merely deals with sex realistically?
6. Can you cite examples of the principle of likeness-and-difference
in any of the nonverbal arts, such as music, painting, architecture, sculpture, and photography?
7. Does the principle of the plurisign imply that all interpretations
of a creative work are equally valid? Why or why not?

B. Study the *form* of the following short poems and be prepared to discuss some of the ways in which each exhibits the principle of likeness-and-difference:

1.

Nursery Rhyme

Pease porridge hot,
Pease porridge cold,
Pease porridge in the pot
Nine days old.

Some like it hot,
Some like it cold,
Some like it in the pot
Nine days old.

(ANONYMOUS)

2.

Presentiment

Presentiment is that long shadow on the lawn
Indicative that suns go down:
The notice to the startled grass
That darkness is about to pass.[7]

(EMILY DICKINSON, 1830–86)

3.

Nursery Rhyme

Hickory, dickory, dock,
The mouse ran up the clock,
The clock struck one,
And down he run
Hickory, dickory, dock.

(ANONYMOUS)

4.

The Span of Life

The old dog barks backward without getting up.
I can remember when he was a pup.[8]

(ROBERT FROST)

5.

The Old Philanthropist

His millions make museums bright;
Harvard anticipates his will;
While his young typist weeps at night
Over a druggist's bill.[9]

(PHYLLIS MC GINLEY, 1905–   )

[7] "Presentiment" by Emily Dickinson. Reprinted by permission of Little, Brown & Company.

[8] "The Span of Life" by Robert Frost, from *Complete Poems of Robert Frost.* Copyright 1923, 1930, 1939 by Holt, Rinehart and Winston, Inc. Copyright 1936 by Robert Frost. Copyright renewed 1951 by Robert Frost. Reprinted by permission of Holt, Rinehart and Winston, Inc.

[9] "The Old Philanthropist," from *The Love Letters of Phyllis McGinley* by Phyllis McGinley. Copyright 1952 by Phyllis McGinley. Reprinted by permission of The Viking Press, Inc.

6. *On Limited Warfare*

Don'tcha worry, honey chile.
Don'tcha cry no more,
It's jest a li'l ole atom bomb
In a li'l ole lim'ted war.

It's jest a bitsy warhead, chile,
On a li'l ole tactical shell,
An' all it'll do is blow us-all
To a li'l ole lim'ted hell.[10]
(ANONYMOUS)

7. *Song*

The year's at the spring,
The day's at the morn;
Morning's at seven;
The hillside's dew-pearled;
The lark's on the wing;
The snail's on the thorn;
God's in his heaven—
All's right with the world!
(ROBERT BROWNING,
1812–89)

C. Find a professional book review which seems to you to err in one or more of the ways discussed on pages 139–41. Then write a brief analysis of the review, showing what is wrong with its approach.

D. Find a poem which you consider fairly good. Then write an analysis of it, showing the interdependence of verbal structure (language and form) and virtual life (content or meaning).

E. Pick a poem which seems to you quite rich in meaning, and describe some of the "circles of meaning" which it sets up in your mind.

F. Write a short essay on likeness-and-difference as a formal feature of some nonverbal art with which you are familiar. You may either discuss that art as a whole, in general terms, or focus on a single work.

G. Write an essay which analyzes the differences between an abridged version of a play, a story, or a novel and the original version.

H. Do the same thing as in G with two versions of the same poem. You will probably have to write your own abridged version in this case.

[10] "Limited Warfare," from *The Silver Treasury of Humorous Verse*, Mentor Edition, edited by Oscar Williams. Reprinted by permission.

9. Some Aspects of Poetry

> Poetry is life at the remove of form and meaning;
> not life lived but life framed and identified. So the
> criticism of poetry is bound to be occupied at once
> with the terms and modes by which the remove was
> made and with the relation between—in the ambiguous
> stock phrase—content and form.
>
> R. P. BLACKMUR, *The Double Agent*

The "Types" of Creative Writing

Like so many things in the groves of academe, creative literature is conventionally divided into three parts: poetry, fiction, and drama. And then it is usual to show that each part has various subdivisions. Every schoolboy knows about these categories, the main ones at least, and understands the principal distinctions among them. Indeed he could scarcely avoid doing so. A mere glance at the printed pages is enough to prove that most poetry is different from most prose, that fiction designed to be read is different from fiction designed to be enacted on a stage, and that novels are different from both novelettes and short stories (even though no one has ever defined the boundaries precisely). Furthermore, there are other, less obvious and less superficial, differences among the "types" which it is sometimes profitable to discuss.

But seldom is a discussion of the "types" as profitable as text-books and courses in literature frequently imply. For most of the distinctions among the types involve differences of degree only, not of kind. More important, the distinctions tend to break down. To mention just a few examples: all drama is by definition more or less fictitious; much of the best fiction and drama, especially in the older literatures, is also poetry; lyric poems contain—though less obviously—most of the elements of fiction and drama; and most drama and fiction contain many of the elements and techniques of poetry.

This overlapping of the traditional categories has become especially apparent in our time, because contemporary writers have done so much experimenting with the older forms and inventing of new ones: a modern novel like Joyce's *Ulysses* is far closer, despite its 768 pages, to lyric poetry than it is to the ordinary run of realistic fiction; similarly, many contemporary plays ostensibly written in prose, such as those of Tennessee Williams, are essentially dramatic poems; the kind of poetry known as free verse is likely to be indistinguishable, except typographically, from the more lyrical prose of writers like D. H. Lawrence, Thomas Wolfe, or William Faulkner; and many modern novels and short stories rely so heavily on dialogue that they read almost like plays. On the other hand, some plays, such as G. B. Shaw's and the later works of Eugene O'Neill, contain such elaborate stage directions and other intrusions by the dramatist that they read almost like novels; and the most characteristically modern short stories, such as most of Hemingway's, are in subject, word use, and form more akin to lyric poetry than to the bulk of pre-twentieth-century prose fiction. Sometimes it seems as if, in our time, the best writers themselves had deliberately set out to refute the standard methods of classifying literature.

But even if the conventional categories were far more valid and useful than they are, in this book we would largely ignore them. For our province here is the whole of literature—informative, persuasive, *and* creative; and in this context the differences among poetry, fiction, and drama become very minor in comparison with their similarities. For our purposes, the key points of interest are the characteristics which the three creative types have in common, characteristics which separate all three from the other uses of language and which link all three to the nonverbal arts.

Poetry as a Magnifying Glass

Accordingly, we shall pay no attention to the customary distinctions between fiction and drama; instead, we will lump all plays, novels, novellas, and short stories together under the general category of fiction. We shall, however, preserve the distinction between lyric poetry and fiction (both poetic and prosaic, narrative and dramatic), simply for convenience. The fact is that some aspects of creative literature can be most readily observed in lyric poetry, others in fiction. But we must remember that most of the features of poetry are also found in all kinds of fiction, and that most of the features of fiction and drama which we will get to in Chapter 11 also occur in lyric poems. In other words, a more accurate title for the present chapter would be "Some Aspects of Creative Writing Which Are Especially Apparent in Lyric Poetry." For we will begin with poetry, again for convenience.

If one is primarily interested in a few very basic principles of creative literature, as we are here, these can be illustrated most easily in lyric poems. Poems are briefer and more compact than plays or even short stories and are therefore handy examples of complete verbal structures. Furthermore, most lyric poetry is by nature more obviously unlike the noncreative kinds of writing and is, for this very reason, more obviously akin to the nonverbal art forms.

Thus, in many ways lyric poetry is an ideal starting place for a closer examination of creative writing as a whole. To study poems is to see this use of language through a magnifying glass. That is precisely why in the last chapter we opened our discussion of the art of literature with Frost's "Stopping by Woods" as a case in point. And again in the present chapter we shall focus on lyric poetry, not merely to learn a little more about poems, about what makes them tick and how to handle them, but to explore certain elements, techniques, forms, and devices which also occur, less conspicuously, in the various species of fiction and drama, in creative essays, and even in some kinds of informative and persuasive writing.

Finally, both here and in Chapter 11, we shall want especially to note the relation between each element and the basic principles already introduced in the last chapter. In particular, we shall be observing various ways in which creative writers work language far harder than informative writers normally do, in which likeness-and-difference is everywhere present as the main formal principle in creative writing, and in which poems and novels and the rest always tend toward the plurisign (in both the narrow and the broad senses of that term). The reader will then be in a position to see that other elements, not discussed in this book, also can be understood in terms of the same principles.

Words

Our discussion of informative language began, appropriately, with conceptual knowledge—with propositions; but any introduction to creative writing should begin, as ours already has, with words. And in general this is truer of lyric poetry than of any other creative genre, for nowhere else in literature is the importance of the individual word more constantly apparent. The lyric poet works in such limited space that he has relatively little room to make much of the larger elements—character and action and setting—upon which the dramatist and storyteller largely depend. The poet must make every *word* count, as heavily as possible. Even more than other creative writers, therefore, the poet is preoccupied with words themselves. Hence W. H. Auden's comment:

> A poet is, before anything else, a person who is passionately in love with language. Whether this love is a sign of his poetic gift or the gift itself—for falling in love is given not chosen—I don't know, but it is certainly the sign by which one recognizes whether a young man is potentially a poet or not.

Of course, Auden's remark would also apply, with somewhat less force, to all creative writers.

But we have already spent two full chapters (3 and 4) on words and will be noting many new examples of poetic diction as we go along. At this stage it is perhaps enough to remind ourselves of two key points: that poets push the resources of words to the limit, and that especially in poetry, words must be expected to carry multiple meanings, and hence to make more than ordinary demands on the reader. Then there is one new point to be stressed, which arises from the principle of likeness-and-difference: words in poetry not only function together in the usual conceptual sense but at the same time they are linked to each other in all sorts of extra ways, through the operation of parallelism and contrast, repetition and variation. The use of words as plurisigns, and for their thingness, greatly complicates their formal interrelationships. In examining Frost's "Stopping by Woods" we have already seen a few such extra-conceptual linkages, but we will note many more as we go along.

All of these points apply, to a lesser extent, to the use of words in fiction and drama. For the individual word assumes far greater importance in all creative writing than in most other kinds. This is certainly one basic reason why creative literature is so much harder to translate into another language. But poetry is notoriously the hardest of all to translate. The lyric poet deals with aspects of experience which can best be rendered through the exploitation of language itself, especially of its evocative potentialities and its thingness. The poet's "subjects" are normally the most personal, subtle, and intangible kinds of experiential knowledge—feelings, moods, attitudes, sense impressions, momentary visions, intuitions of value. Only the most delicate and subtle of instruments will serve at all in treating these areas of human experience. And the most subtle and responsive instruments at the writer's disposal are words themselves. In proportion as the dramatist or fiction writer also concerns himself with these kinds of experiential knowledge, and many modern prose writers do, he likewise makes the most of words.

Rhythm

The individual word, then, is the most important single element in lyric poetry. But certain other aspects of creative writing also are magnified in poetry. One of these is rhythm. In fact, many people feel that rhythm is *the* hallmark of poetry: if a piece of writing has rhythm, especially the regular kind of beat that stirs the blood and activates the muscles, it must be poetry; and if not, it can't truly be called poetry. Actually, rhythm alone will not produce poetry, any more than it will music. Doggerel verse is no closer to genuine poetry than the monotonous pounding of a machine is to true music.

On the other hand, all poetry *is* rhythmic, as to a lesser extent is most creative writing and, for that matter, all art, verbal or visual or musical. For rhythm is present whenever anything recurs more or less regularly. Thus we even speak of the "rhythms" of nature, meaning the alternation of day and night, the cycles of the seasons, the ebb and flow of the tides, the recurring pattern of birth and maturation and death, the succession of generations. Rhythm in this broad sense is a feature of all artistic form. There is rhythm in the repetition of the arch motif in a Gothic cathedral, of certain colors or lines or shapes in a painting, of particular angles or curves or planes in a piece of sculpture. Rhythm is everywhere present in music, not only as metronomic beat but in the recurrence of melodic, harmonic, contrapuntal, and instrumental patterns.

And so it is in literature: rhythm is produced whenever any element—a particular word or word-cluster, an image, a refrain line, a symbol, a pattern of beats or rhymes, or whatever—keeps reappearing at more or less fixed intervals. Thus, in poetry—as in music —rhythm takes innumerable forms, and—again as in music—several kinds of rhythm are usually present at once. But, since for most readers it is the very systematic sort of rhythm called *meter* which is most striking in poetry, and which seems to differentiate it from prose, we will look at that first.

From our point of view here, the most interesting aspect of meter (as of all rhythm) is its relation to the principle of likeness-and-difference. In fact, almost everything that is worth saying about meter involves this principle in one way or another. To begin with, the essence of meter is the regular repetition of a pattern of units called *feet*. (Here we have likeness.) Each foot consists of some combination of strong and weak (stressed and unstressed) syllables. (Here we have difference.) A metrical line consists of one or more feet, usually of the same kind. (Here we have both likeness and difference.) For instance, the most common English meter—Shakespeare's favorite one—is called *iambic pentameter*, because each line is made up of five feet, each of which is an *iamb* (a foot comprising one weak beat followed by one strong one):

> The time is out of joint: O cursèd spite
> That ever I was born to set it right!

The meter of this couplet can be shown by *scanning* it, which means dividing each line into feet and indicating the makeup of each foot, as follows:

w s	w s	w s	w s	w s
The time	is out	of joint:	O curs	èd spite

w s	w s	w s	w s	w s
That ev	er I	was born	to set	it right!

There are various kinds of feet. In English, the *iamb* is most common, but we also have the *trochee* (one strong beat and then a weak one), the *anapest* (two strong beats and then a weak one), the *dactyl* (a strong beat and then two weak ones), and other measures less frequently used. Each line may consist entirely of one kind of foot or it may include two or more kinds. The kind of foot which predominates gives each meter half of its name; the number of feet gives it the other half. The most common meters in English verse range from trimeter (three feet per line) to hexameter (six feet per line). The same meter may be used throughout a stanza or a whole poem, or the meter may vary within each stanza or from stanza to stanza, according to a regular pattern or irregularly.

The use of meter gives the poet not only one of the intrinsically pleasing elements of music—rhythmic beat—but also an infinitely flexible means of expression. A fixed rhythm sets up expectations which it is pleasant to have fulfilled; it also permits pleasant surprises. Furthermore, psychologists have learned that a regular beat, in verse as in music, tends to induce in the reader a state of "hyperaesthesia" which makes him supernormally receptive to sensory, emotional, and imaginative stimulation. All of these advantages the "free-verse" poet—the poet who dispenses with meter—tends to lose. However, no poet ever discards rhythm entirely.

Now, these technical terms and details need not concern us here: every good handbook on versification treats all of them, and a great many others, far more fully than we can here. What does concern us is how the poet uses meter to create parallels and contrasts, repetitions and variations, beyond those inherent in meter itself. No one could possibly list all the ways, and the reasons for them, so we will note only a few.

A poet may introduce metrical variations, according to some fixed system, merely for variety's sake, to avoid the sing-song monotony of perfect regularity. This is true of all poetry, but is most obvious in nonsense verse or children's rhymes:

> Pease porridge hot,
> Pease porridge cold,
> Pease porridge in the pot
> Nine days old.

> Some like it hot,
> Some like it cold,
> Some like it in the pot
> Nine days old.

Here the extra foot in each third line serves no other function than to change the pattern a little, each stanza then winding up with the basic three-foot meter. The number of syllables per foot is also varied a bit so that the last line of each stanza consists entirely of one-syllable feet. The poem would be much less interesting rhythmically if the meter were more regular, for example:

> Pease porridge hot,
>> Pease porridge cold,
> Soup in the pot
>> Twenty days old.
>
> Some like it hot,
>> Some like it cold,
> Some like the lot
>> Twenty days old.

Metrical variation can also help to underline, by paralleling, some other element, such as the rhyme scheme:

> Hickory, dickory, dock,
> The mouse ran up the clock;
>> The clock struck one,
>> And down he run,
> Hickory, dickory, dock.

In this nursery rhyme the shift from trimeter to dimeter and back again is also dictated by the traditional form used here, namely the limerick. In "Hickory," change of meter also parallels the reversal of "action"—in trimeter the mouse runs up the clock (which ought to take longer), in dimeter he quickly scurries back down.

Thus, even in verse as simple as Mother Goose, we find the anonymous poets varying their meters, for various reasons. In more sophisticated poetry the same elementary reasons may also figure, but they are likely to be implemented by the need for special effects which rhythm can help to produce. This is where meter becomes most interesting—where it is used expressively. Almost any good poem could be used to illustrate this point. For example:

Eight O'Clock

> He stood, and heard the steeple
>> Sprinkle the quarters on the morning town.
> One, two, three, four, to market-place and people
>> It tossed them down.
>
> Strapped, noosed, nighing his hour,
>> He stood and counted them and cursed his luck;

And then the clock collected in the tower
Its strength, and struck.[1]

(A. E. HOUSMAN, 1859–1936)

Here the lines of each stanza rapidly increase in length until the sharply contrasting last line, which in its terse brevity helps to suggest the irrevocable doom awaiting the man on the scaffold and then the terrible finality of the event itself. The final line may even evoke a picture of the body dropping through the trap door of the scaffold.

Housman's stanzas follow a set metrical pattern and even a fixed rhyme scheme. Controlled variation of rhythm for expressive purposes is even more apparent in most free verse. In the following poem the basic contrast is between two pictures: the opening one, which also is brought back at the end, depicts hunters returning from the chase; the second, which is created by the middle stanzas, depicts the same hunters as they had originally set out, to a flourish of trumpets. At least, this is the ostensible contrast; some readers may also see the hunters as soldiers returning from war exhausted, injured, disenchanted, in contrast to the same soldiers (the "leash-men" being their officers) who had embarked with such high zest for battle overseas. In any case, this basic contrast is aided immeasurably by the use of contrasting rhythms:

The Return

See, they return; ah, see the tentative
Movements, and the slow feet,
The trouble in the pace and the uncertain
Wavering!

See, they return, one, and by one,
With fear, as half awakened;
As if the snow should hesitate
And murmur in the wind,
          and half turn back;
These were the "Wing'd-with-Awe,"
Inviolable.

[1] "Eight O'Clock" by A. E. Housman, from *Complete Poems* by A. E. Housman. Copyright 1922 by Holt, Rinehart and Winston, Inc. Copyright renewed 1950 by Barclays Bank Ltd. Reprinted by permission of Holt, Rinehart and Winston, Inc., and by The Society of Authors as the literary representatives of the estate of the late A. E. Housman and Messrs. Jonathan Cape, Ltd., publishers of A. E. Housman's *Collected Poems*.

> Gods of the wingèd shoe!
> With them the silver hounds,
>   sniffing the trace of air!
>
> Haie! Haie!
>   These were the swift to harry;
> These the keen-scented;
> These were the souls of blood.
>
> Slow on the leash,
>   pallid the leash-men! [2]
>   (EZRA POUND, 1885–   )

Pound uses shifts in rhythm to help evoke, by parallelism and contrast, the disintegration of the men—physical and mental and spiritual.

The use of rhythmic variations to support other elements is found in all good poetry. In fact, poems with perfectly regular meter are quite rare, so rare as to make us wonder when we find such a poem whether the regularity is not in itself intentionally expressive.

Joyce Kilmer's "Trees" may be seen as an example of such a poem. One of the most widely known poems by an American writer, it is generally condemned by the critics for its stock phrases, its inconsistent images, its sentimental tone and its appeal to stock responses. Without denying that it is a bad poem (a careful analysis will show that the critics are right about many of its flaws) one may still grant that regularity of form and rhythm and simplicity of diction are appropriate to Kilmer's theme.

Trees

> I think that I shall never see
> A poem lovely as a tree.
>
> A tree whose hungry mouth is pressed
> Against the earth's sweet flowing breast;
>
> A tree that looks at God all day
> And lifts its leafy arms to pray;
>
> A tree that may in summer wear
> A nest of robins in her hair;

[2] "The Return" by Ezra Pound, from *Personae: The Collected Poems of Ezra Pound.* Copyright 1926, 1958 by Ezra Pound. Reprinted by permission of New Directions, Publishers.

Upon whose bosom snow has lain;
Who intimately lives with rain.

Poems are made by fools like me,
But only God can make a tree.[3]
(JOYCE KILMER, 1886–1918)

This is not a "nature" poem, but a religious poem. The triviality of man's achievements (represented by poems) is contrasted with the grandeur of God's achievements (represented by trees, nature). Kilmer could and did write more intricate verse, but having chosen as his symbols poems and trees, he was almost forced to make his own poem seem a humble, childish, trivial accomplishment.

Thus, even when a poet uses a standard meter (such as Kilmer's iambic tetrameter) he has the choice of either sticking to it (thereby creating parallelism both within his rhythm and between it and other elements) or of deviating from it (thereby creating contrasts and irregularities). Usually he does both, playing all sorts of variations on his basic metrical scheme, but coming back to it often enough to remind the reader of its presence as the norm. Any good poem would illustrate this, but here is one by the same author as "The Return," which is similar enough in form and meter to "Trees," and yet different enough in tone, to make a nice contrast:

An Immorality

Sing we for love and idleness,
Naught else is worth the having.

Though I have been in many a land,
There is naught else in living.

And I would rather have my sweet,
Though rose-leaves die of grieving,

Than do high deeds in Hungary
To pass all men's believing.[4]

This is a far more delicate and sophisticated poem than Kilmer's, and a great deal more interesting technically. Each of Pound's couplets involves two different standard meters, the first line in

[3] "Trees" by Joyce Kilmer used by special permission of copyright owner, Jerry Vogel Music Co., Inc., 112 West 44th Street, New York 36, New York.
[4] "An Immorality" by Ezra Pound, from *Personae: The Collected Poems of Ezra Pound*. Copyright 1926, 1958 by Ezra Pound. Reprinted by permission of New Directions, Publishers.

each being iambic tetrameter and the second iambic trimeter. And yet almost none of the lines, if read properly (which means as the sense demands rather than in a child's metronomic fashion), is perfectly regular. (Of course, "An Immorality" also has other interesting features—the alternation of nonrhyming first lines with half-rhyming and later fully-rhyming second lines, alliteration, and an effective use of slightly archaic wording.)

One final point about rhythm in relation to likeness-and-difference: in selecting his meter in the first place, the poet may also follow this principle. He may (consciously or unconsciously) choose a rhythm which is appropriate to his other elements (a meter which fits the mood, helps to create the action or to evoke the desired images, reinforces the tone); or he may purposely choose one which is incongruous (gay when it ought to be solemn, clumsy when it ought to skip, and so on). But even within the chosen meter he will usually introduce variations, not merely because the natural accents of the words he needs don't happen to fall right, but deliberately, for special effects of all kinds.

We should beware, though, of making too much of this notion of a "right" meter (or a deliberately "not right" one); for standard meters, like words themselves, can change their character with context. Shakespeare, for instance, uses the same *blank verse* (unrhymed iambic pentameter) for many different purposes, from the most frivolous to the most profoundly tragic. And both of the following poems are based in part on essentially the same meter (anapestic trimeter)—actually Tennyson varies this basic meter considerably—but they evoke totally different moods:

Break, Break, Break

Break, break, break,
   On thy cold gray stones, O sea!
And I wish that my tongue could utter
   The thoughts that arise in me.

O well for the fisherman's boy.
   That he shouts with his sister at play!
O well for the sailor lad,
   That he sings in his boat on the bay!

And the stately ships go on
   To their haven under the hill;
But O for the touch of a vanished hand,
   And the sound of a voice that is still!

> Break, break, break,
>   At the foot of thy crags, O sea!
> But the tender grace of a day that is dead
>   Will never come back to me.
>
> (ALFRED, LORD TENNYSON, 1809–92)

A *Limerick*

> There was a young woman named Bright,
> Whose speed was much faster than light;
>   She set out one day
>   In a relative way
> And returned on the previous night.
>
> (ANONYMOUS)

In the next chapter we will be noting various uses of meter. But it is well to keep in mind that meter is only one, rather special form of literary rhythm. In reading not only poetry but any type of creative writing we should keep our ears and minds alert for rhythm of all sorts, for repetitive patterns—and for variations on them—of every kind.

Rhyme, Alliteration, Onomatopoeia

Among other things, rhythm is one instance of the poet's normal tendency to take advantage of the thingness of language. Of the many other ways in which creative writers, and especially poets, exploit the sound of words, we will note only three here.

The first is *rhyme*. The end-words of poetic lines either rhyme or don't rhyme. Rhyme can also occur within lines (internal rhyme). But rhyming words are not identical; they are both alike and unlike (*hill-still, bright-light-night*). And words may nearly rhyme but not quite, as in consonance (*apple-supple*) or in assonance (*story-holy*), where again we have both similarity and difference. Some lines may rhyme, while others do not. Certain rhyme sounds may carry over from one stanza to the next, thus linking the stanzas together. Any regular rhyme scheme results, of course, in another kind of rhythm, in addition to the basic meter.

Rhyme, like rhythm, can be enjoyable quite for its own sake, as witness the nursery rhymes and game verses that delight children. Again like rhythm, rhyme can also contribute in valuable ways to the rest of the poem, considered both as a verbal structure and as a piece of virtual life. Rhyme may help to define the poem's structure, pointing up its divisions and the connections among them; it can be used to make certain words or lines stand out from the rest, thus indicating their importance as plurisigns; and rhyme can be employed to create all sorts of special effects. Ogden Nash has invented a humorous and satiric poetic style of his own largely out of incongruous or ironic end-rhymes, as in this piece:

Lines in Dispraise of Dispraise

I hereby bequeath to the Bide-a-Wee home all people who have statistics
    to prove that a human
Is nothing but a combination of iron and water and potash and albumen.
That may very well be the truth
But it's just like saying that a cocktail is nothing but ice and gin and
    vermouth.
People who go around analyzing
Are indeed very tanalizing.
They always want to get at the bottom
Of everything from spring to ottom.
They can't just look at a Rembrandt or a Bartolozzi
And say, Boy! that's pretty hozzi-tozzi!
No, they have to break it up into its component parts
And reconstruct it with blueprints and charts.
My idea is that while after looking around me and even at me
    I may not be proud of being a human
I object to having attention called to my iron and water and potash and
    albumen.
In the first place, it's undignified,
And in the second place, nothing by it is signified.
Because it isn't potash etcetera that make people Republicans or Democrats or Ghibellines or Guelphs,
It's the natural perversity of the people themselfs.
No, no, you old analysts, away with the whole kit and kaboodle of you.
I wouldn't even make mincemeat to give to a poodle of you.[5]

(OGDEN NASH, 1902–   )

Rhythmic variations also help to account for many of the comic effects in this poem. Incidentally, Ogden Nash illustrates another point worth keeping in mind: when we call poets or other creative writers *serious,* we don't mean that they are necessarily solemn.

What counts is how faithful the artist is to his sense of life. He may see life as comic or as tragic, as senseless or as profoundly meaningful, and still be a "serious" artist if his primary loyalty is to his personal vision of reality. Conversely, he is a nonserious writer, however solemn he may be, if his main business is concocting a vision of reality which his readers would prefer even though both he and they knew it to be a false vision.

A second, closely related way of using sound is *alliteration*. Like rhyme, this involves the repetition of similar sounds, though here the similar sounds are at the beginnings of words, as in these lines from Stevenson's "Requiem":

> Home is the sailor, home from the sea,
> And the hunter home from the hill.
>
> (ROBERT LOUIS STEVENSON, 1850–94)

The English poet Swinburne, who was notoriously over-fond of alliteration, once wrote a parody of his own style which contained the line

> Made meek as a mother whose bosom-beats bound with the bliss-bringing bulk of a balm-breathing baby.
>
> (ALGERNON SWINBURNE, 1837–1909)

Alliteration can be silly, and, more seriously, it can lull us into unresponsiveness to other dimensions of language. (This is one reason why informative writers usually avoid it.) But alliteration, like rhythm and rhyme, can also be both musically pleasing and expressive. Used appropriately it can reinforce all of the other elements, either through parallelism-and-contrast or by linking the unlike through likeness of sound.

When alliteration contributes directly to the virtual life of a poem, it often functions as *onomatopoeia*, which is language that sounds like what it means (that is, language in which sound parallels meaning). Some words are naturally onomatopoetic (*bang, jolt, murmur, whinny, slushy, tinkle*), and poets of course use them where convenient, because, as Conrad puts it, the creative writer's task is always "to make you hear, to make you feel . . . to make you see." But onomatopoetic words don't always fit the poem in all the other ways required (fit the rhythm and rhyme schemes, the evocative context, and so on). Writers therefore have to depend less often on naturally onomatopoetic words than on combinations of words which are made to function onomatopoetically, suggesting sound and tempo. In these lines from Browning we find natural onomatopoeia (in *slushy*) and invented combinations which express the sound and rhythm of the action:

> As I gain the cove with pushing prow
> And quench its speed i' the slushy sand.

The first line conveys the quick, strong pull of the oars; the second slows and comes to a halt that is audible in *slushy sand*.

These three uses of sound—rhyme, alliteration, and onomatopoeia —are merely common examples of a great many devices through which poets—and other creative writers—capitalize on the fact that words are sounds as well as symbols. The reader of creative writing, and especially of poetry, should not confine his attention to these easily nameable sound patterns. The principle of likeness-and-difference operates in innumerable ways, and we should notice its presence whether we can name the relationship or not. As far as sound is concerned, this means reading poems aloud and with attention to every kind of repetition and variation, parallelism and contrast.

Here are two poems by Wilfred Owen in both of which sound is worked heavily, though for radically different effects. The first is a love poem with the Biblical title "Song of Songs":

> Sing me at morn but only with your laugh;
> Even as Spring that laugheth into leaf;
> Even as Love that laugheth after Life.
>
> Sing me but only with your speech all day,
> As voluble leaflets do; let viols die;
> The least word of your lips is melody!
>
> Sing me at eve but only with your sigh!
> Like lifting seas it solaceth; breathe so,
> Slowly and low, the sense that no songs say.
>
> Sing me at midnight with your murmurous heart!
> Let youth's immortal-moaning chords be heard
> Throbbing through you, and sobbing, unsubdued.[6]

Properly read aloud, this poem should appeal even to a child unaware of the sense of the words. By using all the elements we have looked at, and many other kinds of audible patterns, Owen has created an unusually interesting fabric of verbal sounds. There are the half-rhymes at the ends of the lines (*laugh—leaf—life, day— die— -dy, sigh—so—say*) except in the last stanza, where the pattern varies slightly to *heart—heard— -dued,* giving the last word—*unsub- dued*—extra weight. There are all sorts of internal half-rhymes (*Love—laugheth—Life, voluble—leaflets—do—let—viols—die, Throb- bing—through—you—sobbing—unsubdued*). There is alliteration in every line and of various kinds. There is onomatopoeia, combined with alliteration, especially in the last two stanzas:

> Sing me at eve but only with your sigh!
> Like lifting seas it solaceth; breathe so,
> Slowly and low, the sense that no songs say.

And there is a very elaborate interweaving of identical consonants and of related but slightly different vowels throughout the poem. Finally, beneath all these sound patterns there is the basic iambic pentameter rhythm, varied in several places to change the pace of the poem and for special effects. This sort of weaving of words as sound is so intricate as to defy analysis. And yet this fabric of sounds at the same time serves to evoke several facets of the complex human relationship which is the poem's "subject." The verbal music is not there merely for its own sake, but as one means of creating virtual life.

Now here is the same poet in a totally different mood, but still working with the sound values of words:

Greater Love

> Red lips are not so red
>   As the stained stones kissed by the English dead.
> Kindness of wooed and wooer
> Seems shame to their love pure.
> O Love, your eyes lose lure
>   When I behold eyes blinded in my stead!
>
> Your slender attitude
>   Trembles not exquisite like limbs knife-skewed,
> Rolling and rolling there
> Where God seems not to care;
> Till the fierce Love they bear
>   Cramps them in death's extreme decrepitude.
>
> Your voice sings not so soft,—
>   Though even as wind murmuring through raftered loft,—

Your dear voice is not dear,
Gentle, and evening clear,
As theirs whom none now hear,
    Now earth has stopped their piteous mouths that coughed.

Heart, you were never hot,
    Nor large, nor full like hearts made great with shot;
And though your hand be pale,
Paler are all which trail
Your cross through flame and hail:
    Weep, you may weep, for you may touch them not.[7]

Here many of the resources of sound used in the last poem are enlisted for ironic purposes. Rhymes bring together and thus emphasize the violent contrast between man-and-woman love and the love of country, the "Greater Love" which ends in death on the battlefield. Thus *slender attitude* contrasts with *death's extreme decrepitude, sings not so soft* with *piteous mouths that coughed.* And the sounds of the words in these and other contrasting phrases express on the one hand the smooth sweetness of young love and on the other the harsh awkwardness, ugliness, unnaturalness of bodies destroyed by war. *Red lips are not so red* and *your slender attitude* fall easily from the tongue in contrast to *stained stones kissed by the English dead* and *trembles not exquisite like limbs knife-skewed* where alliteration, internal half-rhyme (*stained stones*), irregular rhythm, and the repetition of similar vowel sounds express audibly the ugliness and unnaturalness of death.

But harsh, cacophonous sounds and awkward, irregular rhythms can also be employed to celebrate a joyous vision of life, as in our final example of how all these ways of exploiting the thingness of language can combine. This poem, by Gerard Manley Hopkins, is in honor of variety, diversity, and eccentricity, and of the Creator who presumably meant things to be this way:

Pied Beauty

Glory be to God for dappled things—
    For skies of couple-colour as a brinded cow;
      For rose-moles all in stipple upon trout that swim;
Fresh-firecoal chestnut falls; finches' wings;
    Landscape plotted and pieced—fold, fallow, and plough;

And áll trádes, their gear and tackle and trim.
All things counter, original, spare, strange;
  Whatever is fickle, freckled (who knows how?)
    With swift, slow; sweet, sour; adazzle, dim;
He fathers-forth whose beauty is past change:
              Praise him.[8]
            (GERARD MANLEY HOPKINS, 1844–89)

The expressiveness of this poem depends on the united effect of a number of the devices or elements which we have been discussing, notably rhythm, rhyme, alliteration, and onomatopoeia. The hesitant, jerky, uneven rhythm is paralleled by the awkward juxtaposition of cacophonous sounds, the irregularity of the rhyme scheme, and the unbalance in the last line. All of these uses of the sound qualities of words help to evoke the basic image of "dappled things"—objects, creatures, and folkways which are peculiar, asymmetrical, off-beat. The special decisiveness of the final command—"Praise him"—derives mainly from its brevity and simplicity, in contrast to the very complex longer lines that come before.

The reason for giving so much space here to some of the audible elements in poetry is that these are often misunderstood: sometimes they are regarded as mere devices, tricks of the trade, rather than as inevitable products of the poet's need to tap the full expressive resources of language; or they are regarded as mere decoration, a tasty but unnutritious frosting on the cake. We will treat a few other elements more briefly, not because they are less important but because they are less liable to such misconceptions.

Metaphor

The dictionary defines *metaphor* as "a figure of speech in which a term or phrase is applied to something to which it is not literally applicable, in order to suggest a resemblance, as 'A mighty fortress is our God.'" In modern criticism the term metaphor is used more broadly, to include various kinds of poetic comparisons, not only metaphors in the narrow sense but similes (comparisons using *like* and *as*), personification, and so on. We shall treat metaphor here

---

[8] "Pied Beauty" from *Poems of Gerard Manley Hopkins*, third edition, edited by W. H. Gardner. Copyright 1948 by Oxford University Press, Inc. Reprinted by permission.

in a very general way as an assertion (or implication) of similarity between two phenomena not usually thought of as similar:

(a) O my luve is like a red, red rose

(b) Though rose-leaves die of grieving

(c) lady through whose profound and fragile lips
the sweet small clumsy feet of April came

into the ragged meadow of my soul.[9]

(E. E. CUMMINGS, 1894–   )

There is no doubt that all language tends to be metaphorical: we talk about the teeth of gears, the life-blood of commerce, the heart of a problem. We talk about cold wars and iron curtains, and we call each other skunks, angels, and squares. Most of these expressions have become what are sometimes called *dead metaphors,* meaning that we no longer think of them as metaphors at all. What the poet—or other creative writer—manages is to produce live metaphors, comparisons which suggest likenesses we would never have thought of.

In the context of this book, metaphor is of special interest as another instance of the principle of likeness-and-difference. When Robert Burns writes:

O my luve is like a red, red rose,

his metaphor is expressive partly because his girl (or his feeling for her) is in many ways not at all like a rose (or his feeling for roses). On the other hand, the assertion "My dory is like a boat" is not a metaphor but a crude definition, because the two things compared are too much alike.

By nature, then, metaphors always involve parallelism; but at the same time they also imply contrast. Thus metaphors help to evoke phenomena in two ways at once: by suggesting resemblances and by reminding us of differences.

Allusion

Technically, an allusion (not to be confused with an *ill*usion) is merely a reference to something apart from the immediate subject,

---

[9] Copyright 1926, 1954 by E. E. Cummings. Reprinted from *Poems: 1923–1954* by E. E. Cummings by permission of Harcourt, Brace & World, Inc., and the author.

such as history, other literature, legend, mythology, or contemporary affairs. But in effect an allusion is really a special kind of metaphor, because it always implies comparison (and contrast) between the subject at hand and the thing alluded to. The comparison may be seriously intended or it may be comic, satiric, ironic, or a mixture of these things. An example of irony is the title of Owen's poem "Arms and the Boy" (p. 67, Chapter 4). This alludes ironically to the famous opening line ("Arms and the man I sing") of Vergil's *Aeneid,* which is a glorification of the heroics of war written in the classical epic form of Homer's *Iliad* and *Odyssey.*

When a writer uses allusions, he is always taking a calculated risk: the reader may not know anything about what is alluded to, may not even recognize that he is faced with an allusion; for example, many American readers probably would not know that eight o'clock—the title of Housman's poem—is the traditional hour for public execution in England. Or the reader may take offense at what seems needless showing off by the author. On the other hand, the great virtue of allusions, which makes them worth the risk, is their tremendous economy. They enable a writer, by the mere mention of a name or phrase, to bring into play a whole new range of associations, thus adding immeasurably to the richness of his work. This is one reason why poets like T. S. Eliot and novelists like James Joyce (in his later work) take the gamble of depending very heavily upon learned allusions to older literature.

Imagery

This is a poetic element to which scholars have given much attention in recent years. Actually, imagery is an ingredient of all creative writing, because an image is simply any fragment of virtual life which involves the reader's *senses* (sight, hearing, touch, smell, taste, and so on). The term *image* can be applied to units of any size, from individual words to entire works. Thus the whole poem "Stopping by Woods" presents an image, and so do many of the individual lines, such as

> He gives his harness bells a shake

or

> The woods are lovely, dark and deep.

It should be obvious that images can be produced by any or all of the elements discussed earlier—separate words, rhythm, all of the techniques based on sound, metaphors, allusions.

Some poets work even more with images than they do with sounds. It has even been suggested that poets might be classified in terms of their affinity to different kinds of nonverbal artists: the poet who relies heavily on sound is like the musical composer; the "imagist" is more like a painter or sculptor. Here is an imagist poem by Stephen Crane which depends, for its irony, on the picture it paints:

The Heart

In the desert
I saw a creature, naked, bestial,
Who squatting on the ground,
Held his heart in his hands,
And ate of it.
I said, "Is it good, friend?"
"It is bitter—bitter," he answered;
"But I like it
Because it is bitter,
And because it is my heart." [10]

(STEPHEN CRANE, 1871–1900)

One aspect of imagery that is especially intriguing is the fact that every good creative writer seems to be partial to particular kinds of imagery, and even to particular patterns of images. These tend to recur in all of his writing, and hence constitute a distinctive feature of his "style." The greatest writers—such as Shakespeare—possess imaginations of such scope that the patterns of imagery vary from one work to the next, thus contributing in important ways to the uniqueness of the virtual life of each work. *Hamlet,* for instance, has been found to be full of images related to disease, corruption, and death, whereas in *Macbeth* the dominant recurrent images involve blood, fog, confusion, and madness.

Indirection

Each of the aspects of poetry we have looked at so far—words, rhythm, rhyme, alliteration, onomatopoeia, metaphor, allusion, and

[10] "The Heart" by Stephen Crane. From *Stephen Crane: An Omnibus,* edited by Robert Wooster Stallman. Reprinted by permission of Alfred A. Knopf, Inc.

imagery—is also an *element* of poetry. But poetry exhibits other hallmarks which are not so much elements as general characteristics.

For example, there is the tremendous economy, conciseness, condensing power of good poetry. To state in prose just the ideas imbedded in a first-rate poem usually takes many more words than the poem itself contains; and yet these "ideas" are only one strand in the poetic fabric, only a layer of the poem's total meaning as experience.

This compactness is one of the most striking features of poetry; but it confronts us with a paradox: for another, even more striking feature of poetry is its fondness for *indirection*. This is the quality, or kind of strategy, which Robert Frost (speaking metaphorically) calls "metaphor" in his famous remark:

> There are many things I have found myself saying about poetry, but the chiefest of these is that it is metaphor, saying one thing and meaning another, saying one thing in terms of another, . . . the pleasure of ulteriority.

The poet uses remarkably few words and yet he does everything indirectly. It is as if he took the old, meandering, high-crowned road and yet got to his destination more quickly than he could have on the thruway. There is a magic about this which no amount of analysis can ever quite explain. For instance:

London

I wander thro' each charter'd street,
Near where the charter'd Thames does flow,
And mark in every face I meet
Marks of weakness, marks of woe.

In every cry of every Man,
In every Infant's cry of fear,
In every voice, in every ban,
The mind-forg'd manacles I hear.

How the Chimney-sweeper's cry
Every black'ning Church appalls,
And the hapless Soldier's sigh
Runs in blood down Palace walls.

But most thro' midnight streets I hear
How the youthful Harlot's curse
Blasts the new born Infant's tear,
And blights with plagues the Marriage hearse.

(WILLIAM BLAKE)

Any adequate "interpretation" of this famous poem would run to many times the number of sentences Blake needed. For his subject is not merely London, but also Western civilization; the action the poem depicts is not merely a stroll through London's midnight streets, but a lifetime of angry scrutiny of the weaknesses of modern society; the images evoked are not merely the casual impressions of a transient, but symbols for conditions that have inspired two or three centuries of debate and gradual reform—social, economic, political, medical, religious, and philosophic. In fact, the basic viewpoint from which Blake indicts organized society here is not unlike that from which the modern Beats write ("In every voice in every ban/The mind-forg'd manacles I hear"), though his poem is infinitely better than anything the Beat movement has turned out so far.

Both the economy and the power—they are related, of course—of Blake's poem derive largely from its indirectness. Like all good poetry—like all good creative writing—"London" attacks its subject from an angle, obliquely, in roundabout fashion. At least, the approach is indirect from the point of view of the informative writer, which is the instinctive point of view of most of us. An artist might argue otherwise—that nothing could be more straightforward than a direct appeal to the imagination, the senses, and the feelings.

But from our vantage point the strategy of creative writing is always one of indirection. In fact, a little thought will show that all of the "elements" we have been discussing are essentially devices for indirection, means whereby the poet can *suggest* things, via the nonintellectual faculties, instead of *stating* them in the direct manner which the intellect usually prefers.

Indirection helps to explain, of course, why creative literature is often so hard to reduce to conceptual terms. Concepts are usually present (sometimes as an important element in the poem, sometimes relatively unimportant); however, they appear in disguise, are suggested rather than stated, are implicit rather than explicit. But this is simply the artist's way, and reminds us again of a principle we noted back in Chapter 2: that the *primary* target of the creative writer is not the intellect but the senses and imagination and feelings, the imagination through the senses and feelings, and back to the senses and emotions by way of the imagination.

In "London," Blake is not deliberately trying to make it hard for the reader; *good* creative writers seldom play such games with their readers. He is writing as explicitly as he can without losing some of what he has to say or without so radically changing his way of saying it that, in Bertrand Russell's phrase, "the stream of his experience will be lost in a dusty desert."

The crucial role of *form* in creative literature is one major example of indirection: structure or pattern largely takes the place of direct statement, in the informative sense. We have already looked in this chapter at various ways in which form expresses meaning indirectly: the varying rhythms in Housman's "Eight O'Clock" and Pound's "The Return," the contrasting smoothness and harshness of Owen's "Greater Love," and the "dappled" "asymmetrical" pattern of Hopkins' "Pied Beauty." Another major example is the constant presence of *plurisign,* in both senses of that term. In other words, throughout our study of creative writing we have been talking about various kinds of indirection, without calling them that. But there are certain special kinds of indirection which we have hardly mentioned up to this point. Among them are *understatement, overstatement,* and *irony.* The first two are probably self-explanatory, but a note on the third is in order because irony is so much discussed in modern criticism.

In irony, as in both comedy and tragedy, we find incongruity, inappropriateness, discrepancy. This is true whether the irony is of language, of situation, or of tone.

Irony of language occurs when the literal meaning of words is the reverse of their intended meaning. Irony of situation exists when the relationship between characters or the outcome of events seems the reverse of what would normally be expected or appropriate. Irony of tone exists when one is made to feel that the author's own point of view is the reverse of his narrator's. These definitions are too simple, and there is no room here to illustrate the many kinds of irony, but we will be noting some examples in the next few chapters.

The Interplay of the Elements

This chapter's rapid survey of a few aspects of poetry may be misleading in several ways. For instance, in the interest of simplicity we have omitted many important things; some of these will be worked in as we proceed. Again, by talking about poetry exclusively we may have obscured the fact that all of these things can readily be found in other types of creative writing and also in much informative and persuasive writing. And finally, any such parading of elements one by one, no matter how elaborate, tends to imply that these things exist for their own sake. But this is true only of bad writing.

In good creative writing, all of the elements work together to perform the poem's total task. Nothing is nonfunctional. This is what the critics mean by the "organic unity" of any successful work of art. Only the incompetent or fake creative writer adds a dash of alliteration, or a sprinkling of metaphors and images, simply to doll up his work.

There are many ways of demonstrating this interplay of the parts in poetry. One good way is to try stripping a poem down, element by element, until we have reduced it to a prose paraphrase; an exercise at the end of this chapter suggests that the reader attempt this experiment. It will reveal many subtle aspects of poetry that we have had to ignore here, just as stripping down a complex piece of machinery can teach us many fine points about how it works.

Another way of showing the organic unity of good poetry is through formal analysis of a few individual poems. This will be the business of the next chapter.

EXERCISES

A. Think about the following questions for class discussion:
  1. Can you think of more examples, besides those mentioned at the beginning of the chapter, of works which show the blurring of distinctions between types of creative writing?
  2. Can you offer some possible reasons why rhythm is an ingredient of all art, not only verbal but also visual and musical?
  3. Be prepared to discuss the function of rhythm and other sound effects in Owen's "Greater Love," Housman's "Eight O'Clock," Tennyson's "Break, Break, Break," and Blake's "London."
  4. Make a collection of dead metaphors from everyday speech.
  5. Be prepared to analyze, in terms of the general principle of likeness-and-difference, the *over-all* structure of each of the following poems: Owen's "Song of Songs" and "Greater Love," Housman's "Eight O'Clock," Pound's "The Return" and "An Immorality," Tennyson's "Break, Break, Break," Hopkins' "Pied Beauty," and Blake's "London."

B. Find a short poem that seems to you both striking and good. Then try the experiment of stripping it down, element by element, to a mere prose statement. In your first revised version try to avoid spoiling anything but the rhythm; then write a second version which also spoils the rhyme scheme; in your third version eliminate all the other sound effects; in your next get rid of all the most evocative words in the original by substituting synonyms; and finally eliminate all of the basic metaphors, allusions, and images. You should now have a very flat, possibly even trivial, piece of prose. Next, consider these questions: Which elements matter most in this poem? Do all of the elements work together? Are there any elements which seem quite unimportant, which contribute very little to the poem as a whole?

C. Find two poems which are written in the same meter but which create very different kinds of virtual life. Then try to explain what makes the two poems so different.

D. Find a short poem (or paragraph of creative prose) in which you feel that *sound effects* are especially important, and write a short analysis of the various ways sound is used there.

E. Find a short poem (or paragraph of creative prose) in which the *metaphors* seem to you unusually striking, and write a short analysis of how they function.

F. Do the same thing (as in E) with a poem (or paragraph of creative prose) which depends heavily on *allusions*.

G. Do the same thing (as in E and F) with a poem (or prose paragraph) in which the *imagery* strikes you as particularly interesting. Then try to explain what other elements are mainly responsible for the creation of this imagery.

H. Find a short passage of *creative prose* which exhibits several of the poetic elements described in this chapter, and write an account of what they are and how they combine to produce the total effect of the passage.

I. Do the same thing (as in H) with a passage of *informative* prose.

10. Some Poems Analyzed

Critics are rarely faithful to their labels and their
special strategies. . . . For the poem is like the monstrous Orillo in Boiardo's *Orlando Innamorato*. When
the sword lops off any member of the monster, that
member is immediately rejoined to the body, and the
monster is as formidable as ever. But the poem is even
more formidable than the monster, for Orillo's adversary
finally gained a victory by an astonishing feat of dexterity: he slashed off both the monster's arms and quick
as a wink seized them and flung them into the river.
The critic who vaingloriously trusts his method to account for the poem, to exhaust the poem, is trying to
emulate this dexterity: he thinks that he, too, can win
by throwing the lopped-off arms into the river. But he
is doomed to failure. Neither fire nor water will suffice
to prevent the rejoining of the mutilated members to
the monstrous torso. There is only one way to conquer
the monster: you must eat it, bones, blood, skin, pelt,
and gristle. And even then the monster is not dead,
for it lives in you, is assimilated into you, and you are
different . . . for having eaten it.[1]

ROBERT PENN WARREN, "Pure and Impure Poetry"

Why Analyze Poetry?

If what Warren says above is true, why are some people forever
trying to analyze poems and—for that matter—stories and plays and
other works of art? They do it for various reasons. A few people,
artists themselves, analyze in order to learn more about their craft.
Others are driven by simple curiosity, the natural desire to better

[1] FROM "Pure and Impure Poetry" by Robert Penn Warren, from *Selected
Essays* by Robert Penn Warren. Copyright 1958 by Random House, Inc. Reprinted by permission of the publisher.

understand, just for its own sake, how the poem works. Others would go beyond understanding to appreciation. If things are very complex, or a little out of our line, we *have* to understand them before we can appreciate them; but even things which seem too simple to be interesting may turn out, on analysis, to have fine points which make them well worth our attention. Still others analyze because they know that the better they understand how a thing is made, and how it works, the better prepared they are to use it properly.

Contrary to popular opinion, analysis can do very little harm to a good poem. The only work of art that permanently suffers from critical analysis is a bad one. Even when we get tired of a creative work after seeing it torn apart too often, or too wrong-headedly, if the work is really any good it usually outlasts the temporary unpleasantness. Almost always we come back to it with deeper pleasure than before; and invariably we are better equipped than before to enjoy new works.

Ideally, of course, literary analysis eventually becomes something the reader performs instinctively, just as in time he learns to analyze his tennis form or his fly-casting technique without conscious thought. But this kind of skill comes later. In the beginning, a little deliberate intellectual effort, and even some coaching, can help a great deal.

In this chapter we will analyze several poems, bringing to bear on them some of the theories presented in the last two chapters. None of the analyses will even try for completeness. An occasional question will invite the reader to carry the analysis further, either on his own or through class discussion. The poems themselves are an arbitrary selection from among a great many which have to do, in one way or another, with the general theme of Time. However, most of them, being poems, also deal with other subjects as well. This is especially true of the more complex ones. In general, we will progress from simpler poems to more complicated ones.

Our first specimen, which is about as short as a good poem could be, shows how deceptive an apparent simplicity can be in poetry:

The Span of Life

The old dog barks backward without getting up.
I can remember when he was a pup.[2]

(ROBERT FROST)

On the most literal level, the piece of virtual life evoked here is simply the speaker's perception that a dog he has known since puppyhood is growing old. But even without the title, we at once see these two lines also as a metaphor for all mortal life. We, like Frost, recognize that this dog is a symbol for man and for everything which grows old. We sense this meaning because of the vividness of Frost's *contrast* between enfeebled-dog-now and vivacious-puppy-then.

The poem is based on contrast, both visual and auditory. The first line gives us a sharp slow-motion picture of the reclining dog turning his head back over his shoulder to bark a greeting; the second line evokes an equally rapid motion picture of a bounding, leaping puppy all too eager to welcome his master home. However, these visual images are not created simply by the meanings of the words. Normally we would not expect rhythm to be very important in a two-line poem, but it is here, and so are other sound effects. There is distinct contrast in the movement of the two lines: the first limps along, haltingly, wearily, as if crippled; the second bounces by in normal good health and is gone with a switch of the tail. The first line takes twice as long to read, is rhythmically irregular, has three words of more than one syllable, and contains an awkward pattern of hard consonants interspersed with long vowels, so that we have to slow up if we read it properly. The second line is far shorter even to look at, is rhythmically regular, and is made up entirely of monosyllables—except for *remember* which fits into the metrical scheme so naturally that we are not aware of its length.

Thus the sound parallels the sense, auditory images reinforce the visual ones, and the two together create the basic contrast. And yet the contrasting lines are at the same time linked together through basic meter and rhyme.

But all this ignores the title, which introduces an extra dimension. "The Span of Life" is too pretentious a title, in a sense, for a mere couplet about a mere dog; it might lead us to expect a more elaborate (and pompous) kind of poem about life and death. By over-titling his little poem, Frost introduces a mildly humorous note into a poem that is otherwise quite noncommittal and which deals with a serious subject. One can even see the title as a sly dig by the "realistic," conversational Frost at the solemn way his more "romantic" literary predecessors treated such themes.

Question: In what ways does this poem violate the straight chronological form often found in "biographical" pieces? (After all,

Frost's couplet *is* a fragment of biography, even though its immediate subject is a dog.)

Our second specimen is a very famous treatment of essentially the same theme Frost is dealing with—the ravages of Time—but in a totally different manner:

Ozymandias

I met a traveller from an antique land
Who said: Two vast and trunkless legs of stone
Stand in the desert. Near them, on the sand,
Half sunk, a shattered visage lies, whose frown,
And wrinkled lip, and sneer of cold command,
Tell that its sculptor well those passions read
Which yet survive, stamped on these lifeless things,
The hand that mocked them and the heart that fed:
And on the pedestal these words appear:
"My name is Ozymandias, king of kings:
Look on my works, ye Mighty, and despair!"
Nothing beside remains. Round the decay
Of that colossal wreck, boundless and bare
The lone and level sands stretch far away.

(PERCY BYSSHE SHELLEY, 1792–1822)

Frost is a "realist" among poets, fond of the simple, the unpretentious, the commonplace, and the homespun, in both his images and his language; Shelley, on the other hand, is the epitome of romanticism, with his love of the awesome, the grandiose, the exotic, the superlative. Whereas Frost's technique usually is that of understatement, Shelley's is usually that of overstatement. Both techniques work.

"Ozymandias" is a powerful image of the futility of man's efforts to conquer Time. The basic contrast, around which the whole poem is organized, is primarily a pictorial one: the shattered fragments of some ancient tyrant's attempt to imprint his own ego forever on the earth's face are set off against a desolate waste of sand. Time and the forces of nature have almost obliterated even this massive gesture of vanity. But the irony of the poem does not stop there. For the human ego still speaks in the expression on the sculptured face and the arrogance of the inscription, whereas the lone and level sands remain forever silent and speechless. And there is still more: Time has rendered the tyrant's message itself ironically ambiguous. It had been meant to point to the matchless grandeur of one man's works; instead it now points to the ultimate futility of all of man's works.

Thus Shelley piles irony on irony, just as he piles up exorbitant language: *antique, vast, visage, sneer of cold command, passions, king of kings, my works ye Mighty, nothing beside remains, colossal, boundless and bare, stretch far away*. This is grandiose diction quite unlike the language of Frost, but in this context, and in a great romantic's hands, it works magnificently, because although the central contrast is basically visual, the oversize language greatly enhances it. So do the variations in rhythm. Compare the insulting terseness of the dead king's ultimatum with the flowing expansiveness of the final sentence.

Questions: Can you find the name Ozymandias in any reference work? Why did Shelley use it? What does he mean by the line: "The hand that mocked them and the heart that fed"? What extra contrast does this line add to the poem? This poem is a sonnet, of the Italian or Petrarchan type (which always consists of an "octave"— an eight-line section—followed by a "sestet"—a six-line section, each section having its own rhyme scheme); what role does the sonnet-form play in this poem?

Both Frost and Shelley deal quite directly with Time as an agent of destruction. Frost is content with a small-scale instance of the change brought about by Time; Shelley's vision of its inexorable power is on a grander scale. Our next poet, Andrew Marvell, combines the two scales in an amusing and yet impressive way:

To His Coy Mistress

Had we but world enough, and time,
This coyness, Lady, were no crime.
We would sit down and think which way
To walk, and pass our long love's day;
Thou by the Indian Ganges' side
Shouldst rubies find; I by the tide
Of Humber would complain. I would
Love you ten years before the Flood;
And you should, if you please, refuse
Till the conversion of the Jews.
My vegetable love should grow
Vaster than empires, and more slow.
An hundred years should go to praise
Thine eyes, and on thy forehead gaze;
Two hundred to adore each breast,

But thirty thousand to the rest;
An age at least to every part,
And the last age should show your heart.
For, Lady, you deserve this state,
Nor would I love at lower rate.
    But at my back I always hear
Time's wingèd chariot hurrying near;
And yonder all before us lie
Deserts of vast eternity.
Thy beauty shall no more be found,
Nor in thy marble vault shall sound
My echoing song; then worms shall try
Thy long preserved virginity,
And your quaint honor turn to dust,
And into ashes all my lust.
The grave's a fine and private place,
But none, I think, do there embrace.
    Now therefore, while the youthful hue
Sits on thy skin like morning dew,
And while thy willing soul transpires
At every pore with instant fires,
Now let us sport us while we may;
And now, like amorous birds of prey,
Rather at once our time devour,
Than languish in his slow-chapped power.
Let us roll all our strength, and all
Our sweetness, up into one ball;
And tear our pleasures with rough strife
Through the iron gates of life.
Thus, though we cannot make our sun
Stand still, yet we will make him run.
                    (ANDREW MARVELL, 1621–78)

On a first reading, this famous poem seems to have a simple logical form. Its three parts follow the pattern of a commonplace sort of argument: If . . . But . . . Therefore. Very few of Marvell's lines are actually needed to present the *conceptual* backbone of the poem:

Had we but world enough, and time,
This coyness, Lady, were no crime.
But at my back I always hear
Time's wingèd chariot hurrying near;
Now therefore, while the youthful hue
Sits on thy skin like morning dew,
Now let us sport us while we may.

This sums up the poem's "argument," though scarcely in pure conceptual language. Few informative writers would call chastity a "crime," nor compare "hue" (which implies color) to "dew" (which is colorless). Nor can we, without serious loss, change *hurrying* to *drawing*, even though the latter would fit the meter better; nor change *sport us* to *make time*, even though this would give us an extra play on the idea of Time. In short, even our condensation of "To His Coy Mistress" remains a poem, because the language itself is all-important and will not submit to the rewording test which most informative writing passes so easily.

Our abridgement of the poem reveals its "logic" clearly enough; but it also reveals how much more than logic even an intellectual poem contains. Reducing a poem (or a work of fiction) to its bare conceptual (or narrative) skeleton usually helps us to see its overall *structure;* at the same time, it reminds us of the enormous importance of *texture* in works of art. Someone once wrote a piece, entitled "How to Be Efficient with Fewer Violins," which pretended to be the report of an imaginary efficiency expert after an evening at a symphony concert. His "report" read in part as follows:

> For considerable periods the four oboe players had nothing to do. The number should be reduced and the work spread more evenly over the whole concert, thus eliminating peaks of activity.
>
> All the twelve violins were playing identical notes; this seems unnecessary duplication. The staff of this section should be drastically cut. If a larger volume of sound is required, it could be obtained by means of electronic apparatus.
>
> Much effort was absorbed in the playing of demi-semi-quavers; this seems to be an unnecessary refinement. It is recommended that all notes be rounded off to the nearest semi-quaver. If this were done it would be possible to use trainees and lower-grade operatives more extensively.
>
> There seems to be much repetition of some musical passages. Scores should be drastically pruned. No useful purpose is served by repeating on the horns a passage which has already been handled by the strings. It is estimated that if all redundant passages were eliminated, the whole concert time of two hours could be reduced to 20 minutes and there would be no need for an interval [intermission].[3]

This time-and-motion man might well prefer our abstract of "To His Coy Mistress" to the original; no doubt he would fail to see

[3] FROM "How to Be Efficient with Fewer Violins," reprinted from *Harper's Magazine.* By permission of *Harper's Magazine.*

that the pattern of ideas in a poem is only one thread or layer in a complex and multi-level design. Even the form of Marvell's poem involves a number of other patterns, each recognizable in terms of the principle of likeness-and-difference.

For instance, there is a series of images of Time and Space. In Part I, both Time and Space are pictured (fancifully, of course) as being boundless. Then, in Part II, real Time and Space are shown to be narrowly bounded: mortal Time is the brief interim before the "wingèd chariot" inevitably catches up with us; and mortal Space, at that moment, is reduced to the narrow confines of the grave. (By contrast, *im*mortal Time and Space are a quite different matter: both are brought together in the single image of "Deserts of vast eternity," but it is a most unappealing image.) Finally, in Part III, the speaker proposes that he and his mistress beat the "wingèd chariot" by voluntarily confining themselves to the narrowest space possible ("Let us roll all our strength, and all our sweetness up into one ball"), thus gaining at least a moral triumph over Time. This very rich and suggestive pattern of images is presumably one of the things which the time-and-motion man would have eliminated from the poem, because it is by no means implied by the intellectual argument.

Then there is a second pattern of images, involving nonhuman organisms. In the first part, the speaker imagines an "ideal" mode of love-making which he describes as "vegetable"—infinitely slow, almost mindless, and ultimately inhuman. It is therefore impossible, and his mistress must wait—but not long—for another kind of sub-human love-making—the depredations of the grave-worms. Unless, of course (third part), she is willing to join him in a kind of love-making which is like that of "amorous birds of prey."

But there are still other threads in the design. For instance, the tone and technique change with each part. In Part I the tone is frivolous and mildly satiric. Marvell begins by labeling her reluctance a crime, but then shows it to be merely silly. The technique is overstatement; her wish to wait is exaggerated to absurd proportions. Then, quite abruptly, the tone changes with Part II, becoming serious, even portentous. The language is still high-flown, but the matter is solemn. And the technique is essentially that of understatement. And finally, in Part III, the tone becomes both serious and excited, importunate, sensual rather than philosophic. And the technique is neither overstatement nor understatement, but direct. Actually, the pattern is not quite as simple as this, because the nonserious first part ends on a serious note (the sincere compliment to the woman), the serious second part ends on a humorous note ("The grave's a fine and private place/But none, I think, do there embrace"), and the eager and sensual third part ends with a bit of philosophical whimsy.

Thus a number of the speaker's most powerful arguments are not stated explicitly at all, but are suggested by the texture of the poem: that her hesitance is ridiculous, that neither virginity nor honor make much sense in the grave, and that she is far too lovely in her passionate youthfulness to waste herself or to deny him.

In short, Marvell's poem is a great deal more complex than any simple abstract of it could suggest. The interested reader will find many things in it which have not been mentioned. For example, consider these questions: In what sense does the poem involve the theme of passiveness versus active willing? What is the effect of Marvell's peculiar intermingling of levity and gravity in this poem? In what ways do rhythm, pace, and other sound effects reinforce some of the formal patterns we have looked at?

The next poem, by Archibald MacLeish, was suggested by Marvell's "Coy Mistress," in particular by the lines "But at my back I always hear/Time's wingèd chariot hurrying near." It has been justly praised as a technical *tour de force,* but as we shall see is much more than just that:

You, Andrew Marvell

And here face down beneath the sun
And here upon earth's noonward height
To feel the always coming on
The always rising of the night:

To feel creep up the curving east
The earthly chill of dusk and slow
Upon those under lands the vast
And ever-climbing shadow grow

And strange at Ecbatan the trees
Take leaf by leaf the evening strange
The flooding dark about their knees
The mountains over Persia change

And now at Kermanshah the gate
Dark empty and the withered grass

And through the twilight now the late
Few travelers in the westward pass

And Baghdad darken and the bridge
Across the silent river gone
And through Arabia the edge
Of evening widen and steal on

And deepen on Palmyra's street
The wheel rut on the ruined stone
And Lebanon fade out and Crete
High through the clouds and overblown

And over Sicily the air
Still flashing with the landward gulls
And loom and slowly disappear
The sails above the shadowy hulls

And Spain go under and the shore
Of Africa the gilded sand
And evening vanish and no more
The low pale light across that land

Nor now the long light on the sea:

And here face downward in the sun
To feel how swift how secretly
The shadow of the night comes on . . .⁴
      (ARCHIBALD MACLEISH, 1892–   )

If in "To His Coy Mistress" the most obvious unifying device is a logical argument, here it is geography. MacLeish picks up Marvell's image of "Time's wingèd chariot" and depicts the gradual arrival of darkness over one country after another, from east to west, as the earth turns. This sense of the march of night is located in the consciousness of an American—which MacLeish himself is—because night's advance first appears in the Middle East, then progresses across the Near East, the length of the Mediterranean, and the Atlantic. The poem concludes where it started, in the mind of the American, who is still prone in the light of the declining sun.

On the surface, this is the whole poem: a remarkable evocation of an imaginative man's sense of the turning of the earth on its axis. The meter is very regular, the pace is constant, and practically all punctuation is omitted to enhance the impression of this cycle's in-

---

⁴ "You, Andrew Marvell" by Archibald MacLeish. Reprinted by permission of Houghton Mifflin Company.

evitability. Each stanza is linked with the preceding one in some way, to further reinforce the sense of a continuous and inexorable natural process.

But this geographic pattern, like the syllogistic pattern in "To His Coy Mistress," is merely the starting point, the reader's opening wedge into the poem. Why does MacLeish arbitrarily begin with the Middle East and end with America? Why did he elect to follow the sun's setting along a path that falls roughly between the thirty-fifth and the fortieth parallels? And why does he mention these particular place-names? The answer to all three questions is that the poem's structure is not merely geographic but historic. The poem begins and ends not only here—in America—but now—at this moment in world history. And the middle seven stanzas not only trace the advance of night from Iran to America, but they trace the successive decline of the great dynasties of the past. The flash back begins with the earliest civilizations we know of, those of the ancient Mesopotamians, Medes, and Persians, then follows the progress of civilization westward through Arabia, Damascus, Phoenicia and Palestine, the Aegean Sea (the Minoan and later the Greek empires), Italy (the Roman Empire), Spain (the great Christian empires of the Middle Ages and early Renaissance), and Africa (the great Mohammedan civilization of the same era). Then we cross the Atlantic and are in America.

Is MacLeish suggesting that the Western world is following in the footsteps of the great earlier civilizations? Night in the narrower sense must inevitably envelop our hemisphere as it already has, in the poem, Asia and Europe and Africa and the Atlantic. But how about "night" in the broader sense also? We may now find it interesting to speculate as to why MacLeish's Western observer of these diurnal and millennial movements is pictured, both first and last, as lying "face downward in the sun." Is this merely a gently satiric dig at Andrew Marvell's lover with his philosophy of "Eat, drink, and be merry, for tomorrow you die"? Or is MacLeish's intent more serious here? Is he implying that to lie prone in the sun, luxuriating in the pleasures of the moment, is no way to cope with the perhaps imminent destruction of this latest of history's great civilizations? Seen in this light (or twilight) a word like *secretly* (in the next-to-last line) begins to make more than alliterative sense. So does the title—"You, Andrew Marvell"—which carries a note of accusation, not necessarily of Marvell's lover's amoral attitude toward sex, but of the implications of this attitude when carried into the spheres of political, social, and economic action.

The reader will find it interesting to look more closely at several aspects of MacLeish's poem which we have ignored so far: for example, just how do various kinds of sound effects contribute to the poem's power to evoke all of these speculations? Why does MacLeish keep alternating between pictures of specific, concrete objects (close-ups, in effect) and broad panoramic shots? Do you notice other similarities here to motion picture technique? Why is there not one complete sentence in the whole poem?

Our next poem, one of Shakespeare's best-known sonnets, takes us back to the joint theme of Love and Time which "To His Coy Mistress" focuses on, but treats it as differently as could be:

Sonnet CXVI

Let me not to the marriage of true minds
Admit impediments. Love is not love
Which alters when it alteration finds,
Or bends with the remover to remove:
O, no! it is an ever-fixèd mark,
That looks on tempests and is never shaken;
It is the star to every wand'ring bark,
Whose worth's unknown, although his height be taken.
Love's not Time's fool, though rosy lips and cheeks
Within his bending sickle's compass come;
Love alters not with his brief hours and weeks,
But bears it out even to the edge of doom:—
    If this be error and upon me proved,
    I never writ, nor no man ever loved.

As always in poetry, it would be a mistake to identify the speaker here with the poet himself, and this kind of identification is especially dangerous in dealing with Shakespeare, who was basically a dramatist and who in the course of his whole work expresses a great many different conceptions of both Love and Time, as of most other perennial themes. So the voice in this sonnet is not Shakespeare's but a nameless speaker's. Of this speaker, we can assert one thing for sure: his notion of love is poles apart from that of Marvell's speaker. To Shakespeare's man, love is more than a physical relationship; love's quality is to be judged by the integrity the lovers demonstrate more than by the pleasure they enjoy.

In fact, the central contrast in the poem involves the difference between these two kinds of love: the partial kind stressed by Marvell, which is bound to be inconstant because it depends entirely on physical factors that are subject to the mutations of Time; and a richer kind which can escape Time's sickle because it is a union of spirits as well as of bodies. (Note that Shakespeare's speaker does not view the two kinds of love as opposite, but as part and whole; his kind remains an invaluable "star" even though its "height be taken"—that is, no matter how fully it may be consummated in a physical sense.)

But this contrast between two kinds of love is supplemented by another contrast: that of the first four lines and the last two, taken as a unit, with the eight lines in between. The lines in the first group are deliberately "factual," pedantic, really legalistic in tone; the middle eight are passionate, full of feeling, grand images, and metaphors. The very bluntness and prosaicness of the concluding couplet intensify the passion of the middle part, as does the ingenious but essentially intellectual play on words in the first quatrain. The shift to the new "poetic" tone of the middle lines is signaled by the emphatic "O, no!" Within the middle part, the poem rapidly builds up to the climactic line "But bears it out even to the edge of doom." This is a long way from Marvell's ironic:

> The grave's a fine and private place
> But none, I think, do there embrace.

Incidentally, Shakespeare's poem illustrates another kind of sonnet form—usually *called* Shakespearean—which consists of three more-or-less parallel quatrains followed by a contrasting and concluding rhymed couplet.

Questions: Does the use of this kind of sonnet form serve any purpose in this particular poem? How do sound effects contribute to the pattern the poem makes?

In the following poem by John Donne, a contemporary of Shakespeare, we return to Marvell's kind of intellectual, witty poetry, but the aspect of love dealt with is one that Marvell's pleader wisely ignored:

Woman's Constancy

Now thou hast loved me one whole day;
To-morrow when thou leav'st, what wilt thou say?
Wilt thou then antedate some new made vow?

Or say that now
We are not just those persons, which we were?
Or, that oaths made in reverential fear
Of Love, and his wrath, any may forswear?
Or, as true deaths true marriages untie,

So lovers' contracts, images of those,
Bind but till sleep, death's image, them unloose?
Or, your own end to justify,
For having purpos'd change, and falsehood, you
Can have no way but falsehood to be true?
Vain lunatic, against these 'scapes I could
Dispute, and conquer, if I would,
Which I abstain to do;
For by tomorrow, I may think so too.

(JOHN DONNE, 1573–1631)

This type of poetry—sometimes called *metaphysical*—is highly
cerebral. One has to follow the pattern of ideas closely, and note
how they interweave. The drama of Donne's poem lies in the
elaborate way his speaker imagines the various reasons his mistress
might invent for breaking off their affair, each new reason being
less obvious and more farfetched than the preceding ones, only to
concede in the last line that he may want to use the same reasons
himself. Thus the title turns out to be ironic, for the subject is not
really "Woman's Constancy"—in fact, we have no evidence that *she*
intends to be either constant or inconstant—but the speaker's own
*in*constancy, of thought if not yet of action.

Question: How does the curious epithet *Vain lunatic* function in
this poem?

In contrast to Donne's rather theoretical treatment of the change
of mood which Time can bring to a love affair, here is a purely
sensual, unanalytic presentation of the same experience. Browning
wrote the poem in two parts, but they really belong together:

Meeting at Night

The gray sea and the long black land;
And the yellow half-moon large and low;
And the startled little waves that leap
In fiery ringlets from their sleep,
As I gain the cove with pushing prow,
And quench its speed i' the slushy sand.

Then a mile of warm sea-scented beach;
Three fields to cross till a farm appears;
A tap at the pane, the quick sharp scratch
And blue spurt of a lighted match,
And a voice less loud, through its joys and fears,
Than the two hearts beating each to each!

Parting at Morning

Round the cape of a sudden came the sea,
And the sun looked over the mountain's rim:
And straight was a path of gold for him,
And the need of a world of men for me.

As the titles indicate, the two parts of the poem contrast two phases, two aspects, of a love affair. Part I evokes the romantic, impatient, nervous, passionate, sensual nighttime world of the lovers, intent only on getting together; Part II suggests the commonplace, disciplined, calm, practical daytime world of routine affairs. The nighttime world is essentially a feminine one, the daytime world masculine.

In its development, the poem follows a narrative pattern, reaching its climax in the last four lines of Part I. But the most interesting thing about this narrative—as in Frost's "The Span of Life"—is how much is left out. It's not merely that there are Victorian asterisks after the lovers' initial embrace, but that we are given no "facts" about these people. We don't even know whether they are sweethearts or husband and wife, whether their relationship is illicit or proper. The whole "story" is told by means of a few carefully chosen images couched in language whose sound is very important. And all of these elements contribute to the basic contrast of mood.

In Part I, Time is intensified, each moment being packed with feeling and excitement; in Part II, Time has assumed its normal daytime dimensions. Thus Part I is three times as long as Part II. The celestial observer in Part I is the moon, feminine, a "yellow half-moon large and low"; in Part II the moon has been replaced by a striding, masculine sun proceeding on its daily course. The sea also is feminine in Part I—"The startled little waves that leap/In fiery ringlets from their sleep"—but masculine in Part II—"Round the cape of a sudden came the sea"—now all business, like the sun. The personification of the waves in the earlier metaphor foreshadows, by parallelism, the eager but apprehensive awakening of the girl (or wife?) from her sleep (or worried waiting?) when her lover arrives.

The rhythm of Part I is irregular, nervous, anticipatory. The pace of these lines accelerates, beginning awkwardly and slowly (as the lover strains at his oars, impatient to beach the cumbersome boat and take off by foot), then speeding up in eager anticipation until it reaches the dramatic climax of:

> A tap at the pane, the quick sharp scratch
> And blue spurt of a lighted match,

and finally relaxing, with a sigh, into the more regular rhythm of

> And a voice less loud, through its joys and fears,
> Than the two hearts beating each to each!

Thus the rhythm and pace of Part I parallel the movements and emotions of the lovers.

Then comes the strong, perfectly regular, masculine rhythm of Part II, which is all business and no pleasure—at least, no loverlike pleasure.

The first part is full of alliteration and onomatopoeia, sensuous language to reinforce the sensuousness of the images and tone:

> As I gain the cove with pushing prow
> And quench its speed i' the slushy sand.

Or, again, there are the four lines that begin with "A tap at the pane" and end with the lovers clasped to each other.

Browning engages in none of the witty intellectual gymnastics that characterize Donne's kind of poetry. His poem makes its appeal almost wholly to the imagination, the emotions, and the senses, to the last both directly and indirectly.

Questions: Try scanning the sixteen lines of Browning's two-part poem. What do you discover? Does the changed mood of "Parting at Morning" mean that this love affair is over, as Donne's speaker anticipates that his affair may shortly be?

We will conclude this chapter with two poems which record the attitudes toward Time of people grown too old to be lovers. Our first speaker has been both lover and man of affairs, but has outlived the heyday of his generation:

The Lamentation of the Old Pensioner

> Although I shelter from the rain
> Under a broken tree
> My chair was nearest to the fire

In every company
That talked of love or politics
Ere Time transfigured me.

Though lads are making pikes again
For some conspiracy,
And crazy rascals rage their fill
At human tyranny;
My contemplations are of Time
That has transfigured me.

There's not a woman turns her face
Upon a broken tree,
And yet the beauties that I loved
Are in my memory;
I spit into the face of Time
That has transfigured me.[5]

(WILLIAM BUTLER YEATS)

The most striking thing about this poem is its great economy,
though it may not be obvious at first how much Yeats gets into
three tight stanzas. Conceptually, the poem is simple enough: in
the first stanza the old man says that in his day he was a leading
figure in both political warfare and love-making; in the second
stanza he takes up the politics, and says that although the wars
still go on he is no longer interested in them, that in fact they now
seem silly to him; then in the third stanza he turns to the matter
of love, insisting that even though he is now out of the running,
he has his memories to keep him warm.

All this is straightforward enough for the least experienced taste.
But it is merely the frame around which Yeats wraps his poem. For
example, it fails even to suggest the power and subtlety with which
Yeats evokes, in order, three very different attitudes towards old
age. The tone of the first stanza is defensive, nostalgic, a little plain-
tive. He seems to be apologizing for his present circumstances and
justifying them by pointing out his past eminence. The tone of the
middle stanza shifts from self-defense to a rather smug offensive
against the younger generation who have displaced him: he pretends to have outgrown such "crazy" pastimes as waging political

warfare, to have matured from an active combatant into a philosopher. The lines:

> My contemplations are of Time
> That has transfigured me

contain a note of complacent self-congratulation that suggests sour grapes. But at least he has shifted the burden of proof to the young men. Then, in the final stanza, he locates his real defense in the fact that he has, in a sense, defeated time, by saving up in memory his past triumphs even though Time denies him new ones.

There are other subtleties in this very human portrait of old age. For example, Yeats surely hopes we will notice the inconsistency between the pensioner's attack on political activity and both his earlier boasting of his former role in politics and his final gesture of defiance in:

> I spit into the face of Time
> That has transfigured me.

If the old man can no longer "rage his fill/At *human* tyranny" he can at least rage at the tyranny of mortality. There's subversive spirit in the old boy yet; he's by no means the bystanding philosopher that he fancies himself. In fact, the last two lines throw the rest of the poem into stark relief, contradicting the traditional and banal with a fierceness that is startling.

Then there is the richness of the plurisign of the "broken tree." The first time, the metaphor refers primarily to his physical environment—the humble living quarters of an old man on a limited pension, and so on. But the next time the "broken tree" is his old man's body in contrast to the still youthful spirit which it houses. Most interesting of all is the refrain line, which takes on new meanings each time it is repeated.

Questions: Can you explain how the word *transfigured* changes in meaning as the poem develops? Why did Yeats use the word *transfigured* anyway? Does its use involve any allusion to its theological meaning? How does the strict stanza form contribute to the poem? (Notice how strict this pattern is; that all of the second, fourth, and sixth lines end in the same long *e* sound; and that the alternation of four-foot and three-foot lines is maintained throughout.)

Our final specimen, also by Yeats, expresses the reaction to the ravages of Time of a very different sort of man from the Old Pen-

sioner. This speaker's approach to life is that of an artist rather than
of a man of affairs, of an inveterate observer and creator rather than
of a natural player and fighter. Also, this old man's eyes are primarily on the future rather than on the past:

Sailing to Byzantium

I

That is no country for old men. The young
In one another's arms, birds in the trees,
—Those dying generations—at their song,
The salmon-falls, the mackerel-crowded seas,
Fish, flesh, or fowl, commend all summer long
Whatever is begotten, born, and dies.
Caught in that sensual music all neglect
Monuments of unageing intellect.

II

An aged man is but a paltry thing,
A tattered coat upon a stick, unless
Soul clap its hands and sing, and louder sing
For every tatter in its mortal dress,
Nor is there singing school but studying
Monuments of its own magnificence;
And therefore I have sailed the seas and come
To the holy city of Byzantium.

III

O sages standing in God's holy fire
As in the gold mosaic of a wall,
Come from the holy fire, perne in a gyre,
And be the singing-masters of my soul.
Consume my heart away; sick with desire
And fastened to a dying animal
It knows not what it is; and gather me
Into the artifice of eternity.

IV

Once out of nature I shall never take
My bodily form from any natural thing,
But such a form as Grecian goldsmiths make
Of hammered gold and gold enameling
To keep a drowsy Emperor awake;
Or set upon a golden bough to sing

To lords and ladies of Byzantium
Of what is past, or passing, or to come.[6]

We will leave the reader to attempt his own analysis of this poem, offering as aids only a few questions:

1. What is the central contrast here?
2. Why does Yeats use Byzantium as his symbolic city?
3. What is the speaker's attitude toward the "sensual" world? Is he like the Old Pensioner, scornful, perhaps a little jealous, of it? Or does he feel differently about it?
4. What role does *color* imagery play in this poem?
5. What poem discussed earlier in this chapter comes closest to expressing the attitude toward Time expressed here?
6. Is this a religious poem? If so, in what sense? If not, why do you say no?

EXERCISES

A. Write an analysis, like those offered in this chapter, of a poem which interests you. In your discussion try to define the over-all form of the poem, explain how the most important elements function, and then try to state what you feel the poem is all about, what it is trying to do.

B. Find another poem, preferably one you like, which also has to do with Time. Then write a discussion of this poem in which you compare its treatment of the theme of Time with that of one or more of the poems analyzed in the chapter. Time, in its innumerable aspects, is a favorite subject of poets, as it is of philosophers, so examples are easy to find. Here are a few suggestions: E. A. Robinson's "Miniver Cheevy," "Mr. Flood's Party," or "Eros Turannos"; G. M. Hopkins' "Spring and Fall: To a Young Child"; Dylan Thomas's "Fern Hill" or "Poem in October"; D. H. Lawrence's "Piano"; Robert Herrick's "To the Virgins, to Make Much of Time"; John Crowe Ransom's "Blue Girls"; many of Shakespeare's sonnets; W. H. Auden's "Musée des Beaux Arts"; Kenneth Fearing's "Dirge."

C. Try analyzing the following poem by T. S. Eliot. You will find it especially interesting to compare it with Marvell's "To His Coy

[6] "Sailing to Byzantium" by William Butler Yeats. Copyright, 1928 by The Macmillan Company. Copyright, 1956 by Georgie Yeats. Reprinted with permission of The Macmillan Company, New York, The Macmillan Company of Canada, Ltd., A. P. Watt & Son, London, and Mrs. William Butler Yeats from *The Collected Poems of William Butler Yeats.*

Mistress" and with the two Yeats poems, "The Lamentation of the Old Pensioner" and "Sailing to Byzantium."

The Love Song of J. Alfred Prufrock

S'io credesse che mia risposta fosse
A persona che mai tornasse al mondo,
Questa fiamma staria senza piu scosse.
Ma perciocche giammai di questo fondo
Non torno vivo alcun, s'i'odo il vero,
Senza tema d'infamia ti rispondo.

Let us go then, you and I,
When the evening is spread out against the sky
Like a patient etherised upon a table;
Let us go, through certain half-deserted streets,
The muttering retreats
Of restless nights in one-night cheap hotels
And sawdust restaurants with oyster-shells:
Streets that follow like a tedious argument
Of insidious intent
To lead you to an overwhelming question. . . .
Oh, do not ask, 'What is it?'
Let us go and make our visit.

In the room the women come and go
Talking of Michelangelo.

The yellow fog that rubs its back upon the window-panes,
The yellow smoke that rubs its muzzle on the window-panes
Licked its tongue into the corners of the evening,
Lingered upon the pools that stand in drains,
Let fall upon its back the soot that falls from chimneys,
Slipped by the terrace, made a sudden leap,
And seeing that it was a soft October night,
Curled once about the house, and fell asleep.

And indeed there will be time
For the yellow smoke that slides along the street
Rubbing its back upon the window-panes;
There will be time, there will be time
To prepare a face to meet the faces that you meet;
There will be time to murder and create,
And time for all the works and days of hands
That lift and drop a question on your plate;
Time for you and time for me,
And time yet for a hundred indecisions,

And for a hundred visions and revisions,
Before the taking of a toast and tea.

In the room the women come and go
Talking of Michelangelo.

And indeed there will be time
To wonder, 'Do I dare?' and, 'Do I dare?'
Time to turn back and descend the stair,
With a bald spot in the middle of my hair—
[They will say: 'How his hair is growing thin!']
My morning coat, my collar mounting firmly to the chin,
My necktie rich and modest, but asserted by a simple pin—
[They will say: 'But how his arms and legs are thin!']
Do I dare
Disturb the universe?
In a minute there is time
For decisions and revisions which a minute will reverse.

For I have known them all already, known them all—
Have known the evenings, mornings, afternoons,
I have measured out my life with coffee spoons;
I know the voices dying with a dying fall
Beneath the music from a farther room.
So how should I presume?

And I have known the eyes already, known them all—
The eyes that fix you in a formulated phrase,
And when I am formulated, sprawling on a pin,
When I am pinned and wriggling on the wall,
Then how should I begin
To spit out all the butt-ends of my days and ways?
And how should I presume?

And I have known the arms already, known them all—
Arms that are braceleted and white and bare
[But in the lamplight, downed with light brown hair!]
Is it perfume from a dress
That makes me so digress?
Arms that lie along a table, or wrap about a shawl.
And should I then presume?
And how should I begin?

. . . . . .

Shall I say, I have gone at dusk through narrow streets
And watched the smoke that rises from the pipes
Of lonely men in shirt-sleeves, leaning out of windows? . . .

I should have been a pair of ragged claws
Scuttling across the floors of silent seas.

. . . . .

And the afternoon, the evening, sleeps so peacefully!
Smoothed by long fingers,
Asleep . . . tired . . . or it malingers,
Stretched on the floor, here beside you and me.
Should I, after tea and cakes and ices,
Have the strength to force the moment to its crisis?
But though I have wept and fasted, wept and prayed,
Though I have seen my head [grown slightly bald] brought in upon a
   platter,
I am no prophet—and here's no great matter;
I have seen the moment of my greatness flicker,
And I have seen the eternal Footman hold my coat, and snicker,
And in short, I was afraid.

And would it have been worth it, after all,
After the cups, the marmalade, the tea,
Among the porcelain, among some talk of you and me,
Would it have been worth while,
To have bitten off the matter with a smile,
To have squeezed the universe into a ball
To roll it toward some overwhelming question,
To say: 'I am Lazarus, come from the dead,
Come back to tell you all, I shall tell you all'—
If one, settling a pillow by her head,
   Should say: 'That is not what I meant at all.
   That is not it, at all.'

And would it have been worth it, after all,
Would it have been worth while,
After the sunsets and the dooryards and the sprinkled streets,
After the novels, after the teacups, after the skirts that trail along the
   floor—
And this, and so much more?—
It is impossible to say just what I mean!
But as if a magic lantern threw the nerves in patterns on a screen:
Would it have been worth while
If one, settling a pillow or throwing off a shawl,
And turning toward the window, should say:
   'That is not it at all,
   That is not what I meant, at all.'

. . . . .

No! I am not Prince Hamlet, nor was meant to be;
Am an attendant lord, one that will do
To swell a progress, start a scene or two,
Advise the prince; no doubt, an easy tool,
Deferential, glad to be of use,
Politic, cautious, and meticulous;
Full of high sentence, but a bit obtuse;
At times, indeed, almost ridiculous—
Almost, at times, the Fool.

I grow old . . . I grow old . . .
I shall wear the bottoms of my trousers rolled.

Shall I part my hair behind? Do I dare to eat a peach?
I shall wear white flannel trousers, and walk upon the beach.
I have heard the mermaids singing, each to each.

I do not think that they will sing to me.

I have seen them riding seaward on the waves
Combing the white hair of the waves blown back
When the wind blows the water white and black.

We have lingered in the chambers of the sea
By sea-girls wreathed with seaweed red and brown
Till human voices wake us, and we drown.[7]

(T. S. ELIOT, 1888–   )

D. Find three or four poems all of which have to do with some one
theme or subject other than Time. Then write an analytical essay
which compares and contrasts them in a fashion similar to that followed in this chapter.

[7] "The Love Song of J. Alfred Prufrock" by T. S. Eliot. From *Complete Poems: 1909–1935* by T. S. Eliot, copyright, 1936, by Harcourt, Brace & World, Inc., and reprinted with their permission and with the permission of Faber and Faber, Ltd.

11. Some Aspects of Fiction and Drama

The difficulty which many people encounter in judging prose fiction lies largely in the medium—discursive language, not even formalized by meter or rhyme—just the same discursive language we use for conversation; it is hard not to be deceived into supposing the author intends, by his use of words, just what we intend by ours—to inform, comment, inquire, confess; in short: to talk to people. But a novelist intends to create a virtual experience, wholly formed, and wholly expressive of something more fundamental than any "modern" problem: human feeling, the nature of human life itself.[1]

SUSANNE K. LANGER, *Feeling and Form*

Relation of Fiction and Drama to Poetry

In turning from lyric poetry to the other forms of creative writing, it is important to realize that we are not really changing the subject. We are still talking about literature as art, about the creating of verbal structures and virtual life, about plurisigns (in both the narrow and the extended senses), and about the kind of form which is based on likeness-and-difference, parallelism-and-contrast, repetition-and-variation.

The differences between poetry, on the one hand, and fiction and drama, on the other, are largely differences in emphasis. As we shall

[1] FROM *Feeling and Form* by Susanne K. Langer. Reprinted by permission of the publishers, Charles Scribner's Sons.

see, poetry and creative prose are even composed of the same elements; only their relative importance differs. David Daiches, in his book *A Study of Literature*, puts it this way: "In prose fiction the disposition of the action carries the greater load, while in poetry it is the use of the resources of language in relation to each other that bears the major burden. *Both aim at achieving the same kind of end.*" To put it even more simply, the one great practical difference is that in reading most poetry we have to pay far more attention to language itself, to the separate words, their sounds, their rhythm, and all of their multiple relationships; in reading most fiction and drama, we pay somewhat less attention to language itself and more to the larger elements which the words create.

But even this general distinction tends to break down. For one thing, a great deal of fiction and drama—especially in the older literatures—is written in verse. An epic poet like Dante or a playwright like Shakespeare has to be attended to on all levels at once: his words are just as important as his characters, his rhythms can no more be ignored than the events he creates. For another thing, much of the best creative prose—especially in modern literature—depends very heavily on minutiae of language. An older novelist, like Dickens or Balzac or Dostoevski, can be translated into another language quite readily; but it is hard to imagine how anyone ever managed to translate a modern novel like Joyce's *Ulysses* (though it has been done, and into several foreign tongues).

We must therefore expect many of the elements which in Chapter 9 we treated as "poetic" elements to appear very frequently in prose fiction and drama; similarly, most of the elements which we are about to discuss here also operate in poems, not only in narrative and dramatic poems but also in lyric poems. In fact, several of these new elements could as well have been mentioned during our discussion of poetry in the last two chapters.

In this chapter, we will look briefly at some of the more important aspects of fiction and drama. Because these represent extremely useful literary concepts, thousands of pages have been written about each. Here, however, we shall see them primarily as further applications of the same two principles which we have observed before, the principles of likeness-and-difference and of the plurisign, because a reader who has grasped these two basic principles can do a respectable job of understanding and experiencing any piece of creative literature. But it will help to further demonstrate these principles if we can see their relevance to such traditional critical concepts as character, action, conflict, setting, point of view, theme, allegory, symbolism, and satire.

Character

Character is perhaps the most familiar of all the concepts which critics use in analyzing stories and plays. Being people ourselves, we can most readily see the "world" which the writer creates in terms of the "people" who "live" in it. However, two preliminary points about character need to be remembered.

There are not really any people in creative works; there are only words. What we call "character" is an imaginative construction based on the words and the forms which the author has put together. However, there are *semblances* of people, and these *semblances* or *virtual people* are what we mean by character. We must be careful, however, not to let "characters" take us in too completely. Authors themselves often have to fight this temptation: virtual people can become so real that they try to run the show themselves. For the reader this danger takes many forms. The TV viewer who identifies herself completely with her favorite soap-opera heroine illustrates one form. But even scholars sometimes succumb, and forget that the "characters" they analyze are only verbal constructions. Thus some modern critics, influenced by Freudian psychology, have treated Hamlet as a patient to be psychoanalyzed. Insofar as this technique shows the complexity of the play and the depth of Shakespeare's conception of his character (though *he* must have seen Hamlet in quite different terms) it can be useful; but the critic is always in danger of losing sight of the fact that Hamlet is, in fact, a *virtual* person.

Every creative work exhibits "character" in some sense. Readers often forget this. We can scarcely ignore the presence of virtual people in stories, novels, plays, and the kind of poems called narrative and dramatic. But we sometimes fail to recognize the element of character in lyric poems and creative essays.

In a lyric poem, there is always at least one character—whom for convenience we (often mistakenly) identify with the poet himself. As we noted in analyzing some of the poems in the previous chapter, this character might better be thought of as the speaker in the poem, who may or may not be the real-life writer. And there is often another character as well—the speaker's sweetheart or mistress or wife, or his dead friend (in an elegy), or God (as in the Psalms). The main point about character with which we are concerned here has to do with the twin principles of likeness-and-difference and the plurisign.

Whether characters are simple or complex, they are developed through parallelism-and-contrast. The "type" figures in Westerns and melodramas demonstrate their "characters" in successive actions which are all basically similar. We sort the "good guys" from the "bad guys" according to these repeated acts. Furthermore, in these simple forms, the goodness of one set of characters is enhanced by contrast with the badness of the other set and vice versa. And within each group, there is usually the same kind of repetition-with-variations. The hero's followers in a Western resemble him in some ways but differ in others, so that he emerges as the best of the good guys; and the villain's gang are all dirty, bearded, and unscrupulous like him, but display less initiative and intelligence.

In more complex fiction and drama, the same principle operates but in a more complex way. Hamlet is brave *and* hesitant, loving *and* callous, ruthless *and* sensitive, idealistic *and* cynical, and so on. And his characteristics are brought out also in relation to those of other characters. We do not divide the characters in *Hamlet* simply into two camps, but we see Hamlet in relation to Fortinbras, Laertes, Horatio, and the King; and we see all *these* characters in relation to each other.

Furthermore, in fiction and drama, characters frequently undergo changes: an indecisive man becomes a resolute one; the heroine outgrows her pride and prejudice or prejudice and pride. Characters may even reverse their roles. There is also often a double view of a single character. The narrator's judgment of a character may be appropriate or ironically inappropriate to what we sense him to be. Or the author's implied estimate may disagree with his narrator's estimate, and so on.

But for this principle of likeness-and-difference to operate in character development, the principle of the plurisign (in both the narrow and the broad sense) must also operate. Unless every detail regarding each character were significant beyond its literal meaning, most of the similarities and differences would fail to emerge. For example, the conversation between characters in fiction and drama is never quite like real-life conversation because in the former every word tells us more than it seems to on the surface. Real life would be unbearable if every sentence we uttered were as meaningful as is the dialogue of these virtual people.

Likeness-and-difference is enriched by the presence of plurisigns; it also produces plurisigns. The creative writer's characters are meaningful in proportion as they stand for something more than themselves. The truly great characters are those who seem to embody so much of human nature or to reveal such depths of human nature, within their merely verbal skins, that they become images or symbols of man himself.

Action

It takes more than "people" to make the virtual world of a poem or story or play; it takes events. The *action* of a creative work is what happens in it, or rather what seems to happen; for these are virtual events, just as the people who cause or are affected by them are virtual people.

The all-important thing to remember about action is that it can be almost anything. To requote Susanne Langer,

> The piece may be great or small—as great as the *Odyssey*, or so small that it comprises only one little event, like the thinking of a thought or the perception of a landscape.

There are other kinds of events besides fist and gun fights, murders and chases, seductions and marriages, the making and losing of fortunes, battles and deaths. Impressions, thoughts, feelings, memories, impulses, and moods are all "events." So is conversation. And a great deal of literature is devoted to creating virtual events of this kind. James Joyce's *Ulysses*, a novel of 768 pages, is concerned almost entirely with such "trivial" events. In fact, one of Joyce's main points in this book is that *no* great and crucial events occur in these virtual lives, whereas Homer's *Odyssey* (which *Ulysses* roughly parallels) is full of virtual action on the grand scale.

Just as every creative work involves virtual people, so it involves events of some kind. This is obviously true of novels and plays and short stories. But it is equally true of poems, including lyric poems, as a glance at any of the analyses in the last three chapters will show. Though we never used the term there, every one of the poems discussed contains *action* in one sense or another. Frost's traveler stops his horse, admires the snow-filling woods briefly, makes his decision, and resumes his journey; Marvell's lover argues with his coy mistress; Shelley's "traveller from an antique land" observes the ruins, reads the inscription, and suddenly senses the manifold irony of the scene; and so on. In discussing many of these poems we actually observed the action, without calling it that. Furthermore, we noted many times that these actions invariably involve likeness-and-difference in some form.

In fiction and drama the role of likeness-and-difference in the action is often quite open and obvious. An essentially good, and hence deserving, hero starts out promisingly, then suddenly is faced with all sorts of adversities (contrast), and finally overcomes his obstacles and wins Gorgeous Gwendolyn (further contrast, but also a return—repetition—to the good fortune of the beginning). Or we have the familiar rising and falling action of stories with *un*happy endings: a good man enjoys a series of successes (repetition) only to commit a fatal mistake (his erring contrasts with his ability) and go down to defeat (reversal).

In many novels and plays a number of actions on different planes are interwoven. Sometimes the different actions parallel each other, sometimes they contrast with and thus set off each other. A tragic action is developed alongside a comic one; a noble story alongside a story of low-life. In Shakespeare's *Henry IV*, Prince Hal is shown alternately at court with his father the king and in a cheap pub in the London slums with the buffoon Sir John Falstaff.

The action of a story or play often concludes by returning us to the opening scene or situation, thus emphasizing, by inviting comparison, the changes that have occurred. Occasionally this circling of the action back to its beginning shows that *nothing* has changed, and this may be the whole point. The significance of a story may lie in the fact that what we expect to happen never does materialize. Or the action may conclude by completely reversing the opening situation. Thus the tender-minded, reluctant, brooding Hamlet finally precipitates one of the bloodiest actions in all of Shakespeare and ends up responsible (more or less) for eight deaths, including his own.

The same basic scene or episode may be repeated several times, with minor variations. Or contrasting scenes and episodes may alternate as the action progresses. Or both. When two or more actions proceed concurrently, we have something like counterpoint in music.

It would be impossible to list all the ways in which the principle of likeness-and-difference operates in the creation of virtual action. But using these examples as clues, the reader will find it useful to look at the action in all stories and plays in terms of repetition, variation, alternation, tension, and counterpoint. He will also find it useful to see action, like character, as a plurisign (in the broader sense of that term). Everything that happens may have meaning beyond itself. As Wallace Stegner puts it,

> Any good piece of serious fiction is collected out of reality, and its parts ought to be vivid and true to fact and to observation. The parts are reassembled in such a way that the architecture, the shape of the action, is meaningful. And if the fiction is good enough that meaning will stretch; the building will throw a shadow longer than itself; the particular will become representative, general, symbolic, indefinitely applicable to other people, other situations.[2]

One kind of significant action should be especially noted, because it appears so often in all creative literature, both the best and the worst. This is what is sometimes called *archetypal* action. *Webster's Collegiate Dictionary* defines *archetype* as, "The original pattern of which all things of the same species are representations or copies; original idea, model, or type." An archetypal action is the sort of virtual action which reflects, consciously or unconsciously, some part of the fundamental cycle of human life. Archetypal events, therefore, function as complex plurisigns. This point is very important to an understanding of the full meaning of many creative works and of their connection with such preliterary symbolisms as myth and ritual.

Modern anthropology is chiefly responsible for our deeper awareness of literature's archetypal dimension. The anthropologists have found that, despite its seemingly endless variety, human life is essentially much the same in all cultures, times, and places. For all men, the basic cycle of life includes birth, coming of age, marriage, a prolonged struggle for self-fulfillment, a decline into old age, and finally death. Each part of this cycle involves major crises. Religious and secular rituals, both primitive and civilized, note and celebrate these crises or high points. Anthropologists call such rituals *rites of passage* because they invariably symbolize the "passing" of the individual from one phase of the cycle to the next, from one life-role to another, or from life to death.

These rituals form a major part of primitive man's life; but even

---

[2] FROM "Fiction: A Lens on Life" by Wallace Stegner, from *Saturday Review*. Reprinted by permission of the author and the publisher.

in our own, "civilized" society we celebrate life's high-points in ritual form: to celebrate birth, we have baptisms and christenings; to celebrate coming of age, we have confirmations, *bar mizvahs*, and graduations; to celebrate marriage, we have engagements and weddings; to celebrate the individual's assumption of leadership and his dedication to communal causes, we have coronations, inaugurations, ordinations, Hippocratic oath-takings, inductions, and commencements; to celebrate the onset of old-age we have retirement and golden-wedding ceremonies; and to celebrate death, we have funerals.

In a sophisticated society like ours, these ceremonies are often pale, rationalized affairs. For primitive men they were (and are) extremely serious business. Primitive men sense deeply that these transitions are both difficult and significant; this is why primitive societies tend to dramatize each crisis as a death and a rebirth, thus in effect symbolizing the whole cycle in each separate ritual. Even we sometimes preserve this element in our rituals; we sense, perhaps rather vaguely, that baptism is not merely a symbolic washing but also a symbolic rebirth; and some initiation rites involve a symbolic death and resurrection.

Furthermore, we members of literate societies continue to celebrate the great crises in the human cycle by means of our literature. It stands to reason that those of our writers who respond most deeply to the human experience should create virtual actions which mirror the central actions in real life. Some writers even draw directly on the older literatures which derived originally from prehistorical myths and legends which were, in turn, narrative renderings of very ancient rituals. Thus it is not strange that so much major literature should involve action which is *archetypal*, either deliberately so or because the writer is instinctively in tune with the basic patterns of life.

The archetypal dimension of a given work may be obvious, as it is in tragedy or in the great epics (for instance, Dante's *Divine Comedy*); or it may be not at all obvious, as in much "realistic" fiction and drama. But if the reader is aware of this special way in which events may function as plurisigns, he will find greater richness in many literary works. Here are a few practical suggestions:

1. We should notice virtual action which centers around any of the perennial human crises, either literally or symbolically. For example, the main action in many novels, plays, and stories is

essentially an initiation or baptism-of-fire for the protagonist. In fact, there is one special class of novel—which the Germans call *bildungsroman*, or development novel—which deals explicitly with a young person's problems in coming of age.

2. We should notice any event which looks at all like a death and rebirth: a descent into some kind of grave or hell, a purification through suffering, imprisonment ending in release, or even a journey and return.

3. We should notice "quests" and tests and other forms of search for self-fulfillment or for permanent values within the flux of life.

4. We should notice the kind of action which springs from a deliberate rejection of accepted values and standards.

5. We should notice ceremonial actions of all sorts, and ask ourselves whether they may be ritualistic: communal meals, runnings of the gantlet, ceremonial fights and killings, departures and home-comings, executions. These are especially noteworthy when they seem to be getting more attention than the literal story calls for.

To get back to our main theme, archetypal action clearly constitutes a special kind of parallelism (between virtual life and real life) and of plurisign (extra dimension of meaning) which *some* creative writing exhibits.

Conflict and Tension

In virtual life, as in real life, people in action generate conflict and tension. The virtual action of a story, play, or novel always involves a conflict or opposition of some sort. Often there are several conflicts at once, of different types and on different levels. It is from these conflicts that the "drama" of the story arises. But, as we have seen, even lyric poems usually involve some kind of tension or at least contrast.

The important point to remember is that the elements in conflict need not be two men with clenched fists. A poem, an essay, or even a story may be organized around the opposition of two or more contrasting moods, attitudes, sets of values, or even ideas. Glance through the poems in the last three chapters and notice how many of them are built on a conflict or tension of some sort.

The most obvious signal to the reader that a creative work is nearing its end is that the conflict or conflicts are finally being resolved. The wanderer finally reaches home, the hero finally wins the heroine, the police finally catch the criminal, the rich uncle finally comes through, the tragic protagonist receives the final blow, the separated lovers are finally reunited, the undecided character finally makes up his mind, the hero finally achieves his place in the sun, and so on.

As even these familiar and relatively crude examples indicate, there are many different types of conflict. It may be useful to think in terms of a half-dozen general types. A classification of this kind is, of course, arbitrary; but it often helps the reader to see in another way the likeness-and-difference, particularly in fiction and drama.

1. *Man against man.* This may be the ordinary hero-villain kind of conflict, or it may occur in much more subtle forms. James Joyce's story "Counterparts," which is analyzed in the next chapter, will illustrate this.

2. *Man against the supernatural.* The great Odysseus was opposed not only by mortal enemies but also by Poseidon, the Greek sea god. Again, Odysseus was befriended by the goddess Athena and the god Hermes. The "supernatural" can also take the shape of an impersonal force, such as "fate" or "destiny," as in many tragedies or in the novels of Thomas Hardy.

3. *Man against nature.* Man's struggle with nature may appear as an intense conflict with hostile forces, the sea, the desert, the frozen North, wild beasts; or it may appear as a patient attempt to wrest a living from the earth, or even as the scientist's effort to probe the secrets of nature. (Science fiction exhibits a man-against-nature conflict.)

4. *Man against society.* The individual is fighting his social environment. The conflict may be an open struggle between the individual and the social group, or a more general conflict with poverty, racial hostility, or unsympathetic cultural conditions.

5. *Man against himself.* Here the conflict is internal: the character is torn between opposing facets of his nature. (*Hamlet* is a classic example of this conflict.)

6. *Two worlds in opposition.* This conflict is usually combined with others; it may be embodied, for example, in a man-against-man conflict. The emphasis, however, is on opposing sets of ideas, values, or whole cultures.

Though a classification like this is helpful in separating the various strands of a creative work, the conflicts in good literature can seldom be neatly pigeonholed. Thus in the list above, the *Odyssey* is cited as an example of a man-against-the-supernatural conflict; but it also contains conflicts of man-against-man, and man-against-nature. Similarly *Hamlet*, although emphasis is placed on internal conflict, also contains conflict of man-against-man, man-against-society, and opposition between worlds or sets of values. As in real life, the virtual life of complex characters is likely to involve several kinds of conflicts at once. This we shall also see in Joyce's story in the next chapter.

It is perhaps obvious that all the types of conflict mentioned above can take the form of archetypal conflicts, thus becoming plurisigns in the broadest sense. For example, the man-against-man conflict nearly always involves a larger conflict, between good and evil, in some sense of these two many-colored terms. But the man-against-man struggle can also embody many other universal human conflicts: youth against adulthood, sons against fathers, have-nots against haves, ruled against rulers, the individual against the group, and so on.

Conflict, or at least tension, is so fundamental to the form of most creative works that the reader should be especially watchful for any trace of it.

Setting

Not even *virtual* people, events, and conflicts can exist in a vacuum; they must have "a local habitation," and this we call the *setting* of the novel, play, story, or poem.

Sometimes the setting plays an important role in the work; sometimes it is scarcely noticeable. Where it is important, its function can best be understood again in terms of the principle of parallelism-and-contrast. Natural setting is often used to help evoke the mood or atmosphere of a virtual world, as in some of Hardy's novels, in which setting parallels action and reinforces characterization. In other works, the setting may contrast with the events, as in Poe's "The Cask of Amontillado," in which a madman's murderous revenge takes place against a Mardi Gras background of gay festivity.

When the central conflict involves man-against-environment, the setting normally becomes, in effect, a character, in fact the chief antagonist whom the hero must overcome. In other works, two contrasting settings may be used to parallel a man-against-man conflict. Thus, in D. H. Lawrence's novel *Lady Chatterley's Lover*, the organic life of the woods is contrasted throughout with the mechanical life of the minepits, thus repeating and emphasizing the basic conflict between the gamekeeper Mellors (who is a "whole" man) and Sir Clifford Chatterley (who is paralyzed from the waist down and spends most of his life in a mechanical chair).

Point of View

Point of view has to do with who tells the story and from what vantage point. It is a technical critical term and should not be confused with the more general idea of philosophical or intellectual position. Thus, the author may elect to tell his story anonymously and with a godlike omniscience: the narrator sees what goes on in the minds of all the characters. Or the author may limit himself to an objective point of view. That is, the story is told in such a way that we are able to see the actions and hear the conversation, but we never enter directly into the minds of any of the characters. Or the author may tell his story through the intelligence of one of his characters, either a major character or a minor one. And he may let this character speak in the first person, or he may use the third person, limiting the perspective to those things this character can know: thus, the narrator will be able to tell us of the other characters only what they say and do; but of himself he can also tell us what he thinks and feels. Or the story may be narrated by various persons from several different points of view, each having its own limitations of knowledge and bias.

In studying fiction and drama it is often useful to ask: How does this particular point of view affect the way in which parallels and contrasts are generated? What would the story be like if told from a different point of view?

One way in which likeness-and-difference is brought out is through a double point of view. The story may be told by a first-person narrator who doesn't fully understand what he is telling, an uncomprehending narrator. Thus we see the story simultaneously from the narrator's restricted point of view and the author's own more com-

prehensive one. This is the technique that Sam Clemens uses in
Huckleberry Finn, and it makes possible all sorts of special effects:
sometimes it heightens the comedy, at other times the pathos; it
sharpens the satire and makes for understatement; it enables Huck
to characterize himself obliquely, without Twain's having to tell
us explicitly what kind of boy Huck is; and it makes for many
kinds of irony. Centuries before Clemens, the Greek tragedian
Sophocles used a similar technique in his play *Oedipus the King,* in
which a double point of view is maintained without the limitations
inherent in first-person narration. Flaubert manages the same double
point of view in his novel *Madame Bovary,* which is told both from
various characters' points of view and also from Flaubert's own
point of view. Thus we are often allowed to see the same events
through the eyes of the romantic heroine *and* through those of the
almost cynically realistic author.

Related to this question of point of view is the use of the *frame
story* device, or story within a story. Joseph Conrad is a master of
this method, and employs it in many ways. Sometimes the frame
narrative parallels or mirrors the main narrative, sometimes the two
contrast, sometimes the effect is a mixture of both parallelism and
contrast.

Theme and Ideas

The term *theme* is used in several different ways in literary
criticism. Sometimes it means the "subject" of the work, what it is
"about." More often it refers to some central proposition, or set of
ideas, which the author presumably had in mind and around which
he built his poem or story or play.

Actually, not many creative works originate in this way, in conceptual knowledge, and we have to be careful that what we call
theme is not merely a generalization produced by our own minds. It
is always possible to draw abstract conclusions from almost any
piece of life, virtual or real; but it is dangerous to treat these conclusions as central. As Wallace Stegner puts it in "Fiction: A Lens
on Life,"

> Ideas, of course, have a place in fiction, and any writer of fiction
> needs a mind. But ideas are not the best *subject matter* for fiction.
> They do not dramatize well. They are rather a by-product, something

the reader is led to formulate after watching the story unfold. The ideas, the generalizations, ought to be implicit in the selection and arrangement of the people and places and actions. They ought to haunt a piece of fiction as a ghost flits past an attic window after dark.

In the same article, Stegner also makes a further point: that creative writers—like other artists—are not, generally speaking, particularly intellectual. That is, they are not by nature the sort of people who care passionately about ideas, theories, intellectual abstractions of any kind. In short, their strong point is more likely to be experiential knowledge than conceptual knowledge.

On the other hand, as Stegner indicates, general ideas may lurk in the background of almost any creative work, and where they do we should be aware of their presence. Furthermore, ideas can also occupy the foreground. As we have seen, every creative writer creates "people," and most people—including virtual ones—just naturally have ideas and just as naturally like to express them, whether they are worth expressing or not. As a result, ideas do appear as *one element* in most poetry and in almost all fiction and drama. But very frequently ideas are not the main element, but rather a means of presenting character, of explaining motivation, of advancing the action, of establishing the social setting, and so on. There are exceptions, of course. Many of the "great" books of all ages naturally reflect the key ideas of their time. And in some creative writing, ideas—expressed by the author in person or through his characters—appear as a major element. This is true, for instance, of plays like Ibsen's and Shaw's or of novels like Aldous Huxley's *Point Counterpoint,* Norman Douglas' *South Wind,* Arthur Koestler's *Darkness at Noon,* and Thomas Mann's *The Magic Mountain.* It is perhaps significant that all six of these writers *are* (or were) intellectuals, and most of them have also written widely in the informative and persuasive modes.

But even in the so-called "problem play" or the "novel of ideas," in which propositions are explicitly and deliberately introduced, they should be regarded as merely one element among many others. Whether the ideas are important or not, they operate as do the other elements in creative writing. That is, the various ideas are made to parallel and contrast with each other, just as characters and events do, and to assist in the creation of the other elements. We should notice the interweaving and interplay of propositions, as we do the interaction of characters, events, setting, and all of these together.

Allegory

One special way in which ideas are made to operate in creative writing is through allegory. In allegory there is a constant parallelism between the virtual life of characters, actions, etc., and a more or less systematic pattern of propositions. Both levels of meaning, the experiential and the conceptual, are continuously present and interacting. The virtual life is intended to embody, dramatize, illustrate, and give imaginative meaning to the conceptual knowledge; and the conceptual meanings are intended to interpret and give general meaning to the virtual life.

We might do well to take our example from the first great allegorical novel in English, Bunyan's *Pilgrim's Progress*, first published in complete form in 1679. On the realistic level, the novel depicts the adventures of its hero, Christian, as he travels on foot about a quite vivid English countryside; on the allegorical level, Christian's journey is a strenuous attempt to lead the good life, despite all temptations, and hence achieve God's Grace:

At last there came a grave person to the gate, named Good Will, who asked who was there, and whence he came, and what he would have.

CHR. Here is a poor burdened sinner. I come from the City of Destruction, but am going to Mount Zion, that I may be delivered from the wrath to come. I would therefore, sir, since I am informed that by this gate is the way thither, know if you are willing to let me in.

GOOD WILL. I am willing with all my heart, said he; and with that he opened the gate.

So, when Christian was stepping in, the other gave him a pull. Then said Christian: "What means that?" The other told him: "A little distance from this gate there is erected a strong castle, of which Beelzebub is the captain. From thence both he and them that are with him shoot arrows at those that come up to this gate, if haply they may die before they can enter in." Then said Christian: "I rejoice and tremble." So when we was got in, the man of the gate asked him who directed him thither.

CHR. Evangelist bid me come hither and knock, as I did; and he said that you, sir, would tell me what I must do.

GOOD WILL. An open door is set before thee, and no man can shut it.

CHR. Now I begin to reap the benefits of my hazards.

GOOD WILL. But how is it that you came alone?

CHR. Because none of my neighbors saw their danger as I saw mine.

GOOD WILL. Did any of them know of your coming?

CHR. Yes; my wife and children saw me at the first, and called after me to turn again; also some of my neighbors stood crying, and called after me to return; but I put my fingers in my ears, and so came on my way.

GOOD WILL. But did none of them follow you, to persuade you to go back?

CHR. Yes, both Obstinate and Pliable. But when they saw that they could not prevail, Obstinate went railing back; but Pliable came with me a little way.

GOOD WILL. But why did he not come through?

CHR. We indeed came through together until we came at the Slough of Despond, into the which we also suddenly fell. And then was my neighbor Pliable discouraged, and would not adventure further. Wherefore, getting out again, on that side next to his own house, he told me I should possess the brave country alone for him. So he went his way, and I came mine; he after Obstinate, and I to this gate.

Allegory represents a special case of both parallelism-and-contrast and the plurisign. Images and generalities exist side by side. Allegory clothes conceptual skeletons not only in flesh but also in appropriate costumes. It makes concepts into people, propositions into events, states of mind into places, moral problems into journeys.

The kind of allegory represented by a novel such as the *Pilgrim's Progress* poses no great problem for the reader. The conceptual meanings are clearly labeled. But there are other, less systematic types of allegory which do present a problem: the reader is sometimes in doubt as to *how much* of the virtual life is intended to be allegorical. Does every detail have an extra, conceptual meaning? Or is the piece allegorical only in a *general* way, the details being there for the sake of the virtual world and not for conceptual purposes?

In this type of semi-allegory, the reader is always in danger of trying so hard to find a conceptual meaning for everything that he fails to experience the virtual world itself. Good examples of this difficulty are the novels of Franz Kafka and Albert Camus.

Loosely speaking, all truly rich and significant creative writing can be said to be allegorical, in that everything has a larger meaning than its surface meaning. In other words, everything is a plurisign. But it is probably wiser to reserve the term *allegorical* for the kind of deliberate and continuous multilevel writing illustrated by Bunyan.

Symbolism

Like allegory, symbolism involves a special type of plurisign. However, unlike allegory it depends on evocative rather than conceptual meanings. In a true allegory, such as *Pilgrim's Progress*, every character, event, and bit of dialogue corresponds to some part of a system of ideas (in *Pilgrim's Progress* the system is Christian theology) that was constantly in the author's mind. In symbolism we do not find this one-for-one correspondence.

A literary symbol is a word or a fragment of virtual life which operates richly, deeply, and consistently in some special way, however difficult it may be to label the special meaning. Thus symbols may be either words themselves or the things the words stand for. Symbols may also be either traditional or personal. When Hemingway, in *The Old Man and the Sea*, introduces the images of the Christian cross and the scarred hands (suggesting stigmata, marks representing Christ's wounds), he is employing traditional symbols. However, in some of his other works, Hemingway creates his own personal symbols. For example, the bull ring is for Hemingway a symbol for human life, which he sees as essentially tragic; mountains are for him good (happy, healthy, free, spiritually satisfying), whereas plains are bad (unhappy, unhealthy, oppressive, spiritually debilitating).

A creative writer establishes personal symbols by means of parallelism-and-contrast, repetition, frequent association. To see this process at work in a single poem, reread Frost's "Mending Wall" (p. 71) and notice how the term *wall*, which starts out meaning simply an ordinary stone fence, gradually acquires new meanings, layer upon layer, until by the end of the poem "walls" are *all* of the barriers (cultural, religious, political, racial, etc.) which men erect between themselves and which impede human understanding.

Satire

This is another "nonrealistic" mode of literature, as are allegory and symbolism. Satire is extremely complex, occurring not only in creative writing but also in informative and persuasive works, and we will not attempt even to define its range here. However, it does involve the principle of similarity-and-difference rather interestingly.

Insofar as satire includes certain kinds of creative writing, it means the kind of poetry, fiction, and drama which is to "realism" as caricature is to "representational" drawing and painting. In other words, like caricature satire calls for likeness, but it also calls for difference, in the form of exaggeration. And its effect depends on the reader's recognition of both the likeness and the difference at once. Here are the opening paragraphs of Aldous Huxley's famous novel *Brave New World*. Huxley's book is both a classic of science fiction, in its picture of a socialistic-scientific "utopia" of the future, and a biting satire on various aspects of our own materialistic, "progressist" civilization.

A squat grey building of only thirty-four stories. Over the main entrance the words, CENTRAL LONDON HATCHERY AND CONDITIONING CENTRE, and, in a shield, the World State's motto, COMMUNITY, IDENTITY, STABILITY.

The enormous room on the ground floor faced towards the north. Cold for all the summer beyond the panes, for all the tropical heat of the room itself, a harsh thin light glared through the windows, hungrily seeking some draped lay figure, some pallid shape of academic goose-flesh, but finding only the glass and nickel and bleakly shining porcelain of a laboratory. Wintriness responded to wintriness. The overalls of the workers were white, their hands gloved with a pale corpse-coloured rubber. The light was frozen, dead, a ghost. Only from the yellow barrels of the microscopes did it borrow a certain rich and living substance, lying along the polished tubes like butter, streak after luscious streak in long recession down the work tables.

"And this," said the Director opening the door, "is the Fertilizing Room."

Bent over their instruments, three hundred Fertilizers were plunged, as the Director of Hatcheries and Conditioning entered the room, in the scarcely breathing silence, the absent-minded, soliloquizing hum or whistle, of absorbed concentration. A troop of newly arrived students, very young, pink and callow, followed nervously, rather abjectly, at the Director's heels. Each of them carried a notebook, in which, whenever the great man spoke, he desperately scribbled. Straight from the horse's mouth. It was a rare privilege. The D. H. C. for Central London always made a point of personally conducting his new students round the various departments.[3]

[3] FROM *Brave New World* by Aldous Huxley. Reprinted by permission of Harper & Brothers and Chatto and Windus Ltd.

Always, in satire, the reader is asked to compare the situation *as it is* (or as it seems to be in the satirist's eyes) with the situation *as it should be* (according to any right-thinking reader's sense of propriety and justice). The discrepancy between the two is the essence of satire. Thus, as has often been noted, within every genuine satirist there lurks a fervent idealist, whose satiric criticisms of people and institutions, ideas and customs, programs and policies, spring from an acute sense of what is right and of how badly things fail to measure up to standard.

Satire is a powerful weapon for the persuasive writer. However, it would be a mistake to regard the presence of satire as a sure sign of persuasive purpose. Authors may write satirically simply because this is how they *see* life; they are not necessarily trying to induce action or even to persuade the reader to their own vision of things. Thus, satire may arise from a satiric sense of the human condition, just as comedy does from a comic sense of life, or tragedy from a tragic sense of life.

Indirection and Interplay Again

In this chapter we have touched on a few of the elements and modes which are most frequently talked about in discussions of fiction and drama. We have purposely omitted certain very important subjects—for instance, comedy and tragedy—because of lack of space. But we have tried, by relating each topic to a few basic principles, to lay a foundation on which the reader can build a more complete and elaborate structure of critical theory if he chooses to. For example, some readers might find it very interesting to re-examine both tragedy and comedy in the light of the principle of likeness-and-difference.

It should be stressed again that the aspects of fiction and drama we have looked at here are also aspects of poetry; that all of these elements and techniques, like those discussed in connection with poetry, are instruments for indirection; and that the parts of fiction and drama interact, in organic fashion, just as the parts of poetry do.

But the best way to demonstrate these points is by analyzing at least one specific work. This we will do in the next chapter.

EXERCISES

A. Think about the following questions for class discussion:
  1. What is the reason for calling things like "character," "action," and "conflict" concepts?
  2. What are some of the ways in which a short-story writer or novelist may appear as a "character" in his fiction?
  3. Does a playwright ever appear as a character in his plays? How?
  4. The text claims that *character* is created by means of similarity-and-difference. Is the novelist or storyteller who simply *describes* his characters an exception to this rule?
  5. In what sense can a character be called a plurisign?
  6. What is the relation between *action* and *conflict* and the more familiar idea of *plot?*
  7. Does all creative literature involve archetypal action and conflicts?
  8. Can the conflict and action in cheap literature be archetypal?
  9. In what sense does even a creative essay sometimes contain action?
  10. Can you cite some kinds of creative writing in which *setting* is actually the main element?
  11. What is the difference between *allegory* and *symbolism?*
  12. Why is *satire* not necessarily evidence of persuasive purpose?

B. Write a short analysis (400 to 500 words) of how *character* is created in a particular story or poem.

C. Write a short comparative analysis of the *action* in two pieces of popular fiction of the same type (e.g., western, murder, gangster, or love stories).

D. Write a short analysis of the *action* in two lyric poems which seem somewhat alike.

E. Analyze the *conflict* or conflicts in a single short story, narrative poem, or play.

F. Find a story, poem, or play in which *setting* seems to be important, and analyze its various functions in the work.

G. Find a story or play which seems to you to have an interesting *point of view,* and show how this point of view contributes to the story's effectiveness.

H. Write a discussion of one realistic story or play in which you show that many *themes* might be found in it.

I. Find a story, poem, or play in which *ideas* (propositions) seem to be an important element, and show how these ideas are dramatized (made to parallel and contrast with each other) as if they were characters.

J. Find an *allegorical* poem, story, or play and discuss it in terms of the statements made on pages 224–26.

K. As in J, discuss the *symbolism* in one story, poem, or play.

L. Write a comparative analysis of the kinds of *satire* found in two stories, two essays, two or three poems, or two plays. Mention to what extent each work seems to be persuasive in purpose.

12. A Story Analyzed

The Story

Now we will put to use some of the theory we have been developing. This will give us a chance to test our basic principles and to clarify some of our analytical concepts; it will also enable us to see how one actually proceeds in reading a moderately subtle creative work. The work, a short story by James Joyce, is from his collection *Dubliners*, first published in 1914. Incredible though it may seem, official and unofficial censorship forced Joyce to wait nearly ten years before any publisher could be persuaded to bring out this book. Even today, *Dubliners* is still black-listed in Ireland.

Counterparts

The bell rang furiously and, when Miss Parker went to the tube, a furious voice called out in a piercing North of Ireland accent:

"Send Farrington here!"

Miss Parker returned to her machine, saying to a man who was writing at a desk:

"Mr. Alleyne wants you upstairs."

The man muttered "*Blast* him!" under his breath and pushed back his chair to stand up. When he stood up he was tall and of great bulk. He had a hanging face, dark wine-coloured, with fair eyebrows and moustache: his eyes bulged forward slightly and the whites of them were dirty. He lifted up the counter and, passing by the clients, went out of the office with a heavy step.

He went heavily upstairs until he came to the second landing, where a door bore a brass plate with the inscription *Mr. Alleyne*. Here he halted, puffing with labour and vexation, and knocked. The shrill voice cried:

"Come in!"

The man entered Mr. Alleyne's room. Simultaneously Mr. Alleyne, a little man wearing gold-rimmed glasses on a clean-shaven face, shot his head up over a pile of documents. The head itself was so pink and hairless it seemed like a large egg reposing on the papers. Mr. Alleyne did not lose a moment:

"Farrington? What is the meaning of this? Why have I always to complain of you? May I ask you why you haven't made a copy of that contract between Bodley and Kirwan? I told you it must be ready by four o'clock."

"But Mr. Shelley said, sir . . ."

"*Mr. Shelley said, sir* . . . Kindly attend to what I say and not to what *Mr. Shelley says, sir.* You have always some excuse or another for shirking work. Let me tell you that if the contract is not copied before this evening I'll lay the matter before Mr. Crosbie . . . Do you hear me now?"

"Yes, sir."

"Do you hear me now? . . . Ay and another little matter! I might as well be talking to the wall as talking to you. Understand once for all that you get a half an hour for your lunch and not an hour and a half. How many courses do you want, I'd like to know . . . Do you mind me now?"

"Yes, sir."

Mr. Alleyne bent his head again upon his pile of papers. The man stared fixedly at the polished skull which directed the affairs of Crosbie & Alleyne, gauging its fragility. A spasm of rage gripped his throat for a few moments and then passed, leaving after it a sharp sensation of thirst. The man recognized the sensation and felt that he must have a good night's drinking. The middle of the month was passed and, if he could get the copy done in time, Mr. Alleyne might give him an order on the cashier. He stood still, gazing fixedly at the head upon the pile of papers. Suddenly Mr. Alleyne began to upset all the papers, searching for something. Then, as if he had been unaware of the man's presence till that moment, he shot up his head again, saying:

"Eh? Are you going to stand there all day? Upon my word, Farrington, you take things easy!"

"I was waiting to see . . ."

"Very good, you needn't wait to see. Go downstairs and do your work."

The man walked heavily towards the door and, as he went out of the room, he heard Mr. Alleyne cry after him that if the contract was not copied by evening, Mr. Crosbie would hear of the matter.

He returned to his desk in the lower office and counted the sheets which remained to be copied. He took up his pen and dipped it in the ink but he continued to stare stupidly at the last words he had written: *In no case shall the said Bernard Bodley be* . . . The evening was falling and in a few minutes they would be lighting the gas: then he could write. He felt that he must slake the thirst in his throat. He stood up from his desk, and, lifting the counter as before, passed out of the office. As he was passing out the chief clerk looked at him inquiringly.

"It's all right Mr. Shelley," said the man, pointing with his finger to indicate the objective of his journey.

The chief clerk glanced at the hat-rack, but, seeing the row complete, offered no remark. As soon as he was on the landing the man pulled a shepherd's plaid cap out of his pocket, put it on his head and ran quickly down the rickety stairs. From the street door he walked on furtively on the inner side of the path towards the corner and all at once dived into a doorway. He was now safe in the dark snug [1] of O'Neill's shop, and, filling up the little window that looked into the bar with his inflamed face, the colour of dark wine or dark meat, he called out:

"Here, Pat, give us a g.p.,[2] like a good fellow." The curate [3] brought him a glass of plain porter. The man drank it at a gulp and asked for a caraway seed.[4] He put his penny on the counter and, leaving the curate to grope for it in the gloom, retreated out of the snug as furtively as he had entered it.

Darkness, accompanied by a thick fog, was gaining upon the dusk of February and the lamps in Eustace Street had been lit. The man went up by the houses until he reached the door of the office, wondering whether he could finish his copy in time. On the stairs a moist pungent odour of perfumes saluted his nose: evidently Miss Delacour had come while he was out in O'Neill's. He crammed his cap back again into his pocket and re-entered the office, assuming an air of absentmindedness.

"Mr. Alleyne has been calling for you," said the chief clerk severely. "Where were you?"

The man glanced at the two clients who were standing at the counter as if to intimate that their presence prevented him from answering. As the clients were both male the chief clerk allowed himself a laugh.

"I know that game," he said. "Five times in one day is a little bit . . . Well, you better look sharp and get a copy of our correspondence in the Delacour case for Mr. Alleyne."

This address in the presence of the public, his run upstairs and the porter he had gulped down so hastily confused the man and, as he sat down at his desk to get what was required, he realised how hope-

---

[1] The drinking space next to the bar.
[2] A glass of porter, a heavy dark beer.
[3] Not a clergyman, but the bartender.
[4] The caraway seed is to hide the odor of alcohol on his breath.

less was the task of finishing his copy of the contract before half past five. The dark damp night was coming and he longed to spend it in the bars, drinking with his friends amid the glare of gas and the clatter of glasses. He got out the Delacour correspondence and passed out of the office. He hoped Mr. Alleyne would not discover that the last two letters were missing.

The moist pungent perfume lay all the way up to Mr. Alleyne's room. Miss Delacour was a middle-aged woman of Jewish appearance. Mr. Alleyne was said to be sweet on her or on her money. She came to the office often and stayed a long time when she came. She was sitting beside his desk now in an aroma of perfumes, smoothing the great black feather in her hat. Mr. Alleyne had swivelled his chair round to face her and thrown his right foot jauntily upon his left knee. The man put the correspondence on the desk and bowed respectfully but neither Mr. Alleyne nor Miss Delacour took any notice of his bow. Mr. Alleyne tapped a finger on the correspondence and then flicked it towards him as if to say: *"That's all right: you can go."*

The man returned to the lower office and sat down again at his desk. He stared intently at the incomplete phrase: *In no case shall the said Bernard Bodley be . . .* and thought how strange it was that the last three words began with the same letter. The chief clerk began to hurry Miss Parker, saying she would never have the letters typed in time for post. The man listened to the clicking of the machine for a few minutes and then set to work to finish his copy. But his head was not clear and his mind wandered away to the glare and rattle of the public-house. It was a night for hot punches. He struggled on with his copy, but when the clock struck five he had still fourteen pages to write. Blast it! He couldn't finish it in time. He longed to execrate aloud, to bring his fist down on something violently. He was so enraged that he wrote *Bernard Bernard* instead of *Bernard Bodley* and had to begin again on a clean sheet.

He felt strong enough to clear out the whole office single-handed. His body ached to do something, to rush out and revel in violence. All the indignities of his life enraged him . . . Could he ask the cashier privately for an advance? No, the cashier was no good, no damn good: he wouldn't give an advance . . . He knew where he would meet the boys: Leonard and O'Halloran and Nosey Flynn. The barometer of his emotional nature was set for a spell of riot.

His imagination had so abstracted him that his name was called twice before he answered. Mr. Alleyne and Miss Delacour were standing outside the counter and all the clerks had turned round in anticipation of something. The man got up from his desk. Mr. Alleyne began a tirade of abuse, saying that two letters were missing. The man answered that he knew nothing about them, that he had made a faithful copy. The tirade continued: it was so bitter and violent that the man could hardly restrain his fist from descending upon the head of the manikin before him:

"I know nothing about any other two letters," he said stupidly.

"*You—know—nothing.* Of course you know nothing," said Mr. Alleyne. "Tell me," he added, glancing first for approval to the lady beside him, "do you take me for a fool? Do you think me an utter fool?"

The man glanced from the lady's face to the little egg-shaped head and back again; and almost before he was aware of it, his tongue had found a felicitous moment:

"I don't think, sir," he said, "that that's a fair question to put to me."

There was a pause in the very breathing of the clerks. Everyone was astounded (the author of the witticism no less than his neighbours) and Miss Delacour, who was a stout amiable person, began to smile broadly. Mr. Alleyne flushed to the hue of a wild rose and his mouth twitched with a dwarf's passion. He shook his fist in the man's face till it seemed to vibrate like the knob of some electric machine:

"You impertinent ruffian! You impertinent ruffian! I'll make short work of you! Wait till you see! You'll apologise to me for your impertinence or you'll quit the office instanter! You'll quit this, I'm telling you, or you'll apologise to me!"

．　．　．　．　．

He stood in a doorway opposite the office watching to see if the cashier would come out alone. All the clerks passed out and finally the cashier came out with the chief clerk. It was no use trying to say a word to him when he was with the chief clerk. The man felt that his position was bad enough. He had been obliged to offer an abject apology to Mr. Alleyne for his impertinence but he knew what a hornet's nest the office would be for him. He could remember the way in which Mr. Alleyne had hounded little Peake out of the office in order to make room for his own nephew. He felt savage and thirsty and revengeful, annoyed with himself and with everyone else. Mr. Alleyne would never give him an hour's rest; his life would be a hell to him. He had made a proper fool of himself this time. Could he not keep his tongue in his cheek? But they had never pulled together from the first, he and Mr. Alleyne, ever since the day Mr. Alleyne had overheard him mimicking his North of Ireland accent to amuse Higgins and Miss Parker: that had been the beginning of it. He might have tried Higgins for the money, but sure Higgins never had anything for himself. A man with two establishments to keep up, of course he couldn't.

He felt his great body again aching for the comfort of the public-house. The fog had begun to chill him and he wondered could he touch Pat in O'Neill's. He could not touch him for more than a bob [5]— and a bob was no use. Yet he must get money somewhere or other: he had spent his last penny for the g.p. and soon it would be too late for getting money anywhere. Suddenly, as he was fingering his watch-chain, he thought of Terry Kelly's pawn-office in Fleet Street. That was the dart! Why didn't he think of it sooner?

He went through the narrow alley of Temple Bar quickly, muttering to himself that they could all go to hell because he was going to have a good night of it. The clerk in Terry Kelly's said A *crown!* [6] but the cosignor held out for six shillings; and in the end the six shillings was allowed him literally. He came out of the pawn-office joy-fully, making a little cylinder of the coins between his thumb and fingers. In Westmoreland Street the footpaths were crowded with young men and women returning from business and ragged ur-chins ran here and there yelling out the names of the evening editions. The man passed through the crowd, looking on the spec-tacle generally with proud satisfaction and staring masterfully at the office-girls. His head was full of the noises of tram-gongs and swishing trolleys and his nose already sniffed the curling fumes of punch. As he walked on he preconsidered the terms in which he would narrate the incident to the boys:

"So, I just looked at him—coolly, you know, and looked at her. Then I looked back at him again—taking my time, you know. 'I don't think that that's a fair question to put to me,' says I."

Nosey Flynn was sitting up in his usual corner of Davy Byrne's and, when he heard the story, he stood Farrington a half-one, saying it was as smart a thing as ever he heard. Farrington stood a drink in his turn. After a while O'Halloran and Paddy Leonard came in and the story was repeated to them. O'Halloran stood tailors of malt, hot, all round and told the story of the retort he had made to the chief clerk when he was in Callan's of Frownes's Street; but, as the retort was after the manner of the liberal shepherds in the eclogues, he had to admit that it was not as clever as Farrington's retort. At this Farrington told the boys to polish off that and have another.

Just as they were naming their poisons who should come in but Higgins! Of course he had to join in with the others. The men asked him to give his version of it, and he did so with great vivacity for the sight of five small hot whiskies was very exhilarating. Everyone roared laughing when he showed the way in which Mr. Alleyne shook his fist in Farrington's face. Then he imitated Farrington, saying, "And

---

[5] A shilling (about 25¢, in those days).
[6] Five shillings.

here was my nabs,[7] as cool as you please," while Farrington looked at the company out of his heavy dirty eyes, smiling and at times drawing forth stray drops of liquor from his moustache with the aid of his lower lip.

When that round was over there was a pause. O'Halloran had money but neither of the other two seemed to have any; so the whole party left the shop somewhat regretfully. At the corner of Duke Street Higgins and Nosey Flynn bevelled off to the left while the other three turned back towards the city. Rain was drizzling down on the cold streets and, when they reached the Ballast Office, Farrington suggested the Scotch House. The bar was full of men and loud with the noise of tongues and glasses. The three men pushed past the whining match-sellers at the door and formed a little party at the corner of the counter. They began to exchange stories. Leonard introduced them to a young fellow named Weathers who was performing at the Tivoli as an acrobat and knockabout *artiste*. Farrington stood a drink all round. Weathers said he would take a small Irish and Apollinaris.[8] Farrington, who had definite notions of what was what, asked the boys would they have an Apollinaris too; but the boys told Tim to make theirs hot. The talk became theatrical. O'Halloran stood a round and then Farrington stood another round, Weathers protesting that the hospitality was too Irish. He promised to get them in behind the scenes and introduce them to some nice girls. O'Halloran said that he and Leonard would go, but that Farrington wouldn't go because he was a married man; and Farrington's heavy dirty eyes leered at the company in token that he understood he was being chaffed. Weathers made them all have just one little tincture [9] at his expense and promised to meet them later on at Mulligan's in Poolbeg Street.

When the Scotch House closed they went round to Mulligan's. They went into the parlour at the back and O'Halloran ordered small hot specials all round. They were all beginning to feel mellow. Farrington was just standing another round when Weathers came back. Much to Farrington's relief he drank a glass of bitter this time. Funds were getting low but they had enough to keep them going. Presently two young women with big hats and a young man in a check suit came in and sat at a table close by. Weathers saluted them and told the company that they were out of the Tivoli. Farrington's eyes wandered at every moment in the direction of one of the young women. There was something striking in her appearance. An immense scarf of peacock-blue muslin was wound round her hat and knotted in a great bow under her chin; and she wore bright yellow gloves, reaching to

[7] "My lordship," in the humorous sense.
[8] A liqueur.
[9] A "nip" or "shot."

the elbow. Farrington gazed admiringly at the plump arm which she moved very often and with much grace; and when, after a little time, she answered his gaze he admired still more her large dark brown eyes. The oblique staring expression in them fascinated him. She glanced at him once or twice and, when the party was leaving the room, she brushed against his chair and said "*O, pardon!*" in a London accent. He watched her leave the room in the hope that she would look back at him, but he was disappointed. He cursed his want of money and cursed all the rounds he had stood, particularly all the whiskies and Apollinaris which he had stood to Weathers. If there was one thing that he hated it was a sponge. He was so angry that he lost count of the conversation of his friends.

When Paddy Leonard called him he found that they were talking about feats of strength. Weathers was showing his biceps muscle to the company and boasting so much that the other two had called on Farrington to uphold the national honour. Farrington pulled up his sleeve accordingly and showed his biceps muscle to the company. The two arms were examined and compared and finally it was agreed to have a trial of strength. The table was cleared and the two men rested their elbows on it, clasping hands. When Paddy Leonard said "*Go!*" each was to try to bring down the other's hand on to the table. Farrington looked very serious and determined.

The trial began. After about thirty seconds Weathers brought his opponent's hand slowly down on to the table. Farrington's dark wine-coloured face flushed darker still with anger and humiliation at having been defeated by such a stripling.

"You're not to put the weight of your body behind it. Play fair," he said.

"Who's not playing fair?" said the other.

"Come on again. The two best out of three."

The trial began again. The veins stood out on Farrington's forehead, and the pallor of Weathers' complexion changed to peony. Their hands and arms trembled under the stress. After a long struggle Weathers again brought his opponent's hand slowly on to the table. There was a murmur of applause from the spectators. The curate, who was standing beside the table, nodded his red head towards the victor and said with stupid familiarity:

"Ah! that's the knack!"

"What the hell do you know about it?" said Farrington fiercely, turning on the man. "What do you put in your gab for?"

"Sh, sh!" said O'Halloran, observing the violent expression of Farrington's face. "Pony up, boys. We'll have just one little smahan more and then we'll be off."

A very sullen-faced man stood at the corner of O'Connell Bridge waiting for the little Sandy-mount tram to take him home. He was full of smouldering anger and revengefulness. He felt humiliated and discontented; he did not even feel drunk; and he had only twopence in his pocket. He cursed everything. He had done for himself in the office, pawned his watch, spent all his money; and he had not even got drunk. He began to feel thirsty again and he longed to be back again in the hot reeking public-house. He had lost his reputation as a strong man, having been defeated twice by a mere boy. His heart swelled with fury and, when he thought of the woman in the big hat who had brushed against him and said *Pardon!* his fury nearly choked him.

His tram let him down at Shelbourne Road and he steered his great body along in the shadow of the wall of the barracks. He loathed returning to his home. When he went in by the side-door he found the kitchen empty and the kitchen fire nearly out. He bawled upstairs:

"Ada! Ada!"

His wife was a little sharp-faced woman who bullied her husband when he was sober and was bullied by him when he was drunk. They had five children. A little boy came running down the stairs.

"Who is that?" said the man, peering through the darkness.

"Me, pa."

"Who are you? Charlie?"

"No, pa. Tom."

"Where's your mother?"

"She's out at the chapel."

"That's right . . . Did she think of leaving any dinner for me?"

"Yes, pa. I—"

"Light the lamp. What do you mean by having the place in darkness? Are the other children in bed?"

The man sat down heavily on one of the chairs while the little boy lit the lamp. He began to mimic his son's flat accent, saying half to himself: *"At the chapel. At the chapel, if you please!"* When the lamp was lit he banged his fist on the table and shouted:

"What's for my dinner?"

"I'm going . . . to cook it, pa," said the little boy.

The man jumped up furiously and pointed to the fire.

"On that fire! You let the fire out! By God, I'll teach you to do that again!"

He took a step to the door and seized the walking-stick which was standing behind it.

"I'll teach you to let the fire out!" he said, rolling up his sleeve in order to give his arm free play.

The little boy cried *"O, pa!"* and ran whimpering round the table, but the man followed him and caught him by the coat. The little boy looked about him wildly but, seeing no way of escape, fell upon his knees.

"Now, you'll let the fire out the next time!" said the man, striking at him vigorously with the stick. "Take that, you little whelp!"

The boy uttered a squeal of pain as the stick cut his thigh. He clasped his hands together in the air and his voice shook with fright.

"O, pa!" he cried. "Don't beat me, pa! And I'll . . . I'll say a *Hail Mary* [10] for you . . . I'll say a *Hail Mary* for you, pa, if you don't beat me. . . . I'll say a *Hail Mary* . . ." [11]

Getting into the Story

"Counterparts" is the sort of creative piece that most people who care about literature will read more than once. Not that the story is so difficult as to baffle even an inexperienced reader the first time over; but it is rich enough to yield much that is new on rereading. The second time, an attentive reader is bound to see the story's over-all structure far more clearly than the first; and he should notice many details of its texture which escaped him before. This, of course, is what normally happens when one re-experiences any good work of art—a painting or a play or a sonata. If the work is very rich, it will withstand a great deal of repeated use before wearing thin.

So it is not really unnatural that in the following analysis we shall in effect be rereading "Counterparts." However, let's begin by going back, in imagination, to our *first* reading, and noting some of the things that took place as we initially worked our way into the virtual life which Joyce has created here. At least, this is something like what *should* have occurred. Incidentally, we shall assume that we started out knowing next to nothing about Joyce or about his other writings.

The first item to catch our eye should have been the title. Like many creative writers—especially modern ones—Joyce chose his titles with great care. He wanted each title to serve as a gateway

[10] A Roman Catholic prayer that goes as follows: "Hail Mary, full of grace! the Lord is with thee; blessed art thou amongst women, and blessed is the Fruit of thy womb, Jesus. Holy Mary, Mother of God, pray for us sinners, now and at the hour of our death. Amen."

[11] "Counterparts" from *Dubliners* by James Joyce. Reprinted by permission of The Viking Press, Inc. All rights reserved.

into the unique virtual world of the particular story, novel, play, or poem. It is always safest to assume that this is the author's practice, and therefore to note the title. And "Counterparts" is a title especially worth noting, because, being a perfect plurisign here, it warns us in advance of the pattern which the story will follow. It even announces the specific kind of character relationships to watch for and suggests the general "thematic" content of the story.

Now, the average reader probably will not know all of the conceptual meanings of the term *counterpart,* nor is he expected to consult a dictionary, but at the very least, the title word should suggest things which are somehow alike. Almost everything in this story is connected with the notion of "counterparts." The characters, the action, the conflicts all stress the idea of parallelism, as we shall see as we go along. (Even much of the textural detail involves this idea, in one way or another.) If we did bother to look up *counterpart* in a dictionary, we might find the following:

> 1. a copy; duplicate. 2. a part that answers to another, as each part of a document executed in duplicate. 3. one of two parts which fit each other; a thing which complements something else. 4. a person or thing closely resembling another.
>
> (*American College Dictionary*)

Incidentally, Farrington's job at Crosbie and Alleyne's law offices is to copy legal documents. (See definition 2.)

Thus, Joyce's title alone orients us with remarkable accuracy toward his story, but of course we pause only an instant before reading the opening paragraph. And "Counterparts" is the type of story that wastes no time getting going:

> The bell rang furiously and, when Miss Parker went to the tube, a furious voice called out in a piercing North of Ireland accent:
> "Send Farrington here!"
> Miss Parker returned to her machine, saying to a man who was writing at a desk:
> "Mr. Alleyne wants you upstairs."
> The man muttered "*Blast* him!" under his breath and pushed back his chair to stand up.

This is a brilliant opening because it tells us so much without holding us up. Taking a close look at these eight lines we may be surprised at how much they tell us. They establish a man-against-man conflict, between someone called Farrington (obviously a subordinate) and someone called *Mr.* Alleyne (obviously the boss). Thus they point up a difference between the two men; but they also tell us that the two are alike, both being violent, hot-tempered people who apparently hate each other. They also tell us that Mr. Alleyne has absolute authority over Farrington. (This is shown in Alleyne's tone and in the promptness of Farrington's obedience.) They tell us that, much as Farrington hates Alleyne, he also fears him and does not dare curse him aloud in the presence of the woman clerk. It looks very much as if Alleyne is a tyrant, and as if Farrington is a cowardly menial. Farrington's status in the office is further defined by the way Alleyne refers to him, simply as "Farrington," and by the way Joyce does, as merely "a man" and "the man." One more point: Mr. Alleyne's "furious" voice has "a piercing North of Ireland accent"; as it turns out, this apparently minor detail actually introduces a motif that recurs several times throughout the story.

We could go on with this detailed analysis of the opening paragraphs, but the idea should be clear: much of the whole story, in "Counterparts," is presented in embryo on the first page. The early sentences, scenes, or stanzas of a good creative work are likely to be especially revealing. An experienced reader pays close attention to the beginning, because it furnishes him with an aerial photograph of the terrain. It sets up key plurisigns and main parallels and contrasts. It inducts the reader imaginatively into the author's virtual world.

But, since we have already read through the whole story at least once, let us now look at "Counterparts" as a complete work, using some of the critical concepts discussed in the last chapter.

The Characters

Our interest centers around Farrington; it is his story. The events that occur happen to him, and they are seen mostly through his eyes. Furthermore, one senses that this small fragment of his life, merely a single afternoon and evening, is intended to sum up and stand for his whole pathetic existence. As a matter of fact, though the reader would not know this from "Counterparts" alone, Farrington's story, like the other stories in *Dubliners,* is intended to typify all of Irish life, as Joyce saw it. Joyce conceived of the book as ". . . a chapter in the moral history of my country." And he adds (in a letter to his publisher), "I chose Dublin for the scene because that city seemed to me the centre of paralysis." Some critics have gone much further than Joyce himself, finding in these stories an image of modern man in general, trapped in his self-created waste-land of bourgeois, urban "civilization."

Farrington's personality is rendered swiftly and deftly. Physically he is immense, but also overweight, out of condition, and inclined to drink. Emotionally he is equally unhealthy—immature, self-centered, unstable, bitter, irresponsible, vile-tempered, vindictive, full of self-pity. Mentally he is a mediocrity (though he fancies himself rather bright) and given to compensation-fantasies of sex and self-assertion. Morally he is a coward and incurably dishonest, with others and above all with himself. Spiritually he is empty. He is an unhappy failure in his job, in his marriage, in his family life. Though he is a man in body and age, he has never outgrown his attachment to his "gang." Only in the alcoholic conviviality of pub-crawling does he manage any "successes," and these are artificial, tenuous, and temporary. The first impression we get of him is that of an overgrown schoolboy, too big for his grade because he has failed so often, and chafing under the authority of a ruthless headmaster. His need to show off before his peers and his erotic daydreaming further reinforce this impression of neurotic adolescence.

His fellow workers, we gather, tolerate him but secretly perhaps despise him. His only "friends" are his drinking buddies, who apparently more or less resemble him.

Farrington suffers from the bullying of two bosses, Mr. Alleyne at work and his wife Ada at home. He, in turn, bullies each of them when he dares to: Mr. Alleyne under the inspiration of the porter, Miss Delacour, and his anger; Ada under the false courage of alcohol.

In the three episodes which make up the story, the main characters aside from Farrington himself fall into two groups. The first group are his antagonists—Alleyne, then Weathers (the vaudeville acrobat), and finally the son Tom. All of these intended victims (actually his vanquishers) are male, and all are small. Joyce emphasizes this point: Farrington, though small in every other respect is (by contrast) physically big; each of his opponents, though bigger than he in other ways, is physically unimpressive: Alleyne is "a little man" (so short he can hardly see over the pile of papers on his desk), "fragile," a "manikin," a "dwarf"; Weathers, though powerfully muscled, is "young," "a stripling," "a mere boy"; and

Tom is "a little boy," "the little boy," "the little boy," "the little boy," "little whelp," and "the boy."

The second group of main characters includes the two women who intrigue Farrington, first Miss Delacour (Mr. Alleyne's perfumed client) and later the actress from the Tivoli. Both are buxom, vaguely exotic, sensual, and possibly accessible—but not accessible to Farrington. Both of these women arouse vague erotic longings in Farrington, but Farrington lacks the courage to approach either. Both women contrast sharply with Farrington's wife Ada, who is described as "a little sharp-faced woman who bullied her husband when he was sober and was bullied by him when he was drunk," and who spends much of her time at the neighborhood chapel (as Farrington spends his in the Dublin pubs).

Within Farrington's character, the only interesting complexity is the contrast between his delusions of superiority and his actual mediocrity. Especially under the stimulation of drink, he imagines himself not only as a great lover but also as a man about town, a man "who had definite notions of what was what"; and yet, like all bullies, he picks on those who are less consequential than he is, for instance bartenders. Thus, in O'Neill's bar, "He put his penny on the counter; . . . leaving the curate to grope for it in the gloom." And later, after Weathers has beaten him wrestling, he snarls fiercely at the onlooking bartender, who unwisely has complimented the victor: "What the hell do you know about it? . . . What do you put in your gab for?"

The Action

The action of "Counterparts" is the distance between Mr. Alleyne's furious shout through the speaking tube—"Send Farrington here!" —and the dying fall of a child's pleading voice in "O, pa! . . . Don't beat me, pa! And I'll . . . I'll say a *Hail Mary* for you . . . I'll say a *Hail Mary* for you, pa, if you don't beat me . . . I'll say a *Hail Mary* . . ."

The events, which cover only four or five hours in Farrington's life, consist of three episodes separated by brief transitional passages. The first episode takes place in the office, the second in various pubs, and the last in Farrington's kitchen. Thus we are given glimpses of this man at work, at play (in society), and at home (in "the bosom of his family").

In each episode, Farrington is pitted against an individual opponent and is defeated by him; and yet in each Farrington manages in one way or another to score a counter-blow, avenge himself partially, and salvage some bit of self-esteem. But in each successive "round" his opponent is less formidable, the prize at stake is less important, Farrington's self-redeeming blow is dirtier, and his position at the bell is more ignoble. Thus each new round repeats the basic action of the preceding one, but with significant variations. The effect is that of a descending spiral.

In the opening round, Farrington puts up what is for him a pretty good fight against a relatively worthy antagonist. In fact, the action see-saws back and forth. Mr. Alleyne scores first with his "furious" order over the speaking-tube. Farrington counters with a (characteristically) muttered curse. Then Alleyne pummels him verbally in his office. Farrington considers asking him for a pay advance, but typically lacks the courage. Alleyne scores again with a repetition of the threat to propose to his partner that they fire Farrington. Farrington retreats to his own desk, then scores a sneak counter-blow by slipping out to O'Neill's for a quick drink. On Farrington's return, Mr. Shelley takes up where Alleyne left off. Significantly, Shelley's tirade is delivered "in the presence of the public," whereas Alleyne had abused him in privacy. Farrington's humiliation is becoming more and more public. And on Farrington's second trip to Alleyne's office, the abuse is again public, delivered in the presence of Miss Delacour, whom Farrington would much more like to impress than he would anyone in the office outside. This time Alleyne's attack is more cutting because of the woman. Mr. Alleyne treats Farrington as the lowest menial. By now Farrington is getting groggy, literally and figuratively. Farrington is too befuddled from porter and rage even to copy.

The final phase of this first round takes place in the main office and in the presence of both Miss Delacour and Farrington's fellow clerks. This time Alleyne's abuse is really sadistic: he is out not only to humiliate Farrington publicly but to show off his strength to Miss Delacour. Farrington counters with an inspired retort. In answer to Alleyne's stupid question, "Do you think me an utter fool?" he comments, "I don't think, sir, . . . that that's a fair question to put to me."

This blow, in the first round, is Farrington's only real triumph of the day. But Joyce makes it clear that it is an accidental punch, and it astonishes everyone, "the author of the witticism no less than his neighbors." In effect, Farrington scores only because Alleyne stuck his chin out. However, it is a telling counterpunch, and amuses the "amiable" Miss Delacour.

But Farrington's victory is both short-lived and unreal, because he is forced at once to apologize, in front of the same public (including Miss Delacour); and he knows that Alleyne will now hound him out of his job. Though this is Farrington's best round, he loses even it. However, his one solid punch gives him the false courage to go on to the next round.

After a transitional passage, in which Farrington pawns his watch to get drinking money, we proceed with Round Two. Farrington starts well for Farrington—or seems to, from an outsider's view—reliving vicariously, and with improvements, his brief success of Round One. And his buddies are willing to cooperate as long as Farrington can buy his share (with money from the pawned watch). The reader recognizes by now that Farrington's position is becoming increasingly false with each new move. At the moment he is accepted as a hero, but he is a doomed hero, and even he knows it. For a while, however, Farrington holds up well, doling out his artificial wealth with care because he knows how completely this good fellowship depends on it.

Even the vaudeville player Weathers seems more friend than foe in these glowing hours, despite his being an Englishman. Farrington's best moment in this round comes when the actress seems interested in him; but as usual he lacks the courage to follow up her apparent invitation. And now comes the crusher: Farrington, the local strongman and in this case also Ireland's hope against the English, is defeated twice in a row by young Weathers. Once again, Farrington's counterattack is a sneak one and indirect: it is thrown at a rather stupid but otherwise innocent onlooker, the bartender. Thus once more both his defeat and his victory (equally a defeat in terms of his morale) are public; but this time the public is composed, not of his fellow clerks (whom he despises anyway) but of his own best "friends." Further, his vanquisher is merely a traveling acrobat and a boy; and the prize at stake is not his livelihood, but merely his local prestige as a strongman.

Thus, as Joyce summarizes between-the-rounds (p. 239), Farrington has now been stripped of everything: his job (almost certainly), his watch, the few shillings he got for it, his "honor," his temporary feeling of self-esteem, his alcoholic glow, most of his self-delusions, and his cronies. He is now alone and headed homeward, and "he loathed returning to his home." The Miss Delacours and the Tivoli actresses have disappeared even from his world of fantasy; ahead of him waits only "a little sharp-faced woman" named Ada by whom he has had five children through some trick of fate unfathomable to him.

But not even Ada is awaiting him, to give him the satisfaction of receiving the abuse of his vengeance. Ada has gone to chapel, the dinner is cold, the fire is out. And the third and final round is fought against his little son Tom, in a desperate effort to reestablish his ego.

This round Farrington wins—in a sense. The boy is a small child and helpless before his father's rage. But there is no public to witness Farrington's victory. And what a "victory" it is! Not even a man as adept at kidding himself as Farrington could take much pride in this conquest. Furthermore, doesn't the child win anyway? Doesn't the boy, in his terrified pleading at the story's end, reveal that he possesses hidden resources which his father, for all his brutal strength, can never touch? And this is quite apart from the probability that the injustice of this beating will destroy any trace of respect which the son may still feel for the father.

Thus the action of "Counterparts" consists of a series of blows, both material and psychological, which temporarily destroy Farrington's ego, reducing him from a pseudo-man to a cornered and enraged animal. The action is deliberately initiated by Alleyne, then inadvertently carried a step further by Weathers, and concluded by Farrington himself, with the passive assistance of his other bully (his wife) and the innocent child Tom. Or it can almost be seen as a story of self-mutilation, with Alleyne merely triggering a sequence of events in which Farrington himself increasingly becomes his own destroyer.

One final point about the action in "Counterparts": our use of the round-by-round analogy in some ways oversimplifies Joyce's "plot" here. For example, it is quite certain that Joyce also intended us to see the last scene as a return to the opening scene, with of course ironic differences. The first and last scenes are counterparts, the last becoming an ironic parody of the first. Farrington finally achieves a position of absolute authority which parallels that held by Mr. Alleyne in the first episode. The end of the story takes us back to the beginning, with Farrington reenacting Alleyne's role and Tom replacing himself. Nothing has really happened: we have simply come full circle, and the cycle is ready to repeat itself the following day.

These two views of the action are not mutually exclusive. Joyce undoubtedly wanted us to see it in both ways at once, for only then do we perceive all of the ironic implications of this story.

The Conflicts

The main conflict in "Counterparts" may be viewed in various ways; or, to put it differently, there are three or four levels of conflict in this story.

We have already seen in detail the man-against-man conflict, or rather conflicts, for there is a series of three. They might be described as: first, man-sized schoolboy against child-sized bully; second, man-sized bully against boy-sized man; and finally, man-sized animal against child-sized child. However, this summary takes into account only physical size, and therefore tells only part of the story. The other part might be summarized in this way: first, half-man versus half-man; second, quarter-man versus full man; and finally, no-man versus God's child. It should be pretty apparent by now that this is a far more complex short story than it may at first have seemed.

But there are still other ways to see the central conflict. For instance, we can see it as Farrington against his social environment. His three individual antagonists represent, respectively, his professional colleagues, his social colleagues, and his domestic relations. Thus, we see Farrington in each of his chief life-roles in turn: as worker, as player, and as family man. In each of these roles, he is worse than a failure. So we have Farrington versus his world, or, if one prefers, versus life itself; and by his world or his life he is defeated.

Again, we can read "Counterparts" as a picture of a man in conflict with himself. On the one hand, there is Farrington's desire for independence and self-assertion. On the other hand, there are his cowardice, his unwillingness to work, his emotional instability, his selfishness, his alcoholism, his temper, his bitterness, his general incompetence. He is by nature incompetent to achieve even *his* elementary ambitions.

Finally, it is even possible to see in "Counterparts" a conflict between man and the supernatural. "Naturalistic" critics, with their deterministic philosophy, might well regard Farrington as the victim of "destiny" or "fate." By now he stands helpless in the face of forces beyond his control. From another point of view it could be argued that Farrington is an image of man without God (Joyce himself, though not a believer, undoubtedly saw him this way, for he saw all of Dublin as largely a city without any real spiritual life, with only institutionalized religion and empty rituals.) Thus Farrington is a man devoid of Grace, in any sense of that term.

Which of these views of the central conflict is right? Luckily there is no need to choose: the story as a whole is a plurisign and can easily carry all these meanings and more.

The Setting

Though Joyce spends relatively few words on it, the setting, both physical and social, plays several interesting roles in "Counterparts." In the first place, the general setting—the city of Dublin—is itself a counterpart to Farrington. Like him, it exudes an atmosphere of slovenliness, ill health, dreariness, murkiness, and false gentility. Like him, it appears furtive, bleak, defeated. The city is a sort of shabby jungle, and Farrington seems perfectly adapted to it, its product and creature. He knows all of Dublin's alleys and back-doors, though the knowledge avails him nothing.

Second, there are the physical settings of the three main scenes. We are not told much, but each brush-stroke counts. Our general impression of the law offices where Farrington works is that they are rather stodgy and shopworn, an impression created by a single detail—the stairs are rickety. Otherwise, we picture the scene in the image of the people who inhabit it. The same point applies to the final setting, Farrington's kitchen, about which we are told only that it is empty and dark, and the fire is out.

However, the various pub scenes in between are created quite vividly, though in an unusual way. We know next to nothing of how the pubs are arranged or furnished, but we do know their characteristic sounds and smells and that they are brightly lighted. Thus, Farrington at his desk thinks longingly of "drinking with his friends amid the glare of gas and the clatter of glasses"; and "his head was not clear and his mind wandered away to the glare and rattle of the public-house." Then, having pawned his watch, he strides through the streets, "and his nose already sniffed the curling fumes of punch." Throughout the scenes that follow, the air of the pubs seems thick with the odor of hot punch and other liquors and crackling with the sounds of glasses, banal talk, and raucous laughter. Finally, as Farrington waits for his streetcar he longs to be back in the "hot reeking public-house." By contrast, of course, his own kitchen is empty even of the odors of a cheap stew, for dinner is long over and the fire has gone out.

A third interesting use of setting in "Counterparts" concerns the weather. Here again, there are few specific references, but the weather seems to parallel and reflect Farrington's personal situation, both external and internal. As he comes out of O'Neill's pub, near the beginning, "Darkness, accompanied by a thick fog, was gaining upon the dusk of February." A bit later, as he tries to copy the contract, he muses that "the dark damp night was coming." After the last set-to with Alleyne, as Farrington waits in the gloom outside for someone he can touch for a loan, "He felt his great body again aching for the comfort of the public-house. The fog had begun to chill him." As he and his cronies leave their first pub, "Rain was drizzling down on the cold streets." One wonders if this nasty February weather doesn't mirror perfectly the state of Farrington's own mind and soul. Furthermore, the oppressiveness of the weather intensifies our sense that life is rapidly closing in on Farrington and that his momentary glow of self-esteem is indeed an illusion already threatened.

The Point of View

On the surface, "Counterparts" is told from Farrington's point of view; the camera-eye is Farrington's. But actually we have here a double point of view. We witness the events and the characters (including Farrington) through Farrington's eyes (and ears and nose), but we also understand everything (especially Farrington himself) from Joyce's vantage point.

That the two points of view are very different is important to the story. Farrington is by nature an uncomprehending observer, especially of himself, for he is a self-deluder. One doubts that even at the end of the story Farrington realizes how complete a fool (or worse) he has made of himself. This incapacity for self-discovery is one thing that bars Farrington from the status of tragic hero. For a growing awareness of himself, of his tragic situation, and of the tragic possibilities of life is a basic characteristic of a tragic protagonist. Farrington is not tragic, merely pathetic.

By means of the double point of view Joyce manages to tell us a great deal more than Farrington himself could ever understand. Furthermore, the discrepancy between Farrington's view of things and Joyce's is a primary source of irony. Farrington gives himself away in the very moments when he is trying hardest to preserve some semblance of personal dignity. In the final scene Joyce strips him of his last shred of human decency and exhibits him as a caged brute. It is a cruel unmasking, but we feel, with Joyce, that Farrington has brought it on himself.

Some Symbols

"Counterparts" is obviously not an allegory, however many "themes" different readers may choose to find in it; nor is it an especially symbolistic kind of story. Yet, for all his realism, Joyce was by gift a poet, and all genuine poets tend to employ language symbolically. "Counterparts" therefore contains several interesting though not especially obtrusive bits of symbolism.

One of them involves a play on *accents*. Each of Farrington's "enemies" has an accent different from his, which is presumably standard Dublin Irish. Thus Mr. Alleyne's accent is a "piercing North of Ireland," the acrobat Weathers' is presumably English, and the boy Tom's is "flat" (perhaps like his mother's). On the other hand, the Tivoli actress, whom Farrington finds very attractive also has "a London accent," but in her case this adds to her fascination. Like many provincial people, Farrington seems both attracted to and antagonistic toward things which are foreign to his world.

Another symbol, this one associated with Miss Delacour, is *perfume*. Joyce has Farrington notice this perfume three separate times, until it seems to become a general symbol for all of Farrington's sensual and romantic longings. He craves a life full of "moist pungent . . . perfumes," but has to settle for an occasional few hours amid the fumes of hot punches.

One of the most interesting symbols in "Counterparts" involves *eyes* and *faces*. On the first page, Joyce writes that Farrington's eyes "bulged forward slightly and the whites of them were dirty." Several times this description is repeated. (The reader may be reminded of the ancient notion that the eyes are mirrors of the soul.) Farrington's eyes and face are incidentally contrasted with Mr. Alleyne's, who is "wearing gold-rimmed glasses on a clean-shaven face . . . The head itself was so pink and hairless it seemed like a large egg reposing on the papers." Farrington, on the other hand, "had a hanging face, dark wine-coloured . . ." Joyce makes the most of the idea that Alleyne's head is egg-like, as when Farrington "stared fixedly at the polished skull . . . , gauging its fragility." Again, later on, Alleyne's tirade becomes "so bitter and violent that the man could hardly restrain his fist from descending upon the head of the manikin before him." However, he does refrain, and instead glances "from the lady's face to the little egg-shaped head and back again," and then delivers his "felicitous" answer to Alleyne's stupid question. This emphasis on Alleyne's egg-shell fragility conveys to us vividly the intensity of Farrington's frustration.

Joyce also uses *money* symbolically in this story. How much money Farrington has on him is an exact barometer of his emotional climate. When he stands penniless outside the office trying to play a loan, "He felt savage and thirsty and revengeful, annoyed with himself and with everyone else." But the moment he is handed six shillings for his watch, "He came out of the pawn-office joyfully, making a little cylinder of the coins between his thumb and fingers . . . [He] passed through the crowd, looking on the spectacle generally with proud satisfaction and staring masterfully at the office-girls." Three bars later we find Farrington nearly broke again, and "He cursed his want of money and cursed all the rounds he had stood, particularly all the whiskies and Apollinaris which he had stood to Weathers." A few minutes after this, having been defeated by Weathers, he stands alone waiting for his tram: "He was full of smouldering anger and revengefulness. He felt humiliated and discontented; he did not even feel drunk; and he had only twopence in his pocket. He cursed everything." Thus Farrington's money-possession parallels his self-possession; this in itself tells us something about his values.

But by far the most dramatic use of symbolism in "Counterparts" occurs when Tom offers his father the bribe of a *Hail Mary*. This gesture also brings the irony of the story to a climax. In fact, it would be impossible to list all the ways in which the *Hail Mary* prayer is a plurisign here, but we might note a few. A *Hail Mary* is a plea for compassion, which, heaven knows, Tom needs from his father at this moment; but Farrington at this moment is as devoid of compassion, for anyone or anything, as man can get. Again, ever since Farrington's first words in the story (*"Blast* him!") many of his most heartfelt thoughts have been curses, and blasphemous ones at that. Furthermore, Tom could scarcely have picked a less appropriate member of the Holy Family than the Virgin Mary to intercede for *his* father. Then there is the fact that the *Hail Mary* prayer appeals to the Virgin as a parent; Tom is being savagely beaten by his father. Again, Tom is using the offer of a sacred prayer as a bribe: he is rendering unto Caesar a thing that is God's. Yet again, Tom is relying on his father's religious convictions, whereas the reader must wonder if Farrington has any. Finally, Tom is ironically unaware of all the points just mentioned.

He is also unaware of the extent to which his father *does* need divine intercession, of the extent to which Farrington *is* a sinner and to which this, in a sense, *is* the hour of his death.

The very inadequacy of this partial analysis should at least show the inexhaustible richness which an inspired literary symbol can take on. Try to imagine how much less of a story "Counterparts" would be without the *Hail Mary* passage.

Conclusion

The sample analysis offered in this chapter is of one creative work only, and it represents but two readers' experience. You should feel free to take issue, on the basis of your own experience of the story, with anything which has been said. But you should remember that anybody's "interpretation" is valid and valuable only insofar as it helps to account for what is in the work. The ultimate test of an interpretation of any work of art is how satisfactorily it translates into conceptual terms the actual experience represented by the specific notes one hears, the specific colors, lines, and forms one sees, the specific words one reads.

A number of further points about the texture of "Counterparts" —about, for example, Joyce's use of irony—are raised in the first exercise on page 254.

EXERCISES

A. Think about the following questions for class discussion. In general, they are designed to bring out fine points in the texture of "Counterparts" which were deliberately excluded from the preceding analysis.

1. In what ways are the situations in "Counterparts" ironic?
2. Where is the language itself ironic?
3. The real-life person on whom Farrington was modeled was not a particularly big man. Why does Joyce make so much of Farrington's massiveness?
4. What extra touch is gained by having the brass nameplate read *Mr. Alleyne?*
5. How does Joyce reveal Farrington's lack of physical fitness? Why does he stress it?
6. There are many detailed similarities between the opening episode and the final episode. Name some.
7. What part does the idea of mimicry play in the story?
8. Why does Joyce so often apply the word *furtively* to Farrington's actions?
9. Why does Joyce make Miss Delacour "middle-aged"?
10. How does Joyce use the many images of light and darkness in this story?
11. Why (on p. 235) does Joyce have Farrington recall that Higgins has "two establishments to keep up"? (Incidentally, this was one of several details in this story which the publishers objected to.)
12. What is the function (on p. 236) of the brief description of the crowded Dublin streets?
13. How does Farrington (on p. 236) revise his retort to Alleyne in preparing it for recital to "the boys"?
14. What, beyond its literal meaning, does the following passage (on p. 237) tell us?

    When the round was over there was a pause. O'Halloran had money but neither of the other two seemed to have any; so the whole party left the shop somewhat regretfully.

15. What is the function of this detail (on p. 237)?

    The three men pushed past the whining match-sellers at the door

16. Why does Joyce make Weathers and his friends theater people?

17. Why does Joyce arrange for Farrington's wife to be away at chapel when Farrington gets home?

18. In the last few paragraphs, Joyce stops using Farrington's name, and refers to him simply as "the man." Why?

19. Why does Joyce never actually *show* us Farrington's apology to Mr. Alleyne?

20. In what ways does Joyce prepare us imaginatively for Farington's final reduction to animality?

21. "Counterparts" was one of the stories in *Dubliners* to which various publishers objected most strenuously. Can you suggest possible reasons why?

22. One critic has proposed the theory that Farrington's wife, like Alleyne, is a North of Irelander and probably a Protestant. If so, the boy Tom is probably a Protestant too, whereas his father is almost certainly a Roman Catholic, like most Dubliners. What is your reaction to this theory? How would you test it?

23. Why does Joyce bother with Farrington's mistake in writing *Bernard Bernard* instead of *Bernard Bodley?*

24. How does Miss Parker tie into the story?

25. What, in your opinion, is the "theme" of this story? In what sense is it a "theme"? Can you see other possible "themes"?

26. Why do "ideas," as a formal element, not figure prominently in this story?

27. Do you think Joyce would have accepted your notion of his "theme"? Why or why not?

28. To what extent do you feel that the present authors have "read things into" Joyce's story?

29. Can you think up a better title than "Counterparts" for this story?

B. Write a paper (1800 to 2000 words) on another short story, short play, or novelette in which you analyze the work along the lines followed in this chapter, though of course in less detail. Build your generalizations on specific references to the text.

13. Informative and Creative: Fusion and Matrix

> The scientific use of language is the highest development of human speech *in one direction*, and it is important that the student of literature understand it so that he will not confuse its aims, methods, limitations, and criteria of success with those of literature, which is the highest development of human speech *in another direction*. It is also important for the student of science to understand the use of language which is literature, so that he in turn may not confuse its aims, methods, limitations and criteria of success with those of scientific communication.[1]
>
> THOMAS C. POLLOCK, *The Nature of Literature*

The Middle Ground

The passage quoted above states the rationale of the last eight chapters. We have discussed, in turn, two basic uses of language; to avoid extra complications, we have purposely stuck to relatively pure forms of each use. But now, before turning to persuasion—our third use—we should remind ourselves that neither informative writing nor creative writing is always that "pure." There is a great middle ground of literature where the two uses coexist in all sorts of combinations and blends. This is true even today, when literature like everything else has gone in for specialization; it was truer still ten centuries or even as recently as two centuries ago.

[1] FROM *The Nature of Literature* by Thomas C. Pollock. Published in 1942 by the Princeton University Press. Reprinted by permission of the publisher.

A middle ground will always exist, for three basic reasons. In the first place, as we have seen, language itself is by nature both conceptual and evocative, and try though he may, the writer can never wholly eliminate either kind of meaning. Secondly, the two kinds of knowledge—conceptual and experiential—are intimately related: they coexist in everyone's consciousness and they depend on and modify each other in very complex ways which psychologists and linguists are just beginning to understand. And finally, human purposes are seldom pure: it's a rare lyric poet who is not at least secretly fond of some of the ideas he builds into his poems, however artistic; and there has probably never been a reporter who didn't find it painful and unnatural to have to keep his personal feelings, impressions, and intuitions out of his reports.

So it is not at all strange that the informative and creative uses intermingle in many forms of literature which we have deliberately bypassed up to now. To begin with the obvious, there are even certain recognized literary genres, some of them very old, whose very reason for existence is the fact that they consciously combine concept and experience, information and virtual life. For instance, there is the historical novel; it is by definition a "mixed" form from our point of view, but what could be more natural than for a learned and talented creative writer to try to integrate his knowledge of history with his vision of what it was like to live in the skin of those famous figures and to undergo their experiences? Then there is the fictional biography, a contradiction in terms but an inevitable result of our lack of genuine information about so many important people who actually lived. For example no fully developed biography of Shakespeare is possible unless it be a fictional one.

In Chapter 11 we considered allegory and satire as aspects of fiction. But allegories—along with parables and fables—are a very ancient combination of conceptual and experiential knowledge—natural products of our impulse to give imaginative life and emotional meaning to ideas. And satire is likewise a combination of uses, in this case of the creative and the persuasive. It is normally written by men whose interests are divided between social and psychological (or some other) criticism and commentary, on the one hand, and creative literature, on the other. And this has been true from the time of Aristophanes or the great Latin satirists, through Ben Jonson, Jonathan Swift, and Voltaire, to such moderns as George Bernard Shaw, Aldous Huxley, and George Orwell. Such men are by nature intellectuals and artists at once.

In our own day, the proliferation of the social sciences—which are concerned, though in a different way, with the same subject that has always intrigued artists: man as individual and as institutional creature—has produced an enormous amount of serious creative writing, both good and bad, which is half case study and half fiction or drama and occasionally poetry. Even the best critics are not entirely used to this peculiarly modern development, as their reviews clearly show: one critic reviews a novel like Arthur Koestler's *Darkness at Noon* as if it were pure novel, the next one sees it mainly as popularized political science and psychological analysis. But the critics may as well reconcile themselves to this latest mixture of the conceptual and the creative, and recognize it as such; for it is certain to be with us for a long time to come. Science fiction is still another current blending of the two uses, though only half-serious—so far—because the science and the fiction are seldom in balance: the science, often being quite sound, is usually taken seriously by the critics, while they scorn the fiction as generally incompetent.

But all of these standard hybrids are obvious and deliberate combinations of the informative and the creative, the conceptual and the experiential. More interesting, because less obvious, is the large quantity of good writing in which the two kinds of knowledge and the two literary purposes are unconsciously and inevitably fused. The rest of the chapter will be given to this portion of the middle ground.

A Single Example

We will begin with one short example of what might be called *pure blending*, a passage from Thoreau's *Walden*:

Time is but the stream I go a-fishing in. I drink at it; but while I drink I see the sandy bottom and detect how shallow it is. Its thin current slides away, but eternity remains. I would drink deeper; fish in the sky whose bottom is pebbly with stars. I cannot count one. I know not the first letter of the alphabet. I have always been regretting that I was not as wise as the day I was born. The intellect is a cleaver; it discerns and rifts its way into the secret of things. I do not wish to be any more busy with my hands than is necessary. My head is hands and feet. I feel all my best faculties concentrated in it. My instinct tells me that my head is an organ for burrowing, as some creatures use their snout and forepaws, and with it I would mine and burrow my way through these hills. I think that the richest vein is somewhere hereabouts; so by the divining rod and thin rising vapors I judge; and here I will begin to mine.

Thoreau is dealing here with abstract concepts of the kind which have occupied philosophers for two thousand years: time and eternity, appearance and reality, and the function of the intellect. But the same themes, as we noted in Chapter 10, are also perennial elements in poetry. So it is really quite natural for Thoreau, who was both philosopher and poet, to present his concepts in images and metaphors: time is a stream; eternity its sandy bottom—a metaphor which is suddenly inverted as if Thoreau were looking at the sky reflected in the stream. The eternal bottom of the sky is pebbly with stars. Confronted with such a picture, Thoreau sees all learning as losing, and offers a series of personal paradoxes. Then more metaphors: the intellect is a cleaver; the head is an organ for burrowing. Knowing involves penetrating, mining in the hills, seeking a rich vein. But how to know where to dig? Through the intuition of divining rod and thin rising vapors.

Apart from *these* words, *these* images, what is it that Thoreau is trying to say? His metaphors are fully as important as his concepts. In fact, we find ourselves, as we read, *thinking in metaphors*. And if we look closely we discover that not only images and metaphors but sounds play a part in the over-all effect. Thoreau is using the thingness of words much as the poet does. The whole passage is rhythmical. The first two sentences—except for the last two words —actually scan; from there on, the rhythm is one of phrases and sentences much like the rhythm of free verse. Thoreau makes little use of alliteration—because if he soothes us we may stop thinking— but his words are rich with interrelated sounds—sounds which taken together sometimes suggest their subject matter. Look at and listen to the sentence: "The intellect is a cleaver; it discerns and rifts its way into the secret of things," and notice the repetition of short *i* sounds in *i*ntellect, *i*s, *i*t, d*i*scerns, r*i*fts, *i*ts, *i*nto, and th*i*ngs, and the hard *c* sounds in intelle*c*t, *c*leaver, and se*c*ret. Notice also the alternation of the impersonal and the personal: *time, I; intellect, I; my head, I;* and so on.

A passage like this recalls some of the poetry discussed in Chapter 10. Even the theme of Time appears here. Yet this is as much philosophy as poetry. We would find it hard to classify not only this passage but the whole of *Walden:* Is it informative or creative? Fortunately we do not have to decide; the categories we have been dealing with overlap and combine, in this case as naturally as living by Walden Pond and thinking did for Thoreau.

The Creative-Informative Matrix

Many modern readers brought up on contemporary poetry, fiction, and philosophy have considerable trouble not only with works like *Walden* but with a great deal of literature—much of it very old, and some of it quite new. Many of the books of the Bible do not fit neatly into our informative and creative categories. In fact, most of the "scriptures" of the great world religions are both experiential and conceptual. Plato deals in abstract concepts, but often through the medium of myths and images. Most of the classical philosophers use language that is poetic. And so on into more recent times: the novel in the eighteenth century is frequently a vehicle for the expression of the writer's ideas, directly addressed to his audience; and poetry, until the romantic movement at least, was thought of partly as a mode of instruction. Even today, essays, columns, "reportage," and interpretive news stories frequently combine the creative and the informative.

We can compare this development of literature to a tree: the roots are planted in conceptual and experiential knowledge, and the trunk—that is, the earliest literature—is a combination of the creative and the informative. Later on, branches develop—some purely informative, some purely creative; but the trunk continues upward, though diminished in comparison with the branches.

Some literary historians see the common ancestor of poet, philosopher, historian, scientist, and lawmaker as the seer. Helen Chadwick, in her book *Poetry and Prophecy,* describes the work of these earliest intellectual leaders in these words:

> . . . it is clear that the function of the seer was practically universal in early Europe. For centuries before Christ it was important in the south—in Thrace, in Greece, and doubtless in Etruria. During the Roman period and the Dark Ages it was held in high estimation in central Europe. Long before the close of the first millennium it had left a rich store of legends to the Celtic and Teutonic populations of the outer fringes of Europe.

The fundamental elements of the prophetic function seem to have been everywhere the same. Everywhere the gift of poetry is inseparable from divine inspiration. Everywhere this inspiration carries with it knowledge—whether of the past, in the form of history and genealogy; of the hidden present, in the form commonly of scientific information; or of the future, in the form of prophetic utterance in the narrowest sense.

If we look at some early writings from several different cultures, we can see clearly what Mrs. Chadwick is talking about, though the distribution of the following examples is even more widespread than Mrs. Chadwick indicates. All of the passages present visions of life as it might be, should be, or once was, and all of them are combinations of conceptual and experiential knowledge and of informative and creative expression. It is unfortunate that we must read them in translation, but even in translation their evocative power is apparent. The first is from Hesiod's *Works and Days,* and was written in Greece in the eighth century B.C.

> . . . they who give straight judgments to strangers and to the men of the land, and go not aside from what is just, their city flourishes, and the people prosper in it: Peace, the nurse of children, is abroad in their land, and all-seeing Zeus never decrees cruel war against them. Neither famine nor disaster ever haunt men who do true justice; but light-heartedly they tend the fields which are all their care. The earth bears them victual in plenty, and on the mountains the oak bears acorns upon the top and bees in the midst. Their woolly sheep are laden with fleeces; their women bear children like their parents. They flourish continually with good things, and do not travel on ships, for the grain-giving earth gives them fruit.

The second is from the Hebrew prophet Amos, and was probably written during the same century:

> In that day will I raise up the tabernacle of David that is fallen, and close up the breaches thereof; and I will raise up its ruins, and I will build it as in the days of old; that they may possess the remnant of Edom, and all the nations that are called by my name, saith Jehovah that doeth this. Behold, the days come, saith Jehovah, that the plowman shall overtake the reaper, and the treader of grapes him that soweth seed; and the mountains shall drop down sweet wine, and all the hills shall melt. And I will bring back the captivity of my people Israel, and they shall build the waste cities and shall inhabit them; and they shall plant vineyards and drink the wine thereof; they shall also make gardens and eat the fruit of them. And I will plant them

upon their land, and they shall be no more plucked up out of their land which I have given them, saith Jehovah thy God.

The third is from the Chinese Tao Tê Ching, written perhaps in the third century B.C.

Given a small country with few inhabitants, he could bring it about that though there should be among the people contrivances requiring ten times, a hundred times less labor, they would not use them. He could bring it about that the people would be ready to lay down their lives and lay them down again in defence of their homes, rather than emigrate. There might still be boats and carriages, but no one would go in them; there might still be weapons of war but no one would drill with them. He could bring it about that the people should have no use for any form of writing save knotted ropes, should be contented with their food, pleased with their clothing, satisfied with their homes, should take pleasure in their rustic tasks. The next place might be so near at hand that one could hear the cocks crowing in it, the dogs barking; but the people would grow old and die without ever having been there.[2]

These passages are similar in subject matter, but they produce rather different effects; and they do not all represent the same proportions of conceptual and experiential knowledge. Amos probably strikes us as being closest to poetry; the Tao Tê Ching as most conceptual. It is unfortunate that we cannot study the language of each directly, but the dependence of all three on images is apparent, as are the personification in Hesiod and the parallelisms in Amos and in the Tao Tê Ching.

All may be taken as examples of the relatively unspecialized writing of seer or prophet: they combine thought with feeling, poetic vision with philosophic content. In every culture such writing is the matrix out of which the more specialized forms develop as seer gives way to poet, on the one hand, and to philosopher and historian, on the other. It is interesting to note that this specialization of functions had gone so far by the time of Plato that the philosopher proposes to ban the poets from his Republic, chiefly because they operate *as* poets and hence purvey a brand of knowledge that is not sufficiently pure and conceptual—though Plato himself often wrote his philosophy in the language of poetry. The movement toward specialization was well underway by Plato's time,

[2] Reprinted with permission of The Macmillan Company and George Allen & Unwin, Ltd., from *The Way and Its Power* translated by Arthur Waley.

a movement that has culminated in some poetry which is non-conceptual and some art which is nonobjective on the one hand, and in "objective" reporting and a highly abstract science and philosophy on the other.

Some Later Examples

But it may be well to carry yet further the discussion of combinations. Any number of examples could be produced from earlier literature, but let us turn instead to the seventeenth and eighteenth centuries, and to English so that we can see more clearly the role of language in the combination. Here, for example, is a short passage from John Milton's *Areopagitica*, the poet's plea for freedom from censorship.

> I cannot praise a fugitive and cloistered virtue, unexercised and unbreathed, that never sallies out and sees his adversary, but shrinks out of the race, where that immortal garland is to be run for, not without dust and heat. Assuredly we bring not innocence into the world, we bring impurity much rather; that which purifies us is trial, and trial is by what is contrary. That virtue therefore which is but a youngling in the counterplots of evil, and knows not the utmost that vice promises to her fellows, and rejects it, is but a blank virtue, not a pure; her white is but an excremental whiteness.

Milton is certainly dealing in concepts—in fact, *Areopagitica* is one of the great philosophical statements on freedom of the press—but Milton has clothed his ideas in figurative language; and we may well feel that the statements are fully as important as the propositions they embody. We can translate, if we want to, and we will get a somewhat simpler kind of statement about the superiority of a virtue which has been tested through acquaintance with vice and the necessity for purification through trial. But a good deal will have been lost, and not mere decoration but knowledge.

And here is a passage from Fielding's *Tom Jones*, in which the writer is speaking to the reader in his own person:

> And here we shall of necessity be led to open a new vein of knowledge, which, if it hath been discovered, hath not, to our remembrance been wrought on by any ancient or modern writer. This vein is no other than that of contrast, which runs through all the works of the creation,

and may probably have a large share in constituting in us the idea of all beauty, as well natural as artificial: for what demonstrates the beauty and excellence of anything but its reverse? Thus the beauty of day, and that of summer, is set off by the horrors of night and winter. And, I believe, if it was possible for a man to have seen only the two former, he would have a very imperfect idea of their beauty.

This passage appears in a novel, but its language is clearly somewhat more conceptual than that used by Milton in his philosophical essay. We could, of course, find similar passages in novels today, but they would usually be spoken by the characters, not presented by the author himself.

For a final example let us look at a piece of eighteenth-century verse, a passage from Pope's *Essay on Criticism:*

> 'Tis with our judgments as our watches, none
> Go just alike, yet each believes his own.
> In poets as true Genius is but rare,
> True Taste as seldom is the Critic's share;
> Both must alike from Heav'n derive their light,
> These born to judge, as well as those to write.
> (ALEXANDER POPE, 1688–1744)

There is no doubt about either the creative or informative characteristics of these lines. The form is verse, iambic pentameter couplets. The whole figure is built on comparison, between judgment and our watches, between poet and critic, between genius and taste, and so on. The lines depend for much of their effect on the witty juxtaposition of ideas and images. Yet there is conceptual content. We can rephrase, and the propositions are still quite meaningful:

> We each trust our own judgments just as we trust our own watches;
> yet both real creative ability and real critical judgment are rare.

These examples, of course, do not mean that the purer forms of creative and informative writing did not exist in earlier centuries. Lyric poetry has a history as long as literature itself has, and some of the poems that we looked at in Chapter 10 are earlier than Milton, Pope, or Fielding. And we can, of course, find lyrics that are earlier than Plato and the Tao Tê Ching. Yet the tendency to separate and to "purify" has become markedly stronger in the last two centuries. Philosophy has moved closer to science and even to mathematics, while both the novel and short story have moved closer to poetry. And poetry itself—which was once used for all sorts of purposes—as witness Pope—is now used almost exclusively for lyrical moments of experience.

The Combination Today

But again we need to be quite clear about what has actually happened, because the tendency to "purify" does not mean that the combinations which are the subject of this chapter have disappeared in our own day.

Most of us, if we were asked to think about where the combination now exists, would probably suggest the essay, that rather amorphous catchall form whose obituary is always being written (usually in essays), but which continues to survive, to be published in journals and magazines, and to be anthologized. From Charles Lamb to the *New Yorker,* the essay combines conceptual with experiential knowledge; it contains recognizable propositions, expressed in words which function as plurisigns; and it usually creates "character" through the self-revelation of the author.

The essay may be as light and casual as many of the bits in the *New Yorker's* "The Talk of the Town." In the sentence below note the satirical effect of *dote, fond, happy week, string of stunning firsts.*

> Since newspapers dote on recording first times—almost anything done for the first time is, by definition, news—and since they're especially fond of first times involving famous people, the press had a happy week or so describing President Eisenhower's recent trip abroad, in the course of which they ran up a whole string of stunning firsts.[3]

Or the essay may be as serious as the critical or philosophical material in a literary review. Witness this passage from Gerald W. Johnson's *The Man Who Feels Left Behind:*

> It is hard for us to manage a clear perception because of a very ancient error, which began to be corrected only with the introduction of the scientific method. It was the error of applying our emotional powers to purposes they were never fit to serve. The March Hare, in *Alice in Wonderland,* tried to correct his watch by applying butter to

[3] FROM "The Talk of the Town," reprinted from the Notes and Comment in *The New Yorker,* September 19, 1959. By permission of the publisher.

the works and would not be convinced of his error because, as he pointed out, it was the very best butter. The March Hare was mad. Draw your own conclusions about people who expect to understand the physical universe by an act of faith.[4]

If this passage does not strike us as philosophy, this is only because we now think of philosophy as being something else—something more conceptual, more technical, less evocative.

The combination is also the stock-in-trade—or the occasional diversion—of columnists. Look, for example, at this paragraph from a column by Joseph Alsop, entitled "In a Green Shade":

> Great beauty, long enduring, ought to be more noteworthy than public folly, long persisted in. So there will be no apology here for writing about the Garden of the Moss Temple. It is certainly one of the most beautiful gardens in the world. It must also be one of the half-dozen oldest gardens in the world, having been laid out over six centuries ago. Discovering it is almost like seeing the Parthenon for the first time without advance warning—if one can imagine such a thing. Hence the impulse to share the discovery is irresistible.
>
> Imagine, then, a country road meandering into a little Japanese village that nestles at the foot of Kyoto's craggy, tree-clad western hills. The Saihoji stream, a clear, swift-rushing brook, runs along the road. There is a simple bridge. Beyond the bridge there is a low gate. Pass through the gate, and you enter the enchantment which is so strong that you feel spellbound even as you walk.[5]

Alsop has turned from his usual subjects, politics and international relations, not merely to describe a garden in Japan but to give us some idea of what the experience of the garden meant to him. This kind of writing is a variety of journalism, on the border line perhaps between the thoroughly serious integration of modes of knowing and the mere instrumental use of technique to make writing interesting. "Technique" is what we usually find in such specialized forms as the feature article, the profile, and the columnist's interpretation of events. The evocative effects are not part of the writer's thinking but planned devices. They sugar-coat the pill of information, a charitable act for which we can sometimes be grateful. But too much sugar can so cloy our appetites that we cease to be interested in plainer, more essential food, and will accept only sweets.

[4] FROM *The Man Who Feels Left Behind*, by Gerald W. Johnson, copyright © 1960, 1961 by Gerald W. Johnson, by permission of William Morrow and Company, Inc.

[5] FROM "In a Green Shade" by Joseph Alsop, reprinted from the New York *Herald Tribune*. By permission of the author.

Yet the genuine combination of modes of thought—a perfectly natural and unforced combination—is not at all rare. And it even appears in writing which is as scientific as that of Margaret Mead's *Coming of Age in Samoa,* a scholarly study in anthropology:

The life of the day begins at dawn, or if the moon has shown until daylight, the shouts of the young men may be heard before dawn from the hillside. Uneasy in the night, populous with ghosts, they shout lustily to one another as they hasten with their work. As the dawn begins to fall among the soft brown roofs and the slender palm trees stand out against a colourless, gleaming sea, lovers slip home from trysts beneath the palm trees or in the shadow of beached canoes, that the light may find each sleeper in his appointed place. Cocks crow, negligently, and a shrill-voiced bird cries from the bread-fruit tree. The insistent roar of the reef seems muted to an undertone for the sounds of a waking village. Babies cry, a few short wails before sleepy mothers give them the breast. Restless little children roll out of their sheets and wander drowsily down to the beach to freshen their faces in the sea. Boys bent upon an early fishing start collecting their tackle, and go to rouse their more laggard companions. Fires are lit, here and there, the white smoke hardly visible against the paleness of the dawn. The whole village, sheeted and frowsy, stirs, rubs its eyes, and stumbles toward the beach. "Talofa" "Talofa!" "Will the journey start today?" "Is it bonito fishing your lordship is going?" Girls stop to giggle over some young ne'er-do-well who escaped during the night from an angry father's pursuit and to venture a shrewd guess that the daughter knew more about his presence than she told. The boy who is taunted by another, who has succeeded him in his sweetheart's favour, grapples with his rival, his foot slipping in the wet sand. From the other end of the village comes a long drawn-out, piercing wail. A messenger has just brought word of the death of some relative in an- other village. Half-clad, unhurried women, with babies at their breasts, or astride their hips, pause in their tale of Losa's outraged departure from her father's house to the greater kindness in the home of her uncle, to wonder who is dead. Poor relatives whisper their requests to rich relatives, men make plans to set a fish trap together, a woman begs a bit of yellow dye from a kinswoman, and through the village sounds the rhythmic tattoo which calls the young men together. They gather from all parts of the village, digging sticks in hand, ready to start inland to the plantation. The older men set off upon their more lonely occupations, and each household, reassembled under its peaked roof, settles down to the routine of the morning. Little children, too hungry to wait for the late breakfast, beg lumps of cold taro which they munch greedily. Women carry piles of washing to the sea or to the spring at the far end of the village, or set off inland after weaving materials. The older girls go fishing on the reef, or perhaps set themselves to weaving a new set of Venetian blinds.[6]

This is almost entirely observational writing. But the language is highly evocative: we see and hear the life of the village, and we have some sense of what it is like to be a Samoan. Yet few people would argue that Margaret Mead is merely dressing up her observations to make them more interesting; she has entered imaginatively into the Samoan's daily routine, and the knowledge she is presenting is both conceptual and experiential. Here is one more example, this one from D. W. Brogan's *The Free State:*

> There is attributed to an American conservative, Fisher Ames, a contrast between democratic and non-democratic government. "Monarchy is like a splendid ship, with all sails set; it moves majestically on, then it hits a rock and sinks forever. Democracy is like a raft. It never sinks but, damn it, your feet are always in the water."
>
> Fisher Ames lived in the age of the American and French Revolutions; of one he approved a little, of the other he did not approve at all. But for all his dislike for the new forces loose in the world, for all his nostalgia for the past, he was too intelligent not to see the great new fact, that monarchy in the old sense had struck a rock and sunk for ever. He saw too the untidiness of democracy—amid its permanence.
>
> In the modern world, the historical background to the dictum of Ames has been forgotten. Men have forgotten the old world of the rule of custom, of the acceptance of the divine right, not only of kings but of republics. They have forgotten too the enthusiasm with which men welcomed the coming of the new age, the enthusiasm for a new world that greeted the news of the breaking of the cake of custom in France:
>
>> *Bliss was it in that dawn to be alive,*
>> *But to be young was very heaven.*[7]

This passage is a mixture of the conceptual and the experiential. Part of the effect is achieved by the selection of quotations, from Fisher Ames in the beginning and from Wordsworth at the end. But Brogan either echoes or anticipates these quotations in his own words: "struck a rock and sunk for ever," "untidiness of democracy,"

[6] FROM *Coming of Age in Samoa* in *From the South Seas* by Margaret Mead, copyright 1928, 1930, 1935, 1939, 1956, 1958 by Margaret Mead, by permission of William Morrow and Company, Inc.

[7] FROM *The Free State* by D. W. Brogan. Reprinted by permission of Hamish Hamilton, Ltd.

"coming of the new age." And it is clear that Brogan thinks—and wants us to think—not merely in concepts but in images. He *feels* the radical transformations of the age of revolutions and he is trying to convey some of that feeling to others.

Two More Points

We could go on multiplying examples indefinitely, each a slightly different blend of the informative and the creative, but those we have looked at should make the point clear that blends exist, that they take various forms, and that it is worth our while to be aware of them. In fact, unless we are aware of them it is difficult to make sense of much older literature. But two points still need to be considered briefly, even though both will be developed more fully in later chapters. The first point concerns the kind of combination which is used primarily to attract and keep the reader's attention; the second concerns persuasion.

Much contemporary writing exhibits a combination of techniques. Facts and ideas are clothed in words which have evocative effects. Attention is paid to the thingness of words: there is rhythm, alliteration (as in some newspaper headlines). Images and metaphors play a part; parallelism and contrast are used consciously, often violently. One example will suffice. Here is a sentence from the New York *Mirror's* account of the death of movie actor Errol Flynn:

> The end came for Flynn at fifty in an atmosphere of his fondest fancy—aged whiskey (Dr. Gould's) and a young girl (Beverly Aadlund, 17, his latest protégé) who accompanied him here from Los Angeles.

This, most of us will agree, is a deliberate and familiar attempt to play upon our appetite for the scandalous. Note the contrast between death and life, between youth (17) and age (50); and note the alliteration of "Flynn at fifty . . . fondest fancy"; note the parallelism between the whiskey and the young girl, each followed by a parenthesis which implies more than it says. We shall have another look later at this kind of combination. Here it is enough to note that it is basically different from the other examples we have been looking at, in which there is a genuine union of two kinds of knowledge. In passages like that from the *Mirror,* the devices of creative writing seem rather to be a means toward an end. In other kinds of popular reporting we find a wide range, from lazy reliance on stock epithets and metaphors to highly evocative and original recreation of the events of the day.

The second point concerns persuasion. We have paid very little attention to persuasion since introducing it in Chapter 2, but we shall be turning to it in the next three chapters. Before we do, it may be well for us to notice that the element of persuasion is strong in many of the passages we have looked at in this chapter. Milton, Hesiod, Amos, and the anonymous author of the Tao Tê Ching are conceivably interested in the implications of their knowledge for action—not specific actions but general modes of action; or at least they had an eye on the possibility of shaping attitudes. In other words, the union of experiential and conceptual knowledge may also be a union of knowledge and action.

EXERCISES

A. Analyze each of the following passages as a combination of the informative and the creative. Summarize the conceptual content and explain the evocative effects. Try to reword a sentence or two, and note all creative elements: rhythm, alliteration, images, metaphors, and so on.

   1. The night of March 10 was a night of blowing, broken clouds and bitter cold. At 9:30 the radio warned of the approach of the bombers and the people hurried from their houses with their sleeping mats and their pots and pans and their slim stores of rice and soya paste to the *bokugo,* the shallow holes they had dug beside their houses where there was room, or in the little strip of earth between street and sidewalk in those sections where the houses were jammed closely together. For the people of Japan, in their fatalism, did not dig holes to shelter themselves. They dug only shallow caches to hide their goods, and roofed them over with tin and sticks and earth.

   Then, when the bombers came they stood in the streets and watched the fall of the bombs, and the direction of the flames, and ran to save themselves, dodging down the narrow streets until they came to a pond or stream, or to an area that was not bombed. At first they did not even dig holes for their goods, but wrapped everything in straw mats and ran with their burdens strapped upon their backs. But blowing sparks which would have gone out on a tile-roof fell on these mats and caught them afire and the people ran through the streets like blazing torches, spreading fire to parts of the city where it otherwise might not have come. So they stopped carrying these burdens when they ran. But even this did not save them sometimes, for the fire would cut them off. Then they would succumb to the spirit of *shikada go nai,* which means "It is hopeless to try to do more," and kneel in the streets, whole families together, facing toward the palace of the Emperor, and die there as the fire swept over them.[8]

(HAROLD H. MARTIN, "Black Snow and Leaping Tigers,"
Harper's Magazine)

2. There is nothing strictly immortal but immortality. Whatever hath no beginning may be confident of no end; all others have a dependent being and within the reach of destruction; which is the peculiar of that necessary Essence that cannot destroy itself; and the highest strain of omnipotency, to be so powerfully constituted as not to suffer even from the power of itself. . . . But man is a noble animal, splendid in ashes, and pompous in the grave, solemnizing nativities and deaths with equal lustre, nor omitting ceremonies of bravery in the infamy of his nature.

(THOMAS BROWNE, *Hydriotaphia; Urn-Burial*)

3.   *The Killer Whale*

Of this whale little is precisely known to the Nantucketer, and nothing at all to the professed naturalist. From what I have seen of him at a distance, I should say that he was about the bigness of a grampus. He is very savage—a sort of Feegee fish. He sometimes takes the great Folio whales by the lip, and hangs there like a leech, till the mighty brute is worried to death. The killer is never hunted. I never heard what sort of oil he had. Exception might be taken to the name bestowed upon this whale, on the ground of its indistinctness. For we are all killers, on land and on sea; Bonapartes and sharks included.

(HERMAN MELVILLE, *Moby-Dick*)

4. During the exhibition games, Gentile looked awful. The only thing he hit consistently was his rump—with that furious backlash of the bat which Dodger coaches had tried for years to modulate. Nobody in the state of Florida looked worse than Diamond Jim during March, unless it was the weatherman. If Gentile had been sold outright to Baltimore, no strings attached,

---

[8] FROM "Black Snow and Leaping Tigers" by Harold H. Martin, reprinted from *Harper's Magazine*. By permission of the publisher.

there is no doubt he would have been farmed to the minors by Paul Richards before the season began. But Richards had 30 playing days to make up his mind, so he not only kept Diamond Jim; he played him.

Sure enough, as soon as the season opened, Gentile started hitting. He knocked in runs; he won ball games. Now, because of a 30-day-look clause, it looks like the big leagues for Jim Gentile—pronounced to rhyme with steal, which, at $25,000, is what he appears to be.

(AN ANONYMOUS SPORTS WRITER)

B. Select several passages from early literature (the Old Testament, a Greek philosopher, the choruses of a Greek tragedy) and discuss them as examples of the fusion of conceptual and experiential knowledge.

C. Do a thorough analysis of an essay, article, or sports column. (Your instructor may specify.) Is it primarily informative, primarily creative, or is it a mixture? Do you detect any element of persuasion? If there are evocative effects, are they part of the writer's way of thinking about the subject, or are they intended to dress it up and make it more attractive?

D. Select an idea or event which for you involves both conceptual and experiential knowledge, and write an essay on it. Do not try to dress up your ideas with evocative effects, but concentrate on the way you think *and* feel about it; try to embody thought and feeling in appropriate words.

E. Using the ideas suggested by the passages from Hesiod, Amos, and the Tao Tê Ching, write an essay on one of the following subjects (or on any other which the passages may suggest). Agree, disagree, compare, analyze—or use the passages simply as a means of stimulating your own thought processes.
  1. The idea of utopia
  2. The primitive and provincial as an ideal
  3. The good life
  4. War and peace

14. The Persuasive Use of Language

The superior man is liberal towards others' opinions, but does not completely agree with them; the inferior man agrees with others' opinions, but is not liberal towards them.

CONFUCIUS

A Fable for Persuasion

Here is a situation which calls for persuasive action: Mr. Smith, sitting lazily on the porch of his summer camp at Blue Lake, suddenly notices the smell of smoke. He gets up to investigate and discovers a brush fire, some distance away but apparently moving quite rapidly. If it is not stopped, it may well destroy not only his camp but most of those on the west side of the lake. His first impulse is to grab a shovel and ax and try to put out the fire himself. But he soon realizes he can't possibly do the job alone. He must round up some of his neighbors and get them to help.

Now, fighting the fire and getting the neighbors to help are both forms of action, the first a kind of direct, individual action, the second, persuasive action. There is, however, neither time nor need for an elaborate persuasive campaign. All Smith has to do to persuade most of his neighbors to join in fighting the fire is to point out that the danger exists: the information that there is a fire may be persuasive enough; and Smith's excitement and sense of urgency are conveyed not only by his words but by his manner and tone of voice. Where Smith encounters reluctance or resistance, however, he will probably change his tactics instinctively. He may remind one neighbor who thinks it can't come his way that "we all have to help each other." He may tell another neighbor who is reluctant to stop painting his house that "fresh paint will burn just fine!" He may have to encourage the man who stands worried and indecisive and argues that "there isn't much we can do." And he may bawl out the coward who is so panicky that he's ready to load his family into the car and drive away from Blue Lake forever.

What Persuasion Is

This fable, simple as it is, will serve as a starting point for a study of the third use of language which we are concerned with in this book, the *persuasive*. We have mentioned persuasion from time to time, and we took a brief preliminary look at it back in Chapter 2. It is now time for a closer look. Using the story of Mr. Smith and the fire as an example, we shall consider the relation of persuasion to *action* and to *knowledge;* and we shall look at the *attitudes* with which it works, the *audience* on which it works, and its *value* as one of the uses of language.

First, all persuasion is concerned in some way with *action*. It is itself a form of action and its ultimate purpose is to enlist the action of others. The situation that Smith faces when he discovers the fire requires that he do something. Two courses of action appear open to him: to put out the fire himself, or to persuade his neighbors to help him put out the fire. He soon realizes that he can't act directly and alone; he must persuade others to act with him. In this case the action which the persuasion aims at is both specific and immediate. In some cases, as we shall see later, it is much less specific: it may be so general that it means different things to different people; it may not even be mentioned in the persuasion; it may be very remote—as it is for example in the kind of institutional advertising which simply calls attention to a company without making any direct effort to sell merchandise.

Second, as we have indicated elsewhere, all persuasion is based—to some extent at least—on *knowledge,* or something which might pass for knowledge. All Smith's actions stem from his knowledge of the fire. And he uses this knowledge, which is both conceptual and experiential, as a means of stirring others to action. He knows certain facts about the fire, and facts themselves may be immensely persuasive under the right circumstances; but Smith also has a great sense of excitement and urgency, which he conveys to his neighbors by his words, his tone, his actions. Thus he creates an experience in his listeners which is akin to his own experience; and this experience moves them to action just as it moves him to action. Persuasion, then, may be said to build on knowledge, both conceptual and experiential. This knowledge may be authoritative or it may be very unreliable. It could be that Smith was actually mistaken about the fire, or that he is so excitable that he conveys a sense of panic quite out of keeping with the actual threat.

Third, all persuasion works on and through *attitudes*. We shall define attitude here simply as a bent toward action. Very urgent persuasion, of the kind Smith is using, may move so quickly through attitude to action that we are hardly conscious of the intermediate process. Most persuasion, however, is somewhat less urgent; and attitude may actually appear much more important than action. The persuader not only works on and through the attitudes of others; he frequently involves his own attitudes in the persuasion. In some kinds of professional persuasion, however, the persuader may not even share the attitudes he is working with and toward. And even Mr. Smith encounters attitudes which he does not share, varying his approach with the varying attitudes of his neighbors.

This variation in approach to meet varying attitudes in the audience suggests a fourth point about persuasion: persuasion tends to place great emphasis on *audience*. This does not mean that every persuader has his eye on his audience all the time—though some of them do. But the actions and attitudes which are central to persuasion are the actions and attitudes of the audience, and the attitudes are the mechanism through which the actions are produced. The persuader, therefore, has to concern himself with the attitudes of his audience; and he will tend to vary his approach with different audiences. In informal persuasion this variation may be quite spontaneous—a reaction to the reactions of the others. Smith uses different appeals with his different neighbors simply because he encounters different attitudes, to which he responds in different ways. On one man he uses an appeal to the common good; on another sarcasm; a pep-talk on a third; and a scolding on a fourth. Some persuaders, of course, work much more deliberately on their audiences. Professional propagandists and advertisers, working through the mass media and with large sums of money at their disposal, study the attitudes of audiences by means of sampling techniques and "depth" interviews, test audience response through various kinds of polls, and prepare elaborate campaigns to manipulate attitudes.

It is this sort of attention to audience that has made many of us suspicious of all persuasion, and we shall discuss the problem of manipulative persuasion in a later chapter. It may be well at this point merely to indicate that conscious manipulation of the audience is not confined to persuasive writing but is also characteristic of certain kinds of informative and creative writing.

The final point about persuasion—a point related to what has just been said—concerns *value*. Most of us are so weary of the constant flood of commercial propaganda that we are inclined to be cynical about anything which affects actions and attitudes. Yet persuasion is not necessarily insincere, dishonest, or contrived; and it is sometimes—as the story of Mr. Smith adequately demonstrates—absolutely essential. What Smith does in arousing his neighbors is at least as socially useful as the actual fighting of the fire would be: in fact, it is one way of fighting the fire. If we could all do everything necessary for our own good and the good of others without the assistance of others, persuasion would be superfluous. Since we cannot, we must all use persuasion on occasion, and we must be responsive to it. The alternatives to persuasion are either a wholly individualistic society or a completely coercive one—a society in which force has replaced persuasion. In all other forms of society it is necessary for people to secure the cooperation of other people, and this implies the use of persuasion. This does not mean, of course, that all persuasion should be taken on its face value. Smith may be crying "Fire!" when there is no fire; or he may be urging his neighbors to fight when it would be wiser to run. His listeners in response to his persuasion cannot afford to put aside critical judgment. But neither can they afford to sit quietly on their porches while they tell each other that "it's all propaganda anyway."

Persuasion and the Other Uses of Language

This general description of persuasion leaves two questions unanswered. First, what is the relation of persuasion to informative and to creative writing? And second, what forms does persuasion take?

In a sense, the persuasive is a less basic category than are the other two uses of language we have been studying. We may even feel that the persuasive is not really a separate use of language at all, but an extension of the informative and the creative into action. For it uses the same kinds of knowledge with which informative and creative writing are concerned—that is, conceptual knowledge and experiential knowledge—and there is no third kind of knowledge peculiar to persuasion. As a matter of fact, almost any piece of informative or creative writing may function—in the right context—as persuasion. Smith's statement that there is a fire, a purely informative statement, may stir his neighbors to action; and his obvious excitement would probably evoke excitement in others even if they could not understand his words. Or, to return to the examples of Chapter 2, Clemens' account of Pap's bout with delirium tremens and Roueché's informative discussion of alcoholism could both be used persuasively to promote the cause of temperance.

Furthermore, a piece of writing may serve a persuasive purpose without losing its informative or creative character. Very often, of course, informative and especially creative forms do become radically different when they are used for persuasive ends. A novel such as *Uncle Tom's Cabin* may be of much interest as a persuasive document; as a novel it is less interesting. But we have only to recall Owen's "Dulce et Decorum Est" to recognize the possibility that the creative and the persuasive may be thoroughly blended. Owen is attacking the chauvinistic attitude of those who regard war as glorious, but his poem remains a rich and unified poetic work as well as a strongly persuasive one. It embodies Owen's experience and it evokes an experience in his readers—an experience which includes indignation and rage against the glorification of death in battle. Similarly Lincoln's Gettysburg Address has outlived its immediate persuasive purpose, but it retains its value as a creative expression of Lincoln's vision of the decisiveness of our Civil War to the survival of democracy.

Thus persuasion is often blended and combined with the other two uses of language. At times we see it as a clearly distinguishable third use of language; at times it *is* informative or creative writing in a context in which knowledge, either conceptual or experiential, demands action. Because of this ambiguity and elusiveness, much persuasion can be fully understood only in context—not only in verbal context but in social context as well. We have to know what is going on, or we may not be able to identify a piece of writing as persuasion at all.

Two Modes of Persuasion

Our analysis of the relation of persuasive writing to the informative and the creative suggests a first major distinction within persuasion itself. Persuasion employs knowledge of two different kinds, and it is useful to classify persuasion in terms of the kind of knowledge it uses. Some persuasion is based more on conceptual than on experiential knowledge and is related to informative writing; other persuasion is based more on experiential knowledge and is related to creative writing. This fact, incidentally, partially explains the tremendous range in persuasive writing—a range which is as great as that of informative and creative writing taken together.

We have already seen in Owen's "Dulce et Decorum Est" a good example of the kind of persuasion which is based on experiential knowledge. Even the form is a traditional creative one; and the poem is a complete union of the creative and the persuasive. But a fresh example of experience-based persuasion may be useful at this point in our discussion. The following poem was written by Malcolm Cowley at the time of the execution of Nicola Sacco and Bartolomeo Vanzetti, two Boston anarchists convicted of the murder of a paymaster. (Many people believe that they have since been pretty thoroughly exonerated of the crime.)

For St. Bartholomew's Eve
(August 23, 1927)

Then die!
　　　　　Outside the prison gawk
the crowds that you will see no more.
A door slams shut behind you. Walk
with turnkeys down a corridor
smelling of lysol, through the gates
to where a drunken sheriff waits.

St. Nicholas who blessed your birth,
whose hands are rich with gifts, will bear
to you no further gifts on earth,
Sacco, whose heart abounds in prayer
neither to Pilate nor a saint
whose earthly sons die innocent.

And you that never for God's grace
once pleaded, black Bartholomew,
no God will raise you from this place
nor Virgin intercede for you,
nor bones of yours make sweet the plot
where governors and judges rot.

A doctor sneezes. A chaplain maps
the roads of heaven. You mount the chair.
A jailer buckles tight the straps
like those that aviators wear.
The surgeon makes a signal.
                                        Die!
lost symbols of our liberty.

Beyond the chair, beyond the bars
of day and night your path lies free;
along an avenue of stars
march on, O dago Christs, while we
march on to spread your name abroad
like ashes in the winds of God.[1]
                    (MALCOLM COWLEY, 1898–   )

A powerful expression of Cowley's anger at what he feels is a
rank miscarriage of justice, the poem calls for action to vindicate
the martyrs. But the technique is wholly creative, and the poem,
like Owen's, has outlived its persuasive purpose because it is as
much an eloquent act of self-expression on Cowley's part as it is
an appeal to action on the part of other people. Words are used as
plurisigns; there is likeness-and-difference, conflict, irony. Anarchists
have become saints, Nicholas and Bartholomew. Themselves atheists,
they are described as "dago Christs," a phrase which brings together the conflicting aspects of the situation and which is further
ironically underscored in the last two lines:

> . . . to spread your name abroad
> like ashes in the winds of God.

Persuasion may, of course, be based on experiential knowledge
without taking on any of the traditional creative forms. The Gettysburg Address is neither lyric poem, nor prose essay, nor drama, nor
fiction; but if we look at it now in the light of our knowledge of
creative writing, its relation to that use of language becomes ap-

---

[1] "For St. Bartholomew's Eve" by Malcolm Cowley, from *Blue Juniata*, copyright 1929 by Malcolm Cowley. Reprinted by permission.

parent. Not only can it not be rephrased without losing its effect (try rewriting the opening sentence as "Eighty-seven years ago our ancestors established a new country in the Western hemisphere"), but there is a consistent all-pervasive imagery. The motifs are birth and death, the living and the dead, they and we, then and now—all interacting through parallelism and contrast. Notice the sequence: *brought forth, conceived, dedicated, created, consecrated, hallowed,* and finally *new birth of freedom.* This is birth-death-rebirth, and it echoes, consciously or unconsciously, the age-old rituals which lie behind some of our greatest drama and fiction.

But let us look at one more example of persuasion which uses experiential knowledge. Here is the last sentence of one of Winston Churchill's most famous speeches, his address to Parliament in 1940 following evacuation of British and French forces at Dunkirk:

> We shall go on to the end, we shall fight in France, we shall fight on the seas and oceans, we shall fight with growing confidence and and growing strength in the air, we shall defend our Island, whatever the cost may be, we shall fight on the beaches, we shall fight on the landing grounds, we shall fight in the fields and in the streets, we shall fight in the hills; we shall never surrender, and even if, which I do not for a moment believe, this Island or a large part of it were subjugated and starving, then our Empire beyond the seas, armed and guarded by the British Fleet, would carry on the struggle, until, in God's good time, with all its power and might, the new world steps forth to the rescue and the liberation of the old.[2]

Lincoln's language is perhaps closer to poetry, but Churchill's is fully as evocative. What he creates is a vision of a defensive war on British soil carried out through slow withdrawal—an action which is all of a piece with Dunkirk itself. He creates this vision through the incessant and climactic repetition of *we shall* (nine times in the first half of the sentence) coupled with a contrasting shift in tone which introduces a note of positive hope for assistance from overseas—a shift which is actually a shift in audience as well, for the last phrase is clearly addressed not to the British people alone but also to the American people. Churchill does not convey much conceptual knowledge in this passage; what he tries to do is to mobilize the wills of others by expressing his own will. (In this respect he is acting, on a grander scale, much as Mr. Smith did in our fable.)

[2] FROM "Dunkirk" by Winston S. Churchill. Reprinted by permission of G. P. Putnam's Sons, from *Blood, Sweat and Tears* by Winston S. Churchill. Copyright 1941 by Winston S. Churchill.

Now let's turn from the creative mode of persuasion to the conceptual-informative mode. The following paragraphs are taken from Federalist Paper No. 10, by James Madison. They were written as part of a concerted campaign to win support for the new Federal Constitution. Madison is here arguing for a representative republic (such as the United States now is) rather than a "democracy" (meaning here a loose association of sovereign states), and for a large political organization (a federal government) rather than a small one (a state government):

The two great points of difference between a democracy and a republic are: first, the delegation of the government in the latter to a small number of citizens elected by the rest; secondly, the greater number of citizens, and greater sphere of country over which the latter may be extended.

The effect of the first difference is . . . to refine and enlarge the public views, by passing them through the medium of a chosen body of citizens, whose wisdom may best discern the true interest of their country, and whose patriotism and love of justice will be least likely to sacrifice it to temporary or partial considerations. Under such a regulation, it may well happen that the public voice, pronounced by the representatives of the people, will be more consonant to the public good than if pronounced by the people themselves, convened for the purpose. . . .

The other point of difference is, the greater number of citizens and extent of territory which may be brought within the compass of republican than of democratic government; and it is this circumstance principally which renders factious combinations less to be dreaded in the former than in the latter. The smaller the society, the fewer probably will be the distinct parties and interests composing it; the fewer the distinct parties and interests, the more frequently will a majority be found of the same party; and the smaller the compass within which they are placed, the more easily will they concert and execute their plans of oppression. Extend the sphere, and you take in a greater variety of parties and interests; you make it less probable that a majority of the whole will have a common motive to invade the rights of other citizens; or if such a common motive exists, it will be more difficult for all who feel it to discover their own strength, and to act in unison with each other. . . .

Hence, it clearly appears, that the same advantage which a republic has over a democracy, in controlling the effects of faction, is enjoyed by a large over a small republic—is enjoyed by the Union over the States composing it.

The language of this statement is almost entirely conceptual. The words have clearly been chosen with great care; the style is elegant and even eloquent. But concepts are more important than words, propositions than statements: the whole passage could be reworded quite successfully. The structure, furthermore, is logical. There is no progression of images, as in Lincoln, no series of repeated resolves as in Churchill, but a sequence of logically related propositions. We may, of course, question the validity of some of these propositions, but their logical intent is plain. Madison imagines two alternative political systems, a small democracy and a large representative republic. He first argues that elected representatives are more likely to act reasonably than are numbers of people assembled in one place for direct action. He then turns his attention to the charge that a federal government is likely to produce centralized tyranny. Tyranny, he argues, is the natural result of the existence of strong well-organized majorities. But such majorities are more likely to appear in small democracies than in large republics, partly because of the greater variety of opinion in the larger group, partly because of the physical difficulty of getting together an oppressive majority in so large a territory. Therefore, Madison argues, a representative republic is preferable to a small democracy; and therefore, a federal government is better than a loose confederation of small democracies.

The Combination of Modes

We have looked at some rather extreme examples of creative and informative persuasion. There is very little conceptual knowledge in Lincoln or Churchill, very little use of experiential knowledge in Madison. But such extremes are probably less common than is the combination of modes. In the last chapter we looked at the ways in which informative and creative writing overlap and blend. Two tendencies, however, work to keep informative and creative writing proper somewhat apart, especially in our own day. First, we have become very conscious of the differences between conceptual and experiential knowledge; and so long as the emphasis is on knowledge, we set up for ourselves ideals of "purity" which keep the uses of language separate. In our time, creative writing has become less conceptual and more experiential than it was in the eighteenth century, for example; while informative writing has become more conceptual and less experiential: the short story approaches poetry; philosophy approaches mathematics. Second, the rather specialized forms of creative writing tend to set it apart from informative. We recognize a limited number of literary types, such as the short story, the lyric poem, the drama, the novel; and we do not ordinarily use these types for informative purposes.

Neither of these tendencies, however, operates with the same force in persuasive writing simply because neither knowledge nor form is primary. Mr. Smith in our fable conveys information and evokes a sense of urgency at the same time because both kinds of knowledge are instrumental to action: they are used quite naturally and spontaneously as part of a total situation which calls for action. Persuasion, furthermore, is in no way restricted by formal considerations. The persuasive writer uses whatever form is most appropriate to the situation: speeches, letters, essays, poems, plays, novels, editorials, recommendation reports, and memoranda.

Furthermore, the persuasive situation itself frequently demands both conceptual and experiential knowledge. Attitudes are naturally compounded of facts, ideas, feelings, and judgments about value. We do not act readily until we are moved to act by factors which are not entirely intellectual—basic emotions, an imaginative vision of possibilities or dangers, a sense of what is good or fitting. And we can be moved by these nonintellectual factors alone; but except in the most elemental situations, conceptual knowledge is needed to give direction to our action. If Mr. Smith is merely incoherent and excited, he may provoke panic in his neighbors, but he will not be able to channel their action in a useful way.

We usually find, therefore, that persuasive writing mingles the two kinds of knowledge—in varying proportions, of course—and uses language in a way which is partly informative and partly creative. Sometimes this combination is apparent throughout a speech or editorial. Sometimes it appears in different parts of the same piece of writing. Here is another sentence from Churchill's Dunkirk speech:

> The Royal Air Force engaged the main strength of the German Air Force, and inflicted upon them losses of at least four to one; and the Navy, using nearly 1000 ships of all kinds, carried over 335,000 men, French and British, out of the jaws of death and shame, to their native land and to the tasks which lie immediately ahead.

This passage is much more conceptual than Churchill's concluding sentence, which we looked at earlier. The statements could be checked by comparing them with other reports; and the propositions could be stated in other words and still be impressive. At the same time, the words Churchill has chosen express pride and resolution: the Air Force engaged the *main strength* of the German Air Force; the Navy carried men *out of the jaws of death and shame* to *tasks which lie immediately ahead.*

Other Variations in Persuasion

So far in this chapter we have noted the principal characteristics of persuasion, its close relation to both informative and creative writing, the two modes of persuasion—informative and creative—and the tendency of the two modes to combine. We now need to examine some of the other ways in which persuasion varies and which make persuasion the most wide-ranging of the three uses of language. The most significant of these variations may be grouped under four headings: relation to audience, immediacy of action, generality of action, and directness.

Relation to Audience. In our fable, Mr. Smith uses a different approach with different neighbors. This kind of spontaneous variation is normal in persuasion, particularly in face-to-face persuasion, where the response of the audience is continuously fed back to the persuader. We have no reason to feel that Mr. Smith—or most other amateur persuaders, for that matter—is consciously manipulating the attitudes of the audience. But manipulation of the audience is common in professional persuasion, especially in advertising and in political propaganda. Skilled propagandists make themselves aware of the dominant attitudes of various segments of the population, and they prepare campaigns which they hope will work on and with these attitudes. They watch sales records to determine response to particular advertising appeals, and they run public opinion polls to test the effectiveness of particular strategies.

We shall later devote a whole chapter to manipulative persuasion, but it may be well to characterize it briefly at this point. It is distinguished chiefly by the fact that the interests of the persuader and the interests of the audience are essentially different: what the persuader is trying to get the audience to do may be ultimately for their benefit, but he is himself motivated largely by his own interests (or the interests of his client). He is not trying to get his audience to help him fight a fire which threatens everyone, or to help fight a war in which all are involved, but to buy something he has to sell, to elect him to office, or the like.

Now this fact does not necessarily make the manipulative persuader an antisocial person, but it does change radically the entire situation. He becomes a conscious manipulator of his audience simply because he is separated from them in interests: he works *on* them, not *with* them. And since he is motivated by a desire to gain something for himself or his client (though he may be giving good measure in return), his argument is almost inevitably somewhat insincere: he does not say, "Elect me mayor. I need a job"; instead he thinks up reasons which will appeal to the electorate. In manipulative persuasion, action is not the outgrowth of knowledge; the action is usually predetermined and the knowledge is introduced as a means of implementing the action.

Immediacy of Action. Persuasion also varies in the immediacy of the action which it promotes, and, consequently, in the relative emphasis on action and attitude. Mr. Smith, for example, is concerned with immediate and urgent action. Churchill, Lincoln, Madison, and Cowley are more interested in laying the groundwork for action, in encouraging attitudes which may eventually lead to action. This emphasis on attitude rather than immediate action is characteristic of most persuasion. Usually, in fact, there is a delay between the persuasive appeal itself and the action which follows. This does not mean that no action is intended; it simply can't take place immediately. The political campaigner cannot persuade us to go to the polls immediately and vote for his party: the polls won't be open until election day. The advertisement in the magazine or newspaper seldom finds us in a spot where we can immediately buy the merchandise which is advertised. The advertiser has merely prepared the way for action, wound up the spring, as it were; the sight of the merchandise (he hopes) will touch off the appropriate response. Since he is aware of the dangers of delay, the advertiser sometimes proposes some kind of intermediate action which can be carried out at once—filling out a coupon, asking for a free sample, entering a contest.

Generality of Action. Persuasion also varies as to the action itself: Is it a specific kind of action, the same for everyone? Or is the appeal more general, one which will result in different kinds of action by different people? The political campaigner urges us to vote for him and his party—a very specific act. The advertiser usually tries to get us to buy a particular product—another specific act. Mr. Smith urges his neighbors to go and put out a fire—also a specific act, though it may well require somewhat different actions from different people.

On the other hand, Lincoln, Churchill, and Cowley are proposing actions which will certainly mean different things to different members of their audiences. Lincoln is calling for a rededication to a cause, a matter first of will and attitude. The action will depend on the relation of the individual to the conduct of the war. For the soldier the action may mean hardship and perhaps death. For his wife it may mean separation and perhaps widowhood. For others it may mean only giving up certain luxuries. Similarly Churchill calls for actions which will not only mean different things to different people in the British Isles but also different things to people in the British Dominions beyond the seas, and to people in the United States who are still watching from the sidelines. And Malcolm Cowley's poem calls not for something specific, such as the signing of a petition asking a reprieve for Sacco and Vanzetti—they are already dead—but for a variety of acts which may bring about a moral vindication of the two men, and more important, for fundamental changes which will promote greater justice in the courts and greater freedom of expression for all who disagree with the opinions of the majority.

Directness. Persuasion also varies in the directness of its appeal. Churchill, Lincoln, and Madison—and Mr. Smith (except in one instance)—all make direct appeals. Owen, Cowley, and Mr. Smith in his sarcastic remark about how well wet paint will burn—use somewhat indirect appeals. Indirect appeals, and they are very common, cannot be taken literally. They include irony and paradox, as in Cowley's poem; sarcasm, as in Mr. Smith's remark to his house-painting neighbor; light humor, as in some advertisements; and—

sometimes—satire, gentle or biting. They may reduce a position to absurdity by pushing it to an extreme. They may push the reader away from what they appear to be advocating by sheer disgust. Indirect appeals have one serious disadvantage: they may be completely misunderstood. Thus Swift's savage attack on English policies in Ireland, *A Modest Proposal,* which pretends to recommend the selling and eating of children, was taken seriously by some of Swift's contemporaries; and many have read Franklin's letter advising a young man to take an old mistress as a serious recommendation, completely missing the fact that he is really trying to persuade the young man to marry a suitable wife.

Indirect appeals, by their very nature, bring creative and persuasive writing very close together. They produce their effect through paradox, irony, satire—all special cases of the likeness-and-difference which we have seen to be characteristic of creative writing. Much satire may, in fact, be viewed as a complete blend of the persuasive and the creative. When the object of the satire is general, however—the ways of the world or the foibles of mankind—we think of it as creative, since the action which would follow from it is general and diffuse; when the object is more specific, the action is also likely to be specific, and we are likely to think of the writing as persuasive. But often it is impossible to determine whether the satirist really hopes to accomplish anything by his writing or whether he is merely expressing a naturally satiric sense of life.

The Element of Argument

One more point needs to be made in this general survey: it concerns what is sometimes called *argument*. Some writers on rhetoric distinguish between persuasion and argument, viewing persuasion as primarily emotional in its appeal, argument as primarily intellectual. We shall, however, consider argument, not as a special form of writing but as an element which appears in some persuasion, especially in the conceptual-informative variety. Argument is simply the logical element in persuasion: in any piece of writing in which it appears, the argument is a logical structure of propositions. The element of argument is not very prominent in most of the examples we have looked at in this chapter. The one exception is the passage from Madison. Since it is only a fragment of a much longer paper, the total logical structure may not be clear; but it is clear that there are a number of propositions and that they are logically related.

The element of argument is very strong in formal debates, in the discussions which go on in committee meetings, in policy memoranda and proposals, and in reports with recommendations, as well as in many less formal discussions of policy matters over the coffee cups or around the dining room table. Argument is the aspect of persuasion with which all of us are most often concerned as writers and speakers. Comparatively few people spend much of their time writing creative persuasion or preparing sales letters, advertisements, or speeches of the sort delivered by Churchill and Lincoln. Most people, however, are involved in presenting arguments, formal and informal.

In the next chapter, therefore, we shall focus on the element of argument in persuasion, its logic and its rhetoric. But we must keep in mind that the presence of argument in persuasion does not automatically make the persuasion serious and trustworthy; nor does its absence make the persuasion nonserious and untrustworthy. Neither Cowley's poem nor Lincoln's address is strongly argumentative. And though much argument is highly learned, thoughtful and wholly serious, argumentative persuaders sometimes employ manipulative devices which are just as tricky as anything in commercial advertising. We must always ask whether the propositions which are presented really do support the conclusions they are supposed to support.

Summary

Persuasion differs from informative and creative writing chiefly in its emphasis on action: it may be thought of as an extension of the informative and creative toward action. Different pieces of persuasion vary greatly, however, in their relative emphasis on conceptual and on experiential knowledge. They also vary in the attitude of the persuader toward his audience, in the immediacy and generality of the action proposed, and in directness of appeal. Much extended persuasion also contains what we are calling argument. In the next chapter we shall investigate more thoroughly the logic and rhetoric of argument.

EXERCISES

A. Write an account of another situation, like the story of Mr. Smith and the fire, which involves persuasion, and analyze it in terms of the characteristics and varieties of persuasion described in this chapter.

B. Make a collection of persuasive pieces which illustrate the following variations:
   1. Conceptual persuasion
   2. Experiential persuasion
   3. A mixture of conceptual and experiential persuasion
   4. Manipulative persuasion
   5. Indirect persuasion

C. Write a detailed critical analysis of Cowley's "St. Bartholomew's Eve" and Lincoln's Gettysburg Address as *creative* pieces.

D. Study the following examples of persuasive writing in terms of the variations suggested in this chapter, with a view to discussing them in class. Try to answer the following questions about each selection: Is it based mostly on conceptual knowledge, or on experiential knowledge, or on a mixture of both? What is the attitude of the persuader toward his audience? What is the action demanded? Is it immediate or remote? Is it general or specific? Is the appeal direct or somewhat indirect?

1.   *The Crisis*
                (*December 19, 1776*)

These are the times that try men's souls. The summer soldier and the sunshine patriot will, in this crisis, shrink from the service of their country; but he that stands it *now*, deserves the love and thanks of man and woman. Tyranny, like hell, is not easily conquered; yet we have this consolation with us, that the harder the conflict, the more glorious the triumph. What we obtain too cheap, we esteem too lightly: it is dearness only that gives everything its value. Heaven knows how to put a proper price upon its goods; and it would be strange indeed if so celestial an article as freedom should not be highly rated. Britain, with an army to enforce her tyranny, has declared that she has a right (*not only to* Tax) but "to BIND us in ALL CASES WHATSOEVER," and if being *bound in that manner,* is not slavery, then is there not such a thing as slavery upon earth. Even the expression is impious: for so un-limited a power can only belong to God.

I have as little superstition in me as any man living, but my secret opinion has ever been, and still is, that God Almighty will not give up a people to military destruction, or leave them unsup-portedly to perish, who have so earnestly and so repeatedly sought to avoid the calamities of war, by every decent method which wisdom would invent. Neither have I so much of the infidel in me, as to suppose that he has relinquished the government of the world, and given it up to the care of devils; and as I do not, I cannot see on what grounds the king of Britain can look up to heaven for help against us: a common murderer, a highwayman, or a housebreaker, has as good a pretence as he.

(THOMAS PAINE, 1737–1809)

2.   *An Editorial*

In announcing the appointment of a new member to the board of the Tennessee Valley Authority, President Kennedy urged that organization to "study ways in which the lessons it has learned in the Tennessee Valley may be exported abroad." While few dispute the accomplishments of TVA as an engineering achievement, it would be less than accurate to send abroad the impression that only by tax-consuming, semisocialistic projects have we taken "long leaps forward."

Actually, the most striking progress in this industry, as in most others, has been made by private-investor companies. Despite taxes and interest rates which favor public power, with more to come in the new Administration, at least 80 per cent of our electric power is produced by private-enterprise companies. The Idaho Power Company's Hell's Canyon dams add enormously to the power resources of the area and, incidentally, pay $10,000,000 in Federal, state and local taxes. Experimentation in the use of nuclear fuel for electric-power production is being carried on—with the money of American savers and investors—by a number of power companies. Seventeen nuclear plants are in construction at a cost of about $700,000,000.

Obviously a vast publicly financed and virtually tax-exempt enterprise like TVA can produce electricity, but the message which one might expect an American Government to send abroad is the fact that the most significant American economic progress, includ-ing that in the electric-power industry, has been made by private corporations and individuals. Sometimes one is tempted to believe that many American politicians have forgotten this fact. On the other hand, it is difficult to find much public support for socialized industry. Last November in the so-called public-power states in the western part of the country—despite the effort of Democratic candidates to make public power an important campaign issue— Republicans won in most of these states. It is not insisted that efforts to plug public power accounted for the defeat of Democratic candidates in these states—only that the alleged issue did not generate enough steam to elect them.

It is curious that politicians should place so much emphasis on public power and public projects generally when in other countries the passion for socialist adventures is fading. Great Britain's exercise in denationalizing its formerly nationalized industries has given that country a new birth of economic freedom which has left the Labor Party with no issue worth fighting for except getting the Americans and their Polaris missile off the island! New Zealand has retired its Socialist regime of many years' standing, and West Germany, whose prosperity is driving the Communists crazy, is well launched on a series of "privatizations" of its government-owned industries, including Volkswagen.

What the West Germans have been doing ought to be of great interest to Americans, because it suggests a page out of our own "people's capitalism." In the recent denationalization of Volkswagen, investors were limited to those with incomes of no more than $3200 a year. They were encouraged to hang onto their stock by promise of a big dividend after two years. The program, worked out by Economic Minister Ludwig Erhard, is called *Eigentum für Jedermann* (Property for Everybody) and up to now has been an enormous success. Already some 216,000 Germans own pieces of Preussig, a mining-and-smelting firm long owned by the government. They bought the shares for thirty-four dollars each and, according to *The Wall Street Journal*, the recent price is about sixty-five dollars. The Volkswagen deal went through in January and resulted in the distribution of ownership of Hitler's prize state corporation among probably 500,000 people. This of course, isn't "everybody," but after all, investing isn't compulsory.

Coming soon will be a public offering of stock in Prussian Electric, the nearest thing in Germany to our TVA. A few years back former Sen. Edward Martin of Pennsylvania proposed a similar disposal of TVA, arguing, among other things, that this would give the Government and local authorities a chance to tax TVA revenues and properties. The German Government appears to lack that reason for denationalizing Prussian Electric, for that power complex in 1958 paid 37 per cent of its gross revenues in taxes.

This compares with an average of 23 per cent paid by American investor power companies and, of course, outdistances TVA completely.

If the New Frontier wants to do something handsome for other countries, why not let them in on some of the things our people have been doing for themselves without bureaucratic interference? Actually delegations from all over the world visit our private power plants, as well as TVA, to get ideas on engineering, management and finance. It looks as if some other countries have done their homework on this subject and may wonder why the "capitalistic" United States should attempt to educate them on the virtues of socialism.[3]

(*Saturday Evening Post*)

3. *Address to the Constitutional Convention*
(*September 17, 1787*)

Mr. President,

I confess, that I do not entirely approve of this Constitution at present; but, Sir, I am not sure I shall never approve it; for having lived long, I have experienced many instances of being obliged, by better information or fuller consideration, to change my opinions even on important subjects, which I once thought right, but found to be otherwise. It is therefore that, the older I grow, the more apt I am to doubt my own judgment of others. Most men, indeed, as well as most sects in religion, think themselves in possession of all truth, and that wherever others differ from them, it is so far error. Steele, a Protestant, in a dedication, tells the Pope, that the only difference between our two churches in their opinions of the certainty of their doctrine, is, the Romish Chuch is *infallible,* and the Church of England is *never in the wrong.* But, though many private Persons think almost as highly of their own infallibility as of that of their Sect, few express it so naturally as a certain French Lady, who, in a little dispute with her sister, said, "But I meet with nobody but myself that is *always* in the right. *Je ne trouve que moi qui aie toujours raison.*"

In these sentiments, Sir, I agree to this Constitution, with all its faults,—if they are such; because I think a general Government necessary for us, and there is no *form* of government but what may be a blessing to the people, if well administered; and I believe, farther, that this is likely to be well administered for a course of years, and can only end in despotism, as other forms have done

[3] FROM "Socialism Would Be a Strange Export for the USA," from *The Saturday Evening Post.* © 1961 by The Curtis Publishing Company. Reprinted by permission.

before it, when the people shall become so corrupted as to need despotic government, being incapable of any other. I doubt, too, whether any other Convention we can obtain, may be able to make a better constitution; for, when you assemble a number of men, to have the advantage of their joint wisdom, you inevitably assemble with those men all their prejudices, their passions, their errors of opinion, their local interests, and their selfish views. From such an assembly can a *perfect* production be expected? It therefore astonishes me, Sir, to find this system approaching so near to perfection as it does; and I think it will astonish our enemies, who are waiting with confidence to hear, that our councils are confounded like those of the builders of Babel, and that our States are on the point of separation, only to meet hereafter for the purpose of cutting one another's throats. Thus I consent, Sir, to this Constitution, because I expect no better, and because I am not sure that it is not the best. The opinions I have had of its *errors* I sacrifice to the public good. I have never whispered a syllable of them abroad. Within these walls they were born, and here they shall die. If every one of us, in returning to our Constituents, were to report the objections he has had to it, and endeavor to gain Partisans in support of them, we might prevent its being generally received, and thereby lose all the salutary effects and great advantages resulting naturally in our favor among foreign nations, as well as among ourselves, from our real or apparent unanimity. Much of the strength and efficiency of any government, in procuring and securing happiness to the people, depends on *opinion*, on the general opinion of the goodness of that government, as well as of the wisdom and integrity of its governors. I hope, therefore, for our own sakes, as a part of the people, and for the sake of our posterity, that we shall act heartily and unanimously in recommending this Constitution, wherever our Influence may extend, and turn our future thoughts and endeavours to the means of having it *well administered.*

On the whole, Sir, I cannot help expressing a wish, that every member of the Convention who may still have objections to it, would with me on this occasion doubt a little of his own infallibility, and, to make *manifest* our *unanimity*, put his name to this Instrument. [At this point Franklin moved that the Constitution be adopted by the Convention.]

(BENJAMIN FRANKLIN, 1706–90)

15. The Logic and Rhetoric of Argument

> But since belief is a rule for action, the application of
> which involves further doubt and further thought, at
> the same time that it is a stopping-place it is also a
> new starting-place for thought. That is why I have per-
> mitted myself to call it thought at rest, although thought
> is essentially an action. The *final* upshot of thinking is
> the exercise of volition. . . .
>
> C. S. PEIRCE, "How to Make our Ideas Clear"

The Fable Again

In the last chapter we imagined a situation in which Mr. Smith, a summer resident of Blue Lake, found it necessary to call on his neighbors to help put out a brush fire. We saw that Mr. Smith used both conceptual and experiential knowledge, and that he varied his approach somewhat depending upon the responses of his different neighbors. Mr. Smith's situation was unusual, however, in one important way: he had no time to plan a logical presentation nor to deliver long speeches—there was a fire which had to be put out at once.

Now let us imagine a situation in which the required action is less immediate and less urgent. Smith and his friends have managed to extinguish the fire, but the experience has convinced some of them that fire fighting cannot be left to such haphazard arrangements: what Blue Lake needs is a volunteer fire company, with adequate equipment and some practical training. Smith takes it upon himself to find out all he can about such organizations, how they are set up, kinds and costs of equipment, and so on. He then calls a meeting and presents his plans. He spends some time in the beginning talking about the danger of a major fire at Blue Lake and reminding his neighbors of the very real threat of a few weeks earlier. He then produces his proposal for a volunteer fire company, a very detailed proposal which he has had mimeographed in his city office. And he tries to show that the proposed organization will constitute a real safeguard to the residents of Blue Lake, and that it can be set up at once if there is a will to do so.

Some residents agree—and many disagree. One man argues that the fact that an unorganized group managed to put out the only fire at Blue Lake in years is good evidence that no organization is necessary: "We can always rally 'round if we have to." Another man argues that while unorganized efforts will do the job if the fire is a small one, even a well-trained fire company will be of little use if it is a big one: therefore there is no point in organizing such a company. A third neighbor is most concerned about the time required for training. "I have three weeks' vacation," he says. "I come up here for a rest, and I don't want to spend my time playing fireman." Another remarks that the town of New Milford never had a serious fire until *after* it organized a fire company. "Therefore . . ." Still another asks what good the company will be in the off-seasons: "If there's a fire in the fall or spring, it'll burn up not only our camps but all our expensive fire-fighting equipment too."

The mention of cost touches off yet more objections: "The whole scheme is too expensive; it's cheaper simply to carry enough insurance, and let the place burn." There are also practical questions about the legal status of such an organization: "What would the fire company have a right to do? Could it start backfires without being sued for damages if they got out of hand? Could it break fences and cut down trees?"

The Nature of Argument

This discussion—and we shall leave Smith and his neighbors in the midst of it—contains an element which was almost wholly absent from the persuasive appeals of the earlier story, the element of argument. At the end of the last chapter we saw argument simply as the logical element in persuasion—the structure of propositions upon which a conclusion rests. Argument is, therefore, most apparent in the conceptual variety of persuasion, and it is likely to play an important part only in fairly extensive pieces of persuasion or in discussion. A man does not present an argument by shouting "Fire!" Mr. Smith *is* presenting an argument as he tries to persuade his neighbors to organize a fire company.

Now the notion of logical structure should already be quite familiar. Much informative writing is made up of propositions which are logically related to each other. Mr. Krutch's "A Modern View of Man," which we examined back in Chapter 7, contains a number of propositions whose relations to each other might be studied analytically. We did not treat Mr. Krutch in the rigorous fashion which is often needed in dealing with persuasive writers, because we recognized the tentative, exploratory nature of his talk. He is concerned with the consequences of ideas, with the relation between some propositions of science and some political systems. If he is asking us to *do* anything, it is simply to *think* about these relations, to explore them for ourselves.

Our failure to apply a logical analysis to Mr. Krutch does not mean, however, that we are not interested in the logical relations which appear in informative writing. We often are, especially when there is a more definite conclusion than we found in Mr. Krutch; and we are most interested when the conclusion involves action—that is, when the argument is basically persuasive. We then want to know whether the argument justifies the conclusion.

Mr. Smith's conclusion is that the residents of Blue Lake should organize a fire company. This conclusion rests logically on some other propositions—for example, that there is real danger of fire at Blue Lake; that a volunteer group with proper training and equipment can reduce this danger; that the proper equipment will cost X number of dollars. And these propositions, in turn, rest upon others. For example, the assertion that there is danger of a serious fire rests upon the fact that there was a fire a few weeks earlier, and that it was extinguished with great difficulty. We shall keep this argument about a fire company in mind as we go on now to consider the *logic* and *rhetoric* of formal argument.

The distinction between logic and rhetoric—and it is basic to this chapter—is closely related to the distinction between propositions and statements, which was first made back in Chapter 5. Logic is concerned with propositions and their relation to each other. Rhetoric is concerned with the language in which the propositions are expressed—that is, with the statements that are made, and with the order in which the statements are presented. We shall begin by looking at argument from the logical point of view and then go on to consider it from the rhetorical point of view, paying particular attention to some formal rhetorical patterns.

Some Logical Principles

Anyone who knows anything about formal logic will recognize the impossibility of treating it adequately in a few pages; and the introduction of a mere smattering of technical terms is not only useless but downright insidious, since it may lead the reader to believe that he knows more about a very technical subject than he actually does. Fortunately, the groundwork for a nontechnical discussion has already been laid in Chapters 5–7. In these chapters we examined the distinction between propositions and statements, and the notion of levels of generality among propositions and the ways in which these levels are used in the development of conceptual knowledge. We also discussed the reading of informative literature. Most of these ideas are directly applicable to the study of persuasive argument, though some need to be amplified.

For example, we can apply many of the suggestions for the reading of informative literature quite directly to persuasive argument. In Chapter 7 we suggested that the first step was to define the subject: What is the writer writing about? In the analysis of persuasive argument this is a very easy first step. We usually do not have to wonder what the persuader is driving at. He makes his conclusion clear—sometimes in the beginning of his argument. Thus Mr. Smith's subject is the organization of a fire company; the conclusion of his argument is that such a company *should* be organized. The second step, as we saw in Chapter 7, is to isolate the main propositions and to try to see their relation to each other. Here again, the fact that we usually know what the conclusion of a persuasive argument is greatly simplifies our problem. We have only to look for the propositions which immediately support the conclusion, and at the other propositions which support *them*. The third step is to consider the unstated propositions, the assumptions which lie behind the argument. The technique for discovering unstated propositions is the same for persuasive as for informative writing: we trace an argument back until we find a break in the reasoning; we then construct the proposition which must have been assumed as an unstated part of the argument. Thus Smith's argument that it is desirable to organize a fire company is based partly on the unstated proposition that if something *can* be done to provide fire protection at reasonable cost, it *should* be done. (Not everyone in the group, incidentally, agrees with this assumption; one man, for example, objects to spending his vacation playing fireman.)

But useful as this general method of analysis is, it is sometimes necessary to go beyond it in either analyzing a persuasive argument or constructing one. Two new principles need to be considered at this point: *sufficient evidence,* and *valid reasoning.*

Sufficient Evidence. We have called these new principles, but, again, they are not completely new. Back in Chapter 7 we asked, "Where do the propositions come from?" And we noted that many propositions are generalizations based ultimately on some kind of observation. Persuasive arguments usually rest in part at least on propositions of this kind, and the question then is: What do these propositions themselves rest on?

The answer is that they rest on something called *evidence.* There are, however, a number of different kinds of evidence: the reports of eyewitnesses, observers, and participants constitute one kind of evidence; surveys and statistical studies constitute another kind; experimental investigations of all kinds constitute a third kind. Whatever kind of evidence is offered we are always interested in knowing whether it really supports the proposition it is supposed to support—whether it is, in other words, *sufficient evidence.*

If the evidence consists of the reports of witnesses, we want to know who these witnesses were and under what conditions they made their observations. In addition we want to know whether they have a general reputation for competence and reliability, and whether they agree with one another. And we are also interested in knowing whether anything might have rendered a witness incompetent in this particular case: Is he personally involved in such a way that it would be difficult for him to be wholly objective? Incidentally we prize especially statements by witnesses which seem to us to be contrary to their own interests.

If the evidence comes, on the other hand, from surveys or statistical studies, additional problems enter into our evaluation. (We will still want to know who made the survey, under what circumstances and why.) Most surveys make no attempt at complete coverage of the population. If an investigator wishes to collect statistics on a large group, he actually interviews or questions what he hopes is a "representative sample," that is, a much smaller group which he believes has the general characteristics of the whole. If he has done his job well, the results he obtains from his sample are approximately the same as those he would have obtained from a study of the whole group. The question, of course, is whether the sample was actually representative: Was it large enough? Was there any automatic preselection which would make it unrepresentative? A student, for example, may have been assigned the job of writing a report on student living costs at his university. He prepares a questionnaire and gives it to fifty people to fill out. This sample may be large enough for his purposes; but the student, perhaps because he knows only freshmen anyway, circulates it only in the freshman dormitories. But the occupants of the freshman dormitories are obviously a preselected sample. Living costs for freshmen may be somewhat different from those for the student body as a whole.

Finally, if the evidence comes from an experimental investigation, we want to know all we can about how the investigation was conducted and what "controls" were used. Sir John Lubbock, in another of his series of experiments with ants, wanted to find out whether ants could communicate from a distance. He set out six small pillars and on top of one of them placed some honey. As ants discovered the honey, he imprisoned them so that they could not return to the nest but where, he thought, they could communicate their discovery by sound if they were able to do so. He then kept track of the number of ants going to each pillar; and he continued the count after he had released his prisoners. The pillars without the honey served as controls in his experiment. He wanted to know how much visiting of pillars should be set down to random investigation and how much to "information" that food was available in a particular spot.

Valid Reasoning. When we talk about sufficient evidence we are talking about the "truth" (or probable truth) of propositions which are based for the most part on observations of various kinds. When we talk about validity of reasoning, however, we are concerned *with the form of an argument.* Propositions may be thought of as being true or false; arguments are valid or invalid.

Now it is possible to arrive at a "true" conclusion by invalid reasoning from a "false" premise. That is, we may come up with the right answer even if we have worked the problem the wrong way using some wrong numbers. This, however, is merely a chance result; and in either analyzing or constructing an argument it is worthwhile to look closely at the reasoning process and to try to determine whether *this* conclusion does follow from *these* premises.

Logicians like to illustrate the distinction between "truth" and "validity" with examples which are obviously absurd, believing that the absurdity may help make the distinction clearer. Let us follow this policy by imagining a very simple example. George Sanders has been acquainted with only three red-headed girls in his whole life; and all of them had very bad tempers. George has therefore concluded that all red-headed girls have bad tempers. (This is, of course a generalization based on insufficient evidence: three do not constitute a fair sample of the red-headed female population of the world.) At this point George meets a fourth red-head named Mary Burns, and he promptly concludes that she has a bad temper. Now let us suppose that this conclusion is actually correct. George has begun with a false premise (we will assume); he has used it in a valid argument; and he has come up with a conclusion which happens to be "true." But now let us suppose that George hears about Miss Burns' bad temper before he meets her or knows that she has red hair. When he hears about her bad temper, he says: "She must have red hair." His informant says, "She does; but how did you know?" "Oh," says George, "all red-heads have bad tempers." George is still starting with his false premise; he is still reaching a true conclusion; but his argument this time is *in*valid because the premise that all red-heads have bad tempers (true or not) does not imply that all people with bad tempers are red-heads.

We could continue this discussion of validity by introducing a great many additional complications, but the main point has probably been illustrated sufficiently, and we can now turn briefly to some of the special kinds of logical fallacies—that is, of invalid arguments. Many of these have names, and some knowledge of them is useful both to the person who is trying to analyze an argument and to the one who is trying to construct a valid one of his own.

One of the most troublesome is what is called a *non sequitur*. In the discussion at Blue Lake, one of Mr. Smith's opponents says that a fire company should not be organized because it will be of no use in the off-season. Now it is true that fire equipment cannot be used when there is no one around to use it; but it does not follow that the residents of Blue Lake should not take what steps they can to provide protection. A *non sequitur* is simply an argument in which the conclusion does not follow from the premises.

Another kind of invalid argument is the *post hoc* argument. (The full Latin name is *post hoc ergo propter hoc,* meaning after this, therefore because of this.) It is exemplified in our discussion by someone's remark that New Milford never had a serious fire until after it had organized a fire company, "therefore . . ."; the conclusion in this case, that fire companies cause fires, is so manifestly absurd that the speaker must be regarded probably as a mere heckler. A *post hoc* argument confuses sequence in time with causal relationship. It is true that if B does not come after A, then A cannot be the cause of B; but it does not follow that because B does come after A, then A must be the cause of B.

Another kind of invalid reasoning is the *false analogy.* As we noted in Chapter 6, analogy is a very useful device for presenting information, and even, to a very limited extent, for working out ideas. But we can never be quite sure how far an analogy actually holds.

At this point it may be well to try to pull some of these general logical principles together. We have separated the problem of sufficient evidence from the problem of valid reasoning. Actually the two are closely related (as the story of George Sanders and the four red-heads indicates). Much reasoning involves a comparison of two events, relationships, or categories. We examine part of a group—a sample—and then conclude that what we have found applies to the whole group. We notice a constant connection between two events in time, and we conclude that there is also a causal relationship between them. We notice that one process is analogous in some ways to another process, and we conclude that the two are analogous in other ways as well. We know that something has happened in the past and we conclude that it will happen again in the future. From a strictly logical point of view all these arguments are fallacious. In practical argument, however, we accept them and use them, only asking how we know that these further relationships exist.

Logic Plus Rhetoric

The construction and analysis of arguments is not a matter of logic alone, however, but of logic *plus* rhetoric. We have said that rhetoric is concerned not with propositions but with statements and with the order in which the statements are presented. It is also concerned with whole situations in which actual discussions take place. The logical structure of an argument must be sound. If it is faulty, its effect may be to *mis*lead the audience. And as readers and listeners we should be sufficiently alert to argument to detect the flaws within it, whether intentional ones or unintentional. Otherwise we can only say of a piece of argumentative persuasion: "I agree with it," or "I disagree with it." At the same time the logic of an argument often fails to convince unless the person who is using the argument has learned to take other matters into account as well. From the persuader's point of view, at least, it is a mistake to assume that all he need do is to construct a sound, logical argument. He cannot afford to forget that he *is* a persuader, that he *does* have an audience, that this audience must be able to take in his argument, to see its relevance to their interests, and thus to be convinced by it.

This does not mean that the persuader should falsify his argument or that he should abandon logical reasoning. The same logical argument may be presented in a number of different ways, using different words, different statements, different arrangements of statements, and different over-all patterns. What the good persuader does is to put his argument in the most favorable light so that it will have the best chance to convince the audience. In other words, he pays attention to rhetoric as well as to logic.

Now rhetoric grows out of actual situations, and there is no such thing as standard rhetorical pattern. Nevertheless many of the principles of rhetoric can be observed within certain rather common patterns of presentation. In what follows, we shall look at three common patterns—the pattern of formal debate, the problem-solving pattern, and the ends-means-results pattern.

The Pattern of Debate

Formal debate, as it is practiced by school and college teams, is an extreme example of a rhetorical pattern applied to the problem of conducting discussion. It is controlled by rules, time limits, and conventions which are designed to turn discussion into a game. Nevertheless the kind of analysis which has become traditional in formal debate can be applied to less formal situations—such as Mr. Smith's meeting to discuss the organization of a fire company.

Formal debate always revolves around a carefully worded question, or resolution. In the Blue Lake meeting, the question, if it were worded in debate fashion, would be: "Resolved, that the residents of Blue Lake should organize a volunteer fire company." In the logical sense, it should be clear that a resolution of this kind is simply the conclusion of the argument stated in a special way.

Most formal debates center around what are called *policy questions,* as distinguished from questions of fact or questions of theory. Questions of fact, incidentally, are the sort of question which appears in informative writing: the conclusion of an argument in a scientific paper is a question of fact. Questions of theory may also appear in informative discussions. Joseph Wood Krutch's paper is in part a discussion of theory which might be phrased as follows: "The conclusions of mechanistic science are incompatible with the principles of democracy." Policy questions differ from both questions of fact and questions of theory in that they have practical consequences. They lead, or should lead, to action. Other kinds of questions may, of course, also be involved in a policy question in a subordinate position. Much of a policy argument may rest on a question of fact, the kind of question which we have already discussed briefly in talking about sufficient evidence.

Some policy arguments rest also on questions of value. One of Smith's opponents in our introductory story introduces such a question when he argues that a leisurely summer vacation is more important than adequate fire protection. A question of value implies or asserts that A is good or that A is better than B. Often values are assumed; but sometimes they become the subject of discussion. We shall look at them again once we have had a more complete picture of the patterns of policy debates.

We have said that the policy debate in our example revolves around the question, "Resolved, that the residents of Blue Lake should organize a volunteer fire company." In formal debate terminology, Mr. Smith and those who support him are presenting the "affirmative" side of the resolution; his opponents are upholding the "negative" side of this resolution.

This distinction between "affirmative" and "negative" is a useful one for understanding formal debates about policy. We may define the "affirmative" as the side which is initially proposing a change in policy; the "negative" is the side which supports the *status quo.* Madison, in *The Federalist Papers,* is on the affirmative in that he is supporting a new kind of government. His opponents are supporting the *status quo,* as represented by the Articles of Confederation.

Now, it is almost axiomatic that people prefer to leave things as they are unless there are overriding reasons for a change. To be sure there *are* people who like change for its own sake, but most of us cling to the *status quo.* This natural conservatism makes the affirmative's job basically more difficult than the negative's. In the terminology of formal debate, the affirmative is said to have "the burden of the proof." It must prove its case or lose by default, and even if no one argues against it, an affirmative may in effect lose simply because it has not proved its case.

In a formal policy argument, the affirmative case rests—like an old fashioned milking stool—on three legs: necessity, desirability, and practicality. It must show (1) that a change is necessary, (2) that the change proposed is desirable, and (3) that it is practical. Smith, incidentally, follows this pattern point by point. He begins by showing that a change is necessary: the present situation is fraught with dangers which cannot be met by impromptu action. He then presents his specific proposal and tries to show first that it is desirable (it will eliminate most of the dangers) and second that it is practical (it is within the financial reach of the residents of Blue Lake and can be carried out if there is a will to do so).

But since the affirmative must establish three points—necessity, desirability, and practicality—it follows that the negative need only prevent the establishment of any one of these points: it can upset the affirmative case by breaking any one of the three legs on which it rests. Smith's opponents have, therefore, several possible "strategies," though we may imagine that they are not consciously using "strategy" at all, but merely expressing their various unorganized, opposition views. They may argue against all of Smith's points, or they may concentrate their attack on one or two of them. Or they may make a counterproposal of their own. Or they may combine these strategies in various ways. They may, for example, minimize the dangers of serious fire without denying the possibility that a fire *may* take place; and they may then center their attack on practicality: "The idea is an interesting one. Mr. Smith is a fine, public-spirited citizen. But has he considered the cost?"

Smith's opponents may even admit that Smith is quite right about the danger of fire and still oppose him, arguing that there is really nothing which *can* be done: "Some problems have no solution." Usually, however, a negative which admits the evils in the present situation feels obliged to offer a remedy of its own, a counterproposal.

One of Smith's opponents, for example, may suggest that the summer residents of Blue Lake petition to be included in an adjacent fire district, agreeing to pay their share of the costs for this protection. When such a counterproposal is made, the situation changes automatically: two plans now stand in opposition to each other; the negative has become a second affirmative, arguing for a change but a different change; the plans must now be compared as to desirability and practicality.

Arguments over rival proposals, incidentally, may often be very constructive. A group of citizens, for example, are opposed to the construction of a new highway across their property. Their opposition in the beginning may be based solely on self-interest: they do not even face the question of whether such a highway is necessary. Later they may come to see the need, and they may propose a new route which they think will do less damage to themselves and perhaps to others in the community. This counterproposal may actually be better than the other.

So far we have been imagining a situation which calls for a complete policy argument. Many arguments, however, revolve around very small portions of this over-all pattern—single issues or even subissues. One of the most common arguments *against* a proposal, for example, may turn on a subissue within the issue of desirability. Opponents of a measure argue that the proposal, which was designed to remedy certain evils, will, in fact, produce even greater evils. Whole speeches, articles, letters, and even books may center on a subissue of this sort. In a sense, Madison is dealing with such a subissue in the passage quoted in the last chapter. He is answering the argument that the new Constitution will generate a centralized tyranny; at the same time he is turning the argument against his opponents by showing that the tyranny of majority rule is more likely in small democracies. Exchanges of this kind constitute rebuttals and counter-rebuttals and are very common in the kinds of long-range policy arguments which involve many contestants, writing and speaking over a period sometimes of years or even decades. A great deal of attention may thus be concentrated on a point which is logically in a subordinate position.

Every four years we in this country are treated to the spectacle of an elaborate and carefully planned policy debate which follows closely the pattern we have been examining. The affirmative in this debate is the party which is out of power at the moment: it advocates a change. In its platform it may also present a detailed picture of what this change will mean in various areas of government; this is its plan or proposal. This kind of political debate involves, first of all, an attempt to demonstrate the "need for a change." If the party in power has held the reins of government for several terms, the need for a change may be stated as a matter of principle: the two-party system demands alternation in power. But if the party in power has had a more limited term of office, the "need" can be established only by showing that it is incompetent, corrupt, wasteful, and so on. The cry then is to "throw the rascals out." Since the action involved is simple, the debate may stay very close to this single issue (the need for a change), with the party in power "standing on its record." Usually the "outs" must go on to the other issues, however, and demonstrate that what they propose is desirable and practical.

The Problem-Solving Approach

Debate invites controversy. It is built on the assumption that there is going to be an opposition which must be overcome or brought around. But arguments are often presented in such a way as to be less contentious. What we are here calling the *problem-solving approach* is just as logical as the debate approach but much less contentious.

Problem-solving calls for a three-step presentation: (1) a presentation of a problem, (2) a statement of a solution, and (3) a justification of the solution. It is clear that the presentation of a problem is "necessity" in a different guise, and that justification of a solution involves both "desirability" and "practicality." The effect of the problem-solving approach can be quite different however. Instead of arguing the need for a change, an approach which is calculated to antagonize some people—especially those who have a stake in the *status quo* or are in some way responsible for it—the speaker or writer suggests that his audience "look at the problem." He helps them with the "looking," and then proposes a solution. His solution is not, however, an affirmation of a formal debate resolution but a set of recommendations. And he usually tries to show how his recommendations will operate to solve the problem. Thus he moves toward action without actually inviting debate.

This is the sort of thing Mr. Smith may have been *trying* to do in his meeting. But there is, of course, no guarantee, especially in an open meeting, that this approach will work. If there is real opposition, the debate will come anyway—as it does in our story—and the issues will have to be argued out in public.

The problem-solving approach is common, especially in organizations with well-defined structures and purposes, such as educational institutions, businesses, and industries. Recommendations are made in the form of a report, perhaps at the request of the whole organization or of its executive. The writer, or the committee he is reporting for, has been given a definite "charge," a problem to analyze and to try to solve. The report repeats this charge, analyzes the problem, and suggests a solution. Sometimes, of course, a writer acts on his own initiative. He has no "charge," merely some original ideas, some suggestions which he offers in a letter or memorandum, following the problem-solving pattern.

Ends, Means, and Results

A third kind of pattern is built on a causal analysis of ends, means, and results. Behind it is the recognition that most acts have not single but multiple consequences. The "means" may be a highway planned to bypass a small urban community. The "end" (or object) is to facilitate the flow of through-traffic. But one "result" is to isolate the community in such a way that stores and restaurants are forced out of business. If this result is not discovered until after the road has been built (the means developed), it may be too late to do anything about it. But prior to the building of the highway a discussion of ends, means, and results may be useful in making clear the issues involved.

In one sense, an analysis based on ends-means-results is especially useful for developing "negative" cases, just as a problem-solution analysis is useful for developing "affirmative" cases. Its effect is to place special emphasis on results, on all the things which a change may cause to happen. It therefore invites a restatement of the problem, usually in broader terms. Thus the problem of speeding up through-traffic may be seen as that of speeding up through-traffic *without* destroying the business of the urban community.

But the ends-means-results analysis may also be used affirmatively, especially in the development of various sorts of proposals. An educational institution decides that it wants to experiment with larger classes. Its purpose (end) is to find a more efficient way of teaching its own students. It presents this plan to a foundation which, it hopes, will provide funds for the experiment. In so doing it emphasizes not only the objective of efficiency but the possibility that the program will result in greater independence on the part of the students. It also emphasizes the idea that the findings, whatever they are, will be of value to other educational institutions.

Questions of Value

One kind of question we have noted as basic to a discussion of policy is the question of value. Whether we think of ourselves as stating a problem, discussing the evils of the *status quo*, or formulating ends or objectives, we are working with "values." In fact, it is difficult to see a problem as a problem except against the background of some value system. When a speaker argues that the income tax should be repealed because it may deprive a rich man of ninety per cent of his income, he reveals a very definite value system—which his opponent may challenge with the simple question: "What's the matter with that?"

Sometimes, of course, values are simply assumed or tacitly agreed upon. Even Smith's strongest opponents are not likely to question the value judgment that a serious fire in the Blue Lake neighborhood would be a bad thing. Values may, of course, be open to question without being questioned. In recommending changes in work methods an engineer may simply assume that increased productivity is a desirable goal. And this assumption *may* go unchallenged.

Questions of value are more likely to become issues, however, in a discussion of desirability. As we have noted, it is at this point in a policy argument that the question of "new evils" is most likely to arise: granted, the proposal will remedy certain evils; but it will produce additional evils which far outweigh those which it has eliminated. It is here that conflicting value systems sometimes come into play. The proposal which will increase productivity may at the same time increase unemployment. At this point, a management value system and a labor value system may conflict.

Often, however, the question of values is less immediately practical than this analysis would suggest: the problem is not merely to compare probable results; principles are also involved. In one sense, principles may be thought of as general policies which serve as guides in the formulation of other policies. We decide that something is worth doing regardless of results because our over-all value system demands it. In another sense, we may view the principles themselves in a more practical way: in the long run, adherence to certain principles will "work" best—we cannot afford to abandon them in order to achieve short-run objectives. We may argue, for example, that in opposing totalitarianism we must not become totalitarian ourselves. If we do so we shall lose the very things we are fighting for. To this an opponent may argue that if we are destroyed in the process, we are lost anyway: better to sacrifice principle than to lose our very existence.

In considering the role of value in argument, it is well to recognize that discussions about value almost inevitably involve feelings and emotions. Insofar as there are issues of value in an argument, the presentation is likely to use creative methods. Words will be employed with attention to their evocative meanings, especially those evocative meanings which reflect value judgments. This does not necessarily mean that the persuader is trying consciously to manipulate his audience: he may be merely expressing his own strong beliefs in appropriate language.

EXERCISES

A. Prepare a detailed outline for a talk presenting the entire case *for* a policy proposal. Suggestions as to subjects:
   1. That an honor system be introduced in all courses in the college
   2. That the UN be converted into a world federal government
   3. That the US adopt a policy of unilateral disarmament
   4. That the minimum voting age in Federal elections be eighteen years

   (Your instructor may suggest additional subjects.)

B. Decide what line of approach you would use in *opposing* one of the policy proposals in A and write a five-minute speech concentrating your attention on those points which you think are most vulnerable or objectionable.

C. Prepare and conduct a formal debate on one of the above topics or on some other policy question. Unless your instructor specifies otherwise, the debate should be carried out by two teams of two students each, speaking in the following order:

    1. Constructive speeches (6 minutes each): first affirmative, first negative, second affirmative, second negative.

    2. Rebuttals: (3 minutes each): first negative, first affirmative, second negative, second affirmative.

The first affirmative will normally introduce the subject and argue the issue of *necessity;* the second affirmative will present the detailed plan and will argue *desirability* and *practicality.* No new basic arguments may be introduced in rebuttal.

D. Write a memorandum addressed to the president of an organization to which you belong suggesting major changes in its purpose or over-all structure.

E. Write an editorial for the college newspaper supporting (or opposing) one of the following:

    1. An unlimited cut system for all students

    2. The building of a new student union building

    3. A change in library hours

    4. Official censorship of all student publications

F. Assume that you have been appointed a committee of one to investigate one of the following (or a problem of your own choosing):

    1. The establishment of a college literary magazine (or some other publication or organization)

    2. The establishment of a student-run, all-campus lecture series

    3. The over-all program for freshman week

Write a report addressed to the appropriate committee or official setting forth your recommendations and justifying them.

G. Write a letter to the college newspaper on an issue that is of current interest. (Note: this letter may be written as a reply to the memorandum, editorial, or report called for in Exercises D, E, or F.)

H. Write either a critical analysis of one of the following editorials, or a letter to the editor answering points with which you disagree in either of the following statements:

    1. The 25,000 American physicians attending the American Medical Association meeting in New York are stressing the importance of scientific research to help them ease the ills of humanity. Medicine and research are two branches of endeavor which go hand in hand.

       As if to emphasize the keynote, the University of Michigan Medical Center reports a new anesthetic which is effective in

15 seconds and which may be carefully controlled. This is a tremendous advance from the opium and chloroform of a century ago. What it can mean in saving lives in time of emergency cannot be calculated.

Unfortunately research is slowed by lack of adequate funds. This shortcoming has been criticized by Arnold Toynbee, the British historian, who questions the wisdom of the space race to the moon and urges the funds be spent to improve the living conditions of mankind all over the world.

It is true that a few billions spent on space, if diverted to research, might bring lasting benefit to humanity. It could speed the day when the long awaited cure for cancer is found and it could ease many of the ailments which plague people.[1]

(*Troy Record,* June 27, 1961)

2. The villain in the education of American youth is that little technique known as the "curve." Although applied in a thousand different ways by individual school systems and individual teachers, the curve is a flexible device with just one aim: to guarantee passing grades to all but the two or three most nearly moronic students taking any given academic subject. Individual teachers use it because "I couldn't flunk 25 percent of the class." School administrators re-use it to change even those poor grades the teachers do give because "we have to put these students somewhere and get them through." The position of the schools is understandable; America says they must educate all youth through high school regardless of academic intelligence. Yet every time a curve is used to pass very poor students, every student above them must be upgraded accordingly. As long as students are graded not on the basis of their comprehension but on their relative standing in a given class, the actual rate of accomplishment will continue to go down, down, down.[2]

(DOROTHY SAMUEL, "The Villain in Education,"
The Progressive, May, 1960)

I. The following statements propose general systems of values. Either analyze one of these systems or select the point or points with which you disagree and write a letter to the editor of the publication presenting your disagreement:

  1. The conflicts that involve twentieth-century man are not solely ideological or political. They are personal, historic, transcendent.

[1] FROM the *Troy Record,* June 27, 1961. Reprinted by permission of the publisher.

[2] FROM "The Villain in Education" by Dorothy Samuel, from *The Progressive,* May, 1960. Reprinted by permission of the publisher.

They involve his relationship to others—all the way from the immediate community that surrounds him to the human commonwealth as a whole.

These conflicts can be resolved in terms of first principles:

If there is a conflict between the security of the sovereign state and the security of the human commonwealth, the human commonwealth comes first.

If there is a conflict between the well-being of the nation, and the well-being of mankind, the well-being of mankind comes first.

If there is a conflict between the needs of this generation and the needs of all the later generations, the needs of the later generations come first.

If there is a conflict between the rights of the state and the rights of man, the rights of man come first. The state justifies its existence only as it serves and safeguards the rights of man.

If there is a conflict between public edict and private conscience, private conscience comes first.

If there is a conflict between the easy drift of prosperity and the ordeal of peace, peace comes first.[3]

(NORMAN COUSINS, Editorial, *Saturday Review*, August 20, 1960)

2. It was a favorite and no doubt sound argument among early twentieth-century reformers that "playing the game" as the gentleman was supposed to play it was not enough to make a decent society. They were right; it is not enough. But the time has come to add that it is nevertheless indispensable. I hold that it is indeed inevitable that the so-called social conscience unsupported by the concept of personal honor will create a corrupt society. But suppose that it doesn't? Suppose that no one except the individual suffers from the fact that he sees nothing wrong in doing what everyone else does? Even so, I still insist that for the individual himself nothing is more important than this personal, interior sense of right and wrong and his determination to follow that rather than to be guided by what everybody does or merely the criterion of "social usefulness." It is impossible for me to imagine a good society composed of men without honor.

We hear it said frequently that what present-day men most desire is security. If that is so, then they have a wrong notion of what the real, the ultimate security is. No one who is de-

---

[3] FROM an editorial by Norman Cousins, reprinted from the *Saturday Review*, August 20, 1960. By permission of the publisher.

pendent on anything outside himself, upon money, power, fame, or whatnot, is or ever can be secure. Too much is being said about the importance of adjustment and "participation in the group." Even cooperation, to give this thing its most favorable designation, is no more important than the ability to stand alone when the choice must be made between the sacrifice of one's own integrity and adjustment to or participation in group activity.[4]

(JOSEPH WOOD KRUTCH, "The New Immorality,"
Saturday Review, July 30, 1960)

[4] FROM "The New Immorality" by Joseph Wood Krutch, reprinted from the *Saturday Review*, July 30, 1960. By permission of the publisher.

16. The Analysis of Propaganda

> No matter how propaganda is defined, it is clear at
> the outset that the term refers to an attempt by some-
> body to influence somebody else. The crusading that
> propaganda implies characterizes a state of conflict,
> conflict over ideals, supremacy, or merchandise. . . .
> Even the most optimistic of the present generation see
> no end to conflict; many of them, in fact, regard con-
> flict as a necessary source of human motivation.[1]
>
> LEONARD DOOB, *Propaganda—Its Psychology
> and Technique*

Why Study Propaganda?

It would be reasonable to ask at this point: Why take time to
study propaganda? We have looked at serious writing of various
kinds—informative, creative, *and* persuasive. If propaganda is what
most of us take it to be—a nonserious, manipulative kind of writing
—wouldn't it be better simply to ignore it? Or, if we are going to
look at propaganda, shouldn't we also look at its informative and
creative counterparts—the kind of manipulative writing which appears in sensational journalism and slick fiction?

There are several reasons for studying propaganda. Most important is the fact that propaganda, or manipulative persuasion, to
which we have referred a number of times in the last two chapters,
bulks so large that it threatens our view of persuasion as a whole.
We have been stressing the usefulness of some kinds of serious
persuasion, and we have argued that it should be taken seriously—

---

[1] FROM *Propaganda—Its Psychology and Technique* by Leonard Doob. Reprinted by permission of Holt, Rinehart and Winston, Inc.

as seriously as good informative and creative writing. But we have only to pick up a magazine, or listen to the radio, or drive through the country between rows of billboards, or open the day's mail to be convinced all over again that much persuasion is pretty shoddy stuff. It might be well therefore to look at this shoddy stuff, closely and analytically—and partly so that we may better appreciate the serious persuasion of a Churchill, a Lincoln, or a Franklin.

Moreover, the propaganda which confronts us daily, however much we may dislike it, plays a very large part in our everyday decisions. We do buy, vote, oppose, support, fight, and give as a result of the appeals of various kinds of very skillful propagandists. And we do so partly because it is almost impossible to do otherwise. The problem is not merely to detect propaganda. In fact this is often—but not always—the easiest part of the whole business. Most advertisements are labeled as such; brochures and campaign appeals are plainly marked. The real problem is to know what to think about the propaganda we encounter, and what to do as a result of it—because propaganda is, like all persuasion, directed toward action, and even a *refusal* to act is itself a kind of action.

Finally, the study of propaganda is useful as an introduction to nonserious informative and creative writing—to any kind of writing which is less concerned with transmitting or generating knowledge than with manipulating readers. All manipulative writing—whether informative, creative, or persuasive—works in much the same way; and it all deserves at least a casual examination. At the end of this chapter we shall look at informative and creative writing of this sort; and in the next chapter we shall go on to the more general questions of how to evaluate all three uses of language.

The Propaganda Situation

We can best understand propaganda—and the other manipulative forms—if we begin with the kind of situation within which propaganda normally operates. We have said already that manipulative persuasion (which we are now calling *propaganda*) is characterized by a particular relation between the persuader and his audience. Perhaps it will help us to see this relation if we return briefly to Mr. Smith and his neighbors.

Two weeks after the first meeting to discuss the organization of a fire company, Smith calls a second meeting. This time he has arranged for a speaker who, he hopes, will be able to answer some of his neighbors' questions. The speaker is a Mr. Stone, a sales representative for a company which specializes in fire-fighting equipment. Mr. Stone proves to be personable and well-informed. He brings with him quantities of attractive brochures, showing stalwart, keen-eyed men in red helmets and black raincoats battling menacing orange flames with great courage and apparent success. These brochures he simply sets out on a table, however, where they can be picked up by those who want them (nearly everyone takes a copy), and he spends most of his time answering questions. Only at the end of the talk—and then in response to a request—does he go out to his car, accompanied by volunteers from the group, and bring back sample pieces of equipment—a fire extinguisher, several kinds of axes, nozzles, and a length of canvas hose. He is, everyone agrees, an interesting visitor, and he is heartily applauded by even the most skeptical in the audience.

Yet Stone's relations to this audience are quite different from those of Smith, who has brought him here. Smith, in trying to persuade his neighbors to help put out a fire and, later, to organize a fire company, has been exercising leadership in a cause with which he is himself identified. Stone, on the other hand, however honest and even dedicated a salesman he may be, is primarily interested in selling a particular line of equipment. To put it another way, Smith is "in the same boat" with his audience; Stone is not. This fact does not, however, make Stone a menace to the residents of Blue Lake or a dishonest character. The chances are that the information he provides is thoroughly reliable, and it is certain that he is the best-informed man in the room. And if Smith's efforts are in the right direction, so also are Stone's, since Stone's arguments support those of Smith. Nevertheless, the residents of Blue Lake will do well to recognize that the purpose of the amiable Mr. Stone is primarily to sell merchandise. He may help persuade them to go ahead and organize a fire company, but if they are prudent people, they will not rush to sign a contract for *his* line of equipment until they have at least investigated some other lines—listened, that is, to rival propagandists.

In general, we may see all professional persuasion as propaganda; and all of it is characterized by a distinction between the basic interests of persuader and audience. The professional persuader, whether he is an advertiser, a lobbyist, a public-relations expert, a fund raiser, or a professional organizer, may be a thoroughly honest man who is rendering important services to the public as well as to the organization he represents; but his immediate interests and the interests of his audience are never quite the same. In his own interests, or in the interests of his client, he tries to influence other people—to get them to buy something, to give, join, or support. The result is a kind of persuasion which is often very effective and varied in its techniques. Stone, for example, operates as a rather low-pressure salesman using a "soft-sell." He has some high-pressure literature, but he does not distribute it, and he does not plaster the front of the room with advertising posters, nor does he bring in equipment until he is asked to do so. The chances are that he works this way simply because he has gauged the temper of this particular audience. With another audience, in another situation, he might behave somewhat differently.

But because professional persuasion is generally to be equated with propaganda it does not therefore follow that only professional persuasion is manipulative, or that the line between propaganda and what we have been calling serious persuasion is always a clear one. It is quite possible for any of us, at any time, to slip into the propagandist's role. If the public-spirited Mr. Smith suddenly decides to sell his camp at Blue Lake, his approach to prospective buyers will be, almost automatically, different from the approach he has been using in persuading his neighbors to fight a fire or organize a fire company. And political leaders often shift roles. A candidate for public office wants to be elected, and in his role as candidate he is essentially a propagandist, however hard he may try to appear otherwise. But once in office he becomes (or should become) a leader organizing and administering a government which is working in the interests of the people. He and his constituents are now in the same boat: the result may be persuasion as statesmanlike, if not as literate, as any used by a Churchill or a Lincoln. Similarly, a professional organizer acting as the paid secretary of an organization may find himself in a position where his interests and the interests of the people with whom and for whom he works are so closely identified that he ceases to be—at least with the members of the organization—a propagandist. But what of his relations with the same audience when he tries to persuade them to contribute funds to keep the national office operating and to pay his own salary?

The Basic Analysis

We have said that all persuasion pays some attention to the needs and interests of the audience. This is only natural since all persuasion is concerned, directly or indirectly, with actions, and actions cannot be separated from the people who perform them. What we have called manipulative persuasion simply pushes this natural tendency to an extreme. It concentrates on the audience, watches or predicts responses, and modifies its tactics as it goes along. If Mr. Stone in our story is as good a salesman as he appears to be, he is probably conscious of how he is doing at every stage in the discussion: he senses skepticism, hostility, and credulity, and he identifies the specific problems troubling his audience. Even his willingness to answer questions rather than spend all his time on a formal presentation shows the importance he assigns to audience reactions. He is looking for "feedback," so he will know what to do and say next. In more formal situations professional persuaders arrange pilot sales campaigns, conduct opinion polls, and ask listeners to write to them—all for the purpose of obtaining "feedback."

The manipulative persuader, like all other persuaders, is concerned ultimately with action. In his case it is often, although not always, a specific kind of action—purchasing goods, giving money, voting for a candidate or party, joining an organization. His method is to build attitudes in his audience which will move them toward this action. He does this by associating the desired action with other things toward which the audience already has a favorable attitude—or its opposite with things toward which the audience already has an unfavorable attitude. We might examine this procedure under two headings: *attitudes* and *association*.

Attitudes. The propagandist is less concerned with what the reader knows (though this *may* be important to his persuasion) than with how he feels. Professional persuaders go to great lengths to find out all they can about the attitudes of their audiences. Advertisers and other propagandists conduct "market surveys," and carry on "depth interviews," and the most successful ones try very hard to keep abreast of popular taste by studying mass media and best-selling literature.

Manipulative persuaders are interested both in attitudes which are closely related to the actions they are promoting and in more general attitudes. They want to know whether the audience has any feelings about the desired action (product, candidate, or cause) and, if so, whether that audience is generally in favor or opposed; if the audience has no feelings on the subject, they want to know that too. We often think of propaganda as being designed to change attitudes. This seldom is the case, however. Few campaign speeches are directed primarily at members of the opposition party, because it is, in fact, very difficult to reverse an attitude in a single step. Much manipulative persuasion is calculated rather to confirm attitudes which already exist, or at most to swing the audience from a somewhat undecided opinion to a more or less favorable one. When the audience is firmly opposed to the action, the most a propagandist can probably hope to do is to shake their opposition, to make them a little less decided.

But whatever his problem is, the propagandist does whatever he does by bringing into play other attitudes which the audience already has and which may be far removed from the action with which he is concerned. This is his principal technique, and to use it he must have a fair idea of what these other attitudes are. The professional persuader, by the very nature of his job, is therefore much interested in attitudes which are common to large segments of the population. We shall call these *key attitudes,* and they are worth looking at because their obvious employment in a piece of writing—whether persuasive, informative, or creative—is usually a good indication of manipulative intent. In fact, when we can guess at the kind of audience a writer is writing for, we can probably be sure that his attention was primarily *on* that audience.

The key attitudes of different groups are, of course, different; but most professional persuaders working with American audiences would probably accept—and operate on—the idea that Americans in general have favorable attitudes toward America itself, Americans, and American institutions, customs and speech; toward education; toward democracy and the institutions it has created; toward money and physical comfort; toward science and technology; toward "progress"; toward romantic love; and toward monogamous marriage. Americans also are generally in favor of independence, self-reliance, equality, newness, size, power, peace, lack of restriction, togetherness, luxury, and gregariousness. They are against non-American things: totalitarianism (and especially Communism);

all institutions, ideas, and individuals which seem "highbrow" and hence undemocratic; all antiquated and out-of-date things (except antiques and the pies that mother used to make).

The advantages to the professional persuader of understanding key attitudes of this sort is clear. In mass persuasion, these widespread attitudes are probably his most useful tool: they offer an invaluable short cut. Yet it is worth noting that these key attitudes are probably not nearly so general and uniform as any charting of them almost inevitably suggests. In any group there are some individuals who do not share the attitudes of the majority. Moreover, the attitudes themselves are often self-contradictory. Within any group of Americans—and even within a great many individual Americans—there often exists a strongly favorable attitude toward conformity and organization-loyalty on the one hand, and toward self-reliance and individualism on the other. Or the same individual may be in favor of both luxury and physical toughness. Finally, values—no matter how stable they may seem—do change. Changes are produced both by new experience and knowledge on the reader's own part *and* by the efforts of persuaders.

Association. The full significance of attitudes to propaganda is clear only when we begin to look in detail at the methods which are used. The propagandist's basic method is to work on a reader's attitude toward a specific action through the reader's other attitudes. The reader may not feel at all strongly about the action which the propagandist is proposing, but he does feel strongly about some other things. If the persuader knows what these other things are, he may be able to link the specific action to them in the reader's mind.

The actual technique of association varies greatly in different pieces of propaganda. The most obvious kind of association works through simple juxtaposition: the pretty girl in the advertisement for almost anything attracts our attention, of course, but she also provides a pleasant association with the product. We like her; she is in the same advertising space with the product; therefore. . . . Pictures are *often* used in this way. A recent advertisement for tin cans, for example, shows neatly opened cans, all of gleaming metal and all containing savory looking food, arranged on a damask tablecloth and surrounded by a fine silver tablesetting. The cans are thus associated with good food and a rich setting.

Associations of this kind make no assertions. But assertions of various kinds—statements, that is—do appear in propaganda. Some of them certainly contain propositions, but many others will be found on examination to be not very different from the pictorial associations just described. The slogan "Top-Notch Bread will give you more energy" looks like a statement. But if we stop to ask what *more energy* means, we are forced to recognize the ambiguity of the phrase: Will Top-Notch Bread give you more energy than you had before? Or more energy than other bread will give you? Or more energy than other kinds of food will give you? We could show a picture of a boy hitting a home run just after eating some Top-Notch Bread, and the effect on the reader would be approximately the same. What the advertiser is really trying to do is simply to tie together the idea of his product and the idea of more energy.

In the last chapter we noticed some problems of valid reasoning and some examples of logical fallacies. These fallacies were treated chiefly as pitfalls to be avoided in working out arguments, but they are sometimes used, quite consciously, as propaganda devices— along with a few other such devices which may be worth noticing here. Again their primary purpose is to set up associations; and for this purpose an invalid argument may work almost as well as a valid one: "We all know that some members of the OSS had Communist affiliations; Mr. Jones was a member of the OSS; therefore . . ." We can actually draw no conclusion about Mr. Jones on the basis of this argument, but the effect is to associate him with Communism and Communists. Similarly, the *non sequitur,* the *post hoc,* and the *false analogy* may work on the uncritical reader chiefly through association.

Other devices are perhaps even more clearly associational. The *reductio ad absurdum* pushes a proposal to an extreme, and then argues against this extreme as a means of arguing against the proposal itself; or quite frequently, it leaves the obviously undesirable extreme in our minds in association with the milder proposal which is actually the subject of the argument. A special form of *reductio ad absurdum* has been called the *parade of horribles.* One undesirable result is pictured as leading to another yet more undesirable result, and so on. Thus public ownership of the waterworks may be pictured as leading finally to a Communist dictatorship. Another propaganda device is the *argumentum ad hominem.* Not the proposal itself but the man who is responsible for it is attacked: thus an association is set up between a proposal, which may be difficult to assail on logical grounds, and an individual who is in some way vulnerable.

This last example leads to another point about the technique of association. Associations which are set up with a product in an advertisement, or with a proposal in many other forms of propaganda, may be thought of as primary associations. But there is also in every persuasive situation the possibility of secondary associations as well. There are other elements in the situation which are already linked in the reader's mind with the product or proposal—the persuader, for example, and the organization he represents; the persuasion itself; and even the reader who is reading it. The persuader may therefore work through these other elements indirectly, to reinforce the attitude he is promoting. This is also *argumentum ad hominem:* we usually think of that device as employing an attack on a rival persuader, but the principle of indirection is essentially the same. Institutional advertising is a good example of this method. The emphasis is not on buying a particular product but on the organization the persuader represents. The name or the integrity of the company sponsoring the ad is emphasized, and associations are set up with things toward which the reader already has a favorable attitude. ("Goodrich has gone to war." In wartime this is a patriotic act to the credit of the company.)

One final point should probably be made. Secondary associations of the *argumentum ad hominem* variety are not always irrelevant. Where it is possible to check on the reasoning process or to repeat an observation, we may be very little concerned with who is behind an argument. But where we must rely either on the observations of others, or on their judgments, then it is important to know who they are and how they may be motivated.

Open Propaganda

Propaganda analysts often speak as if the detection of propaganda were the major problem in dealing with it, but a tremendous amount of professional persuasion presents no problem of detection at all. An announcer may slide smoothly from the newscast to the commercial, but there is seldom any doubt that it *is* a commercial; advertising copy may occupy pages of a magazine, but it is usually quite clear that it *is* advertising copy; the leaflets distributed by pressure groups ordinarily leave little doubt as to their purpose; and campaign speeches are obviously propaganda —except perhaps in the eyes of the most devoted of the party faithful.

Is there anything then that we need to do about this plainly labeled material? The answer, of course, is "Yes," because even when we know it to be propaganda, we may still have to base important decisions upon it. If the residents of Blue Lake do organize a fire company, they will have to buy equipment somewhere, and they may well have to take into account all the things Mr. Stone has said. And probably the best way of using open propaganda as a means of making decisions is to do the kind of analysis for which we have just prepared the ground. We may have no more actual information when we have finished analyzing an advertisement, a brochure, or a campaign speech; but we are likely to have a much clearer view of what the real questions are and of the value of the propaganda for us.

Let us go on then to analyze in some detail a single example—a full-page advertisement for the Chrysler Imperial. The text occupies the middle third of a magazine page. Above it is a colored picture of an Imperial standing in front of what is obviously a public building. Two men with brief cases are coming down the steps; a liveried chauffeur stands beside the car, waiting, we presume, to open the door for them. The bottom third of the page consists also of a colored picture, showing a young executive riding in the rear seat of an Imperial. He is sitting comfortably, dictating a letter into a recording machine. Through the windows we see street lights, indicating presumably that he is catching up on his correspondence while riding home luxuriously in his chauffeured Imperial. The text is as follows:

You Don't Have to be Rugged to be an Individualist

If you're getting a little bored with meeting your car at half a dozen street corners every time you drive . . . it's probably time you bought an Imperial.

It isn't made in great numbers, simply because we've discovered no way to speed up the patient hand processes that make it America's most carefully built car. Quick, machine body finishing will not give us the mirror luster we get with our slower method of hand sanding. No machine yet invented fits doors and trunk lids with the precision we get by skilled hand adjustment.

No testing machine can be substituted for the final critical road test each of our cars must pass.

Imperial is not only exclusive in quantity, but delightfully uncommon in design and decor . . . and magnificently unmatched in sheer driving virility.

If you're determined to be an individualist . . . you may as well be a comfortable one . . . In an Imperial.[2]

There is no doubt that this is an advertisement and that its ultimate purpose is to persuade someone to buy an Imperial. The appeals which are made and the associations which are set up suggest that this someone—the audience for the advertisement—is a young executive (or someone who would like to be thought of as a young executive), a man who is on his way up but already has enough money so that he can think of buying an Imperial. (The advertisement assumes that he doesn't own one now, though if he does the ad will certainly not offend him.)

A number of attitudes—some of them conflicting—are brought into play by both text and pictures. The central conflict in attitudes is between desire for comfort and individualism, and the copy man has seized on the American shibboleth of "rugged individualism" and boldly divided it in two: "You don't have to be rugged to be an individualist," and, at the end, "If you're determined to be an individualist, you may as well be a comfortable one . . . In an Imperial." This conflict between attitudes also appears throughout the body of the advertisement. On the one hand, there is an obvious snob appeal—the desire to be different. We are told that cars of this kind are produced in very small numbers, that they are handmade. We are also told, however, that they are luxurious. And then, just in case the appeal to luxury and comfort becomes too strong, we are told that Imperials are "magnificently unmatched in sheer driving virility"—whatever that means. The pictures not only show the car, but they show the man who owns one. He enjoys luxury and he can afford it. A liveried chauffeur is opening the door for him, and he is being driven home. But he is no idle rich man. His car is standing outside a large public building, and he is using his time on the way home from the office to dictate letters while he rides.

Thus a whole network of associations is set up with the Imperial at the center—exclusiveness, individualism, luxury, handmade

[2] Reprinted by permission of the Chrysler-Plymouth Division of the Chrysler Motors Corporation and of Young & Rubicam, Inc.

quality, comfort, success, power. This is a car for a man who is on his way to the top. And the man who wants to go to the top will be not only interested but a little flattered by the image which is created for him as he identifies himself with the Imperial owner in the advertisement.

Once a reader has seen the advertisement analytically, he can then ask, "What is it all about really—and what should I do about it?" This advertisement will probably not make the reader rush out to buy an Imperial. Few people make such purchases in so precipitate a fashion. It may, however, make the reader think of himself as a possible Imperial purchaser; he can then investigate further, if he cares to.

Other pieces of open persuasion work, of course, in other ways. But a reader will not go far wrong with any of them if he simply tries to dissect each piece of writing, to note what attitudes are brought into play and how, and then to ask himself what the advertisement has to say to him: "How much do I actually know about this car? Are the attitudes which are brought into play the ones which ought to govern my decision about a car?"

Hidden Propaganda

But if much propaganda is open, much of it also is not. And here the propaganda analysts are right: hidden propaganda may take us in completely unless we detect it for what it is, and detection can be difficult—in fact, sometimes impossible.

Hidden propaganda, like the open variety, is usually the work of professionals. Occasionally it appears in the guise of fiction or even poetry. (The old-fashioned tract which describes the death by drowning of the boy who went fishing on Sunday is an example, and so obvious a one as to call for no comment.) Usually, however, propaganda appears as informative writing. It may be the work of publicity experts in a company or other organization, or the work of the staff of a newspaper which has a special bias. Many papers publish almost unchanged the news releases which are supplied to them by public relations officers. Some of these are very low pressure stories. If they have a propaganda aim at all it is simply to keep the name of the organization in the public eye. But sometimes they are false, or at least greatly distorted. An organization may hold a very small meeting and then issue a press release describing the reactions of a "large and enthusiastic group"—an example both of deliberate distortion and of the *band wagon* device (and a kind of distortion which is almost undetectable unless we have access to other sources of information). And newspapers themselves may also resort to all kinds of slanting. Sometimes the news story simply omits information which the writer does not want to convey. Sometimes the arrangement of the propositions emphasizes a particular point of view. Sometimes headlines and subheads give the story a particular bias or emphasis. Often, of course, the language in such stories will be partly evocative, and the evocative meaning will reinforce the particular slant of the propositions themselves.

In a sense, of course, there is probably no such thing as a completely unslanted story. The mere fact that a news writer must select his information presupposes that he will omit items which would be part of a complete picture. And much selection is a matter of point of view: the writer puts down those items which fit into his picture of things as a whole. In studying the slant of a piece of writing, then, we are really trying to determine what this point of view is and why items were selected and arranged as they are. Fortunately the kind of slanting which involves the intentional omission of significant facts is not nearly so common in important stories as some propaganda analysts would have us suppose. The slant of a publication is most likely to show up in unimportant stories which have nevertheless broad policy implications.

The two stories below have been arranged in parallel columns to show several kinds of divergence in presentation. Each story includes material omitted from the other story; and though the two are completely parallel in some passages, the over-all impressions they leave are quite different.

37 TICKETS JAIL U.N. AIDE AS SCOFFLAW	37 TICKETS GET U.N. AIDE $1,850 FINE
1. A U.N. scofflaw who ignored 37 parking tickets elected to serve a 74 day jail term rather than pay $1,850 in fines Friday as Chief Justice Murtagh teed off on personnel of the world organization who flout this city's laws.	1. A fine of $1,850 or seventy-four days in jail was levied yesterday against Jorge R. Alonso, twenty-one, an employee of the Argentine delegation to the United Nations, for ignoring thirty-seven traffic tickets dating back to July, 1952.

2. The $50 fine or two days in jail for each ticket was imposed by Chief Magistrate John M. Murtagh in Traffic Court. When Alonso after pleading guilty on all counts asked for time to pay the fines, the magistrate ordered him remanded to jail.

3. Later Dr. Armando Bulacia, second secretary of the Argentine U.N. delegation, appeared in court as personal representative of Garcia Olan, Argentine Minister of Foreign Affairs, and asked that the young Argentine be paroled in the custody of Mr. Olan.

4. Dr. Bulacia said the minister would be responsible for Alonso's appearance in court and asked that he be given time to pay the fine. Magistrate Murtagh relented and paroled the prisoner until March 26, ordering him to pay up by then.

2. "The personnel of the U.N. ought to respect the regulations of this country," Murtagh told 21-year-old Jorge R. Alonzo, 22 E. 93rd St., secretary to Rodolfo Munoz, Argentine delegate to the U.N. and now assigned to that nation's Ministry of Foreign Affairs office here.

3. "You have no more right to park illegally than any citizen of this country. Too many U.N. cars are causing us traffic troubles in midtown Manhattan by illegal parking," Murtagh said.

4. Alonzo, whose car was impounded when found parked for the eighth time in front of a hydrant at 2 W. 56th St., had his license suspended after an accident last August but continued to drive.

5. "You personnel of the U.N. ought to respect the regulations of this country and not abuse them," Mr. Murtagh had told the young man earlier.

See paragraph 9.

6. "You have no more right to park illegally than any citizen of this country. Too many U.N. cars are causing us traffic troubles in midtown Manhattan by illegally parking there."

See paragraph 8.

Asked why he ignored the tickets, he said he thought Murtagh's recent amnesty "washed out all tickets."

5. Murtagh told reporters later that the largest number of "diplomatic immunity cards" for top-level aides are held by China with 28 and Russia 27.

6. Every month, Murtagh explained, the U.N. provides him with a list of officials "recognized by the Department of State as entitled to diplomatic privileges and immunity" and identification cards are issued by the department to these persons—as well as their wives.

7. The Argentine list, extending down to third secretary, did not include Alonzo, he said. The Chinese and Russian cards include those of officials accredited to the U.N. and their wives.[3]

See paragraph 4.

7. Alonso said he thought the Magistrate's recent "amnesty" had "washed off violations from my record." Magistrate Murtagh explained that his amnesty was to allow scofflaws to pay for their tickets at a low rate, but did not relieve them from answering the summonses.

8. Alonso was arrested when he tried to reclaim his car from a city pound. It was towed there by Patrolman Louis Reich who saw it parked in front of a hydrant at 2 W. 56th St. and saw two other tickets inside the car. Records showed that Alonso had seven other tickets for parking at the same hydrant, which is handy to the delegation offices at 12 W. 56th St.

9. Alonso, who lives at 22 E. 93rd street, said until last Jan. 1

[3] FROM "37 Tickets Jail U.N. Scofflaw," reprinted from the *New York Mirror*, March, 1954. By permission of the publisher.

See paragraph 2.

he had been personal secretary to Dr. Rodolfo Munoz, the Argentine delegate to the U.N., and is employed as a delegation clerk now. Leaving the court, he said he would never again let a summons go unanswered and added, "I hope I will still be able to hold my position." [4]

(New York *Mirror*)   (New York *Herald Tribune*)

A reader would probably have to study the general policies of the two papers at the time when these articles appeared, and perhaps compare articles in other papers as well, before he could say for sure what divergencies of this kind mean. But if he goes no further than to detect apparent bias, he can at least recognize that there is probably another side to the story and reserve judgment.

Manipulation in Informative and Creative Writing

The two articles we have just looked at are basically informative. If either of them is intended as propaganda, it is the external sort of propaganda, that is, propaganda about an issue outside of the subject of the work itself. These articles may affect our image of the UN or of foreign diplomats. But much informative and creative writing is manipulative in a different way. Its object is not to promote a cause or to sell merchandise—except insofar as the writing itself is thought of as merchandise. Sensational journalism and slick fiction are obvious examples. Their primary purpose is to attract the reader's attention, to whet his appetite for more, and thus to sell newspapers, magazines, or books.

The article on the death of Errol Flynn which was quoted on page 269 is a good example of sensational journalism. Another newspaper put the same story on the obituary page and told it in these words:

Errol Flynn, fifty, film star and playboy, died of a heart attack last night while visiting friends just before leaving for Hollywood at the end of a five-day business-and-pleasure trip.

[4] FROM "37 Tickets Get U.N. Aide $1,850 Fine," reprinted from the *New York Herald Tribune*, March 13, 1954. By permission of the publisher.

The word *playboy* has fairly strong evocative meanings in this context, but the difference between this passage and the other is obvious.

Similarly, the exposé, the confession story, the lurid article in the "men's magazine," the factual account of the horrible or the supernatural (stock-in-trade of the Sunday supplement)—all are essentially manipulative. The writer has his eye on his audience, not on his subject matter, and he selects and arranges with the intention of fascinating his readers. His account *may* be factually correct, but the chances are that if it is, he has achieved this accuracy by an initial and quite deliberate selection: he dug out his lurid tale in order to have something to write about which would attract attention to his magazine or newspaper.

Creative writing of the manipulative sort is similarly diverse. It includes much of the fiction which appears on the newsstands in the form of the pulp magazines and the books with the lurid covers —though many of these are, of course, works of recognized value decked out in flamboyant covers to attract attention. It also includes much of the fiction in the mass-circulation magazines. This nonserious fiction, wherever it appears, *may* exhibit many of the characteristics which we have noted in Chapter 11, including archetypal action, allegory, and symbolism. Usually, however, it is relatively simple: the characters are likely to be stereotypes; the conflict is usually of the more obvious sort—man against man, or man against nature, rather than man against himself, or two worlds in opposition; the action is likely to be open, often violent; ideas or themes are usually trite and conventional. The whole effect is of a story written according to a formula, and this is in fact how many stories of this kind are produced. Stock characters, stock situations, stock conflicts, stock ideas are mixed together in various proportions. Writers of this kind of fiction often show great skill in "plotting," however. They know how to manage suspense, and especially in continued stories—as in the old "cliffhanger" movie serials—they leave the action in a very crucial state just before the "to be continued" line. And it is unwise to assume that such writers are always completely cynical about giving the reader what he wants. Stock conflicts and stock situations may be merely the product of a stock view of life. The results, however, are approximately the same.

In both informative and creative manipulation, as in the persuasive variety, the writer's picture of his reader is very likely to play a large part in what he is doing. Thus he may play on the same conventional attitudes which are used by the propagandist.

In addition he may stress sex and sadism for one kind of reader and a sentimental view of life for another; and he may try to give success to the kinds of characters his readers admire and failure to the kinds they despise. Sometimes the writer's picture of his reader can thus be deduced from the writing itself.

Toward Evaluation

In discussing manipulative writing, which has been the general subject of this chapter, we have of necessity introduced questions of value, of good and bad, of good and better. In general we have seen manipulative persuasion as a kind of writing which should be taken less seriously than other kinds of persuasion. This does not mean, however, that it is necessarily bad or irresponsible; and there is no need to reject all advertising, all organizational propaganda, all campaign speeches, all fund-raising appeals. In fact many of them are extremely useful, quite reliable, and—the only thing we have to go on.

It is clear then that questions of value go beyond the simple differentiation which has been set up in this chapter. Not all manipulative writing can be rejected outright. Not all kinds of serious writing are good—or equally good. But if we are to understand the problem of evaluation we must look at it in a more comprehensive way. This will be the business of the next chapter.

EXERCISES

A. Write a two-page analysis of each of the following advertisements. Try to determine what attitudes are being brought into play and what associational techniques are being used. What is your conclusion about the audience to which each advertisement is directed and the action which the advertisement seeks to promote?

    1. This text appears below a full-color picture of eight slices of cake, all different:

> We've made the flour softer and the sugar finer. We've found out a new rich, creamy shortening. We've come up with a wonderful new way to *pre-cream* all these good ingredients for you.

It all adds up to a rich, moist, tender, honest-to-goodness-home-made kind of cake.

And it's one-step easy! You put everything into the bowl at once—your cake-mix, eggs and water. The batter fluffs up thick and rich in just four minutes . . . ready to bake a cake as fresh and moist and just plain good as grandmother's best butter cake. Bake one for your family tonight, why don't you.[5]

2. The headline to this advertisement says: "I saw myself 10 years from now!" It is flanked by a sketch of a man standing before the pay clerk's window looking ruefully at the money in his hand, while a smartly silhouetted head in the foreground looks on. The text reads:

It happened one pay day . . .

Fred worked on the line next to me. Nice guy. Married. Two children. Been on the same job ten years.

As we walked away from the pay window he said, "Funny, each week I get to feel like I'm letting my family down. You know. Not getting ahead so I can give them all the things they need."

His words hit me all of a sudden. I could see myself saying the same thing—*ten years from now!*

Not only that. I could see the same job. Same thin paycheck. Same worries.

I thought about Fred all day. Then that night I saw an ad for I.C.S. It told about the job opportunities that open up with I.C.S. training. How people had found new careers and job success.

I mailed the coupon and that was the start. In just a few months my boss discovered I was an I.C.S. student. He was so pleased he decided to move me off the line. A year and two raises later I was made an assistant supervisor.

What about Fred? He's still working on the line. Still hoping for the future.

I told him about I.C.S. But so far he hasn't done anything. I guess some people never will.

How about you? [6]

The bottom half of the page is a coupon listing all the I.C.S. schools and inviting requests for additional information.

---

[5] Reprinted by permission of the Betty Crocker Enterprises of General Mills, Inc.

[6] FROM "I Saw Myself Ten Years from Now!" Reprinted by permission of International Correspondence Schools.

3. The text of the third advertisement is as follows:

The High Cost of Killing Time

How quickly the misuse of money—when found out—sparks our moral indignation into fires of investigation.

Yet how slow we are to see that the misuse of man-hours is as morally wrong and harmful as ever the misuse of money.

Padding the hours with a man's mere presence on the job, without using either his mind or his muscles, can be morally crippling to him. In fact, the deliberate waste of a man's power to produce and stand in the dignity of a living fully earned, is waste of a man.

Whoever causes such waste—for another or to himself—would be responsible for damaging not only the person, but would be contributing to weakening the nation's economic strength.[7]

The lower part of the column informs us that the sponsor of the advertisement is Republic Steel and lists the company's products in small print. At the very bottom is a cartoon showing an octopus picking pockets and captioned "Inflation Robs Us All."

4. The text of a fourth advertisement is as follows:

An extraordinary menu
for jaded musical appetites

Beginning twelve years ago, the Louisville Philharmonic Society somewhat startled the music world by commissioning outstanding contemporary composers to write symphonic compositions for the Louisville Orchestra. Ever since, these works have been premiered regularly by the Orchestra under the baton of famed Robert Whitney. Recorded by Columbia technicians, they are offered, by subscription, as fine 12-inch, 33⅓ RPM high-fidelity "First Edition" Records.

During the ensuing years 39 records have been produced, and are now being issued to 2,100 subscribers. (This is to be compared with the *million* subscribers of at least one popular record club!)

Admittedly a very "advanced" project, First Edition Records have won columns of praise from most of America's top critics. The subscription list is a blue-book of music connoisseurs throughout the free world (though Russian composers Shostakovich, Kabalevsky and Khrennikov, visiting the Louisville Orchestra last November, said that First Edition Records were well-known in USSR, too).

[7] Reprinted by permission of the Republic Steel Corporation.

If you are building or wish to build a notable library of the best contemporary music, these records are a must. They are available singly at $7.95 each or by subscription at $5.95. As a special introductory inducement, we are now offering six of the most-requested records for the price of one—$35.70 worth of these connoisseur recordings for only $5.95, upon your agreement to purchase the next six new releases during the next twelve months, at $5.95 each.[8]

B. Select three advertisements which appeal to you very strongly. Analyze their persuasive methods, noting the attitudes which are brought into play and the techniques of association which are used.

C. Write a short (400- to 500-word) analysis of the over-all differences between the ads in a general magazine, such as *Life* or the *Saturday Evening Post*, and those in a technical or trade magazine.

D. Do the same thing as in C for a "pulp" magazine, a middle-class magazine (such as those listed above), and a more highbrow magazine (such as the *New Yorker*).

E. Compare the treatment given by two different publications of a news story in which you suspect propaganda intent, using the parallel-column arrangement employed in the "U.N. Scofflaw" story in this chapter. Try to determine whether differences in treatment are actually the result of deliberate propaganda intentions. Write a 400- to 500-word report on your findings, appending the two stories.

F. Do the same thing as in E for two informative accounts of the same event, one sensational and the other more objective. Write a 400- to 500-word report on your findings, appending the two stories. Notice especially any differences in language.

G. Find a short story in a "pulp" magazine and analyze it first in terms of the ideas presented in Chapter 10 and then with a view to determining the extent to which it seeks to manipulate the responses of the reader.

H. Apply the analytical techniques suggested in this chapter to a piece of serious persuasion: Lincoln's Gettysburg Address, Cowley's "St. Bartholomew's Eve," Franklin's address to the Continental Congress. To what extent does this kind of analysis work? How much does it fail to account for?

[8] FROM "An Extraordinary Menu for Jaded Musical Appetites," reprinted by permission of the Doe-Anderson Advertising Agency, Inc.

17. The Question of Judgment

> To enjoy with discrimination, to discern value, to
> recognize and reject the spurious, to respond maturely
> to the genuine, never to be fooled by the shabby and
> the second-hand—that is the civilized approach. . . .
> We turn to criticism to develop and strengthen that
> approach. . . . Every effective critic sees some facet
> of literary art and develops our awareness with respect
> to it; but the total vision, or something approximating
> it, comes only to those who learn how to blend the
> insights yielded by many critical approaches.[1]
>
> DAVID DAICHES, *Critical Approaches to Literature*

Four Criteria

Earlier in this book we quoted C. S. Lewis's dictum that

> The first qualification for judging any piece of workmanship from
> a corkscrew to a cathedral is to know *what* it is—what it was intended
> to do and how it was meant to be used.

So far we have tried to do little more than develop this first qualification of the competent reader. For many chapters now we have
been exploring in detail three basic purposes which underlie most
formal, public writing and speaking. We have discussed the three
uses of language in general terms, and we have studied various
examples of the three, some specimens relatively "pure" and others
quite obviously alloys or hybrids. But, both in generalizing and in
analyzing, we have usually been satisfied to find out only what these

[1] FROM David Daiches, *Critical Approaches to Literature.* © 1956 by
Prentice-Hall, Inc., Englewood Cliffs, N. J. Reprinted by permission.

uses are, the range of each, how selected pieces of writing actually work, and how to make the most of whatever kind of literature we read. We have usually stopped short of the second and more difficult problem: How should we evaluate things made out of words?

One notable exception to this strategy occurred way back in Chapter 2, when, in setting up a few preliminary distinctions among the three uses, we tentatively proposed that each use might have its own standard. We suggested that maybe the primary criterion for judging informative writing should be its "truthfulness," for creative writing its "richness and unity," and for persuasion its success in promoting worthwhile action.

By now it should be apparent that this neat formula badly oversimplifies the problem. For instance, we have learned that *all three* uses of language, in their serious forms, are concerned with knowledge in some sense—either conceptual or experiential or both, either knowledge for its own sake or knowledge in the interest of inducing attitude and action. Similarly, we have noted that in their *nonserious* forms, *none* of the three uses is much concerned with knowledge but chiefly with "selling" something or other. So how can we say that "truthfulness" applies only to informative writing? Furthermore, we have discovered that truthfulness is itself a very complex notion: that it means quite different things when applied to conceptual knowledge and when applied to experiential knowledge; and that it does not even mean quite the same thing when applied to different kinds of conceptual knowledge.

Again, we have seen that the informative and creative uses tend to overlap and that both of them shade off imperceptibly into persuasion. So how can we say that each piece of writing has its own criterion, however we define that criterion? It is certainly useful to be able to recognize an author's over-all purpose (or purposes), but having done so no reader has a right to arbitrarily judge the writing according to any simple standard.

Instead, there are several *general* standards which, in fact, we do apply, in varying ways, to *all* kinds of reading material. And even these criteria we seldom formulate consciously. Most of our evaluations are performed in a rather casual, intuitive way. However, it may be worthwhile to try to break down the process, if only for purposes of discussion. This could be done in many ways; let us try out the hypothesis that there are four basic criteria involved in all literary judgment:

1. *Integrity,* which may best be thought of as a characteristic of the *writer.*
2. *Effectiveness,* essentially a characteristic of the *writing.*
3. *Truthfulness,* which is a characteristic of the *knowledge* the writing contains.
4. *Significance,* which should perhaps be considered a characteristic of the *work as a whole.*

Whether we think of them in these terms or not, all four of these standards seem to operate, with varying degrees of force, in our everyday critical judgments. For example, however much it may amuse us, we tend to question the *truthfulness* of an overly sensational news report and to suspect its author's *integrity.* We also react unfavorably to an *ineffectively* written story, even when we have no reason to doubt its *truthfulness, integrity,* or even its *significance.* And if we discover that an account is flagrantly inaccurate (*untruthful*) in any way, we may condemn it *in toto* no matter what other virtues it may have.

Or we may put aside a story which has none of the first three faults—which seems accurate, honest, and well written—simply because it strikes us as trivial (*insignificant*). Similarly, we may find a poem by a crude amateur to be sincere—sometimes embarrassingly sincere—but both banal and illiterate. Or we may find it painful to watch soap opera or cowboy shows, however skillfully written and performed, simply because they lack truthfulness: life just isn't like that, and never was. Or we may admire "slick" magazine fiction for its technical competence but find it intolerably dishonest or trivial or both.

In evaluating persuasion, we make similar distinctions. We are concerned not only with the significance of the action involved, but with the author's integrity (does he believe what he says?), the truthfulness of the knowledge he introduces to support his arguments and appeals, and the over-all power (*effectiveness*) of his language.

Thus, all four criteria tend to enter into our specific judgments. We make distinctions, and we balance good points against bad, but in no simple mechanical fashion. In a given instance, any one standard may assume overwhelming importance and outweigh all the others. This is obviously one reason why critics are seldom unanimous. It also explains in part why our judgments change with our maturity and experience. We should probably add that we are seldom willing to give the very highest praise to any work, of whatever sort, which does not meet all four requirements.

Now let's further examine some of these generalizations by looking more closely at each of the four criteria in turn and its relation to each of the three uses of language. We will conclude by suggesting how all four criteria might figure in judging a creative work, where the problem of evaluation is perhaps most complex.

Integrity as a Criterion

The chief thing a writer—any kind of writer—has to offer is the contents of his own mind. He may put down on paper facts he has personally gathered or ideas he has thought out or information he has borrowed from others. He may try to convey some part of his own experience and sense of life. He may offer us his judgments on things, people, and events. Or he may give us some of each, all at once. But whatever he gives, it is of little value unless it is genuine. If he tells us not what *he* knows and feels but what he thinks *we want* to hear, his writing is essentially both false and unenlightening: we have asked for a picture, and he has given us a mirror; we have asked for his judgment of the state of things, and he has OK'd our own prejudices; we have asked for insight into the human condition, and he has given us "entertainment."

Now, there is nothing wrong with "entertainment"—provided we don't mistake it for something else (e.g., for wisdom or truth) and provided we recognize that there are different kinds and levels of entertainment. Animals and children enjoy their own "proper pleasures" (to use Aristotle's phrase), but these are not necessarily the *only* "proper pleasures" of sophisticated adults.

The point here is that the only way we have of discovering the contents of another man's mind (a process which can be highly entertaining) is through the things he says and writes—or composes or paints or designs, and so on. Serious writing, of all kinds, *does* let us enter a little way into the consciousness of another human being, and it gives us thereby a means of understanding better the contents of our own minds. Furthermore, the acquiring of such understanding is one of the proper pleasures of civilized human beings.

Before we go any further, let us look at two pieces of writing. The first is from a speech on the mutual security program; the second is from Vanzetti's last speech to the court which sentenced him to die in the electric chair. Here is the security speech:

> I must make it clear that any foreign aid program which I endorse must submit to the same rigorous tests of fiscal soundness, not only in its entirety, but in each particular thereof, as must any domestic program which elicits my support.
>
> I have, in the past, voted for sewage disposal, airport construction, area redevelopment, and many other eminently worthwhile and valuable programs; but always I have insisted that all waste be first eliminated therefrom. To that end I have not hesitated to cast my vote for cuts wherever I felt that such cuts would effectuate justifiable economies. What I ask for domestic programs, I now ask for the proposed mutual security program.
>
> Let no man impugn my patriotism, for I yield to none in my zeal to preserve the republic from all her enemies foreign and domestic, of which the greatest are waste and corruption.

And here is Vanzetti's last speech to the court:

> I have talk a great deal of myself but I even forgot to name Sacco. Sacco too is a worker, from his boyhood a skilled worker, lover of work, with a good job and pay, a bank account, a good and lovely wife, two beautiful children and a neat little home at the verge of a wood near a brook.
>
> Sacco is a heart, a faith, a character, a man; a man, lover of nature and mankind; a man who gave all, who sacrifice all to the cause of liberty and to his love for mankind: money, rest, ambition, his own wife, his children, himself and his own life.
>
> Sacco has never dreamt to steal, never to assassinate. He and I have never brought a morsel of bread to our mouths, from our childhood to today, which has not been gained by the sweat of our brows. Never. . . .
>
> Oh, yes, I may be more witful, as some have put it. I am a better babbler than he is, but many, many times in hearing his heartful voice ringing a faith sublime, in considering his supreme sacrifice, remembering his heroism, I felt small at the presence of his greatness and found myself compelled to fight back from my eyes the tears, and quanch my heart trobling to my throat, to not weep before him: this man called thief and assassin and doomed.
>
> But Sacco's name will live in the hearts of the people and in their gratitude when Katzmann's bones and yours will be dispersed by time; when your name, his name, your laws, institutions, and your false god are but a dim rememoring of a cursed past in which man was wolf to the man. . . .

If it had not been for these thing I might have live out my life talking at street corners to scorning men. I might have die unmarked, unknown, a failure. Now we are not a failure. This is our career and our triumph. Never in our full life could we hope to do such work for tolerance, for justice, for man's understanding of man, as now we do by accident. Our words, our lives, our pains—nothing! The taking of our lives—lives of a good shoemaker and a poor fishpeddler—all! That last moment belongs to us—that agony is our triumph.

Now, deciding about the integrity—the sincerity, the honesty—of public statements like these is sometimes very difficult. In this case, most of us would immediately raise a skeptical eyebrow over the first speech and sense at once the sincerity of the second. But the first is respectable Congressional oratory, and the second is by a man who was executed for murder. Evidently judging integrity can be tricky business, and in the long run there is probably no substitute for knowing the man personally. But his writing itself often contains some helpful indications:

Tone. Perhaps most reliable, and yet hardest to define, is a quality which might be called *tone.* When we talk with someone we are usually aware of this quality in his personality, in his voice, in his inflection. It requires more perceptiveness to detect *tone* in printed words, but we do it all the time. Read aloud the mutual security speech and the Vanzetti speech, and listen for the voices behind them. Is the voice pompous, inflated, oratorical? Is the tone unctuous and ingratiating? Does it purr in our ears? Or is it self-deprecating, apologetic? Modesty may be a virtue, but mock-modesty is a vice. Similarly any undue self-justification casts doubt on the writer's integrity. "Methinks the lady doth protest too much" is a penetrating observation. Does the Congressman perhaps protest too much? Does Vanzetti? At bottom, tone is a reflection of the writer's attitude toward both his subject and his audience.

Appeals. A less subjective clue to the integrity of the writer is the kind of *appeals* that he uses. The question is: What kinds of attitudes, feelings, sentiments are brought into play? Is the writer working primarily on those attitudes and feelings which can be aroused most easily and cheaply—chauvinism, class or race consciousness, sentimentality, prurient curiosity, the taste for violence, sex, and sadism? These are the standard appeals of the "men's magazines," the "exposés," "romantic love" magazines, cheap newspapers. This test can be applied equally well to all three uses of language—to news stories and editorials (note the appeals of the tabloids), to fiction (note both sensationalism and sentimentality in novels, in movies, and on radio and TV), and to advertisements and political speeches. Sensational appeals usually indicate a cynical attitude toward the reader; the writer is "giving 'em what they want." Sentimental appeals, on the other hand, may indicate either cynicism or merely a stereotyped view of life.

We need to be quite clear about this analysis of appeals. We must always take into account the quality of the sentiments and feelings which are brought into play. Churchill appeals to British patriotism; it would be a mistake to label his appeal as chauvinism. We must also take into account the relevance of the appeal to the central issue, especially in persuasion. An advertiser's appeal to buy something in order to conform to the "American way" is an irrelevant use of what might be under some circumstances, a quite legitimate appeal to patriotism. And in creative works, we must also take into account the place of the appeal in the work as a whole. The presence in a creative work of sex, sadism, violence and so on, *as part of a complex picture*, is no proof that the writer is dishonest. A thoroughly honest creative writer—witness James Joyce in "Counterparts"—may feel that these things are an integral part of the virtual world he is creating; to *leave them out* would be dishonest. Nor is all strong emotion, all feeling, to be equated with sentimentality. The appeals in a literary work must be considered as a whole. Moralists have too often suppressed a book or play because of a single passage which they found offensive but which was an integral part of the whole work; for instance, Joyce's publisher objected to "Counterparts" because of Higgins' "two establishments" and because the Tivoli actress brushes against Farrington's chair. More hard-boiled critics have too often mistaken sentiment for sentimentality. These distinctions are not always easy to draw, but any reader who cares about judging literature fairly must try to draw them.

Formulas. Another indication of lack of integrity is the use of formulas and gimmicks. Formulas are of various kinds. In fiction they may appear as the stereotyped plot, the stock situation, the standard set of characters—the heavy villain, the stalwart hero, the poor-but-honest-workingman, the prostitute-with-a-heart-of-gold, the innocent heroine, the misunderstood heroine, the courageous heroine. It is unlikely that a work which depends heavily on formulas represents the writer's personal vision of life. The chances are that he is a hack grinding out stories to order. It may be, however, that the content of his mind is simply thin, that he sees things this way because he thinks in stereotypes. If this is so, the fault is less a matter of integrity, perhaps, than of truthfulness; but our over-all judgment should probably be the same: the stuff is not worth bothering with.

In informative and persuasive writing, the formula may appear simply as a "gimmick." A conversational opening to an article (especially if it appears contrived), a punch line developed for its own sake, "human interest" which merely dresses up the facts—all are stock devices, part of the formulas of journalistic writing. They are not in themselves bad; and in a sense they are readily forgivable, especially when they reflect, as they sometimes do, real consideration for the reader; but they often suggest that the writer is more interested in "working" his reader than in presenting the contents of his own mind. And they *may* indicate that the writer really has nothing much to say.

Effectiveness as a Criterion

In the last section we have, in general, deplored the use of formulas, gimmicks, and other tricks of the trade. The sincerity of Vanzetti's speech is made more convincing by the artlessness of his language. But this does not mean that a piece of writing cannot be both honest and well-made. The world's greatest literature has both integrity *and* effectiveness. And the finest informative articles, books, and scientific papers not only provide valuable knowledge but do it with elegance and precision. Look for example at these paragraphs from Thomas Henry Huxley's "On a Piece of Chalk":

> Let us try another method of making the chalk tell us its own history. To the unassisted eye chalk looks simply like a very loose and open kind of stone. But it is possible to grind a slice of chalk down so thin that you can see through it—until it is thin enough, in fact, to be examined with any magnifying power that may be thought desirable. A thin slice of the fur of a kettle might be made in the same way. If it were examined microscopically, it would show itself to be a more or less distinctly laminated mineral substance and nothing more.

But the slice of chalk presents a totally different appearance when placed under the microscope. The general mass of it is made up of very minute granules; but, imbedded in this matrix, are innumerable bodies, some smaller and some larger, but, on a rough average, not more than a hundredth of an inch in diameter, having a well-defined shape and structure. A cubic inch of some specimens of chalk may contain hundreds of thousands of these bodies, compacted together with incalculable millions of granules.

The examination of a transparent slice gives a good notion of the manner in which the components of the chalk are arranged and of their relative proportions. But, by rubbing up some chalk with a brush in water and then pouring off the milky fluid, so as to obtain sediments of different degrees of fineness, the granules and the minute rounded bodies may be pretty well separated from one another, and submitted to microscopic examination, either as opaque or as transparent objects. By combining the views obtained in these various methods, each of the rounded bodies may be proved to be a beautifully constructed calcareous fabric, made up of a number of chambers, communicating freely with one another. The chambered bodies are of various forms. One of the commonest is something like a badly-grown raspberry, being formed of a number of nearly globular chambers of different sizes congregated together. It is called *Globigerina,* and some specimens of chalk consist of little else than *Globigerinae* and granules. Let us fix our attention upon the *Globigerina.* It is the spoor of the game we are tracking. If we can learn what it is and what are the conditions of its existence, we shall see our way to the origin and past history of the chalk.

This is informative writing. Huxley is communicating something to an audience, and he is doing it effectively; but he is not using mere gimmicks. The qualities which this piece exhibits—and which all good instrumental writing exhibits—are *functional form, economy, precision of wording,* and *clarity.*

Instrumental Writing. This term is used here to distinguish between informative and persuasive writing, on the one hand, and creative writing on the other. Both informative writing and persuasion have limited and, in some sense, definable objectives of which they are the instruments. Their effectiveness can therefore be measured—at least approximately—if we want to take the trouble to do so. The pulling power of an advertisement, for example, can be measured by increased sales; the impact of a campaign speech by a shift in the public opinion polls; the effect of a class lecture by student performance on a quiz. Most of the time, of course, we do not resort to actual measurement, but content ourselves with evaluating probable effects; and in so doing, we use the criteria of functional form, economy, precision, and clarity.

The first point which may help us to judge how functional the form is, and how economical the wording is the fact that all instrumental writing has an end-product, something which the reader can take away from it. But this end-product, whether it is a package of concepts or a change in attitude, is seldom produced instantaneously. The end-product must be put together a little at a time. When we talk about functional form we are talking partly about the way in which this end-product is put together; and if we look closely at the organization of a piece of instrumental writing, we can usually decide whether the end-product has been put together efficiently and economically.

A second point must also be considered. As we noted in Chapter 6, the mind of a reader is not a blank surface on which ideas may be imprinted, nor is his will a mechanism which can be simply reassembled to do a new job. The reader's mind *works* as he reads— partly on the suggestions provided by the reading, partly on other matters. The writer must, therefore, not merely construct an endproduct in a logical fashion; he must focus the reader's attention on what he is reading and help his thinking process along. In fact, good writing nudges the reader ahead of the text, causing him to raise questions and to formulate his own tentative answers as he reads.

Since the passage from Huxley is a small part of a much longer essay, the end-product may not be clear. We can say roughly, however, that Huxley's purpose is to provide an understanding of the process of chalk formation and of the significance of this process. What Huxley does is to begin with an actual piece of chalk and ask us to think through a series of experiments with him. If we read slowly enough, we can actually see this thinking process. We think of questions and objections; and in the next sentence we find our question stated or the answer given, and our objections recognized and explained away. This, incidentally, is the simplest and best way of testing functional form: try reading a text slowly enough so that questions and observations will arise in your mind as you go along; then notice whether your questions are answered in subsequent statements and your observations commented upon.

In the first part of this chapter we placed so much emphasis on integrity that there may now be doubt about the honesty of a functional form which focuses the reader's attention and keeps him reading. And if this result is achieved by gimmicks, we are probably right in being slightly skeptical. But there is nothing incompatible between good instrumental writing and integrity of purpose. A thoroughly honest writer, thinking his way through a subject or reporting his observations, may involve the reader in the same journey of discovery that he himself is taking. And if the landscape, for the writer, is a very familiar one, he may still think his way along, looking always for something he has not seen before. If he proceeds in this way, his writing is likely to be effective. In earlier chapters the point was stressed that the creative writer often does not know quite where he is coming out. (Remember Frost's "Stopping by Woods.") But in a sense this is also true of the informative writer. What he puts down on paper often turns out to be for *him* exciting and novel, and this excitement is part of what he conveys to someone else.

Effectiveness also involves wording. We can judge the language of instrumental writing much as we judge form and economy: by reading slowly and with attention both to the end-product and to the details of expression. If the end-product is conceptual knowledge, are the words conceptually accurate? If evocative meanings are brought into play, do these meanings help attain the object? Or are the words vague, general, ambiguous?

Here again, an examination of Huxley's passage can be instructive. His wording is precise and even technical. He talks about a "distinctly laminated mineral substance," and he says that "embedded in this matrix are innumerable bodies." At the same time, his words enable us to visualize what he is writing about. He speaks of "rubbing up some chalk with a brush in water and then pouring off the milky fluid," and he describes the chambered bodies as "something like a badly-grown raspberry." He even uses figurative language when it will be useful: "making the chalk tell us its own history"; "it is the spoor of the game we are tracking." And he employs imperatives as a means of fixing attention: "Let us try another method . . ."; "Let us fix our attention . . ."

Creative Writing. In creative writing, effectiveness means something different from what it means in instrumental writing. As we have pointed out in various ways before, there is no end-product in creative writing, at least not in the same sense that one might be found in instrumental writing—no capsule of wisdom, no outline of plot that can be taken away as an adequate summary of the work. The meaning is in the whole work and in one's experience of the whole work as he reads it. Creative writing should be thought of not as *limited*-purpose writing but as *un*limited-purpose writing. Its effectiveness cannot be measured precisely because there is no precisely definable end-product with which we can compare actual results. And the actual results are themselves unmeasurable—perhaps a better word would be immeasurable. In judging effectiveness, what we do is to examine the text with two qualities in mind, *richness* and *unity*. Now, these qualities are not wholly different from those we have just been looking at. In fact, unity may be thought of as the creative counterpart of both functional form and economy: and richness involves, among other things, both precision and clarity of wording, though of a different kind than we look for in informative language.

Both richness and unity are best discovered by the technique of analysis described and employed in Chapters 9–12. At this point we need only summarize. It may be worthwhile, however, to have a couple of examples in front of us as we think about both richness and unity. The first is a fine lyric by Emily Dickinson, the second a poem by her less gifted contemporary, Harriet Liszt. Here is Emily Dickinson's poem:

The Soul Selects

> The soul selects her own society,
> Then shuts the door;
> On her divine majority
> Obtrude no more.
>
> Unmoved she notes the chariots pausing
> At her low gate;
> Unmoved, an emperor is kneeling
> Upon her mat.
>
> I've known her from an ample nation
> Choose one;
> Then close the valves of her attention
> Like stone.[2]

And here is Harriet Liszt's poem:

> Why this longing, this forever sighing
> For the far off, unattained, and dim;
> While the beautiful, all round thee lying,
> Offers up its low, perpetual hymn?

[2] "The Soul Selects" by Emily Dickinson. Reprinted by permission of Little, Brown & Company.

Wouldst thou listen to its gentle teaching,
All thy restless yearning it would still:
Leaf, and flower, and laden bee, are preaching
Thine own sphere, though humble, first to fill.
Poor indeed thou must be, if around thee
Thou no ray of light canst throw;
If no silken cord of love hath bound thee
To some little world through weal or woe;
If no dear eyes thy fond love can brighten—
No fond voices answer to thine own;
If no brother's sorrow thou canst lighten
By daily sympathy and gentle tone.
Not by deeds that win the crowd's applauses;
Not by works that give thee world-renown;
Not by martyrdom, or vaunted crosses,
Canst thou win and wear the immortal crown:
Daily struggling, though unloved and lonely,
Every day a rich reward will give;
Thou wilt find by hearty striving only,
And truly loving, thou canst truly live.

Emily Dickinson's poem is both rich and unified; the other is thin, and though it has a kind of unity, it is a unity of ideas only, and stale ones at that. "The Soul Selects" is subtle and complex in its sound effects. Notice the startling half-rhymes, *society-majority*, *gate-mat*, *one-stone;* and notice the way in which the rhythm is varied. The lines alternate between four and two feet, but in the last stanza, the solidity of the decision is emphasized by the dropping in the two-foot lines of the unaccented syllables: it is *Choose one* and *Like stone*. No such richness, no such interaction of sound and meaning appears in the other poem. Notice also Dickinson's highly original images: "selects her own society," "shuts the door," "divine majority," "low gate," "valves of her attention." Not only are there no such images in the other poem, but the words hardly function as plurisigns at all.

To judge the *richness* of a piece of creative writing, we need first to respond fully to its form and language. We must notice all the elements which make for variety and complexity, and the intricate interactions among these elements and between them and the world of real life outside the work. Thus, as we have seen before, a work's full meaning begins to emerge only in proportion as we sense its *form* in full detail. In other words, recognition of the *richness* of a creative work *depends* on recognition of its *unity*.

To judge the *unity* of a creative work, we must of course perceive its form. In particular, we need to recognize the real nature of the *dominant* formal elements. In fiction and drama, these dominant elements, as we saw in "Counterparts," are such things as the shape of the action, the central conflict (or conflicts), the character-groupings, and the point of view; in lyric poetry, the dominant elements are the key metaphors, the basic contrasts or tensions, the progression of images, and the patterns of sounds and symbols.

However, these elements represent only the large-scale similarities and differences, parallels and contrasts. If the work is truly unified, if the form is thoroughly organic, every detail will be functional. And if our conception of the over-all form is right, we should be able to account for the presence of all parts of the work in terms of this conception. We should be able to explain the function of each character, each scene, each image, every bit of dialogue. This is always on the assumption that the poem or play or novel or story *is* in fact unified.

Occasionally this assumption is unjustified. There are some creative works—including a few great ones—which are deficient in unity, though they may partially make up for it in richness. This is especially true of such naturally amorphous works as novels. Among the masters, Dickens and Dostoevski are two novelists who frequently failed to unify their works as well as lesser writers have. Among moderns, Thomas Wolfe's novels are examples, and perhaps some of Faulkner's.

In a sense, the principles of richness and of unity, of multiple meaning and of organic form, are constantly at war. An author with a great deal to "say" is most likely to have trouble organizing it; and another writer may succeed in giving his work remarkable formal unity largely because he has so little to say. Good and great literature normally exhibits a marriage of the two principles. In creative writing, "effectiveness" is largely a matter of the success of this marriage.

Truthfulness as a Criterion

As we have seen, all serious literature embodies knowledge—of one kind or another, in one form or another, for one reason or another. Therefore the question of the truth-value of knowledge applies to all kinds of writing. It is relevant to the knowledge embodied in creative works, and to whatever kind of knowledge the persuasive writer may introduce in support of his arguments and other appeals.

But truthfulness does not mean quite the same thing when applied to the informative writer's propositions and the creative writer's segments of virtual life.

Conceptual Truthfulness. The sort of truthfulness we expect to find in informative literature was discussed at length back in Chapters 5, 6 and 7. There we found that the assorted hypotheses which we think of as "information" can be checked out in various relatively objective ways. We can test propositions by restating them in other words, sometimes even by embodying them in nonverbal media; we can ask ourselves about their origin; we can compare them with other writers' assertions; we can judge their logic; sometimes we can even verify them by repeating the writer's experiments, observations, or thought processes; and so on. Thus it is relatively easy for people to reach a meeting of minds on how sound a body of information is at a particular point in man's intellectual progress.

What we are concerned with in all this is the probable truth-value—in a fairly literal sense—of propositions. And among our most practical clues are some of the things mentioned earlier in connection with the writer's integrity. But it is worthwhile to separate the two criteria, integrity and truthfulness. A perfectly honest man may make a mistake in observation or inference; and the most well-meaning philosopher often makes bad guesses. Such errors need not imply lack of integrity. On the other hand, the information contained in a piece of sensational journalism may be quite literally true and yet convey a false impression because the writer has been less concerned with giving us the picture than with selling newspapers.

Experiential Truthfulness. In judging creative literature, the question of truthfulness becomes a great deal more complex. Here we are no longer dealing with the intellectual abstractions called propositions but with concrete images of life. These images are by nature at least partly "untrue"; they are invented, fictional, virtual. Furthermore, they "mean" on more than one level at once. They may be quite incredible on one level and profoundly true-to-life on another. Again, a creative writer's vision of life may seem to us to be

wildly distorted, but who is to say that this may not be *his* "truth"?
Thomas Hardy once wrote, "A novel is an impression, not an argument." Wallace Stegner has written, "We can make closer contact
in fiction than in reality; more surely than we know the secrets of
our friends we know how this writer who is something like ourselves
looks upon himself, how he fronts his life, how he, another waif
in a bewildering world, has made out to survive and perhaps be
at peace. . . . Ultimately, I am convinced, he is what we read for.
The work of art is not a gem, as some schools of criticism would
insist, but truly a lens. We look through it for the purified and
honestly offered spirit of the artist." And Walter Allen says that
"every novel is an extended metaphor of the author's view of life."

If what these critics—all of them novelists as well—say is correct,
then it is hard to see how we can rightly apply the criterion of
truthfulness to any creative work. And yet we do apply it, constantly,
both as amateurs and as professional critics. For example, we frequently condemn sentimentality as one form of falsity in creative
writing. We say that the virtual world created by the sentimentalist
is oversimplified. His characters are either pure as angels or wicked
as devils. His plots work out far too neatly. His scenes are either
too pretty or too desolate. He works largely with the pathetic, the
overemotional. To see what we mean by sentimentality, let us look
at two poems, both on the emotion-filled subject of the death of
a child. There is no question in either of the sincerity or integrity
of the writer: there *is* a question of how true to experience the
two versions are. Here is James Russell Lowell's treatment of the
subject:

FROM *After the Burial*

There's a narrow ridge in the graveyard
    Would scarce stay a child in his race,
But to me and my thought it is wider
    Than the star-sown vague of Space.

Your logic, my friend, is perfect,
    Your moral most drearily true;
But since the earth clashed on *her* coffin,
    I keep hearing that and not you.

Console if you will, I can bear it;
    'Tis a well-meant alms of breath;
But not all the preaching since Adam
    Has made Death other than Death.

It is pagan; but wait till you feel it,—
That jar of our earth, that dull shock
When the ploughshare of deeper passion
Tears down to our primitive rock.

Communion in spirit! Forgive me,
But I, who am earthly and weak,
Would give all my incomes from dreamland
For a touch of her hand on my cheek.

That little shoe in the corner,
So worn and wrinkled and brown,
With its emptiness confutes you,
And argues your wisdom down.

(JAMES RUSSELL LOWELL, 1819–91)

And here is a poem we have already looked at, John Crowe Ransom's treatment of a similar subject:

Bells for John Whiteside's Daughter

There was such speed in her little body,
And such lightness in her footfall,
It is no wonder that her brown study
Astonishes us all.

Her wars were bruited in our high window.
We looked among orchard trees and beyond,
Where she took arms against her shadow,
Or harried unto the pond

The lazy geese, like a snow cloud
Dripping their snow on the green grass,
Tricking and stopping, sleepy and proud,
Who cried in goose, Alas,

For the tireless heart within the little
Lady with rod that made them rise
From their noon apple-dreams, and scuttle
Goose-fashion under the skies!

But now go the bells, and we are ready;
In one house we are sternly stopped
To say we are vexed at her brown study,
Lying so primly propped.[3]

[3] "Bells for John Whiteside's Daughter" by John Crowe Ransom, reprinted from *Selected Poems* by John C. Ransom, by permission of Alfred A. Knopf, Inc. Copyright 1924, 1945 by Alfred A. Knopf, Inc.

Now, Lowell's poem is far, far better than most verse on such subjects. There is spirit in it, and defiance, and there are some strong images: notice "alms of breath," and "jar of our earth, that dull shock." And Lowell is writing about the death of his own daughter—we have no reason to doubt the strength of his feelings or the sincerity of what he says. But this should not obscure the sentimentality of:

> Would give all my incomes from dreamland
> For a touch of her hand on my cheek.
> That little shoe in the corner,
> So worn and wrinkled and brown . . .

Compare Ransom's lines (remembering, if you care to, that he appears to be writing not about his own child but about a neighbor's child). Notice the contrast of restless activity with death, and the vexation at the child's "brown study." And notice particularly the unsentimental emphasis on the geese being harried to the pond. The speed in the child's little body, the lightness in her footfall, and her tireless heart contrast with her brown study lying so primly propped. But the contrasting images are muted, played down by the picture of the slow geese, instead of being underscored as is the "little shoe" in the other poem.

Sentimentality, however, is only one kind of falseness in creative writing. It is an especially obvious one, and it is found in a great many places—in magazine stories, in movies, on the radio and TV; but equally false is the extreme of hardboiled "realism." Here is an exaggerated instance from Mickey Spillane's *The Big Kill* [two hired killers have Spillane's "hero," Mike Hammer, cornered in the men's room. Hammer, of course, is the narrator]:

> The goddam bastards played right into my hands. They thought they had me nice and cold and just as they were set to carve me into a raw mess of skin I dragged out the .45 and let them look down the hole so they could see where sudden death came from.
>
> It was the only kind of talk they knew. The little guy stared too long. He should have been watching my face. I snapped the side of the rod across his jaw and laid the flesh open to the bone. He dropped the sap and staggered into the big boy with a scream starting to come up out of his throat only to get it cut off in the middle as I pounded his teeth back into his mouth with the end of the barrel. The big guy tried to shove him out of the way. He got so mad he came right at me with his head down and I took my own damned time about kicking

him in the face. He smashed into the door and lay there bubbling. So I kicked him again and he stopped bubbling. I pulled the knucks off his hand then went over and picked up the sap. The punk was vomiting on the floor, trying to claw his way under the sink. For laughs I gave him a taste of his own sap on the back of his hand and felt the bones go into splinters. He wasn't going to be using any tools for a long time.[4]

"Realism" of this sensational sort is in a sense only the opposite side of the coin of sentimentality.

Sometimes falseness is less a matter of over-all tone than of detail. The fault may lie in the action: coincidence plays too large a part in the working out of the story. The events are highly improbable. Sometimes it is in the characterization: human nature just isn't like this. The motivation is inadequate, and so on. Sometimes it is in the dialogue: people of this sort do not talk this way.

It is important to note, however, that this kind of truthfulness has little to do with conceptual truthfulness. A creative writer is presenting a probable fiction, not a literal history. If the facts of history are necessary to the virtual life, they must be preserved with reasonable accuracy. Thus Joyce insisted, in "Counterparts," on retaining the actual names of the Dublin pubs, over his publisher's strong objections. He felt that they were essential to the air of verisimilitude he wished to create. But if actual details are not necessary in this way, they may be freely altered. Remember how Frost changed from two horses to one in "Stopping by Woods." The emphasis, in other words, is on the truth of experience, not on conceptual truth.

This distinction is especially apparent if we consider the truthfulness of fantasy, allegory, and myth. On the literal level, these forms are not only historically false, but sometimes utterly incredible. We have already referred to Kafka's story, *Metamorphosis,* in which a man wakes up one morning to find that he has been changed into a giant cockroach. Now, this does not happen to people—not literally. Is the story then valid? The answer is that we must look at other levels of meaning. On the literal level the story is fantastic; on a symbolic or perhaps allegorical level, it evokes a virtual world which represents certain aspects of human psychology in a complex and convincing way. Thus *Metamorphosis* is "true" in spite of the fact that it is fantasy. And this same distinction has to be applied to

[4] FROM *The Big Kill* by Mickey Spillane. Reprinted by permission of E. P. Dutton & Co., Inc.

many other stories, ancient and modern, including many primitive or classical myths: the fable is fantastic; but imbedded in the fantasy lies a "truthful" vision of man's condition.

This too-brief discussion suggests some of the complexities involved in applying the criterion of truthfulness to creative writing. Above all, there always remains the question of *whose* experience the image of life is true to. It is entirely possible that Lowell's re-creation of grief is entirely true to *his* experience, however questionable it may seem in terms of *our* experience. It may even be argued that Mickey Spillane's virtual world of violence and sadism is quite true to his personal sense of reality. The practical implications of all this seem to be that the "reality" of creative literature is a highly subjective matter, that personal visions vary a great deal from one individual to the next and from age to age, and that we must handle the criterion of truthfulness most carefully in dealing with creative writing. In general, it is probably safer here to rely on the other three standards.

Significance as a Criterion

Evaluating significance requires us to pass judgment on the importance of the knowledge, conceptual or experiential, which a piece of writing contains, and on the action which it promotes. And this requirement involves us, in turn, both in highly personal judgments and in the most general questions of philosophy. We ask, in effect, "What *is* significant anyway?" "And how is this piece of writing related to it?"

Informative Writing. The question of significance in informative literature was discussed back in Chapter 7 under the heading "Usefulness" (pp. 133–35). Here we will ignore the more obvious, *immediate* kind of usefulness which purely instrumental writing may have, and focus instead on the longer-range significance of less utilitarian forms of informative material.

Our personal judgments about the significance of conceptual knowledge depend largely on the knowledge we already possess. If the new knowledge which is offered us is wholly outside our ken, we are likely to ignore it, or to dismiss it as incomprehensible. If it is something we have known all along, we are likely to dismiss it as superfluous: it's all old stuff. Thus we judge significance by the effect on our own body of knowledge. And this explains why judgments about the significance of pieces of informative writing are so diverse; we each have different bodies of knowledge, different problems, different interests. We don't even read our newspapers in the same order, or notice the same stories.

But besides our individual judgments, there is also a kind of general judgment—an educated consensus. The significance of informative books—historical, philosophical, and scientific—is judged in terms of their effect on a more general body of knowledge. Thus we place a high value on Newton's *Principia*, Locke's *Essay Concerning Civil Government*, Adam Smith's *Wealth of Nations,* and Darwin's *Origin of Species,* to name only a few. This judgment of significance does not mean that we find works of this kind in every respect "true." It does mean that, true or not, they have reorganized or reconstructed whole areas of man's conceptual knowledge. The really significant informative books do so thorough a job that men never see the world quite in the same way afterwards.

Persuasion. Our judgment of persuasion is considerably more complicated. In the first place, we must begin by dealing with whatever informative and creative elements (or both) it may contain. If it is serious persuasion, these elements may be very important; in nonserious persuasion, they are likely to be negligible. In either case, we must then go on to the persuasion proper.

This involves thinking first in terms of how the piece may influence (or has influenced) attitudes and actions, both our own and other people's. Then we must, in turn, judge these influences according to our social, political, and personal value systems. This is a two-step process.

In the first step, using the criterion of influence on attitudes and actions, we readily admit that Marx's *Communist Manifesto,* Hitler's *Mein Kampf,* and Mrs. Stowe's *Uncle Tom's Cabin* are significant pieces of persuasion. And we make these judgments without regard to our personal or political philosophies. We do not have to be communists to call Marx significant, or fascists to call Hitler significant, or abolitionists to call Mrs. Stowe significant.

But we then go on, in the second step, to a further evaluation in terms of our own philosophies or interests. The book may be significant, but we do or do not approve of how it influences actions and attitudes. This further evaluation should perhaps be thought of as a fifth criterion, and it might be better to treat it as such except that the criteria we are looking at in this chapter are general ones, which apply to all three uses of language.

It is worth noting that our judgment of the significance of a work as persuasion should be distinguished from our judgment of the same work as a vehicle for conceptual or experiential knowledge. Thus *Mein Kampf* is undoubtedly significant as persuasion; we would probably not judge it so as political philosophy. *Uncle Tom's Cabin* is significant as persuasion; we would probably not judge it so as creative writing.

Creative Writing. In discussing the significance of conceptual knowledge, we noticed two kinds of judgments, individual judgments and a general educated judgment. This second kind of judgment is largely historical. We look at some works as turning points in man's intellectual development, and if they are contemporary works, we *predict* that they will have important intellectual results.

Now it is possible to draw the same kind of distinction in judging works which convey experiential knowledge. Not only does man's conceptual view of the world change as a result of what other men write; but his experiential view also changes. Literary movements, such as romanticism, realism, naturalism, generate new ways of seeing, feeling, and responding. The literary historian, like the historian of ideas, notes these changes and the works which produce them or at least represent them. He may discuss Chaucer as a significant forerunner of realism. He may note that certain twelfth-century French poets are responsible for a romantic view of woman and love. Or he may place Ibsen's significance in his capacity to view middle-class life tragically. And so on. Thus the historical critic treats these works as documents, which have to be read for the experience they contain but which are significant because they exemplify a particular state of perception and understanding.

There is, however, still a third way of evaluating the significance of creative works—from the point of view not of their historical significance but of their contemporary, immediate value. Creative writing generates experiential knowledge. Its "subject," in a very real sense, is "the human condition." Now, we noted back in Chapter 9 that there is a strong similarity in the human condition at all times and in all places. The great crises of life, especially among primitive men, are dramatized in rituals; and they are narrated in myths. And literature—much of which retells myths and employs ritual symbolism—serves a similar function. It initiates us into the life-pattern and confronts us with questions of the permanent behind the transitory. In judging significance, therefore, it is often useful to consider the ritual symbolism which the work contains, and to notice the way in which it is related to the principal crises in the life pattern.

But ritual parallels are only an *indication* of significance, and they appear in many of the cheapest, most formula-ridden works. For example, here is one serious critic's explanation of the basic appeal of Mickey Spillane's novels:

> In Spillane's books we see, as through a magnifying glass, the drama inherent in the formula of the detective story. Every murder mystery poses symbolically (in the form of the initial murder) the problem of Evil—and resolves it; every detective story therefore meets a deep metaphysical need.

In general, we ask of serious literature such questions as these: How universal is this work? How close to man's central concerns? How comprehensive? How deep in its penetration? These questions should not be taken to imply systematic analysis. Depth, centrality, scope, and universality, as qualities of experiential knowledge, overlap. They all point finally to a single question: What does the work have to do with the central problem of what it means to be a man? I am born. I shall die. Between these two events stretches a life, with its growth and decline, its pains and pleasures, its repetitive details, its insights, its conflicts, its passions, and its monotony. What, if anything, does it "mean"?

These are the most important questions anyone can ask; all other questions—about knowledge, about techniques, about devices—although they may be ultimately related to these, are peripheral. And these questions, the questions about the significance of human experience itself, can be answered only through experience. Answering them through experience is the business of art, of ritual, and of myth. They are sometimes answered conceptually, of course—in philosophy, in science, and in theology. But conceptual answers, useful as they may be, are no substitute for experiential ones. Whatever theories we may have to help us, there is still the span of individual existence, and, in a very real sense, it is all any of us has—to do something with, or just to endure.

In judging the significance of a creative work from *this* point of view, therefore, we ask: What does this work have to do with the fundamental concerns of mankind? For therein lies its significance for all of us. And this is not a judgment about mere historical significance. We find immediate value, in this sense, in ancient as well as in modern works, and in the works of cultures quite different from our own. And it is not merely that these works tell us what life was like in Elizabethan England, or Imperial Rome, or Periclean Athens.

Who would question, for example, the significance *as experience* of a passage of poetry like the following verses from the Ninetieth Psalm? (Note that our reaction to these words as experience may have very little to do with our personal conceptual beliefs.)

> For a thousand years in thy sight are but as yesterday when it is past, and as a watch in the night.
> Thou carriest them away as a flood; they are as a sleep; in the morning they are like grass which groweth up.
> In the morning it flourisheth and groweth up; in the evening it is cut down and withereth,
> For we are consumed by thy anger, and by thy wrath are we troubled.
> Thou hast set our iniquities before thee, our secret sins in the light of thy countenance.
> For all our days are passed away in thy wrath: we spend our years as a tale that is told.

Or who would question the significance *as experience* of these lines from a poem we have already analyzed, Andrew Marvell's "To His Coy Mistress"?

> But at my back I always hear
> Time's wingèd chariot hurrying near;
> And yonder all before us lie
> Deserts of vast eternity.
> Thy beauty shall no more be found,
> Nor, in thy marble vault, shall sound
> My echoing song; then worms shall try
> That long preserved virginity,
> And your quaint honor turn to dust,
> And into ashes all my lust:
> The grave's a fine and private place,
> But none I think do there embrace.

We do not see these passages simply as historical documents. They speak to us now. That is why we continue to read creative writing which is far removed from us in time and place.

Older pieces of *informative* writing, on the other hand, especially those which are based on observation, are likely to have for us mostly an historical or even antiquarian interest. Thus great numbers of people read Chaucer's *Canterbury Tales;* few read his *Treatise on the Astrolabe,* and when they do, they read it for the light it throws on Chaucer the poet, or for its historical interest, not for the knowledge of astronomy which it contains. We can get a better grasp of astronomy from a modern textbook on the subject, learn more about electricity from a contemporary treatment than from the papers of Faraday and Franklin, more about chemistry from a freshman text than from Boyle, Lavoisier, and Dalton. In informative writing, the new tends to supplant the old. The same cannot be said of creative writing. Homer and Sophocles, Chaucer and Shakespeare, Dante and Milton, Flaubert and Dostoevski are still significant in the here and now of our experience.

And so is a fifty-year-old short story about a man in Dublin named Farrington. Perhaps the best way of concluding this discussion of the significance of experiential knowledge is to turn once more to the one long piece of creative writing which we have already analyzed in detail. But if we are not to become hopelessly confused, we must begin by looking briefly at the special problems of evaluating realistic and naturalistic writing.

Literature does its work in two rather different ways. In some literature, our experience, as we read, is essentially the experience of a central character with whom we more or less identify ourselves. We live some part of his life with him. This is true of our relations with most of the great epic heroes, Achilles, Hector, and Odysseus, of the great tragic heroes, Oedipus and Hamlet, and of other heroes as well. But sometimes, especially in realistic fiction, something very different happens. We come to our experience of life, to the question of what it means to be a man, *indirectly.* We may see things as a character sees them; but we also see them in another way. This, as we have already noticed in discussing the point of view in "Counterparts," is exactly what happens in Joyce's story. The camera eye is Farrington's, but there is a double point of view: *we* know more, *much* more, than Farrington does.

We have already called "Counterparts" a *realistic* story. We do not find much in the way of ritual in it, nor is it noticeably symbolistic. And while this is certainly a crisis in Farrington's life, it does not fall into the universal pattern. Farrington is not coming of age. He is not really seeking self-fulfillment. He does not spend any significant part of his time looking for answers to the meaning of life. He is concerned chiefly with making a good impression among his cronies. He wants revenge, domination, escape, a few hours in the Dublin bars. And it would be a hardy critic who would try to prove that "Counterparts" is an allegory.

Yet it is clear that something more is involved in the story than a mere four or five hours in the life of a singularly unpleasant character. We do not identify ourselves with this man, and we sympathize with him only briefly; he is pathetic as he starts home having lost everything, but he forfeits our good will by his vicious attack on young Tom. How can the story have any significance? The answer, of course, is in our response. The story is concerned indirectly with the very values Farrington does not have, does not even want. "Counterparts" forces us to consider what it means to be a man as surely as does the *Iliad* or *Hamlet.* Only it does it in a different way: Joyce holds up to us the image of a damned soul and a meaningless life.

Two other points are worth noticing. First, here is a story which is profoundly concerned with human values. It is completely serious, but it does not preach. There is no moral to be drawn. We don't say when we finish that the point is that a man shouldn't drink on the job, or that he should be kind to his children, or that he should work hard. We do ask, perhaps unconsciously: What is man? What does life mean?

Second, "Counterparts" is a good illustration of the difference between significant experience and entertainment. "Counterparts" is not entertaining in the usual meaning of that word. Farrington may be looking for an escape, but his story is for us, as readers, no escape at all. And the same comment could be made about a large proportion of the world's most significant literature. It does not offer escape. It is not even pleasant reading. It is, however, the embodiment of significant experience. And in the long run, only that part of the world's literature which passes the test of significant experience endures. The lasting, permanent works of the creative imagination are those which, having passed all other tests, have in the long-term judgment of critical readers passed this test as well.

Thus, over the years, a *Moby-Dick* stands higher in critical judgment than a *House of the Seven Gables,* a *Madame Bovary* than a *Count of Monte Cristo,* a *Huckleberry Finn* than a *Tom Sawyer*— a Joyce than an O. Henry.

A Note on Interrelations

At this point, one further comment on creative writing seems called for. In this chapter we have worked systematically, discussing integrity, effectiveness, truthfulness, and significance. And in informative and in persuasive writing these criteria are logically separable, but in creative writing the separation is always somewhat artificial.

A genuine artist experiences life in and through his particular medium—whether it is words, musical sounds, or pigments. His experiencing and his creating are, therefore, parts of the same process; and the way in which he handles his medium is directly related to the way in which he experiences life. Effectiveness, integrity, truthfulness, and even significance may therefore be very much the same thing. Thus stock situations and clichés are signs of a mechanical, stale approach to experience; they are also ineffective —they put us to sleep instead of stabbing us broad awake.

Ultimately, what we demand of any work of art is that it open up new possibilities to us, new depths of meaning, new relations in experience, new ways of seeing life. And in meeting this demand, form and value come together. Plurisigns set up new relationships in experience. Likeness-and-difference is no trick device; it is the only method of establishing and varying an experiential pattern— that is, of generating virtual life. The writer who contents himself with old formulas, old figures of speech, worn-out images, hackneyed plots, and stock characters produces nothing new and valuable, either for himself or for us. He may take us out of ourselves temporarily—and under some circumstances this escape can be therapeutic—but he adds nothing new to human experience.

Thus integrity, effectiveness, truthfulness, and significance in creative writing tend to be simply different aspects of the same criterion of value—a criterion which, in the last analysis, must be applied intuitively.

EXERCISES

A. Write a critical evaluation of a short story of recognized value. Your instructor may ask you to write on a story you have already analyzed or on a new story.

B. Write a critical evaluation of a short story of unknown or doubtful value. Your instructor may specify a pulp magazine story or a story from one of the "slick" magazines.

C. Select a subject for a short informative article. Write the article, keeping in mind the principles of effectiveness suggested in this chapter.

D. Write a critical evaluation of a political speech, considering indications of integrity or lack of it, and considering also effectiveness, validity, and significance.

E. Write an evaluation of a poem which you believe does not measure up to critical standards. (Unless your instructor has a different suggestion, make your selection from the columns of a newspaper or popular magazine.)

F. Write a critical evaluation of a piece of writing which exhibits a genuine mixture of purposes, considering the principles suggested in this chapter and also in Chapter 13.

G. Select a piece of writing in creative form but with strong persuasive intentions, and write an evaluation of it *as creative writing,* noting especially richness and unity. Now evaluate it *as persuasion.*

H. Write an essay evaluating the *significance* for the contemporary reader of a piece of creative writing from the past. (Your instructor may specify.) Note whether it works directly, involving you in the experience of one or more of the characters, or indirectly, as does "Counterparts." Look for ritual significance, relation to the major crises in the "life pattern." Try to decide how close it is, experientially, to the central, universal concerns of mankind.

Index

*(Quoted material is indicated by **boldface** page numbers.)*

363